Cooperative Information Systems

Cooperative Information Systems

Trends and Directions

Edited by

Michael P. Papazoglou and Gunter Schlageter

Tilburg University,
INFOLAB,
Tilburg,
The Netherlands

University of Hagen,
Department of Computer
Science,
Hagen, Germany

ACADEMIC PRESS

San Diego   London   Boston
New York   Sydney   Tokyo   Toronto

Academic Press
525 B Street, Suite 1900, San Diego, California 92101-4495, USA
http://www.apnet.com

Academic Press Limited
24–28 Oval Road, London NW1 7DX, UK
http://www.hbuk.co.uk/ap/

ISBN 0-12-544910-0

A catalogue record for this book is available from the British Library

Typeset by Laser Words, Madras, India
Printed in Great Britain by WBC Book Manufacturers, Bridgend,
Mid Glamorgan

97 98 99 00 01 02 EB 9 8 7 6 5 4 3 2 1

Contents

Contributors   vii

Preface   xi

Introduction

Themes in Cooperative Information Systems Research   3
Michael P. Papazoglou and Gunter Schlageter

Part I
Distributed Object Computing and Open Systems

The Emperor's Clothes are Object Oriented and Distributed   15
Michael L. Brodie

Beyond Objects: Components   49
Theo Dirk Meijler and Oscar Nierstrasz

Part II
Architectures and Language Paradigms

Supporting Cooperation in Enterprise-Scale Distributed Object
Systems   81
*Frank Manola, Dimitrios Georgakopoulos, Sandra Heiler, Benjamin
Hurwitz, Gail Mitchell and Farshad Nayeri*

A Harness Language for Cooperative Information Systems   111
Keith L. Clark and Nikolaos Skarmeas

Part III
Use of Metadata and Ontologies for Information Sharing

Semantic Heterogeneity in Global Information Systems: the Role
of Metadata, Context and Ontologies   139
Vipul Kashyap and Amit Sheth

Dynamic Classificational Ontologies: Mediation of Information
Sharing in Cooperative Federated Database Systems   179
Jonghyun Kahng and Dennis McLeod

Part IV
Communication, Cooperation and the Exchange of Knowledge

Dealing with Semantic Heterogeneity by Generalization-Based
Data Mining Techniques   207
Jiawei Han, Raymond T. Ng, Yongjian Fu and Son Dao

Reflection is the Essence of Cooperation   233
David Edmond and Michael P. Papazoglou

Part V
Modelling Organizations and Systems Requirements

Model-Driven Planning and Design of Cooperative Information
Systems   263
Matthias Jarke, Peter Peters and Manfred A. Jeusfeld

From Organization Models to System Requirements: a
"Cooperating Agents" Approach   293
Eric Yu, Philippe Du Bois, Eric Dubois and John Mylopoulos

Part VI
Visionary Approaches

Cooperative Information Systems: a Manifesto   315
*Giorgio De Michelis, Eric Dubois, Matthias Jarke, Florian Matthes, John
Mylopoulos, Michael P. Papazoglou, Klaus Pohl, Joachim Schmidt,
Carson Woo and Eric Yu*

Index   365

Contributors

Brodie, M.L.
GTE Laboratories Incorporated, 40 Sylvan Road, Waltham,
MA 02254, USA

Clark, K.L.
Imperial College, Department of Computing, London, UK

Dao, S.K.
Networking and Information Exploitation, Hughes Research Laboratories,
3011 Malibu Canyon Road, Malibu, CA 90265, USA

De Michelis, G.
Dipartimento di Scienze dell' Informazione, Università degli Studi di
Milano, Via Comelico 39, 20135 Milano, Italy

Du Bois, P.
CEDITI-FUNDP, University of Namur, 21 av. Georges Lemaître,
B-6041 Gosselies, Belgium

Dubois, E.
Computer Science Department, University of Namur,
21 rue Grandgagnage, B-5000 Namur, Belgium

Edmond, D.
Queensland University of Technology, School of Information Systems,
GPO Box 2434, Brisbane QLD 4001, Australia

Fu, Y.
Computer Science Department, University of Missouri—Rolla,
1870 Kiner Circle, Rolla, MO 65409-0350, USA

Georgakopoulos, D.
GTE Laboratories Incorporated, 40 Sylvan Road, Waltham,
MA 02254, USA

Han, J.
School of Computing Science, Simon Fraser University, Burnaby,
British Columbia V5A 1S6, Canada

Heiler, S.
GTE Laboratories Incorporated, 40 Sylvan Road, Waltham,
MA 02254, USA

Hurwitz, B.
GTE Laboratories Incorporated, 40 Sylvan Road, Waltham,
MA 02254, USA

Jarke, M.
Informatik V, RWTH Aachen, Ahornstr. 55, 52056 Aachen, Germany

Jeusfeld, M.A.
Informatik V, RWTH Aachen, Ahornstr. 55, 52056 Aachen, Germany

Kahng, J.
Computer Science Department, University of Southern California,
Los Angeles, CA 90089-0781, USA

Kashyap, V.
MCC, 3500 W. Balcones Center Dr., Austin,
TX 78759, USA

Manola, F.
GTE Laboratories Incorporated, 40 Sylvan Road, Waltham,
MA 02254, USA (Current address: Object Services and Consulting Inc.,
151 Tremont St, #22R, Boston, MA 02111, USA)

Matthes, F.
Software Systems Institute, TU Hamburg-Hamburg,
Hamburger Schloss Strasse 20, D-21079 Hamburg, Germany

McLeod, D.
Computer Science Department, University of Southern California,
Los Angeles, CA 90089-0781, USA

Meijler, T.D.
Baan Development b.v., Zonnenoordlaan 17, PO Box 250,
NL-6710 BG Ede, The Netherlands

Mitchell, G.
GTE Laboratories Incorporated, 40 Sylvan Road, Waltham,
MA 02254, USA

Mylopoulos, J.
Department of Computer Science, University of Toronto,
10 King's College Road, Toronto, Ontario M5S 3H5, Canada

Nayeri, F.
GTE Laboratories Incorporated, 40 Sylvan Road, Waltham,
MA 02254, USA (Current address: Critical Mass, Inc.,
1770 Mass. Ave. #262, Cambridge, MA 02140, USA)

Ng, R.T.
Department of Computer Science, University of British Columbia,
Vancouver, British Columbia V6T 1Z2, Canada

Nierstrasz, O.
Software Composition Group, Institut für Informatik (IAM),
Universität Bern, Neubrückstrasse 10, CH-3012 Berne, Switzerland

Papazoglou, M.P.
Tilburg University, INFOLAB, PO Box 90153, LE Tilburg,
The Netherlands

Peters, P.
Informatik V, RWTH Aachen, Ahornstr. 55, 52056 Aachen, Germany

Pohl, K.
Informatik V, RWTH Aachen, Ahornstrasse 55, 52056 Aachen, Germany

Schlageter, G.
University of Hagen, Department of Computer Science, Postfach 940,
Hagen D-58084, Germany

Schmidt, J.
Software Systems Institute, TU Hamburg-Hamburg,
Hamburger Schloss Strasse 20, D-21079 Hamburg, Germany

Sheth, A.
LSDIS Lab, Department of Computer Science, University of Georgia,
Athens, GA 30602, USA

Skarmeas, N.
Imperial College, Department of Computing, London, UK

Woo, C.
Faculty of Commerce and Business Administration, University of British
Columbia, Vancouver, Canada V6T 1Z2

Yu, E.
Faculty of Information Studies, University of Toronto, 140 St George
Street, Toronto, Ontario, M5S 3G6, Canada

Preface

This is a ground-breaking book on a topic that is capturing a large part of the current research in information systems, viz. how to make such heterogeneous and autonomous computerized information systems cooperate to achieve goals together that they would not be suited for in isolation. This desired property is known as *cooperation*. Any comprehensive treatment of this issue must address the many aspects of this problem: methodology, theoretical foundations, suitable architectures and practical applicability. In this book, some of the best researchers in the field of databases and information systems present recent work that treats all of these aspects to varying degrees of detail. As the field is still in an emergent state, this work as reported here cannot be seen as definitive, but it clearly has an essential role to play in that fundamental principles are identified through the study of these aspects.

It is not surprising that because of the nature of the field and the vast complexity of the different issues at hand, there is still considerable heterogeneity in the respective approaches chosen by the authors, and therefore the editors must be commended on the excellent job they have done in aligning the material according to a few main lines of force that seem to begin dominating the domain of cooperative information systems (CISs). One of these forces is the study of *semantics*, another one is the emergence of *brokerage architectures*, and a third seems to be the use of specialized *technologies* to tackle the problems raised. One might argue that, as usual, the need for appropriate *methodologies* and techniques is a fourth force and albeit a very important one, it is destined to become developed last, and so it is encouraging to see the first rudiments of methodological approaches for CISs emerge in this book.

For a stimulating and provocative opening, trying to put all the players and their games together, and putting into perspective things seen through the unforgiving glasses of practical applicability and pragmatic constraints, the editors could hardly have done better than with Michael Brodie's chapter on "the emperor's clothes", pitting research against industry in a favourite argument, but supplying us with many a sobering thought to consider for the rest of the book.

Since in CISs, heterogeneity combines with autonomy, this quite literally dictates that researchers as well as future users of a CIS must be aware, among other things, of profound semantical issues when developing such systems. Indeed, no valid application can be imagined for such a CIS where it would not be fundamental to understand, in a formal manner, the meaning of the information that has to be exchanged in order to make the cooperation happen and the common goal achieved; any other approach would be self-contradictory. Unfortunately for the applicators (but perhaps fortunately for researchers?), such research is in its infancy although this book contains some three chapters making inroads on important aspects of the problem. In particular, Kashyap and Sheth argue interestingly that no such treatment can be adequate without a thorough study of the metadata involved.

On the matter of architectures, and again the extremely wide range of systems that may play a role in cooperation, it is not surprising that a multitude of proposals abound in the literature, and this book presents an interesting subset of them. It shows that there are very many ways in which cooperation may be organized, while at the same time it remains hard to establish relative merits for their underlying principles, not to mention merits in absolute terms. Some chapters indeed derive their inspiration from the field of computer-supported cooperative work (CSCW), while others take a more foundational approach (e.g. see the CIS manifesto at the end of the book). The attentive reader undoubtedly will find this a rich supply of discussion material and a source of topics for further research.

Finally of course, there must be considered the matter of method-ologies for introducing cooperative systems. Quite generically, one may define a methodology conveniently as a framework of different representa-tions, which start with the analysis and specification of user requirements, and in which one may fit stepwise procedures that implement specific tech-niques leading to a system that satisfies the user requirements. The stepwise aspect is a fundamental one, as it paves the way for repeatability and teach-ability. Good and usable methodologies require a deep understanding of the problem area as it presents itself to the user of the technology, and therefore large amounts of experience have to be amassed first in order for the underlying principle to be abstracted out of them. Cooperative systems clearly are no exception to this, but the attentive reader will derive some potential *methodological requirements* from the provocative "CIS manifesto" included in this book, and from the chapter on mediation by Kahng and McLeod. Several *techniques* that may play a role in future methodologies are also proposed and treated in detail, such as the use of metamodels (Jarke *et al.*) and a number of representation and specification mechanisms (Yu *et al.*) useful for the design steps of a method.

Robert A. Meersman
Vrije Universiteit Brussel, March 1997

Introduction

Themes in Cooperative Information Systems Research

Michael P. Papazoglou[a] and Gunter Schlageter[b]

[a]Tilburg University, The Netherlands; [b]University of Hagen, Germany

I BACKGROUND

Until a few years ago the dominant computing paradigm was that of mainframe systems and individually built applications. Subsequently, we experienced the introduction of minicomputers running relational databases and their applications. It is only very recently that information technology is characterized by individuals working at PCs or powerful workstations, both stand-alone and in local area networks. Personal productivity tools such as word-processors, relational databases and spreadsheets are still the primary applications, and this software usually comes shrink-wrapped. Naturally, this phase of computing continues today at a very rapid pace. However, nowadays the combination of information technology and communications networks, with inexpensive high-performance computing systems, have the potential to make possible unprecedented modes of collaboration and commerce. Collaborative environments are a new breed of applications of potential widespread utility in medicine, manufacturing, design, banking, training, education, environmental management and so on. These pose major challenges for the development of future enabling technologies in the context of information and communications research and development.

2 COOPERATIVE SYSTEMS TECHNOLOGIES

In the next generation of computing which has just begun, large servers and workstations are all being connected to enable collaborative or cooperative work across corporate boundaries and even across continents. Today's modern computing environments provide access to vast networks of databases, knowledge bases, document repositories — which contain many different types of data — and application software. The essence of these systems is various types of *task-processing* activities, such as business-related

Cooperative Information Systems
Trends and Directions
ISBN 0-12-544910-0

application-dependent processes, which require information of widely distributed nature. These require information that flows over the networks, that is presented to enterprises and end-users, manipulated by computers and stored by information repositories for future use. For this generation of computing systems to become reality, tools and products must emerge to bring together incompatible systems and software. Software must operate across heterogeneous computing platforms working in much the same way across global and public networks as it does within a local network. Access to such widely distributed resources is currently not only hampered by the presence of propriety or legacy systems but also by the rapid expansion of information networks. Information networks include a wide range of users and organizations with a variety of requirements. This capability leads to a requirement for new technologies and tools that with a minimum of effort enable end-users and applications to locate, retrieve, abstract, correlate, combine and process data over vast geographic distances in order to solve a variety of complicated problems. Another major challenge is to develop technology that permits continuous enhancement and evolution of the current massive investments in information systems. This technology is required to build an appropriate infrastructure within which the development of distributed information system applications would be made possible. This infrastructure must support the conversion of large numbers of independent multivendor databases, knowledge bases, and application software into dynamic and highly connected information networks. Such issues are the concern of the next generation of information systems.

The next generation of information systems will be characterized as reconfigurable aggregations of disparate problem-solving components and their underlying information sources. These systems will enable cooperation among a large number of pre-existing information systems in a way that converts a flood of data to useful information, while protecting massive investments in software and leveraging spent capital. A promising approach to this problem is to provide access to a large number of information sources by organizing them into a collection of *information agents* (Papazoglou et al., 1992). The goal of each such computerized agent[1] is to provide information and expertise on a specific topic by drawing on information from already-existing information sources and other such information agents. Information agent capabilities typically include interprocess communication mechanisms and services, such as naming, translation, information discovery, syntactic/semantic reconciliation, partial integration, distributed query processing and transaction management and a variety of other activities that need to be performed to enable information sharing and cooperation between diverse incompatible information systems.

---

[1] In our view information agents should include both humans as well as computerized agents, thus the distinction at this point.

To perform a complex task we expect that an information agent should use an incremental processing style: it would select and entangle other information agents in the process of task execution in a dynamic and opportunistic way, thereby aggregating the solution to a common problem one step at a time. This assumes that an information agent can invoke the functionality of other such agents and that more importantly there is no *a-priori* order of subtask execution.

We consider the communities of information agents that synergistically execute a common information service-related task to form a larger (widely distributed) and more advanced *meta*-information system, a *cooperative information system (CIS)*. Cooperative information system[2] technology aims to enable collaborative or cooperative work across corporate boundaries and even across continents. This type of technology is the logical development of federated and client–server architectures in a large scale and addresses the problem of distributed information exchange on the basis of task decentralization (Papazoglou *et al.*, 1992; Brodie and Ceri, 1992).

CIS technology must able to solve problems relating to the coexistence of a vast number of network-based legacy systems and new information sources. CIS computing is concerned with combining appropriately information agents (both humans and computers) working cooperatively over space and time to solve a variety of complex problems in medicine, engineering, finance, banking, commercial enterprises and so on. Such concerns are characteristic of nearly all systems created today, and are expected to become even more common in the future. They also apply equally well to small companies with network-based information systems and to large organizations seeking to engage in the practices of international electronic commerce. CIS technology aims to develop the concepts and tools that enable cooperation between diverse information resources and processing components — possibly on the basis of information agent technology — while obviating the need to modify the participating systems. In this new computing paradigm, the classical client/server model is extended to a more dynamic and versatile setup. Individual information agents will support users in effectively performing complicated task-processing activities, e.g., medical, engineering, banking processes, efficiently using the most appropriate information and computing resources (e.g., processing, knowledge, and data) available in large computer networks. Moreover, they will be in a position to dynamically change their role in the client–server relationship: at times they will function as requesters of information services of other application-support agents, and at other times they will provide information and services to other information clients.

---

[2]In this brief introduction we will not attempt to provide any definitions of terms such as interoperability or cooperation as these are explained in later chapters of this book.

The advances that culminate in cooperative information system technology will not come from any single area within the field of information technology. Knowledge-based systems, distributed computing systems and database systems have matured to the point that while further enhancements are desirable, the most promising opportunity for technological advancement comes from their integration into a seamless whole. Such multicomponent networks can be based on fast and flexible data communications networks, realized on client–server architectures, and may utilize interactive multimedia services for communicating with users. The development of the research and technology field of CISs relies on the cooperation of researchers in several disjoint research areas, and the appropriate cross-fertilization of concepts tools and methodologies from various rather independent areas. Data(base) engineering contributes to CIS information management techniques, particularly, for distributed or heterogeneous database systems, data warehousing and efficient implementations of information sharing. AI concerns the representation, utilization, and acquisition of knowledge. AI methods and techniques that are particularly relevant for CISs, include data mining, distributed problem solving and multi-agent systems, planning, scheduling and negotiation. Object-oriented systems and techniques will also contribute to the development of appropriate tools and methodologies. Other related technologies include computer-supported cooperative work, distributed computing, inter-enterprise workflow systems, electronic marketing and commerce, decision support and coordination technology. Application domains that are driving the need for this technology include manufacturing, sales and marketing, distribution, collaborative supply chain management, design, banking, training, education and environmental management to mention just a few.

3 COOPERATIVE INFORMATION SYSTEMS IN THE CONTEXT OF MODERN ORGANIZATIONS

CISs are introducing a variety of technological changes that will permit business and engineering processes to cross-organizational, computing and geographic boundaries. We perceive the impact of integrating CIS technologies into the business practice as being twofold. On one hand the existing strategy, governing structures and organizational forms require advanced technological solutions such as those provided by CISs to transact their business effectively and become more competitive in a global market. On the other hand the introduction of this technology should act as a catalyst to trigger new strategies, governing structures, organizational forms and business processes.

CISs will have a major impact on the way that modern organizations are structured and operate: cross-function, cross-business unit and cross-company availability and exchange of information is a cornerstone of any modern organization. The rapidly accelerating rate of change in today's information-based business environments coupled with increased global competition, makes corporations face new challenges in bringing their products and services to the market (National Research Council, 1994; Tapscott, 1996). Modern enterprises are increasingly dependent on the continuous flow of information for virtually every aspect of their operations. An important requirement is to concentrate on how this novel technology should be integrated with the other components of an organization, namely its strategy, its people and its operations. Organizations should think of their business processes and re-engineer them appropriately in response to technology and market changes. Re-engineering business processes should aim for a more enterprise-wide operation, cross-functional and cross-organization coordination. While cooperative processing allows more organizational flexibility, it poses a lot of challenges in connection with business process re-engineering. These are mainly associated with re-engineering and converting traditional monolithic applications — which represent an organization's business process ineffectively — to meet the challenges of new technologies and changes in the organizational context. Mechanisms are required for effectively representing business practices, policies and tactics in a way that they can be effectively engineered or re-engineered.

4 CHARACTERISTICS OF CISs

In the following we outline some of the most important dimensions of functionality and behaviour that we expect CISs to provide us with. The following list is by no means exhaustive, but it is quite representative of our perceptions of the major features of a CIS:

1. A CIS exhibits a flat structure of its component information systems where sources of responsibility alternate depending on where the posed problem originates from. Loosely speaking we can think of this approach as being opportunistic. This should be contrasted with tightly coupled database topologies where there is a single logical source of authority, viz. the global manager.
2. Component systems in a CIS can be used in unanticipated combinations which are determined by the nature of the problem addressed.
3. A CIS comprises a large collection of pre-existing component information systems with each having its own domain of expertise, problem-solving capabilities, structure and terminology. These need to be brought to a bilateral level of understanding (both structurally as well as semantically) in order to be able to interact, coordinate their activities and achieve cooperation in a pairwise manner.
4. CISs are highly dynamic environments. They address a set of problems that are beyond the capabilities and expertise of individual component information systems and which require the synergy of a collection of

such systems to be solved. In these environments, components should know about their capabilities and should exchange knowledge and information with other such systems to achieve cooperation. This should be contrasted with the static approaches taken by federated or multi-database systems which address a fixed set of problems.

5. CISs have an unprecedented impact on all aspects of a modern organization and will have particular influence on how cooperative business modelling should be conducted in distributed organizations. It is necessary to have an understanding of the organizational environment, its goals and policies, so that the resulting systems will work effectively together with human agents to achieve a common objective. Therefore new modelling tools and methodologies are required to address the problems of change management and requirements engineering in the context of large distributed organizations.

5 STRUCTURE OF THE BOOK

The book contains original chapters discussing various aspects of CIS technology and research. It covers most of the aspects of CISs from requirements, functionality and implementation, to deployment and evolution. The chapters are contributed by prominent researchers and practitioners in the field and are divided into six major areas which broadly reflect what we have described above:

Part I: Distributed Object Computing and Open Systems. Part I comprises two chapters discussing trends, issues and challenges regarding the use and deployment of distributed object computing and component-oriented development from the perspective of large organizations and the requirements of open systems, respectively. These two chapters concentrate on such issues as the use of distributed objects on a massive scale, architectural support for distributed computing frameworks, programming language support, software tools and methods for the development of component-based open systems. These chapters relate to items 1 and 2 of the CIS characteristics as mentioned in Section 4 and will provide the reader with a basic understanding of distributed object infrastructure technologies that are required to provide a general technology base for building CISs.

Part II: Architectures and Language Paradigms. Part II comprises two chapters which also relate to items 1 and 2 of the CIS characteristics. These chapters build on concepts and issues described in Part I and consider how to extend the base infrastructure to address higher-level requirements that are necessary to achieve several forms of cooperation among software components and information systems. These chapters cover such topics as business objects, tiered architectures, workflows, application frameworks, brokering agents, advertisement of services, subscription and recommendation messages. All are needed to construct cooperation layers.

Part III: **Use of Metadata and Ontologies for Information Sharing**. Part III relates to item 3 of the CIS characteristics and discusses the classification of information from different component information systems and discovery of semantical related objects in different systems. These chapters discuss such issues as semantic interoperability, metadata representations, the formation ontologies and organization of exported information according to semantic content. These chapters will provide readers with an understanding of how to achieve agreements on the meaning of exported information and key business concepts needed for enterprise-scale cooperative systems.

Part IV: **Communication, Cooperation and the Exchange of Knowledge**. This part presents knowledge-based techniques to turn passive information systems into more proactive and agile systems that can transform heterogeneous low-level data into high-level homogeneous information and can reason about their functionality and competence. These two chapters discuss such issues as the use of data mining, intelligent query answering techniques and reflective object architectures for the construction of CISs. These themes are related to item 4 of our CIS characteristics list and are essential for the construction of more "intelligent" systems.

Part V: **Modelling Organizations and Systems Requirements**. This part comprises two chapters which discuss modelling techniques and strategies for CIS in the context of large organizations. These chapters relate to item 5 in our list and cover such important issues as cooperative business process modelling, the use of metamodels to address change management, forward and reverse mapping methodologies, requirements engineering for CISs, and in general how to understand and redesign organizational processes in cooperative frameworks in terms of strategic relationships and rationales.

Part VI: **Visionary Approaches**. This final part comprises a single chapter written by authors of previous chapters as well as other experts in various CIS facets ranging from technology to business requirements and deployment of CISs within large organizations. The chapter views CISs as stratified systems comprising various interrelated layers whose aim is to organize and coordinate systems, machine and human collaboration, and organizational aspects of CISs. This chapter is the amalgamation of many interesting ideas and threads of research, which were completely segregated until now, into a unique thought-provoking piece of work that paves the way for future CIS research.

As the field of CISs is nascent, in this book we cover only important topics and areas that are most representative of the current research trends and activities. Such topics as design methodologies, expressive modelling tools for CISs, business models for inter-enterprise collaborative applications, cooperative user interfaces, and sophisticated forms of planning and distributed problem solving are exciting and fruitful areas of research and practice not covered in this book; however, we expect that they will constitute the subject of future CIS publications.

6 HISTORY AND OBJECTIVES

This book has its roots in an effort to bring together the people working on diverse themes related to cooperative information systems research and practice. Meetings and discussions between the individuals started at the CoopIS conferences (running successfully since 1993) where it became clearer that the different approaches to a common theme needed a more unified framework. As a result the International Foundation on Cooperative Information Systems (IFCIS) was officially formed in 1995 in an effort to consolidate and unify the many unconnected research threads and approaches to the goals underlying the CIS. This book should be seen within this context. Its goal is to organize important conceptions, technical approaches and methodologies that are relevant to the development of the CIS field into a coherent form. Another purpose of this book is to provide some new and challenging perspectives in studying the problems and approaches of CISs.

The book presents the state of the art (and future directions if we consider Part VI) in CIS technologies, strategies and methodologies to IT researchers and professionals who are involved or interested in the various facets of distributed or cooperative computing environments. Advanced computer science and information systems students who have taken courses in distributed databases and cooperative systems can use this as a reference book. We hope that this book will illuminate some of the assumptions often made in contemporary CIS research, discuss different approaches, and open some new avenues for addressing CIS-related research and problems.

This book is a collaborative effort among leading experts in the field. Contributors have prepared original material in a comprehensive form and discussed the use of their work within the context of CISs. We cannot think of any single person who has the knowledge and experience to write about the wide range of topics and issues covered in this book.

ACKNOWLEDGEMENTS

This book could have not been written without the help of many people to whom we are indebted. First, we are grateful to the authors of the chapters in the book for their inspiring work and for managing to take time out of their hectic schedules to provide us with such superb material. We also thank them for helping us review the chapters in their parts of the book to guarantee consistency and uniformity. Our special thanks go to the numerous reviewers, without whose help and high-quality reviews this book would have not been possible. We will mention them in strict alphabetical order: Mehmet Aksit, Stephen Blott, Athman Bouguettaya, Silvana Castano, Peter Flach, Terry Gaastarland, Michael Huhns, Aranxa Illaramenti, Stefan Kirn, Ling Liu, Aris Ouksel, Zahir Tari, Wolfgang Wilkes. Finally, we wish to thank Kate Brewin, Jo Craig and Bridget Shine of Academic Press for their constant encouragement and reminders regarding deadlines.

REFERENCES

Brodie, M.L. and Ceri, S. (1992) On intelligent and cooperative information systems. *International Journal of Intelligent and Cooperative Information Systems*, **1**(2), 249–290.

National Research Council (1994) *Realizing the Information Future: The Internet and Beyond.* National Academy Press.

Papazoglou, M.P., Laufmann, S.C. and Sellis, T.K. (1992) An organizational framework for cooperating intelligent information systems. *International Journal of Intelligent and Cooperative Information Systems*, **1**(1), 169–202.

Tapscott, D. (1996) *The Digital Economy: Promise and Peril in the Age of Networked Intelligence.* McGraw-Hill.

Part I

Distributed Object Computing and Open Systems

The Emperor's Clothes are Object Oriented and Distributed[1,2]

Michael L. Brodie

GTE Laboratories Incorporated, Waltham, MA, USA

Abstract

Distributed computing, and distributed object computing in particular, holds remarkable promise for future information systems (ISs) and for more productive collaboration between our vast legacy IS base world-wide. This claim is not new to those who have read research, trade, or vendor literature over the past eight years. GTE has made a significant attempt to benefit from this technology. We have found that it is currently considerably more difficult and less beneficial than the literature or its proponents would have had us believe. This chapter outlines challenges that we and others have faced in attempting to put objects to work on a massive scale. The challenges were confirmed in a world-wide survey that I conducted of over 100 corporations that are attempting to deploy distributed object computing applications based on technologies such as COBRA, DCE, OLE/COM, distributed DBMSs, TP monitors, workflow management systems and proprietary technologies.

Distributed object computing has offered a vision, significant challenges, some progress toward a computing infrastructure and some benefits. Whereas distributed computing infrastructure and its interoperability is critical, application interoperability is the fundamental challenge to users of distributed computing technology. More than 10 large corporations spend in the order of $1 US billion annually addressing application interoperability. Although application interoperability is claimed to be the objective of distributed computing infrastructures, there has been little progress toward this critical ultimate requirement.

---

[1]An earlier version of this chapter appeared as "Foundations of Intelligent Systems", in *9th International Symposium, ISMIS'96, Zakopane, Poland, June 1996, Proceedings* (eds Z.W. Ras, M. Michalewicz), Lecture Notes in Artificial Intelligence, Springer-Verlag.
[2]© 1997 GTE Laboratories.

Cooperative Information Systems
Trends and Directions
ISBN 0-12-544910-0

This chapter presents a view of distributed object computing from the vantage point of a large organization attempting to deploy it on a large scale. Requirements are presented in a distributed computing framework that is necessarily more comprehensive than anything currently offered by the distributed object computing vendors and proponents. A *distributed computing framework* is seen as having four parts:

- distributed and cooperative information systems;
- computing environment;
- distributed object computational model;
- domain orientation.

Relative to this framework, I outline GTE's approach to distributed object computing, challenges GTE faces and faced, why it is so hard, alternative distributed object computing infrastructure technologies, and an estimation of the state of these technologies. I conclude with the basic requirement for industrial-strength, enterprise-wide interoperable "applications". This non-technical requirement has always been a fundamental challenge for software.

No, Virginia, there is no distributed object computing, yet.

I THE CHALLENGE

Future computing hardware and software will be scalable, service oriented and distributed. That is, computing requirements, on any scale, will be met by combining cooperating computing services that are distributed across computer networks. Distributed object computing (DOC) is a critical component in this long-term view, particularly for distributed and cooperative information systems (sometimes called CoopISs). The current challenge is to develop an adequate long-term computing vision and a sensible migration toward that vision (Brodie and Stonebraker, 1995; Brodie, 1996). This, however, is a technology-centric view. A more business-oriented, and hence realistic, restatement might be as follows. To efficiently run our businesses, we would like to deal directly with the business process, not ISs, to define, alter and execute them. Ideally, business processes would be directly and automatically implemented by underlying information technology, which we currently refer to as ISs. Business processes cooperate or interact, often in complex ways. Hence, IS must interact correspondingly. Hence, IS cooperation is one of our current key technical challenges. Cooperation is the high-level requirement. Semantic and application interoperability are terms that refer to lower level (e.g., implementation) aspects of the problem.

This chapter presents an evaluation of progress toward the above goals from the point of view of a large "end-user" organization that is attempting to deploy DOC applications on the large scale. Each viewpoint has its biases. This chapter does not share the biases of a DOC technology vendor or consortium, an academic, or a consultant. End users, more directly than the others, pay for and live with the resulting ISs. Specifically, end users are responsible for the entire life cycle of an IS. Characteristic of DOC technology, end users must, themselves, compose a significant number of component parts to achieve their requirements.

We are currently at the beginning of a 20-year cycle, at the end of which some version of DOC will be the technology of choice for ISs. However, from our current status, significant intellectual and behavioural change is required. It may take 5–10 years for the technology to become complete and robust. Methodologies, tools, education and the shift in the user base to the new technology may extend that period to 20 years. This is similar to the 20-year shift to relational database technology, except that DOC has a comprehensive scope (i.e., all of computing) and is orders of magnitude more complex.

The chief architects of 12 successful large-scale DOC applications all agreed that DOC is considerably more complex than previous approaches. DOC may be so hard because it requires a philosophical shift. Theories in computer science are rational (e.g., deductive) and form the basis of programming languages and IS design. ISs are typically designed in a top-down fashion by means of functional decomposition which came from IBM's 360 project. Object-oriented ISs require the philosophical approach on the other side of the dialectic, namely, empiricism. Distributed and cooperative ISs will be composed, bottom up, from existing or newly created components. The rational and empirical approaches are fundamentally different and require different ways of thinking. This age-old dialectic was initiated by René Descartes (1637), who introduced rationalism in 1637, and by John Locke (1690), who introduced empiricism in 1690. Immanuel Kant (1781) attempted to mediate between the two views in 1781. The point is that composing systems from components (e.g., reuse) is a basic premise of distributed and cooperative ISs, and computer scientists are simply not used to thinking about ISs empirically. We do not have empirical theories or tools to assist us with this approach. Our lack of familiarity with and tools for such an approach may lie at the heart of the difficulty of the paradigm shift and explain why reuse has been so elusive. But, then, I digress.

DOC technology is in an early and immature phase. This can be seen in terms of the technology adoption life cycle, defined by Geoffrey Moore (1991) (see Figure 1). Early adopters, called innovators and visionaries, are change agents who get rewarded for instituting change to get a jump on the competition through radical changes, often called improvements. Later adopters, called pragmatists, conservatives and sceptics, need technology to work well in their existing technology base, which they want to enhance, not overthrow. Between the early adopters and the later adopters is a chasm. The chasm represents the challenges in making the cost/benefits obtained by the early adopters acceptable to the later adopters. The chasm also represents a major change in the customer types due to their radically

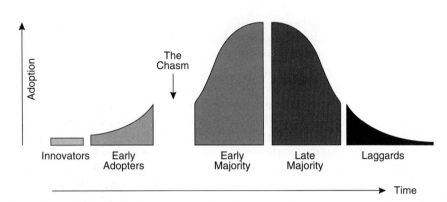

Figure 1.   Moore's technology adoption life cycle.

different motivations. For a new technology to be successfully adopted, it must broach the chasm, since the marketplace is established by the later and not the early adopters. In general, 90% of advanced technology goes down the chasm, at least in the form that it was originally offered. For example, expert system engines went down the chasm, while expert system methodology went into widespread use in a variety of forms, but not in expert system engines.

DOC benefits are often discussed. The costs are not. The DOC vision claims to address current business goals, including improvements in time to market of the target product or service; development, deployment and continuous operations costs; flexibility to accommodate constant changes in business processes, policies and practices; quality; and lowering risk. DOC is also claimed to provide means to overcome problems of previous technologies, including technical (e.g., software crisis (Brodie, 1996)), managerial and administrative. Specific technical objectives include reuse, plug and play, component assembly, workflow-enabled business processes and service or component orientation. The ultimate technical goal is interoperability at all levels and across the entire life cycle. DOC technology is a specific subcase of client/server computing. In the late 1980s, client/server was claimed to provide orders of magnitude improvements in price/performance as well as to address other major information systems problems. By 1997, client/server has not met the claims. Its use is currently at a minimum 20%–30% premium over the mainframe systems it was claimed to annihilate. As with DOC, this may be a temporal issue. As DOC and client/server technology matures, the benefits and cost savings may be realized. Meanwhile, CMOS technology is making mainframes scalable and within 30% of client/server hardware price/performance levels.

DOC technology is in the early adoption stage and is rapidly facing the chasm. DOC technology promoters must now focus on satisfying the requirements of the later adopters. They must address the real state of DOC technology, which our experience and survey suggests is as follows.

DOC is inherently hard, and is not understood. The relevant theory and technology is immature but evolving rapidly. There are rare successes that are due to genius chief architects and their staffs. The claimed benefits (e.g., reuse, productivity) are very hard to realize. Most DOC technology does not meet industrial-strength requirements. Hence, it is not ready for prime time. Since there is currently no dominant DOC infrastructure choice (e.g., CORBA, OLE/COM), how do you design or plan a DOC application? This chapter outlines some of the requirements of the later adopters, based on the experience of an early adopter.

Not surprisingly, there is a pattern here if you replace "DOC" with any "promising advanced computing technology" in the past 20 years (Brodie, 1996; Gibbs, 1994). To address the current challenge of developing an adequate long-term computing vision and a sensible, incremental migration toward that vision, we must act differently than in the past. What is a reasonable time frame for the transition? What are reasonable increments? (Brodie and Stonebraker, 1995.)

2 DISTRIBUTED OBJECT COMPUTING FRAMEWORK

An end user requires a complete distributed computing framework with which to guide an IS through its life cycle. The plug-and-play nature of DOC means that no single vendor provides such a framework since they all produce component parts. Hence, end users of DOC technology must define their own frameworks. There are at least four parts or models that constitute such a framework:

- distributed and cooperative information systems;
- computing environment;
- distributed object computational model;
- domain orientation.

An IS designer must have a conceptual model of *distributed and cooperative information systems*. Such a model (see Figure 2) could consist of a business process that solves a specific business problem. The business process can be expressed in terms of a workflow which, in turn, invokes business services which execute the workflow tasks. Previous-generation architectures were complex and rigid. Next-generation architectures will support the execution time binding of a business service to the workflow task. There may be thousands of such workflows per second, which may mean that the architecture for a given workflow exists only for a nanosecond compared to forever!

The *computing environment* consists of a distributed computing infrastructure and a complete life cycle support environment. The infrastructure provides the services required to support the execution of workflows, the dynamic invocation of business services, and the distributed object space that supports the software components with which the business services

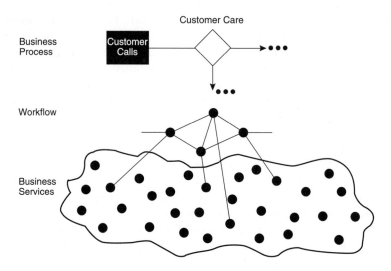

Figure 2.   Next-generation information system: the nanosecond architecture.

and workflows are implemented. These are called CORBAservices® in the terminology of the Object Management Group® (OMG®). The life cycle support environment provides all the necessary tools to support a comprehensive life cycle for ISs–from inception to cradle to grave. Some of these tools are included in what OMG terms CORBAfacilities®. Ideally, these tools will enforce application-specific or domain-specific standards for services at all levels.

The *distributed object computational model* refers to the object model that underlies the computing environment. Rather than being a single object model, it will be a family of interoperable object models, each member of which has a specific role in the computing environment. Due to different computational and programming requirements, there would be different object models for infrastructure services (e.g., persistence service), business services (e.g., telecommunications billing), and applications development (e.g., workflow services, component assembly).

Domain orientation concerns the tailoring of business services with respect to application domain requirements and standards to meet the unique requirements of the domain as well as application interoperability. Domain orientation involves not just standards within one domain (e.g., telecommunications-billing) but also across multiple domains, since few business processes or value chains exist solely within one domain. For example, a telephone call involves billing, routing, possibly advanced services, maintenance and testing, to mention a few. Another example is that most domains contain customers.

In the DOC context, domain orientation involves terminology, ontology, domain (object) models, object/systems interface specifications, and frameworks. Application interoperability requires that two applications mutually understand the messages that they exchange. At least with respect to those messages, they must share (e.g., map to) a common terminology; ontology—definitions of the essential elements of the shared domain; and business processes model—definitions of the way business is conducted in the domain. These shared models can be defined in terms of domain-specific object models which can be standardized in terms of interface specifications for classes from which the IS is composed. A framework for a given application domain is the life cycle support environment (i.e., tools and computing artifacts such as class libraries and interface definitions) that supports and enforces the relevant domain standards. Frameworks are developed by specializing a computing environment with the standard object models of the domain, as manifested in class libraries and interface specifications.

A basis for application interoperability can be defined across application domains by means of families of interoperable object models (see Figure 3) and corresponding interoperable domain frameworks. For example, a generic (domain independent) object model may be extended to produce a billing object model which, in turn, could be specialized to produce a telecommunications billing model as well as others (e.g., a healthcare billing model). Interoperability between healthcare applications and telecom applications (e.g., telemedicine) would be eased by the fact that the corresponding object models were interoperable through the underlying billing object model. Returning to the telecom billing model, it could be specialized to deal with the different sub-domains of telecom billing (e.g., residential, small business, large business and inter exchange). If these object models were developed by a standards body (e.g., the International Telecommunications Union), individual companies would want to specialize them further to support their unique requirements. This results in an interoperable object model family or hierarchy (Manola and Heiler, 1993).

The above domain standards could be enforced, to a degree, by a computing environment that supports the entire life cycle of an IS. The life cycle support environment would ensure that the appropriate domain standards (e.g., object models, classes, interface definitions, business

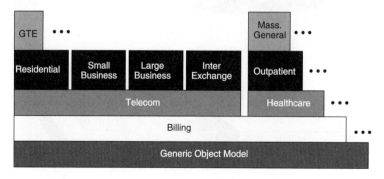

Figure 3.   Object model family.

processes) are used within a domain and between specific domains. Corresponding to the supported object model families or hierarchies, there would be hierarchies of domain-specific life cycle support environments (see Figure 4). Such an environment might be generated or specialized from a generic life cycle support environment by specializing the object model on which it is based (i.e., which it will enforce) (see Figure 5). A number of existing computing environments support such objectives (e.g., DEC's Framework-Based Environment (FBE) product). Another, lower level, example is Expersoft's PowerBroker® Corbaplus for network programming in some specific distributed object computing environments (e.g., it assists in generating interoperability IDL-bridges for C++, SmallTalk, OLE in CORBA 2.0 environments). These bridges include object services such as asynchronous operation, multi-threaded dispatch, and naming.

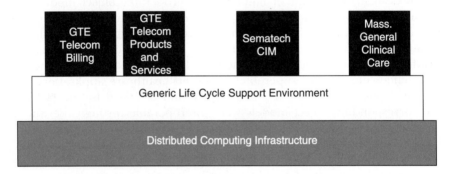

Figure 4.   Interoperable life cycle support environments.

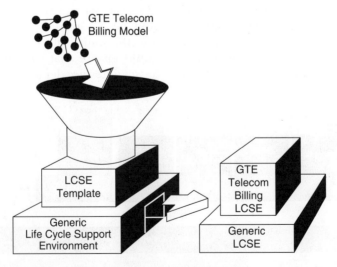

Figure 5.   Life cycle support environment specialization.

Let us turn to the notion of enforcing domain orientation for a moment. Domain orientation should be enforced transparently through the class libraries and the type system on which the class libraries are based. That is, the domain orientation should be enabled by the framework. We should not have to rely on programmer discipline.

Currently, semantic interoperability (i.e., the ability of systems to interoperate, e.g., by exchanging messages that are mutually understood to achieve shared goals) is achieved primarily by the following:

- programmers and designers who must understand system A enough so that when they are programming system B they can design or program meaningful interactions with A (i.e., programmer discipline);
- systems integrators who build bridges between systems to support interoperability.

This low level of solving the problem is labour intensive and error prone. Semantic interoperability should be solved at the highest level possible. For example, if a hierarchy of terminology, ontologies and domain models, such as described above, can be defined to encompass the systems that must interoperate, then the domain models under the ontology can be defined in terms of object models that, in turn, could be used to inform or define a framework with which the systems could be developed. Then, to a very large degree, the developers of the systems can work independently and rely on the fact that the types that they use will be interoperable since they are within the same object model family. It will also be necessary to model the nature of cooperation between the systems. However, this approach reduces the *ad hoc* interoperability approaches (engineering level) to the modelling of cooperation (e.g., through processes, message passing and other cooperation mechanisms).

Consider an example of an underlying, shared theory to enable cooperation between independently developed computing artefacts. Two-phase commit protocols and serializability theory were developed for database transactions so that transaction programmers could develop transactions independently, without any consideration whatsoever of the existence of other transactions to be executed at the same time over the same resources. This independence is required and permitted by transaction theory. Similarly, semantic interoperability and cooperation requires a theory so that an IS can be developed as required without understanding all other ISs with which it might cooperate at some time in the future. This permits flexibility of independent ISs but raises complexity, the current greatest challenge of IS cooperation.

A DOC technology end user requires a comprehensive DOC framework, as described above. Over the past 20 years, the relational database community has developed such a framework, which has resulted in the greatest progress ever made toward application interoperability. In the relational framework, ISs were SQL-based and forms-based applications that shared a common schema. The computing environment consisted of a standardized relational DBMS plus a rich suite of database application programming environments, including CASE environments. The relational computational model has been defined and accepted in national and international standards. There has been little domain orientation in relational database technology. However, it has been discussed in that context for approximately 20 years due to the application interoperability challenges that naturally arose when applications could communicate so readily via a schema. Although it is not stated in terms of domain orientation, the biggest frontier of challenges and related technology advances in database technology lies precisely in this area. The capability of object/relational database management systems to deal with domain-specific data types is the discovery of this new frontier of domain orientation in the database world.

3 GTE'S DOC EXPERIENCE

The decision to use DOC as a fundamental technology of ISs is a complex and expensive one in GTE, due in part to its size. GTE Telephone Operations (Telops) is the largest US local exchange carrier. It is the world's fourth largest public telephone company and has been reported in the *Wall Street Journal* as the 44th largest public company in the USA. It supports 23 million telephone lines, has 100 000 employees, and has annual revenues of $US22 billion. To support this business, GTE's information technology is large scale. The annual information technology expense is in excess of $US1 billion. There are approximately 1500 ISs and over 150 terabytes of data. The legacy ISs are highly interrelated (see Figure 6).

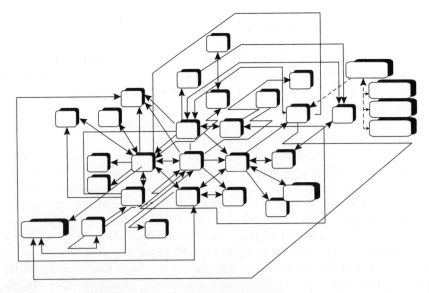

Figure 6.   A legacy IS environment (small example).

In 1993, GTE made a major commitment to re-engineer its business. The goals of business process re-engineering were to permit GTE to respond to rapidly changing business requirements and to the then imminent revolution in the telecommunications business. Other goals included achieving the highest-quality telecommunications products and services and increasing shareholder benefits. These goals are included in this chapter not to advertise, but to reflect the changing demands placed on information technology (e.g., DOC) to be responsive to business needs.

It was in the context of re-engineering that GTE's investigation of DOC turned from research to practice. In 1987, GTE began to investigate distributed object computing infrastructures and applications as a way to significantly improve IS support of its business goals. In 1992, GTE's IT organization began to define a long-term distributed computing framework (see Figure 7) that include distributed and cooperative information systems (e.g., new systems provisioning business process), a computational environment, an underlying object model family and a domain orientation.

In 1993, Telops began the definition of an initial Telops computing environment, as defined in Section 2, and to specify the

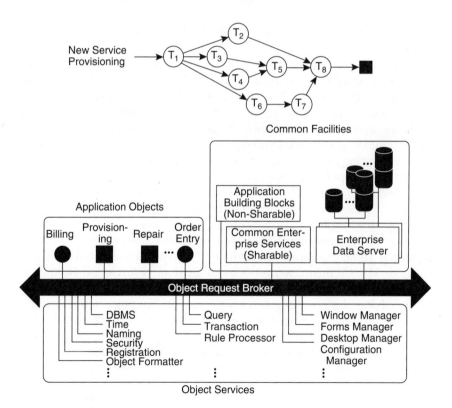

Figure 7. Distributed computing framework.

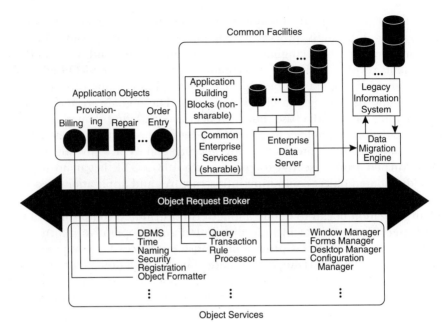

Figure 8. Distributed computing environment plus legacy gateway.

constituent technologies and services (see Figure 8). Initially, the computing environment would consist primarily of non-DOC technology, but would be defined in DOC terms. The non-DOC or legacy technology is included in the architecture via a gateway illustrated in Figure 8. Plans were begun for architecture migration and for corresponding ISs and data servers. Unlike previous technologies, distributed computing encourages resource sharing across applications. Hence, the IT organization and decision-making procedures had to be redefined so that stakeholders across application (e.g., organizational) boundaries could cooperate to achieve a shared technology base. This organizational change was as significant as the technology transition.

The long-term computing environment assumes a model of distributed and cooperative ISs, as defined above and illustrated in Figure 2 and 7, driven by business processes defined in terms of workflows and business services. The work of defining the computing environment and specifying the constituent services was challenging. It was originally assumed that vendors would provide DOC infrastructures. Ideally, there would be a range of vendor products from which to generalize and select. However, this was, and is still, far from the case for DOC technology. Due to the requirement to provide high-quality, robust, reliable products and services, considerable attention was given to a comprehensive life cycle. The minimal services provided in most DOC vendor products focused mostly on the initial 15% of the life cycle, namely analysis, design and development. As a result, GTE focused on the missing services, including class libraries, repository services, comprehensive methodologies, tool support across the life cycle, run-time services, testing and continuous operations support (i.e., the part of the life cycle that consumes 85% of the total IS costs).

A challenge, which can be greater than those of DOC technology, is that of migrating from the existing computing environment and applications base to the corresponding ones for DOC. This is illustrated in Figure 9. This is remarkably challenging not only due to the technical challenges (Brodie and Stonebraker, 1995) but maybe more so due to the business and organizational realignments (Orlikowski and Robey, 1991). The challenges and approaches to their resolution as covered in Brodie and Stonebraker (1995) are not addressed here. Considering the scale of the GTE environment, you can see that key requirements, defined in Brodie and Stonebraker (1995), include the following: ISs cannot be stopped during the migration; the migration must be incremental; the migration will take many years; the computing environment must be designed to support migration; continuous migration will be a way of life; and sequencing of migration increments for shared data and programs requires complex configuration management, to mention a few. Large-scale migrations will proceed incrementally. Hence, the organization

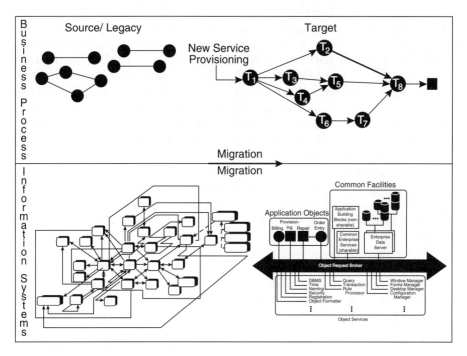

Figure 9.   The migration challenge.

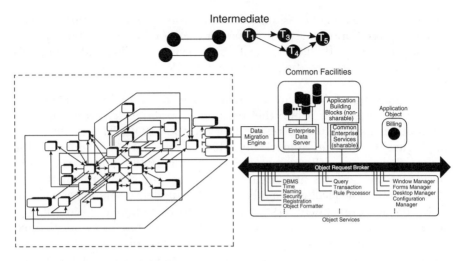

Figure 10.   Migration architecture.

will be in the intermediate stage between the source and target, as illustrated in Figure 10, in which the surviving parts of the old environment, business processes etc., must coexist with the operational parts of the new environment. The critical requirement is that this curious mixture meet the then current business requirements of the organization.

In 1994, GTE began the Carrier Access Billing System (CABS II), its first distributed object computing project, as a joint development between GTE and Ameritech. CABS II was begun after an extensive study to ensure that such a system was achievable. For example, the DOC infrastructure (i.e., TCSI's Object Services Package® (OSP®) — the logical equivalent of an OMG Object Request Broker® (ORB®) plus object services) — was selected based, in part, on the fact that it had been used in several large-scale DOC applications that had been successfully deployed for several years. In addition to OSP, the technical infrastructure included UNIX servers and clients, PC clients and SQL relational DBMS.

A domain-specific distributed object computational model (i.e., a billing object model) was developed for CABS II as well as a corresponding domain-specific (i.e., billing) distributed object framework. Figure 11 illustrates the evolution, through time, of the movement from a domain model that incorporates everything above the operating system level. Introducing a general-purpose application framework reduces the complexity of the CABS domain model. The CABS domain model is further simplified by introducing a billing domain-specific application framework. The resulting CABS domain model consisted of a collection of basic billing object classes. The basic billing object class library assisted significantly in the design and development of CABS II. The rest of the object model family and the corresponding frameworks helped to establish a base for application interoperability across applications and domains. The CABS II

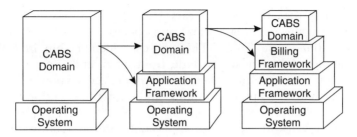

Figure 11.   Billing object model and framework.

Table 1.   CABS II sizes.

Business/domain classes	250
Implementation classes	4500
Class instances (estimate)	
Data	3×10^{10}
Non-usage data	10^6
Servers	50–75
Clients	>1000
TP rate	2200/s
Message rate	6100/s

chief architect claimed that the CABS II billing object model and framework was one of the major advantages of the CABS II project. Using the framework, those developing business solutions work almost entirely with billing objects, not with a general-purpose object model. What is more, all business solutions in CABS II use the same billing objects.

CABS II is a large-scale DOC application, as measured by the statistics in Table 1. These August 1995 numbers have since increased significantly, thus indicating our inability to adequately estimate DOC systems characteristics at the outset. In Table 1, "Message" means an object instance service invocation message plus an object instance service response message (if any).

4 DOC DEPLOYMENT STATUS: A SURVEY

Although I did not start out to do so, I conducted a survey of DOC deployment around the world. Initially, in support of GTE's DOC programme I initiated an information exchange between GTE and a few organizations of comparable size with a comparable commitment and investment in DOC. Following the popular notion from Jack Welch, CEO of GE, we tried to identify and possibly adopt the best DOC practices. Much to my surprise, I found few, if any, comparable organizations with comparable experience. Indeed, two such exchanges ended with the other organizations acknowledging that they were years behind us. A second motivation was to confirm the experiences and approaches followed in CABS II. A third motivation came from GTE's end-user membership in OMG. In OMG meetings, I had heard so little from other end users in terms of technical requirements and challenges. I experienced acknowledgment but little action toward or apparent understanding, by the vendor-dominated organization, of end-user requirements. Specifically, there appeared to be no substantive work in support of application interoperability.[3] This may have been due to the lack of end-user experience with large-scale DOC applications. A survey might shed light on these questions. Finally, I was very interested from the point of view of GTE's nine-year research effort into these topics (Manola *et al.*, 1992) as to the state of technology *vs* the state of research. What are the pragmatic research challenges? The survey was fruitful in each of the above areas.

The survey was informal. I contacted any organization that was an OMG end user or for which there was a rumour or claim that they were attempting to deploy DOC applications (e.g., customers of DOC infrastructure products such as ORBs). A survey form was used which evolved as I learned more about DOC deployment issues. The survey was sent to over 100 end users from whom I received 61 responses on 201 DOC applications in various stages of deployment, as indicated in Table 2.

DOC applications can be built using a wide range of combinations of alternative infrastructure technologies, as indicated in Table 3. Table 3 lists the percentage of systems that used a particular technology. Most systems use more than one technology. These technologies include OMG CORBA-compliant ORBs, Microsoft's OLE/COM®, OSF/DCE® products, a wide range of database management systems (SQL, object-relational, object-oriented, and several flavours of distributed DBMSs), transaction processing monitors, workflow managers, messaging backplanes and proprietary DOC

Table 2.   Survey results.

	CORBA	Proprietary	Total
Large scale			
Deployed 1−3 years	1	13	14
Deployed, not confirmed	25	5	30
To be deployed 0−3 years	6	59	65
Limited scale/features, deployed	6	16	22
Prototype/evaluation/pilot	17	53	70
TOTAL	55	146	201

[3]The first OMG request for proposal in support of application interoperability was issued in January 1996. It is entitled "Common Facilities RFP-4: Common Business Objects and Business Object Facility".

Table 3.   Major infrastructure technology used.

Major infrastructure technology	Applications surveyed (%)
Proprietary	80
DBMS	50
TP monitor	30
CORBA	20
OLE/COM	10
Workflow managers	10
DCE	0

infrastructures (e.g., TCSI's OSP®; SSA Object Technology's Newi®; and NeXT's Portable Distributed Objects®, NextStep®, and OpenStep®).

All successfully deployed large-scale DOC applications that I found ran on proprietary DOC infrastructures. DBMSs are the obvious choice for data management in any infrastructure. However, distributed DBMSs may become the primary DOC infrastructure for some applications. Although distributed DBMS products now meet many distributed computing requirements, they are just beginning to be deployed. TP monitors are in widespread use (e.g., most credit card and ATM transactions). They form the backbone of many distributed computing architectures. During the survey, I found no confirmed large-scale applications deployed on a CORBA-compliant ORB. After the survey, I found one modest-sized ORB-based deployed system (The British Immigration Service's Suspect Index System, which runs on ICL's DAIS®). The ORB-based applications were of limited scale (the largest involved five servers), of limited features (e.g., distribution not used), or were not deployed. Although OLE/COM is in widespread use on desktops, network OLE, the corresponding DOC infrastructure, including Microsoft's Component Object Model (COM), was not yet available. I heard claims of over 100 large-scale applications deployed on workflow management systems (WFMS), but was able to find only 10, and in those, the WFMS did not seem to be the critical infrastructure element. I found no DCE-based applications. Following the survey, I found five modest-scale DCE-based deployments and indications that there are likely to be many more. The clear winner was "combination". Table 3 adds up to 200%, indicating that most applications use a combination of infrastructure technologies. After interoperation is possible, combinations of technologies will likely be the dominant infrastructure. Which will be the component infrastructures, and what degree of heterogeneity will be practical?

Building a DOC application from scratch in a DOC environment can be considerably easier than integrating legacy applications using a DOC technology. I found most DOC applications to be pure, and most

Table 4. DOC application type.

Application type	Applications surveyed (%)
Pure DOC applications	65
DOC for legacy IS integration	30
DOC applications + legacy IS integration	5

of the rest to be legacy IS integrations (Table 4). The challenges include dealing with the complexities of mapping from a DOC environment to a variety of potentially heterogeneous non-DOC environments. This is generally done with DOC wrappers around the legacy applications. Potentially more significant challenges arise in penetrating the legacy application to provide access to the functions and data. Indeed, Jim Kirkley III, an engineer with probably the greatest experience and expertise in such wrappers, advises against penetrating the legacy application at all below its existing API. It is likely that the biggest market, world-wide, for DOC technology will be, at least initially, for legacy IS integration. In the long term, the most obvious requirement is for lots of legacy applications interoperating with lots of DOC applications. This is also clearly the hardest type of application type to build. At GTE, we start with 100% non-DOC applications. CABS II must interoperate with many legacy ISs. Other guidelines from Jim Kirkley include the following: keep the shared objects small (e.g., just interface objects); and do not map legacy functions to externally visible objects. Leave the legacy alone and build an interface with proxies that, in turn, invoke legacy functions. Separate, where possible, the logical model from the distribution model (as supported by DEC's ObjectBroker®) so that you can ignore distribution issues when doing the logical design and you can accommodate changes in the physical/distribution layer without having to change the logical level.

The survey found that CABS II was the largest DOC application, in terms of the statistics listed in Table 5. CABS II is not in production as of December 1996. CABS II was larger than Texas Instruments' TI WORKS®, a suite of applications for running a semiconductor CIM fabrication plant. Based on the information gathered in the survey, TI WORKS was the most successful large-scale DOC application. It does not use an ORB. At the time of the survey, TI WORKS was about to release some small components (e.g., configuration management) of TI WORKS into production, with a plan for major components to be released at the end of 1996. CABS II was larger in all categories, including the number of classes in object instances, the latter by four orders of magnitude. However, this scale is considerably smaller than current large-scale mainframe-based ISs. The "Other" column in Table 5 refers to the 11 large-scale DOC applications that I found which were smaller again than TI WORKS.

Table 5. Scale.

	CABS II	TI Works	HOSIS	Other
Domain classes	300	200	33	100−200
Implementation classes	2243	1000	94	1000−3000
Object instances	10^9	10^6	10^6	$10^4 - 10^6$
Servers	50 to 75	400−1000	100−1000	10−20
Clients	>1000	400−1000	>1000	100−300
TP rate/second	2200		0.1	600−800
Messages/second	6000			>2000

I surveyed the respondents on several issues of significance to GTE's DOC effort. I found that 92% of the successful large-scale DOC applications used asynchronous (e.g., queued) messaging, while 40% of the small-scale ISs and prototypes used synchronous (e.g., RPC) messaging, such as provided in OMG's CORBA. The reasons for asynchronous messaging included robustness (e.g., recoverable queues), performance, scalability, non-blocking behaviour and flexibility (e.g., via queue management). I found only three organizations that were working on an enterprise-wide DOC architecture and three that were working on smaller architectures for divisions or business processes. Four organizations had formal class libraries; four were building ontologies or domain models; and four were developing frameworks, as defined above (including CABS and TI WORKS).

I found only three applications that were built on infrastructures that supported logical–physical object separation. For more than 20 years, DBMS technology has supported a degree of data independence. Programs are insulated from changes in the physical structure, since they deal with logical schema entities which are mapped by the DBMS to the under-lying physical representation. Hence, the physical DBMS can be optimized without impacting programs. In all but three DOC applications, logical and physical object representations are identical. This means that changes to objects' logical or physical representation require changes to the entire system. This is practically infeasible at the scale of CABS II.

There were a few obvious conclusions from the survey of DOC deploy-ment. First, for such a rapidly evolving technology, the situation changes constantly. The premise of this chapter is that DOC technology will be the base of future ISs. However, the current state, at the time of the survey, indicates that considerable maturation is required. Second, there are lots of object-oriented applications, but very few true DOC applications. This survey was not about object-oriented applications; it was about DOC applications. Third, almost all successful DOC applications were based on homogeneous, proprietary infrastructures and were not readily interoper-able with other applications, the antithesis of the DOC vision and of OMG claims, or at least goals. Fourth, DOC is inherently very hard and lacks general solutions and tools (i.e., they must be developed by highly skilled staff). Fifth, there are a few success stories (e.g., HOSIS, TI WORKS), and their success is due largely to the highly skilled staff. Sixth, there may be more significant successful DOC projects that I did not find or which did not respond. For example, the financial community claimed 30 successful large-scale DOC applications, 25 based on CORBA ORBs (see Table 2 "Deployed, not confirmed"). However, they were unwilling to provide the details to substantiate the claims. I did obtain details of one such claimed DOC application and found that it was deployed but was not using distribution (i.e., copies on different machines did not communicate). Finally, claims of success cannot be taken at face value. I followed up on a few public claims of and awards for DOC successes and found them to be either unconvincing, unsubstantiated, or significantly less than claimed. For example, a high level of reuse was claimed for a large-scale deployed DOC application that was built in a partnership between two organizations. I found that one partner, an end user, did not get any reuse. The other partner, a solutions vendor, got considerable reuse since they had sold the system to multiple customers.

The survey seems to suggest the following lessons. First, the major challenge remains the development of an adequate long-term computing vision and a sensible migration toward that vision. Successful large-scale DOC application projects devoted considerable effort to developing a model of distributed and cooperative ISs and a computing environment (e.g., architecture beyond the current application), and planned for a long-duration migration to the vision (e.g., one major application at a time). Second, mission-critical production applications should be pursued using DOC only if the requirements clearly demand it, and then only with great care. Third, small non-mission-critical pure DOC applications are the easiest, while the obvious near-term win, legacy IS integration, is considerably harder. The conventional requirement will be for a substantial mix of both, and that is the hardest type of application to build. Fourth, DOC infrastructures are being developed as products and standardized (e.g., in OMG and OSF's DCE) apparently without having been tested on real DOC application requirements. Indeed, there are few in existence. Finally, the high risk involved in DOC application development and deployment requires explicit risk management. So, how should you design and plan that system today for delivery in three to five years?

5 INDUSTRIAL-STRENGTH DOC REQUIREMENTS

Based on our experience and on the survey, I identify, in this section, a number of requirements that DOC technology must satisfy to meet the needs of large-scale industrial applications. The requirements are given with respect to the distributed computing framework introduced above. As OMG is one of the world-wide foci of DOC technology development,

many of the requirements are given with respect to the current state of
OMG technology. However, the comments can apply equally to any DOC
technology (Microsoft, 1996). Microsoft is also a major focus of DOC technology development. Unlike OMG and vendors of OMG-compliant products, Microsoft has existing products and less than 500 organizations in the
decision process. Indeed, they have significant products on the market (e.g.,
Microsoft® Windows NT® operating system, ActiveX®, Active Server® and
the Microsoft® Transaction Server — formerly known by its code name,
"Viper"). So Microsoft is in a very different position than OMG-based
vendors. One could easily say that OMG is at the beginning of a long,
complex technology development and cannot be expected to provide a
complete solution. Correspondingly, Microsoft is probably further along
but still has a long path to maturity. That is precisely the point of this
chapter. This section looks at some specifics to illustrate the point and, it is
hoped, to encourage effort toward fulfilling end-user requirements.

Industrial-strength applications require that all the pieces be in place,
from the hardware up to the end-user applications and throughout the
entire life cycle. A comprehensive distributed computing framework is
missing and so are the constituent industrial-strength tools and technology.
End users require such a framework and the relevant components since
they must put together all the components to build an application,
let alone an enterprise-wide environment of interoperable applications.
Considerable effort has been invested in DOC infrastructure (i.e., OMG
CORBA, CORBAservices and CORBAfacilities) in the absence of a global
framework or a model of the target ISs that the infrastructure will support.
Work is beginning in OMG's Analysis and Design Task Force to address
application development life cycles, object analysis and design methodology
metamodels, and relevant technologies. Work is also going on in the
Business Object Domain Task Force (BODTF) in the area of business
objects and business object facilities. This work is to be commended. The
fact that they are just beginning, and the difficulty of placing them in the
OMG object management architecture, indicates the current state of DOC
technology. How can you build a DOC application before such technology
is in place? How can you specify DOC infrastructure technology without
understanding the requirements of the business objects that it is intended
to support? My survey found that the optimistic answer is "with highly
skilled people". Another example of progress being made toward business
objects is that SAP, AG developer of SAP R/3®, is developing business
object interfaces and a complete business object approach to the business
objects that constitute SAP R/3. The world-wide usage of SAP R/3 may
well influence the move to business objects. A related development is in
the DBMS marketplace. The growth market is in DBMSs that support
objects. INFORMIX®'s Universal Server is the best example. Although
most DBMS vendors are developing or have competing products. This
technical capability to support objects in the large scale will likely lead

to the increased use of business objects. However, as stated for all such object-oriented technology developments, be they of OMG, Microsoft or DBMS vendors, the cart is before the horse. Business objects and their requirements should precede the technologies that will support them. But, then, it has never gone that way before, and look where we are today!

Industrial-strength applications are often built with large project staffs. The distributed object computational model that the staff uses must be complete and at a level appropriate to the problems being solved. The OMG distributed object computational model could be considered to be the OMG's core object model, augmented by the CORBAservices and some of the CORBAfacilities. DCOM is Microsoft's corresponding distributed object computational model. Collectively, the OMG components, mentioned above, provide the capabilities required by staff to develop DOC applications. CORBAservices will be in development for some years. As of early 1996, some services were not yet adopted (e.g., asynchronous messaging), some were under-specified (e.g., concurrency and transaction services), some require getting some bugs out (e.g., event service), while still others had not yet entered the process (e.g., rules). A significant end-user problem is that OMG-compliant ORBs typically deliver no more than four such services with tens (e.g., 30) of services yet to come. Hence, the computational model is not complete. Further, CORBA services and the OMG distributed object computational model is at too low a level for application programming staff. Figure 12 illustrates the problem. The bottom of the figure indicates low-level basic features of the object model (i.e., objects and messages). The top of the figure illustrates a consistent, high level of abstraction at which a DOC programmer would ideally work. Each line, under the wavy line, indicates a service or facility. The height of a line indicates how close the service or facility is to the desired level of abstraction. Each service or facility has a different height or level of abstraction since, in my view, they have not been designed within a consistent, high-level object model. There is no high-level programming model for CORBA-based application development. Indeed, the services and facilities come from disparate groups or individuals. Hence, the OMG object model, including the services and facilities, provides the OMG

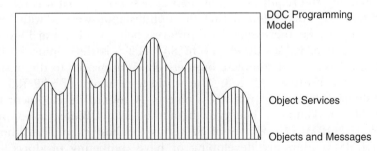

Figure 12.   Distributed object computational model.

technology user with a non-uniform, too low-level model, as indicated by the wavy line.

DOC programming environments such as NextStep, SSA Object Technology's Newi, Forté's Forté® and TI's Composer® provide more complete and higher-level computational models required for industrial-strength applications. OMG's BODTF work on business objects and business object facilities will begin to address some of these issues over the next two to three years. Finally, the recently created OMG Architecture Board is responsible for ensuring the consistency of OMG technology specifications. Its job will be to ensure that the OMG distributed object computational model, as described above, is consistent with respect to a specific and complete OMG core object model. This is a significant challenge. The OMG concept of profile is required to support domain-specific object models but is not yet adequately defined.

In late 1996, Microsoft released Microsoft Transaction Server, for which it claimed (Microsoft, 1996) "Microsoft Transaction Server lowers server development costs up to 40%. Developers use Microsoft Transaction Server to deploy scalable server applications built from ActiveX components, focusing on solving business problems instead of programming application infrastructure. Microsoft Transaction Server delivers the 'plumbing' — including transactions, scalability services, connection management, and point-and-click administration — providing developers with the easiest way to build and deploy scalable server applications for business and the Internet." These claims indicate a concern for the problems mentioned above, and, if true, indicate a significant advance toward the maturity heretofore lacking in DOC.

Industrial-strength applications require a comprehensive life cycle, from inception to design, development, deployment, evolution and ultimately termination or replacement. There is no widely accepted life cycle for DOC applications. It is unlikely that an organization would begin an industrial-strength large-scale application without understanding the entire life cycle and without having an adequate computing environment to support it. OMG does not provide such a life cycle nor do the CORBAfacilities provide the support tools. These will, no doubt, be specified over the next few years. Currently, there is considerable focus on the first 15% of the life cycle. Industrial-strength applications incur 85% of their total costs in that latter 85% of the life cycle. Even within the first 15%, there are significant gaps. There is little support for distribution design for applications, objects/data and execution (e.g., parallelization, load balancing) or implementation. There is no DOC repository. There are no models, metrics or tools to assist in testing. There is almost no support for continuous operations support. Many of these issues are active topics within the OMG. However, this chapter is not addressing the future. It is concerned with what can be used now!

There are other problems with the DOC infrastructure that are related to open research problems and that pose significant challenges for large-scale industrial applications. For example, OMG technology provides several messaging backplanes. There is the ORB, with its basic messaging service. There is the query service for communicating query messages to query processors. Similarly, there is a transaction service and a persistence service. For high-volume transactions, should you use the CORBA messaging service to then access a DBMS transaction service, or should you access the DBMS or TP monitor directly, using SQL, as is done by Microsoft's Active Server and Transaction Server? Similar engineering questions arise for queries and persistence. Hence, there are between one and four messaging backplane choices for application developers. If you choose anything other than the CORBA messaging service, you must then manage the resulting "messaging architecture". You might also consider whether your "objects" should be represented as objects or in the basic representation of the DBMS. A related problem is that you may wish to have persistence, query and transaction services over all objects in the CORBA DOC environment. However, these services are provided over those objects that reside in a component that supports the service. This will not likely include components other than DBMSs and TP monitors for some time. This means that providing those services will mean crossing from the CORBA DOC environment and type system to that of the DBMS and TP monitors. This will generally mean translating between object-type and non-object-type systems. Another performance hit.

Another computing environment problem concerns one of the great successes of OMG, the OMG IDL® (interface definition language). OMG IDL is being adopted widely, independently of, or in anticipation of, the success of CORBA. Hence, IDL is becoming the vernacular API, the interface specification language of many, many systems. Since IDL cannot be all things to all people, it is seen, specifically in my survey, as very limited. Each systems project wants to extend IDL for its own requirements. Unfortunately, many variants of IDL are now evolving.

Our experience with respect to ORB products was confirmed by the survey. These products are at an early stage of development and are incomplete, just as CORBAservices and CORBAfacilities specifications are incomplete. Most ORB products do not support the minimal adopted CORBAservices and CORBAfacilities and may not for some time. In addition, by mid-1996, large-scale industrial-strength applications push the limits of all ORB products with which we or the survey respondents had experience. They did not meet requirements for robustness, scale and reliability. I am aware of no ORB that supports adequate means of testing, quality assurance, appropriate metrics for sizing and tuning, or monitoring and maintenance (e.g., performance tuning — recall the lack of logical–physical separation). What serious organization would go to production without these facilities? Most CORBA products lack an adequate asynchronous queued messaging service as a first-class citizen with RPC. Some of these problems are overcome by proprietary products. For example, Forté provides a wonderful function called the "rolling upgrade", which permits client applications to be upgraded from one version to another while the system is running, all from a single point in the distributed system. Do you want to base a computing environment or even an application on a proprietary product or even a CORBA-compliant product augmented by many proprietary services built either by you or the ORB vendor, awaiting OMG standardization? GTE decided firmly against such a risky strategy.

Synchronous vs. asynchronous messaging is a key issue. Let me speculate in order to illustrate a potential process of maturation and evolution. We are at the beginning of the message-based computing paradigm in which we will be required to understand more deeply the nature of communication protocols and the requirements for communications by the increasingly large number of applications with increasingly complex requirements. Synchronous and asynchronous messaging are two ends of a spectrum, that indeed may be more than one dimensional. As we better understand messaging requirements, we may produce a spectrum of choices for communication protocols in which designers can specify what combination and degree of properties they want from the communication protocol, and the system will automatically generate a corresponding protocol somewhere along the spectrum. Further, the system may be able to optimize the choice. As the system is operational, different communication loads and behaviours could be monitored and the system could alter the communication protocol in order to meet optimization criteria set by the designers. This would require that programmers not specify any specifics of the protocol so that those specifics are not embedded in the program, thus permitting the system to optimize as required (like relational queries). Compare this to the complex programming requirements to use the CORBA RPC mechanisms.

Finally, the fundamental requirement of industrial-strength, enterprise-wide interoperable applications is interoperability. Comprehensive interoperability involves interoperability across the entire life cycle. All artefacts produced during the life cycle should be accessible, in principle, by all tools. All tools should be able to interoperate with others, again, in principle. Interoperability is required from the bottom to the top. At the bottom, there is hardware platform interoperability which is "vendor hard". It is entirely within the capabilities of the platform vendors to resolve the problem. At the next level, infrastructure interoperability is "Turing hard". Whoever solves the problems of interoperable object models and distributed object computing services and facilities should be awarded the Turing Award. It is a very significant challenge. However, interoperability at the next level, application interoperability, is "Nobel hard". A solution here should garner a Nobel Prize. The next section concludes this chapter by illustrating this challenge, indicating its significance, and emphasizing that it is not a technical issue. Indeed, it is a core problem at the interface of computing and real life. It raises, for me, moral and ethical issues such as: What are the limits of technology? To what extent can we genuinely represent real-world (e.g., business) activities in a computer and rely on the system to replicate or become the real-world manifestation of the desired function? This chapter does not pursue these deeper problems. I mention them here to raise the more pragmatic question of what should we expect of DOC as a basis for running our businesses, and can we trust the claims of DOC proponents? To what extent can they verify that their claims are true and reliable since they may influence people to deploy DOC technology in mission-critical contexts not only where business and trade is involved, but where human lives may be at stake?

6 TOWARD INDUSTRIAL-STRENGTH, ENTERPRISE-WIDE INTEROPERABLE APPLICATIONS

In the period 1913–1915, Niels Bohr, the Danish physicist and Nobel laureate, published the papers that defined his new theory of atomic structure, for which he received the Nobel Prize in physics in 1922. The significance of his theory of the erratic changes in energy levels of electrons circling the nucleus was understood almost immediately by physicists world-wide. Within a few years, Niels Bohr's ideas, one man's ideas, had helped to evolve man's understanding of the atom and of elementary matter. This was possible, in part, because physicists world-wide shared a common domain orientation, as defined in Section 2, for elementary particles. There was a common terminology, a shared ontology (i.e., the basic concepts of particle physics) and a number of shared domain models (e.g., Rutherford's nuclear model of the atom). The shared domain models were standardized in mathematical models (analogous to interface specifications of object models) and placed in frameworks (i.e., the larger mathematical models of physics, such as quantum mechanics). The shared domain orientation permitted physicists around the world to cooperate (i.e., interoperate). The shared domain orientation in physics was the result of hundreds of years of science, at least back to Sir Isaac Newton (1643–1727). The process that created it was that of science itself. Now, although there are many differences and constant attempts to change and improve the domain orientation of physics, any two physicists can cooperate based on a mutually shared domain orientation. In 1997, this is being pushed from physics to philosophy and psychology, as the domain orientation in physics is moving more and more from the conventional, particle view of physics to the wave theory.

Following the principles of component orientation motivating DOC technology, consider the creation of a telecommunications billing system from components. The components may be entire subsystems (e.g., a rating system, an account management system, a bill generation system) or one or more class libraries of billing classes (e.g., customer, bill, line item). The use of these components together to produce a single billing system requires application interoperability. Each pair of components must have a shared understanding of the objects (e.g., functions and data) involved in any messages that they exchange. Of course, it is more complex when a communication involves more than two components. Also, a deeper understanding (e.g., of objects that they do not exchange or the business process within which they participate) may be required. However, it is sufficient for this discussion to restrict our consideration to the messages exchanged by two components, the minimal application interoperability requirement.

Mutual understanding of objects in exchanged messages requires a shared domain orientation. The components must share or be able to map to a common terminology. To the degree that it affects their behaviour, they must share a common ontology (i.e., definition of the basic concepts, such as customer). They may also require a shared domain model (i.e., the business process of producing a bill). However, this is dependent on the nature of the functions of the two components. It would be helpful, but not necessary, if the shared domain orientation were enforced by interface specifications and a framework such as is illustrated in Figures 3, 4, 5 and 11.

How can we ensure that the billing system components have a shared domain orientation? Consider the elementary particle domain model shared by physicists world-wide. This was hundreds of years in the making, under assumptions of sharing and cooperation between physicists. Is there a comparable context or history for telecommunications billing? The International Telecommunications Union (ITU) is the international standardization body for telecommunications. It attempts to create shared domain orientations in various domains. It has been most successful in the areas of hardware and network management (e.g., TMN). However, there is no world-wide shared domain orientation for basic telecommunications domains such as billing, provisioning, automation and repair. Work is under way in these areas, using object orientation as a tool to define such models. As you can easily see, the challenge is not technical (i.e., how to define a model in object-oriented models). The challenge involves defining mutually agreeable terminologies, ontologies and domain models. How long will it take to achieve such agreements between thousands of telecommunications companies in countries all over the world, each with different cultures, economic models, levels of sophistication and business models? The models are not static. For example, the landmark US Telecommunications Bill of 1996 will revolutionize the US telecommunications business and related models. Corresponding international agreements are actively under discussion in 1996–1997 within the newly formed World Trade Organization. Unlike physical models, which have the physical world as a basis for verification, billing models are pure abstractions, with no such direct means for empirical verification. A billing model can be verified, but with considerable difficulty, especially when it is undergoing fundamental change.

Let us consider shared ontologies and common object models as a basis for the illusive and much claimed feature of object-orientation, reuse. Reuse is not a technology issue so much as a standards issue, as I will now illustrate. The current essential problem of reuse is that it is not being addressed at the semantic "interoperability" level, but at the systems interoperability level. As long as engineering-level, infrastructure solutions are the focus, the solutions will be too general, and lots of problems will remain to be addressed by programmers and designers. As a result, considerable effort will be wasted, since these individual solutions will be idiosyncratic and will themselves need to be integrated. Generally, semantic interoperability is considered at the engineering level, as an engineering problem. This is analogous to designing automation to scoop up horse manure faster and faster as the number of horses increases rather than solve the problem at the source.

Successful reuse can occur most readily in domains that are well understood and bounded. Examples include: operating systems, DBMSs, spreadsheets and word-processors. Indeed, these are widely reused world-wide. The basic reason is that the domain orientation exists. The related semantics are bounded and well understood. Other aspects that facilitate semantic interoperability, hence reuse, are:

- **Existing domain-orientation:** the domain is widely understood with a standard definition, a widely accepted terminology, ontology or domain model (e.g., as in the physics example above).
- **Market share:** a product becomes widely used, hence its terminology, ontology and domain models become the basis for interoperability. The widespread use of them makes them a standard.
- **Attempts to gain market share:** widely used products become a focal point for products that need to interoperate with them. Hence, vendors build the bridges themselves to facilitate interoperability of their products. For example, Microsoft's ODBC became a world-wide standard within 6 months of its introduction since ODBC provided interoperability with many of Microsoft's products which were *de facto* standards.
- **Modularity:** the domain in which the products are used is well-enough understood that the functionality can be modularized in ways that are universally accepted. This permits the components (i.e., objects) to be reused since their roles are well defined and accepted as a standard (e.g., spellers as components in all text-based systems, RDBMSs in all data-intensive applications).

So we can look at the ease and criticality of establishing a domain orientation to identify the likelihood of establishing general-purpose semantic interoperability, and hence, reuse in a given domain. Let us consider domain-orientation or reuse of telecommunications billing.

- **No market share:** there are no telecom billing applications that have market share. Hence, there is no motivation to semantically interoperate with it (i.e., adopt its domain orientation) to achieve reuse.
- **No modularity:** there is no widely agreed decomposition of the telecom billing domain that would encourage the development of reusable components.
- **No existing domain-orientation:** there is not a widely accepted terminology, ontology or domain model for telecom billing. Hence, semantic interoperability is simply not a realistic issue. All attempts at this will fail, unless the attempt is strong enough to establish itself as the standard.

To conclude this example, telecom billing is a real market opportunity for establishing world-wide standards since the market is vast (e.g., thousands of telecoms world-wide each require billing as a mission-critical business function). However, the plausibility of this must be investigated. What is the likelihood, from a non-technical perspective, of establishing such a standard (e.g., meets customer requirements, intellectual capability of developing a reasonable solution). There are many domains in which this is perfectly reasonable and indeed are well on their way to universal acceptance (e.g., Oracle and SAP financials). Do not hope for reuse until you have established the ease, criticality and feasibility of domain orientation in the domain in which you are working.

A large number of standards bodies or consortia are attempting to create domain orientations. A brief search of the literature and the World Wide Web uncovered activities in the areas listed in Table 6. Within healthcare alone, there are more than 15 such activities in Europe (Table 7) and many in the USA. The RICHE activity has developed an entire healthcare domain orientation, as defined in Section 2. It has defined a terminology, several ontologies, several domain models, interface specifications and a framework which is produced by a consortium. RICHE has been adopted by more than 15 000 hospitals in Europe.

Most of these activities are intended primarily to provide standardization for the domain and not necessarily for the associated ISs. There is significant value to establishing a shared domain orientation, independently

Table 6. Areas pursuing domain standardization.

Manufacturing	Healthcare	Transportation
Engineering	Mathematics	Bibliographic data
Medicine	Retail	DoD
Space	Computer	Software meta-data
Legal insurance	Art	Petroleum
Spatial and multimedia applications		Financial services
Telecommunications management network		
Telecommunications billing		

Table 7.   Healthcare domain standardization activities.

Common Basic Specification (GB)	RICHE (Europe)
READ3	HELIOS II
NUCLEUS	CANON
General Architecture for Languages, Encyclopedias and Nomenclatures	
GALEN-IN-USE	CEN TC251
GAMES	DILEMMA
PRESTIGE: SYNAPSES	SNOMED
The Good European Health Record	
Framework for European Services in Telemedicine	
Strategic Health Informatics Networks for Europe	
Computer-Based Medical Records Institute	
Patient-Oriented Management Architecture (USA)	

of establishing computing standards. However, many of these activities are attempting to extend the agreements to computing. When the activities have been initiated by the computing community (e.g., Great Britain's Common Basic Specification), they have often encountered resistance from the domain (e.g., the healthcare community). This suggests that domain orientations are almost entirely the business of the domain and not the business of the technologist. Technologists can assist with the formulation of the object-oriented domain models, interface specifications, and computing frameworks, but not with the terminologies, ontologies or domain models.

The examples in Tables 6 and 7 illustrate opportunities and challenges. The opportunities are obvious. A shared domain orientation assists all members of the domain, within some limits (e.g., errors and limitations). In addition, the domain orientation could provide a basis for application interoperability of ISs within the domain and a basis for component orientation, class libraries and other benefits claimed for DOC. The challenges are equally obvious. As with the telecommunications standards, it is a challenging, and apparently never ending, human, and not technical, task to achieve a standard. There are all the usual challenges with standards. As illustrated in Table 7, there are multiple standards in any one field. The large number of domains to be standardized only suggests the exponential number of relationships between domains to be standardized. Real-life activities (e.g., value chains and their associated business processes and supporting ISs) cross domains. The needle and the drug being inserted by a nurse into a patient in a hospital had to be manufactured from raw materials, put into inventory, ordered, transported, accounted for, billed for and paid for. The nurse had to be assigned to the task which is part of a medical procedure. And, of course, let us not forget the patient. Figure 13 illustrates an object model family that attempts to capture some domains in this needle example. How do you establish domain orientations across domains? For example, each domain in the needle example may have its

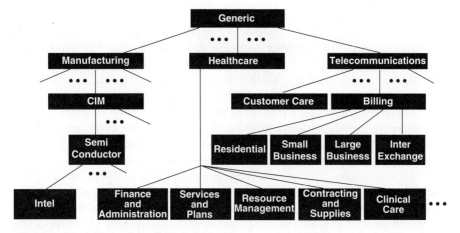

Figure 13. Object model family.

own domain orientation. Each may also have some concepts shared with the others (e.g., customer). To what degree do the domains overlap (i.e., have shared concepts), and how do you achieve agreement on those overlaps, bilaterally or universally? Figure 14 attempts to suggest that a patient care object model and a pharmaceutical object model are specializations or sub-object models of the more general healthcare object model. But the pharmaceutical object model must be interoperable with or be a specialization of other object models (e.g., transportation, manufacturing, finance). How do we standardize just customer across those domains, let alone thousands of other classes?

One final challenge could be termed legacy migration. Let us assume that we have an adequate domain orientation and are able to define new interoperable classes, components and, from them, applications. How do you migrate from the existing heterogeneous "legacy" base of ISs and computing infrastructures to the brave new world? At a minimum, it will be

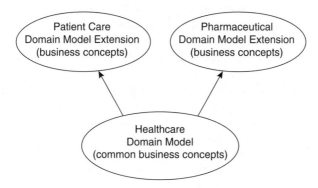

Figure 14. Domain model interoperability.

an iterative, evolutionary transition (Brodie and Stonebraker, 1995). This requires that the legacy ISs, which are unlikely to conform to the domain orientation, must interoperate with the new ISs that do. We are back to square one, a massive IS environment with one DOC application being added, further contributing to the heterogeneity and application interoperability challenges in hopes of ultimately reducing these problems.

Whoever solves the problem of domain orientation, or even application interoperability within a domain, deserves a Noble Prize, perhaps the Nobel Peace Prize, for it will certainly not be a technical achievement, but something far more valuable.

In conclusion, application interoperability is a fundamental requirement for end users of DOC technology. It is not a technical problem. However, DOC technology should be developed to facilitate the definition of the domain models, the interface specifications and the supporting frameworks. The DOC community should understand the nature and full scope of this challenge, work directly with the domains that they should serve, and focus effort accordingly on the relevant domain models (i.e., interoperable domain model families) and supporting frameworks. No small task!

7 CONCLUSIONS

We are at the beginning of a 20-year paradigm shift to distributed object computing. By that time, some variant of DOC will be the dominant computing paradigm and will be effectively and readily deployable. Long before that time, it will have met many of its current claims. Indeed, there are already major successes with large-scale industrial-strength DOC applications.

For the moment, DOC is in its infancy and does not meet industrial-strength requirements or the claims of its proponents. DOC is not yet ready for prime time. There are even very recent claims that a major breakthrough has occurred and that a DOC renaissance is upon us (Microsoft, 1996). Based on our experience, GTE has decided to halt the design, development and deployment of DOC technology and applications, including CABS II. In part this relates to our recognition of the problems described in this chapter. In part, it also relates to our pursuit of commercial off-the-shelf (COTS) applications for which the vendors are largely responsible for the issues raised in this chapter. Following a significant study of and investment in DOC technologies and methodologies, we have concluded that the benefits do not currently warrant the costs to overcome the challenges described in this chapter. The claims for increased productivity, reuse, and lowered costs cannot be achieved with other than very highly skilled staff who must work with immature technology and methods. We will continue to investigate the area and observe its progress and will be prepared to take full advantage of the technology when DOC is more mature. I look forward to a highly competitive market for the DOC infrastructure and highly competitive products. However, I hope that end users such as GTE will be increasingly remote from the technology issues discussed in this chapter so that they can better focus on their businesses and the business requirements and leave as many technology issues to the experts, the vendors, and the COTS suppliers.

Regardless of when DOC technology is deployed, we continue to face on a daily basis the ultimate end-user challenge of application interoperability. Although this challenge is essentially not technical, DOC has the potential to succeed based on its ability to support domain orientation, as described above. The community developing DOC technology should consider establishing application interoperability as its primary goal and defining a comprehensive distributed object computing framework such as outlined above. DOC technology development should be driven by the requirements of industrial-strength applications and specifically to support the requirements domain orientation. Although the Microsoft (1996) announcement is encouraging from a technical point of view, it does not begin to address the application interoperability challenge, the ultimate end-user requirement.

REFERENCES

Brodie, M.L. (1996) *Silver bullet shy on legacy mountain: when neat technology just doesn't work*. (Keynote speech) In *The 8th Conference on Advanced Information Systems Engineering, "Software Engineering Challenges in Modern Information Systems"*, May, Heraklion, Crete, Greece.

Brodie, M.L. and Stonebraker, M. (1995) *Migrating Legacy Systems: Gateways, Interfaces, and the Incremental Approach*, Morgan Kaufmann Publishers, San Francisco, CA.

Descartes, R. (1637) *Essais Philosophiques* (Philosophical Essays), *Discours de la méthode* (Discourse on Method).

Gibbs, W.W. (1994) Software's chronic crisis. *Scientific American*, September.

Kant, I. (1781) *Critique of Pure Reason*.

Locke, J. (1690) *Essay Concerning Human Understanding*.

Manola, F. and Heiler, S. (1993) A 'RISC' Object Model for Object System Interoperation: Concepts and Applications. TR-0231-08-93-165, GTE Laboratories Incorporated.

Manola, F., Heiler, S., Georgakopoulos, D., Hornick, M. and Brodie, M. (1992). Distributed object management. *International Journal of Intelligent and Cooperative Information Systems*, **1**, 1.

Microsoft (1996) The renaissance of distributed computing. Microsoft White Paper, November (www.microsoft.com/pdc/html/p&s.htm).

Moore, G. (1991) *Crossing the Chasm*, HarperBusiness, New York.

Orlikowski, W. and Robey, D. (1991) Information technology and the structuring of organizations. *Information Systems Research*, **2**, 143–169.

TRADEMARKS

The following are registered trademarks of their respective companies: ORB®, CORBA®, CORBAservices®, Object Request Broker®,

CORBAfacilities®, OMG®, OMG IDL® and Object Management Group®
of the Object Management Group; DCE of the Open Software Foundation;
Microsoft® Windows NT® operating system, Active Server® Technologies,
Microsoft Transaction Server®, OLE® and COM® of Microsoft Corpora-
tion; Object Services Package® and OSP® of TCSI Corporation; Forté of
Forté Software, Inc.; DAIS® of International Computers Limited; Newi® of
SSA Object Technology; Portable Distributed Objects®, PDO®, NextStep®
and OpenStep® of NeXT Software, Inc.; ObjectBroker® of Digital Equip-
ment Corporation; and WORKS® and Composer® of Texas Instruments
Incorporated.

Beyond Objects: Components[1]

Theo Dirk Meijler [a] and Oscar Nierstrasz [b]

[a]Baan Labs, Ede, The Netherlands and [b]Software Composition Group, University of Berne, Switzerland

Abstract

Traditional software development approaches do not cope well with the evolving requirements of open systems. We argue that such systems are best viewed as flexible compositions of "software components" designed to work together as part of a *component framework* that formalizes a class of applications with a common software architecture. To enable such a view of software systems, we need appropriate support from programming language technology, software tools, and methods. We will briefly review the current state of object-oriented technology, insofar as it supports component-oriented development, and propose a research agenda of topics for further investigation.

I INTRODUCTION

In large-scale networks, such as the Internet, many different kinds of resources are available. These resources include not only information systems and their contents, but also information processing programs, expert system shells, and other kinds of computational resources. In order to synthesize information from various sources and avoid having to duplicate information processing resources, it is necessary to make information systems and computational resources cooperate. Cooperation can take various forms: in *decentralized* cooperation, resources are agents that cooperate actively (and possibly interactively) to arrive at a common result, and are thus *visible* to each other; in *centralized* cooperation an integrating agent manages underlying resources that are *not* visible to each other, issues requests to the resources, and is responsible for synthesizing the results.

---

[1]Some of the material presented here was previously published in "Research Topics in Software Composition", in *Proceedings, Langages et Modèles à Objets*, A. Napoli (ed), Nancy, Oct. 1995, pp. 193–204.

Cooperative Information Systems
Trends and Directions
ISBN 0-12-544910-0

In order to realize different forms of cooperation, technological support is needed. First of all, an infrastructure is needed to allow heterogeneous resources to communicate either with each other or with an integrating agent. Since there are now several industrial standards available that provide this kind of support (i.e., CORBA, OLE, OpenDoc etc.), we will assume in this chapter that the necessary infrastructure is in place. Second, reliable solutions for coordination and synthesis are needed. This encompasses such aspects as "brokering" (i.e., deciding which requests should go where), coordinating concurrent or simultaneous access to shared resources, establishing a valid execution order for servicing requests, maintaining consistency of persistent state, gathering and integrating results from various resources, and so on. In general we will distinguish *non-functional* behavioural aspects of a system and the functional aspects. In a cooperative information system the latter correspond to the resources that are integrated in a cooperation.

Cooperative information systems are essentially *open* systems: systems that are open in terms of topology, platform and evolution (Tsichritzis, 1989). A key characteristic of open network applications is that requirements continuously change. This implies that coordination and synthesis must not only be reliable, but they must be robust, flexible and configurable. In other words, it is necessary to identify and implement software abstractions that encapsulate efficient and reliable solutions to standard coordination and synthesis problems. These abstractions, or "components", can then be used across many different applications, and can be reconfigured when application requirements change.

Thus "software reuse" is the key to building these systems: not only are the cooperating resources themselves software components that are used across multiple applications, but also the components that realize non-functional behaviour will be used in various configurations to address a variety of requirements.

In this chapter we will summarize the state of the art in software reuse, and evaluate the extent to which available approaches support (or fail to support) the construction of flexible, open information systems. We shall especially focus on the possibilities to configure and specialize non-functional behaviour independently from functional behaviour as needed to realize open cooperative information systems. We shall identify a series of open research problems to be resolved.

We start by noting that object-oriented languages and techniques presently offer the most relevant and promising support for our problem. Objects encapsulate data and operations by providing an interface that only responds to messages. They can therefore hide the fact that they might encapsulate existing programs, act as proxies for remote resources, or even coordinate multiple, concurrent requests. In short, objects provide a uniform way to hide distribution and heterogeneity. If we assume that resources will be encapsulated as distributed objects, the question then becomes how to realize coordination and synthesis abstractions that can be applied in a reusable way to these distributed objects.

It is useful to distinguish between "white-box" reuse — in which the implementation of reused components is exposed to some degree — and "black-box" reuse, in which components can only be reused according a specially provided reuse interface, or *contract*. We will take the position in this chapter that the most desirable form of reuse is "black-box" or compositional reuse, since this frees the application developer from having to study implementation details of components to be reused. Since the reuse contract is explicitly specified, it is possible to check the contract, and to actively support it in a development environment. Furthermore, links and dependencies between black-box components must be explicitly specified, thus making it easier to adapt a composition to new requirements. With white-box reuse, these links are often hidden and implicit in the extension code, and therefore harder to understand and change.

In Section 2 we will give an overview of black-box components, illustrate what problems they address through their support for *variability* and *adaptability*, and provide a scenario for component-oriented application development.

In the next section we shall evaluate how well current object-oriented technology supports this form of black-box reuse, and at the same time indicate what the consequences are for realizing components for non- functional behaviour. We see for example in Section 3.1 that many problems arise when trying to integrate such non-functional aspects in object-oriented programming languages. Furthermore, in Section 3.2 we shall see that subclassing is really a white-box reuse mechanism, which makes it quite difficult to reuse by inheritance classes that implement coordination abstractions.

Section 3 gives us an overview of necessary object-oriented technology, but also shows us the current limitations of that technology. In Section 4 we give an overview of future directions. We focus on the requirements and possible realization of a composition environment. One important aspect of such an environment will be the distinction between two separate roles with separate concerns: (i) *application developers* develop specific applications by composing both domain-specific functional components and generic, coordination components, in a black box fashion; (ii) *component developers* build black-box components by identifying useful software abstractions and factoring out both domain-specific and generic components. The implementation of the components themselves may incorporate white-box reuse, but this should not be visible to application developers. Furthermore, a clear distinction will be made between *extensional* object composition and *intentional* class-level composition, components for non-functional behaviour mostly being part of the latter. In such a composition environment a set of rules, together called the *composition model*, determines what compositions are legal. A composition environment will allow for visual composition, and support the developer to do so in compliance with the composition model.

We conclude by noting that present-day software development methods do not yet support component-oriented development in two important senses: first, component reuse is often considered far too late in the software life cycle, after detailed design is complete, whereas systematic reuse of component requires that software architectures also be reused. Second, none of the well-known methods gives any hint how to develop reusable software components. Methods to support component development are still an open research topic.

2 SOFTWARE COMPOSITION FOR OPEN SYSTEMS

If we examine successful approaches to developing open, adaptable systems — such as 4GLs, application generators, component toolkits and builders, and object-oriented frameworks — we find that there are striking similarities. In each case: (i) the application domain is well-understood; (ii) a generic software architecture captures families of applications; (iii) parameterized software components are designed to be specialized or instantiated to meet specific requirements; (iv) the path from requirements collection to implementation is reduced (at least to some degree) to a recipe or formula.

Each of these points is true to a lesser or greater degree depending on how specialized or general the approach is. For example, software components are clearly visible in the latter three approaches, but are often hidden behind the language in a 4GL. On the contrary, the software development path is most streamlined with a 4GL, and less evident with a framework, since detailed knowledge of the implementation details of a framework is typically required before one can use it to build a specific application.

In each case, *variability* — how much variation can be achieved — is attained by providing components on top of which variations can be introduced. *Adaptability* — how easy it is to adapt existing applications — is achieved by providing a generic application architecture that can be adapted to different needs. Ease of use is achieved by providing "black-box" interfaces to components that on the one hand constrain the ways in which components can be used and on the other hand limit the need to understand implementation details of components.

2.1 Components and Black-Box Reuse

Software reuse addresses two seemingly contrasting sets of requirements: (i) streamlining the development process; (ii) ensuring robustness and run-time efficiency of products. In the introduction we asserted that "black-box" reuse is preferable to "white-box" reuse. We will now try to make this distinction precise by explaining what we mean by the term "component".

We may see a program as a structure: a structure of statements, or of procedures, methods, classes etc. In the most basic form of software development the developer has to create these structures from scratch. We can abstract away from the elements of a structure in order to scale up to various levels of reuse. A programmer who is provided with certain pieces of structure that can be adapted and combined (e.g., a sequence of statements or a group of cooperating classes) can already achieve a certain degree of reuse. We call this "open" or *white-box* software reuse, since the structures that are reused are not encapsulated.

Adapting white-box structures can be very difficult, however: one has to understand what each element in the structure means and how the elements work together in order to reuse the structure. The complexity of adaptation of course depends on the complexity of structure to be adapted. Moreover, putting several complex structures together to form a bigger system (e.g., merging together groups of statements or different class hierarchies) is also difficult. This is where software components help us.

A *component* is an abstraction of a software structure that may be used to build bigger systems, while hiding the implementation details of the smaller structure. Putting together components is simple, since each component has a limited set of "plugs" with fixed rules specifying how it may be linked with other components. Instead of having to adapt the structure of a piece of software to modify its functionality, a user plugs the desired behaviour into the parameters of the component.

There are therefore two important aspects to components: (i) *encapsulation* of software structures as abstract components; (ii) *composition* of components by binding their parameters to specific values, or other components. A simple example is a function or a procedure parameterized by its run-time arguments. An object-oriented example is a generic or "template" (in C++ (Ellis and Stroustrup, 1990)) container class, which can be parameterized by the type of the contained elements. Encapsulation is the means to achieve variability, since the possible variation is expressed in the parameters (or "plugs") of the component. Adaptability is achieved during composition, since a software structure composed from components can be more easily reconfigured than an unencapsulated structure.

We can exchange the open variability of white-box structures for the fixed variability of possible connections to the plugs of the component. This restriction of variability is possible due to the fixed intended purpose of the component; it also includes the possibility to check the correctness of combinations of parameters. We call this "closed" or *black-box* software reuse.

When we build systems by putting together pieces of software, the need for compositionality is even clearer. It is difficult to integrate open pieces of software structure, as anyone who has "cut-and-pasted" software code can testify. Creating new classes through inheritance can pose a similar problem, since object-oriented languages do not support the specification of an explicit, typed "inheritance interface" for programmers who develop

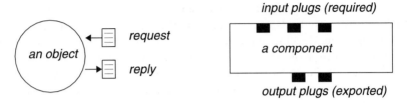

Figure 1. Objects and components.

subclasses (Lamping, 1993). Putting together components is much simpler, due to a well defined composition interface that defines how components may be "plugged" together.

What, if any, are the differences between objects and components? First of all, objects encapsulate *services*, whereas components are *abstractions* that can be used to construct object-oriented systems. Objects have identity, state and behaviour, and are always run-time entities. Components, on the other hand, are generally static entities that are needed at system build-time. They do not necessarily exist at run-time. Components may be of finer or coarser granularity than objects: e.g., classes, templates, mix-ins, modules. Components should have an explicit composition interface, which is type-checkable (see Figure 1). An object can be seen as a special kind of stateful component that is available at run-time.

It is certainly possible to *implement* many kinds of components as objects, which is the source of a great deal of confusion. By encapsulating components as objects, one achieves a great deal of flexibility, since components can then be configured and substituted at run-time. This notion is fundamental to all interactive component-based development environments (such as user interface builders). On the other hand, this does *not* mean that either every object is usable as a component, or that components must be implemented as objects! Functions, modules, templates and even whole applications can be seen as components. Conversely, objects that are not designed to be connected to other objects are not "pluggable", and hence cannot be seen as components.

2.2 Why Do We Need Components?

Let us now consider what specific problems are addressed by components:

- **Fast time-to-market.** Applications that can be built from reusable components can be developed more quickly and thus brought to market and sold more cheaply than custom-made applications.
- **Reliability.** Components that are reused across many applications are bound to be more reliable than new, hand-coded components.

Applications built according to tested frameworks are bound to be more reliable than newly designed and implemented applications.

- **Division of labour.** Components with well-defined interfaces are natural units for distribution to software teams. The development of applications from software components and the development of reusable components themselves are tasks requiring different kinds of skills and experience.
- **Variability.** Families of applications can be developed using a common software base only if the software base can accommodate sufficient variability. Software components support variability through parameterization. Parameters represent functionality that must be provided by the client of the component, or (as is often the case with object-oriented components) default functionality that may be overridden.
- **Adaptability.** A flexible application is one that can be easily adapted to changing requirements. Software components support adaptability if an application can be viewed abstractly as a configuration of components linked together. If the components have been well-designed, many changes in requirements can be addressed at this abstract level by reconfiguring the application's components. In well-understood application domains, many possible changes in requirements can be anticipated and incorporated into the design of the components and the ways in which they may be composed.

  Note that adaptability may be viewed as a form of reusability, since it entails the reuse of an existing application to create a changed version. However, it is a special form since it does not focus on newly building (larger) systems from (smaller) existing software components. Variability is a prerequisite to adaptability but increasing variability in the components may damage adaptability since adaptation becomes correspondingly increasingly complex.
- **Distribution and concurrency.** In order to use hardware resources optimally, systems are becoming more distributed and consequently concurrent. Since distributed systems are notoriously difficult to implement correctly, application developers need software abstractions that can simplify the task. Components offer on the one hand natural units for distribution, and on the other hand may encapsulate protocols and concurrency abstractions, thus hiding the complexity of distributed programming from application developers.
- **Heterogeneity.** Open systems are inherently heterogeneous. Components of a distributed system will be developed using different platforms and programming languages. Components help by hiding differences in implementation platform behind interfaces that are (in principle) independent of programming languages, as in component models such as COM and CORBA (Konstantas, 1995; Pintado, 1995).

A piece of software can be called a *component* if it has been *designed* to be composed with other components. In general this is done to address a particular class of applications. If that is the case[2] we say a *component framework* has been developed for that application area. This notion still needs to be better understood. The key principles, however, are:

- A component framework does not just consist of a library of components, but must also define a generic *architecture* for a class of applications.
- Flexibility in a framework is achieved through *variability* in the components and *adaptability* in the architecture.
- Flexibility in an application is promoted by making the specific architecture *explicit* and *manipulatable*.

2.3 A Scenario for Compositional Development

Since black-box components are not isolated entities, but only become useful in the context of a framework, or at least of an environment (Microsoft, 1993), this form of reuse cannot be achieved by just starting to develop components. So, how should software development be organized in order to achieve compositional, black-box reuse? In an attempt to answer this question, we propose the following scenario for component-oriented software development (see Figure 2):

- A *component framework* is a collection of software artefacts that encapsulates: (i) domain knowledge; (ii) requirements models; (iii) a generic software architecture; (iv) a collection of software components addressing a particular application domain.

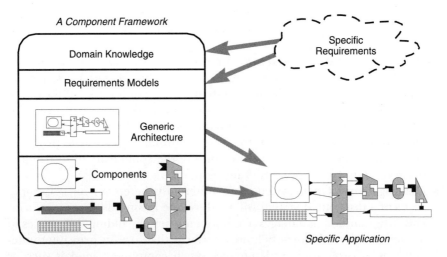

Figure 2.   Component-oriented software development.

---

[2]In the componentware approach (Microsoft, 1993; Udell. 1994) a whole component environment may be said to serve as a "framework".

- Development of specific applications is *framework-driven*, in the sense that all phases of the software life cycle, including requirements collection and specification, are determined according to set patterns formalized within the framework. To a large extent, system design is already done, since the domain and system concepts are specified in the generic architecture.
- The remaining art is to map the specific requirements to the concepts and components provided by the framework. This is in sharp contrast to naive approaches that would apply either a traditional or an object-oriented method for analysis and design, and only during implementation attempt to find "reusable object classes" matching the design specification in a software repository. Experience shows that the most valuable kind of reuse occurs in the early stages of the software life cycle (Gamma *et al.*, 1995; Goldberg and Rubin, 1995).

Such a scenario would therefore correspond to a new, framework-driven method of software development that is much more strongly directed towards software reuse than existing object-oriented development methods.

The scenario assumes that all parts of the component framework are formally specified, and managed by an application development environment. The environment guides the requirements collection and specification activities, and helps to guide the specialization and configuration of the application from available components.

Given this scenario of component-oriented development, we can define software composition as "the systematic construction of software applications from components that implement abstractions pertaining to a particular problem domain". Composition is systematic in that it is supported by a framework, and in the sense that components are *designed* to be composed.

Now let us be more precise about what we mean by a "software architecture":

- A *software architecture* is a description of the way in which a specific system is composed from its components (cf. Shaw and Garlan, 1996).
- A *generic software architecture* is a description of a class of software architectures in terms of *component interfaces, connectors*, and the *rules governing software composition*.

Connectors (Shaw and Garlan, 1996) mediate the interconnection between software components. Connectors may either be *static* or *dynamic*. Static composition entails *interface compatibility* (e.g., type-checking) and *binding* of parameters (e.g., binding of self and super in inheritance). Dynamic connectors additionally entail any kind of run-time behaviour, such as buffering, protocol checking, translation between language/execution models, and service negotiation. Composition often reduces to some combination of: (i) generics/macro expansion; (ii) higher-order functional composition; or (iii) binding of names to resources (e.g., object identifiers, communication channels).

Composition rules formalize the kinds of components that may be composed using the available connectors, and may be expressed in a type system, in the semantics of the programming language used, or as part of a tool or environment. For example, the fact that certain kinds of applications may be composed with "Unix pipes" depends partly on the definition of the components (they must be designed as "sources", "filters" or "sinks"), on the semantics of the shell programming language, and on the run-time environment (i.e., the buffering of input and output by the operating system). All composition rules together, in whatever form, make up the *composition model*.

A component framework helps in the development of open systems by allowing a specific system to be viewed as a generic family of applications in the sense that its software architecture is derived from a generic one. The resulting system is open and flexible if its software architecture is *explicit* and *manipulatable*. (This is clearly a necessary condition, since a system whose architecture is not explicit cannot easily be adapted to new requirements.)

3 OBJECT-ORIENTED SOFTWARE COMPOSITION

From the previous sections we can now distil some requirements for the construction of open information systems in general, and cooperative information systems in particular. In the terminology of Section 2, we see that we need to develop component frameworks. In the context of cooperative information systems, the components of such a framework would include, first of all, the individual systems that cooperate, and, second, the components that realize the coordination and synthesis. This is necessary to keep the cooperation as flexible as possible, allowing us, for example, to have both central and decentralized cooperations. In order to avoid having undesirable and undocumented dependencies between components, it is important that cooperative systems be built from components in a "black-box" fashion.

We assert that the fundamental problem to be addressed by a framework for cooperative information systems and for open systems in general, is to provide black-box components that encapsulate both functional and non-functional aspects of behaviour (i.e., systems and their coordination), that can easily be combined. This separation of concerns is both critical — for ensuring that systems remain flexible and reconfigurable — and non-trivial — since functional and non-functional aspects are typically intertwined in programs.

In our search for technology that supports this, we turn to object-oriented programming languages and methods, where combining functional and non-functional features in a reusable form has been studied extensively in the past. In this section we consider both approaches to reuse and approaches to separating functional and non-functional aspects of behaviour.

3.1 Interference of Object-Oriented Features

Wegner (1987) has proposed a classification of object-based programming languages according to a set of "orthogonal" dimensions:

- Object-based: *encapsulation* (objects) [+identity]
- Object-oriented: +classes + *inheritance*
- Strongly typed: +data abstraction + *types*
- Concurrent: +*concurrency* [+ distribution]
- Persistent: +persistence + sets

An additional dimension not originally considered was *homogeneity*: in a homogeneous object-oriented language, *everything* (within reason) is an object. So Smalltalk is a homogeneous object-oriented language whereas C++ is not.

Dimensions are considered to be *orthogonal* if features supporting them can be found independently in different programming languages. Concurrency is therefore considered orthogonal to inheritance, since some languages support concurrency features but not inheritance, and *vice versa*. Orthogonality in Wegner's sense does not tell us anything about how easy it is to integrate orthogonal features within a single programming language. Numerous researchers have attempted to integrate such features (Nierstrasz, 1992; Briot and Gerraoui, 1996) only to discover that they interfere in unexpected ways (Nierstrasz, 1993) (see Papathomas (1995) for an overview). In fact, most of the problems arise because inheritance is basically a white-box reuse mechanism. Inheritance conflicts with encapsulation since subclasses are dependent upon implementation details of superclasses in a way that is not described by an explicit interface (Figure 3).

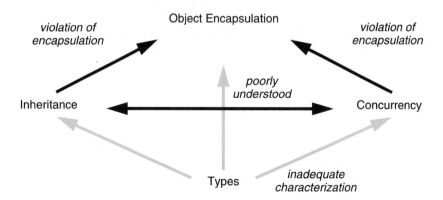

Figure 3.   Interference of object-oriented features.

Concurrency and persistence are examples of non-functional issues. Combining inheritance with concurrency poses problems in that it is difficult to define classes that make use of concurrency mechanisms and can be then inherited and extended in any meaningful way without exposing implementation details (Kafura and Lee, 1989; Matsuoka and Yonezawa, 1993). That one would like to configure these non-functional aspects independently from the functional issues can also seen from the fact that objects that function correctly in a sequential environment may fail when exposed to concurrent clients (Papathomas, 1995). Similarly, one would like to switch persistence "on" and "off" independently of the way functionality is inherited in an inheritance hierarchy. Introducing persistence through the inheritance hierarchy reduces flexibility.

The development of an adequate type model that addresses both objects and inheritance is still an open research problem (Nierstrasz and Dami, 1995), let alone one that addresses type compatibility for concurrent objects (Nierstrasz, 1995).

3.2 Inheritance

Even in approaches where functional and non-functional aspects are separated, both may still be developed independently through inheritance. Although inheritance is an important mechanism for sharing interfaces and implementation in object-oriented design, its principal weakness is that it essentially supports "open", or white-box reuse: the superclass is generally viewed as an open structure of methods and instance variables that the builder of the subclass adapts and extends. This is really a problem since the subclass is not even a copied version of the superclass: the subclass remains dependent on the superclass, and the "openness" thus remains. The superclass cannot be viewed as a component with respect to the subclass, since the implementation of the superclass cannot be changed independently.

There have been several developments that address this problem. Both Eiffel (Meyer, 1992) and C++ (Ellis and Stroustrup, 1990) provide mechanisms for controlling which features are visible to subclasses, and/or for controlling visibility of sets of features to specific client classes. Beta (Madsen et al., 1993) provides a special construct (called "inner") that can be used to control exactly where subclasses may extend inherited behaviour. Lamping (1993) has proposed a discipline for explicitly typing the inheritance interface, which goes a long way towards turning inheritance into a black-box form of reuse.

Bracha (1992) has proposed a finer granularity approach to class composition based on composition of "mix-ins." Mix-ins are comparable to abstract classes, in the sense that they define incomplete sets of methods and instance variables, but then can be combined using a variety of operators, not just by inheritance.

As mentioned above, once functional and non-functional aspects have been combined in a single class, adapting the functional aspects in a subclass requires that the non-functional aspects be adapted as well, so the two become intertwined and can no longer be independently configured. Still, as demonstrated by the ACE toolkit,[3] it is possible to: (i) provide support for non-functional aspects — such as synchronization — in a set of dedicated classes; (ii) provide "pure" functional aspects in a separate set of classes; (iii) finally build a subclass that combines the two. No further subclassing should be done on basis of this latter class.

3.3 Object Composition

A more dynamic approach to separating non-functional and functional aspects is to use object composition. In ACE, for example, both requests and the mechanism for handling requests can be "reified" (made explicit) as objects that are separate from the object that implements the functional part (Lavender and Schmidt, 1995). Having a separate object manage the non-functional aspect of request handling (such as queuing, copying to other server objects etc.) separates this concern, and makes it easier to flexibly substitute different policies.

Object composition provides for more flexible and disciplined reuse than inheritance, since: (i) object compositions may be changed at run-time; (ii) objects are composed according to explicit interfaces. In fact, many of the basic design patterns (Gamma et al., 1995) of object-oriented development introduce flexibility through object composition. For example, the effective behaviour of an object can be changed at run-time if an object delegates some of its responsibilities to other supporting objects, and these supporting objects can be dynamically substituted. Object composition addresses such diverse problems as adaptation of object interfaces, augmentation (or "decoration") of an object's services, dynamically changing the effective behaviour of an object, providing transparent interfaces to remote objects, and so on (Gamma et al., 1995).

Object-composition involves instantiating objects, parameterizing those objects and linking them together. Objects can be parameterized by object-specific methods. Object-composition should take place in the context of a component framework that provides sets of objects that can be linked together. Links have meaning in the sense of a certain corresponding run-time cooperation.

Presently the only way to specify rules for the composition of objects is by means of the type system: objects may be composed if the dynamic type of an object conforms to the static type of the variable used to store the link. There are two shortcomings to this approach.

---

[3]ACE is an object-oriented network programming toolkit for developing communication software; it is well-known for its design and its flexibility.

First of all, in most (typed) object-oriented languages (such as Eiffel) there is "equality" between classes and types. A class is considered to be a subtype of another only if it inherits from the latter (and also satisfies substitutability constraints). This is especially a problem if we want to be able to acquire or replace an implementation later, possibly over the net or from some independent vendor. The Java language (Gosling and McGilton, 1995) shows how the separation between interface and class can allow for this kind of "pluggability". Note that the use of "untyped" linking, as in Smalltalk or in Objective-C, is not really a solution since such mechanisms provide no support for creating correct compositions.

Second, in certain cooperations, instances from one class will not merely play the role of servers for instances of the other class. A more detailed cooperation protocol is involved. Plugging in another class that has the same interface but does not use that protocol, leads again to an incorrect composition. Thus checking on interface only is not enough (Nierstrasz, 1995). So far no object-oriented language supports checking of cooperation protocols.

Although object composition can help to make applications more flexible, it does not necessarily help make application architecture more explicit. The way in which a system is composed of objects is typically hidden in the implementation of the objects themselves. Hiding implementation details is, of course, what objects are good at, but this does not help the system architect who wants to explicitly view a system as a composition of objects. In this sense, object composition is not well supported by existing object-oriented languages.

An environment for object composition (see Section 4) would not only represent compositions of objects explicitly, but would help to manage what kinds of links can be established between components. In a visual tool, type checking may not only be "corrective", that is denying incorrect links, but also "supportive" that is, suggest correct links.

Commercial tools exist that support visual object composition, but these tools are always specialized for a particular composition domain, such as user interface constructing. General commercial tools for visual composition that are adaptable to different component frameworks have not yet been introduced, though some experimental systems have been developed (Mey, 1995).

3.4 Class-Level Black-Box Composition: Genericity

Genericity is a form of parameterization where a component, for example a class or a procedure, has a parameter which is a type (or a class) rather than a value. Genericity can be supported to varying degrees by a programming language. In C++, for example, generic classes, called "templates", are little more than glorified macros, since their parameters must be bound before any type-checking is performed. STL (The Standard Template Library) is a well-known example of the use of templates in C++ (Musser and Saini, 1996). In Ada 95 and Eiffel, on the other hand, generic classes are well-integrated into the language, and can be independently type-checked and compiled. Being a special form of parameterization, genericity can be viewed as separating the variability of a software component from that component.

McHale (1994) has shown that genericity can be used in concurrent object-oriented programming languages to separate the programming of the synchronization control from the "normal" programming of the methods. McHale provides many examples of "generic synchronization policies" that can be independently specified and later bound to arbitrary classes. An example is a "readers–writers" policy, a synchronization policy that allows either several readers to simultaneously access the state of an object, or a single writer at a time. Such a policy is a generic abstraction that can be applied by (i) linking it to a certain class that should have that policy implemented; (ii) describing which methods of the class are readers and which are writers. Using such a policy is purely a matter of black-box parameterization, and totally independent of how the policy is implemented. In McHale's work we see that the policy's dependency on the set of requests (and possibly other parameters) is separated from the component.

Contracts (Helm *et al.*, 1990) provide another example of extending the idea of genericity, and how this can be used to specify cooperation between classes separately from the classes themselves. A contract is basically parameterized by the classes that participate in such a cooperation. Contracts help to make systems more flexible since they make it easier to substitute different classes into a given cooperation pattern. They also make systems more understandable since contracts help to make system architecture explicit and manipulatable.

Genericity has also been applied to federated database systems (Sheth and Larson, 1990) (an area close to cooperative information systems). Generic mechanisms are offered to describe a federated database schema in terms of the external schemas of the various databases constituting the federation: one formally describes an integration contract between the various databases in terms of the data and operations they provide, without a need for programming. These ideas are also related to the ideas described in the chapter "Reflection is the Essence of Cooperation" in Part IV of this book.

If we compare class parameterization — generic classes are a special form of this — and inheritance, we can again note differences in "open" vs. "closed" forms of reuse: the white-box form of reuse supported by inheritance provides more variability, whereas the black-box reuse of class parameterization provides better ease of use and robustness. On the other hand, if we consider how to realize either generic synchronization policies of contracts in existing object-oriented languages, we encounter some difficulties. In fact, both have been supported by means of software generation, since existing object-oriented languages typically support only very weak or restricted forms of genericity.

This leads us to conclude that, contrary to some early opinions concerning the relative expressive power of genericity versus inheritance (Meyer, 1986), the notion of genericity is still underestimated as a simple mechanism for providing variability in the way objects are implemented and the way they cooperate, that works well when the possible purposes of a certain software component (e.g., a synchronization mechanism) can be known ahead, as is often the case in frameworks. Furthermore, there is a need for general mechanisms to define and realize various forms of genericity and class parameterization.

3.5 Genericity and Componentware

There has been a shift in attention in industry from general object-oriented programming systems to so-called "componentware" environments (Udell, 1994). Delphi (Lischner 1996) and Visual Basic (VB) (Microsoft, 1993) are good examples. These approaches are also of interest here due to their black-box approach and their close relationship to class parameterization.

Componentware approaches are closely related to — or may be seen as a form of — class parameterization, since components are typically parameterized by the developer so that they can be easily adapted to different applications. A component with bound parameters is instantiated — in contrast to classes in general only once — at run-time. The parameters are not normally classes or types, but configuration values or in some cases other components. Even if a parameter is another component, this cannot be seen as a form of genericity, since the link is basically an object composition: It means that the instance of the one will be linked to the instance of the other.

Componentware environments provide a visual presentation of components. Since components are black-box entities, a visual presentation is often natural. Furthermore, most components are instantiated just once in an application, making it relatively straightforward to represent applications as static configurations of components. Finally, since many components in environments such as Delphi and Visual Basic are directly concerned with user interaction, it is natural that their visual presentation correspond directly to their interface in the final application (though, of course, the behaviour of the component will differ during application construction and run-time).

Especially interesting aspects are:

- Componentware environments draw a sharp distinction between *programmers*, who implement components, and *developers*, who use components to build applications.

- Components are implemented using relatively standard object-oriented programming techniques. It is therefore possible to develop new components by (white-box) inheritance from existing components. Objects that implement components adapt their behaviour at run-time by interpreting the component parameters.
- There is already quite a large market of available ready-made components for Visual Basic and Delphi.

The basic criticisms we have are the following:

- Neither Visual Basic nor Delphi provides any standard support for (visually) linking components, checking links, or creating correct links. As a result there is not much incentive for creating domain specific component frameworks. In such a framework, standard cooperations between various component are supported. Such cooperations have to be "instantiated" (declaring that two components indeed have a certain cooperation) by linking the components.
- Neither Visual Basic nor Delphi provides any support for subdividing components into separate functional and non-functional aspects.
- Neither Visual Basic nor Delphi provides any extra support for creating the dynamic part (e.g., a tree editor) of a user interface.

3.6 Separating Functional and Non-functional Concerns

In the previously described approaches a separation between functional and non-functional behaviour could be realized by delegating non-functional aspects to a specialized component or object or superclass. Two rather different approaches to separating concerns that should be mentioned are reflection, and aspect-oriented programming.

A well-known mechanism for separating functional and non-functional behaviour is the use of a explicit reflective or "meta" computation. In such approaches, some aspect of the application is explicitly "reified," or represented as an object. One can then reason about this aspect explicitly at the meta-level, and then "reflect" the desired behaviour back into the application. For example, if messages sent to an object are themselves reified as objects, then synchronization policies can be realized by explicitly examining, manipulating, and scheduling messages at the meta-level. In addition to synchronization mechanisms (Briot, 1996; Aksit et al., 1994, McAffer, 1995), many other non-functional aspects have been successfully modelled using reflection, such as transaction mechanisms (Stroud and Wu, 1995), persistence (Paepcke, 1988), and request logging (Demeyer, 1996), to mention but a few.

Aspect-oriented programming (Kiczales, 1997) is a newer approach based on the idea that each functional or non-functional aspect of a application can best be described using a separate, domain-specific language. These different aspects are than "weaved together" to produce a final program.

The specification of each aspect can then be altered or adapted without affecting other, independent aspects. In contrast to meta-level computation, a separation into more than two aspects is possible, and aspects can be described declaratively.

A basic criticism applicable to both kinds of approaches is that neither supports higher-order (generic) parameterization: non-functional behaviour is still inherently described for a specific class (and, of course for its superclasses), and is not a generic mechanism (cf. generic synchronization mechanisms (McHale, 1994), Section 3.4) that can be parameterized by a class or by some cooperating classes. We note however, that the aspect-oriented approach seems to allow for that in principle, since it is based on software generation.

4 REQUIREMENTS FOR A COMPOSITION ENVIRONMENT

We have argued that the development of open systems should be based on component frameworks, and we have shown that object-oriented technology falls short in its support for compositional development in various ways. We consequently identify a set of requirements for an environment to support developers building and using component frameworks:

- Object composition is an essential ingredient of component frameworks, which is needed for creating the static object structures used at runtime. Object composition may be used for linking very large grained objects (complete encapsulated databases) as well as small objects, such as dialogue boxes, buttons etc. Objects can be instances of classes or of "class-level components."[4]
- Genericity, or "class composition" is needed to bind parameters of class-level components, and thus to adapt the behaviour and cooperation of their instances. As in "componentware" approaches (Section 3.5) but in contrast to normal object-oriented approaches that support genericity, a strong separation will be kept between the (black-box) use of a class-level component by the application developer (the user of the component framework) and by the framework developer, who may implement such a component using normal (white-box) inheritance.
- The contrast between object composition vs. class composition is fundamental and necessary. This corresponds to the fundamental contrast between intentional and extensional descriptions. In an intentional description — such as in generic synchronization policies, or in approaches to schema integration — aspects of behaviour are described in terms of "things to be", that is in terms of procedural or

---

[4]A "class-level component" is a component that is used to create object instances, but may not necessarily be implemented as a class. Generic synchronization policies, for example, are class-level components, but are not implemented as classes.

structural interfaces. We note that this kind of intentional composition is not provided by componentware approaches.

- Different component frameworks may require different kinds of connectors. What kinds of connectors there are should therefore be extensible. For example, the link between two interface descriptions might express standard template parameterization: the structural elements of instances of the one (e.g., of lists) must be instances of the other (e.g., visual objects); another kind of link might indicate that all requests handled by instances of the one should be forwarded to instances of the other. We note that most environments and languages only provide a limited "hard-wired" set of connector types.

- Connectors should possibly cover intra-object behaviour, e.g., changing the synchronization policies of instances, as well as inter-object behaviour.

- Following the discussion in Section 3.4 and Section 3.6, the environment should support arbitrary kinds of generic components for non-functional behaviour.

- Both object composition and class composition need some support to ensure that compositions are correctly constructed. The framework developer should be able to define what constitutes a correct composition (the so-called component model); the application developer should be supported in creating compositions that are compatible to the component model. Compositions should of course be made persistent.

- Implementation independence is required and principally possible in a component-based approach. We see compositions as "configurations" that may name components to be used (or name class-level components of which objects should be instances), but due to the black-box approach, implementation choices may be delayed to link- or run-time. As an example, in the approach we propose (see below) we use two complementary implementation mechanisms: one based more on software generation, the other based more on parameter interpretation. Such implementation independence is of course also relevant for portability, dynamic loading etc.

A *visual composition environment* (Mey, 1995) supports the interactive construction of applications from plug-compatible software components by direct manipulation and graphical editing. A general approach to interactive software composition must be parameterized by component frameworks. Existing commercial tools are typically restricted to specific domains (UI, dataflow...), and cannot be adapted to arbitrary domains. Experimental results (Mey, 1995) indicate that general-purpose visual composition is feasible by separating the tool from the component framework and the composition rules. Various technical and pragmatic difficulties nevertheless remain. Complex systems are hard to visualize, and require flexible filtering and representation techniques to support the needed user abstractions. A sufficiently flexible tool requires a framework and composition model *itself* to allow it to be easily adapted to different composition models and application domains.

Since generic composition is one of the novel aspects of the proposed approach we shall now give two examples of generic compositions and the corresponding composition model. We shall use the fact that not only compositions but also composition models are implementation independent. A composition model is itself an intentional description, similar to a database schema, describing what kinds of components may occur and how they may be linked. It may thus also be seen as a "composition" and thus as an implementation-independent configuration.

The diagrams we use to illustrate our examples should give the reader a hint as how the compositions might be represented in a visual composition environment.

4.1 Examples

We shall now consider two examples of generic compositions that make non-functional aspects explicit. Figure 4 represents a generic composition

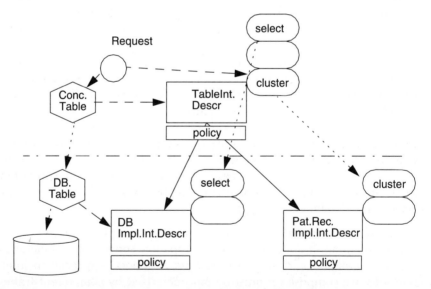

Figure 4. A "conceptual table" is an object that provides a common interface to operations supported by several implementation objects. A "select" request, for example, is forwarded to a database (DB) implementation, whereas a "cluster" request (i.e., to cluster table values according to some statistical properties) is forwarded to a pattern recognition component. How requests are handled is determined by a separate generic "policy" component and through the connections that exist between the elements in the interface description.

for describing a centralized integration between a database system and a pattern recognition package used to perform statistical information analysis. This example has been taken from Meijler (1993). This form of integration is meant to hide for the user of the integrated system the fact that data and operations are located in different packages and possibly different machines. It furthermore hides the fact that in order to apply statistical pattern recognition to numerical data in a database, the data have to be copied and transferred from the database to the pattern recognition program. This means that the data as the user sees them (called the "conceptual objects") may have more than one representation in the underlying packages. Execution of a user request therefore entails relatively complex non-functional behaviour in the integrating system. The choice of a specific generic policy represents the fact that this kind of request execution is used. We note, however, that this policy needs certain information to be available in the generic composition, e.g., which conceptual operation corresponds to which implementation operation. Thus, this policy can only be used together with a composition model that enforces the existence of such links. Figure 5 shows the corresponding composition model.

Figure 6 represents a generic composition describing the coupling of a "readers–writers" synchronization policy (McHale, 1994) to a class component of which instances are objects representing accounts. This example has been taken from Cruz and Tichelaar (1996). In this example we see that a possibility exists to exchange policies. Figure 7 shows the corresponding composition model. We see specifically how for a specific policy, as in this case the readers–writers, a specific part of the composition model is given that specifies how such a policy should be configured.

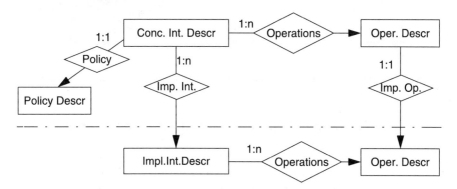

Figure 5. Composition model for the generic composition given in Figure 4. The diamonds are called property descriptors correspond to association descriptors in UML: For instance the descriptor "policy" indicates that a conceptual interface descriptor must be linked to one policy component.

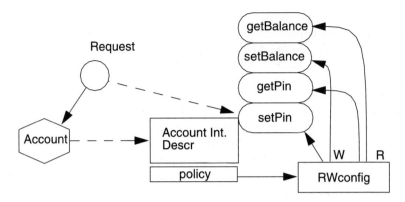

Figure 6. Configuration of synchronization policy for accounts, in this example a readers—writers policy. The readers—writers policy is configured by identifying the set of readers (in this case "getPin", "getBalance") and the set of writers ("setBalance", "setPin").

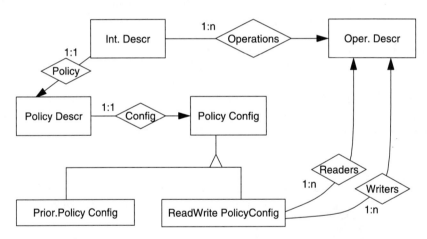

Figure 7. Composition model for the generic composition given in Figure 6.

4.2 Towards a Visual Composition Environment

Visual formalisms are important for specifying and representing software composition because they can support multiple views of the same structures, they can provide important visual cues to aid understanding, and because they can directly represent the final application interface, and hence can conveniently support a direct manipulation paradigm during development.

Framework developers must be able to specify and represent generic architectures, components, component interfaces and glue using a high-level graphical "syntax". Application developers should be able to instantiate architectures by elaborating, binding and linking framework components. Abstractions must be available as explicitly manipulatable (and visually represented) entities in the composition environment. Composition structures must be mappable to language sentences. The visual environment should support the user actively in creating and adapting compositions correctly. The environment should be homogeneous with respect to either object or class-level composition.

The visual environment should be configurable by the composition model and to specifications regarding how the components have to be presented. We note that this need for composition model configurability is surely one of the reasons why there has not yet been any commercial implementation of an open visual composition environment: all existing visual composition tools address a very specific application domain, typically user interface construction.

It is attractive for a visual composition environment to support the possibility to give run-time meaning to compositions by interpreting the information in the structure, [5] since:

(i) it is (should be) relatively simple through composition models to define new kinds of connectors (by just defining a new kind of link between class level components);

(ii) a visual environment "reifies" — represents as explicit object structures — component structures including generically linked class structures;

(iii) some form of run-time testing and/or debugging of compositions is needed in a visual composition environment.

This means that the composition environment should be extensible in this sense as well: for new generic links new interpretation mechanisms must be introduced.

We now briefly illustrate each of these points for the two composition examples.

4.2.1 Visual Composition Support

Supporting visual composition for either one of the examples corresponds to making the diagrams shown in Figures 4 and 6 into explicitly manipulatable structures represented as objects and links between objects. The environment can provide a separate "toolbox" window of components that may be instantiated. In the case of an interface description with its policy, the toolbox will contain, amongst others, possible different policies to be created and operations and interface descriptor components themselves. The environment checks the links the developer attempts to create between components. For example the developer can only create links from the readers property to one of the operations, and not to the interface descriptor itself.

---

[5] Another possibility would be to generate code from (compile) the class composition.

The environment provides a special "global check" operator, it checks whether all connections are consistent with each other; for example, a specific operation cannot be both a reader and a writer. The composition can only be used for run-time execution if all connections are consistent in this global sense.

4.2.2 Adaptability of Run-Time Semantics

Run-time behaviour of a system depends on the properties (composition) of the run-time objects, and the generic information. As mentioned, in the visual composition environment there will be a run-time execution mechanism based on interpretation of that information. In such an approach, run-time behaviours of objects in the system are determined by:

(i) the underlying implementation of the object in a class, which must take into account;

(ii) the properties of the object, and the information in the class structure.

In both examples, the object to which a request is applied has an "execute" method for executing a request. In order to allow for explicit request handling, requests themselves are first class objects, as mentioned in Section 3.3. Requests for an operation are instances of the corresponding interface description of that operation; the request shown in Figure 4 is thus a request for a cluster operation. In both examples, most relevant information for the execution of the request is in the class structure: the policy and the generic links.

In order to allow this information to be interpreted for request execution it has to be explicitly available as an object structure. As mentioned before, this is no problem since the class structure is explicitly represented as an object structure during composition anyhow. We must ask, however, how such a structure can play both the role of an object that can be queried by the run-time objects, and that of a class that they can be asked to generate instances. For this we use the prototype design pattern (Gamma *et al.*, 1995): each class object carries a prototype that is copied when the class object is requested for instantiation.

Interpreting the information in the class structure by the "execute" will delegate the knowledge of how to execute the request (the non-functional part, at least) to the same-named "execute" method in the policy object. It is this method that interprets the knowledge in the class structure; for example in the case of the centralized integration, the method will find which implementation operation has to be executed, on which kind of implementation object (in the example: cluster implementation on a pattern recognition object). It will generate the new object to which the implementation operation must be executed and create a request for that implementation operation. The execution of the implementation request is again determined by a policy.

In general, we say that the adaptation of the behaviour of the run-time objects to the class composition is done through "up-calls" to methods defined in the class objects.

4.2.3 Adaptability of the Visual Composition Support to the Composition Model

A visual composition environment has to adapt itself to the chosen composition model. Since the composition model is itself an intentional "class-level" structure, the environment adapts itself in the same way to the composition model as (other) run-time systems adapt themselves to "normal" class compositions as described in the previous paragraph. Thus, it itself is an example of an application of giving run-time semantics through interpretation to such a class composition. This goes as follows: the composition model is explicitly represented as an object structure and attempted links are checked by querying that structure. When, for example, the developer attempts to link a read–writers policy via the "readers" property to one of the operations, the visual composition environment can query the corresponding "readers" property descriptor to find out if the target of the link is an instance of the right component type, in this case, whether the target is an "operation descriptor".

4.2.4 Current Research

In our latest research on visual composition environments we have achieved the following:

- The principle of interpreting generic class information has been worked out for some smaller examples (Meijler and Engel, 1996; Meijler et al., 1997).
- The principle of having visual composition being checked on basis of a composition model has been worked out and tested (Meijler and Engel, 1996).

Since the composition model is itself a class composition (see above), there must also be a composition model of this composition model etc. This leads to the need for a self-descriptive composition model. This and the need for dynamic adaptation — the environment should be adapted to a new composition model without having to recompile it — poses severe requirements on a kernel implementation in the form of a self-descriptive data model (Meijler, 1993). This kernel data model has been implemented in Self (Ungar and Smith, 1987) and C++ (Ellis and Stroustrup, 1990). Current work is focused on developing more realistic examples and further elaborating our component model.

4.3 Towards Compositional Methods

In addition to the technological issues of component-oriented development, there are difficult methodological issues. First, how can we drive application development from component frameworks? Existing methods ignore reuse, or introduce it too late in the life cycle. Traditional separation of analysis and design is incompatible with a framework-driven approach since framework reuse should be anticipated during requirements collection and analysis.

Second, where do the frameworks come from? Traditional methods do not address the development of generic systems from previously completed projects. Refactoring and framework evolution (Casais, 1995) are not yet well-understood or widely practised.

A component-oriented software life cycle (Figure 8) must take into account that *application development* (the construction of applications from component frameworks) is a separate activity from *framework development* (the iterative development of the framework itself) (Nierstrasz *et al.*, 1992). Framework development is capital investment whereas application development recovers the investment.

Since application development is ideally *driven* by framework development, analysis and design are largely done already. The hard parts are: identifying the appropriate component framework to use, matching specific requirements to available components, building missing components and subsystems, and adapting components to unforeseen requirements. These aspects of object-oriented design and implementation fall outside the scope of today's object-oriented methods.

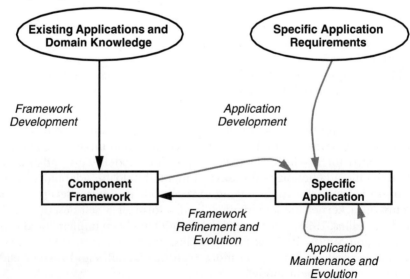

Figure 8.   A component-oriented software life cycle.

5 CONCLUDING REMARKS

Open systems pose special requirements for software development tools and methods. Open systems must be easily adaptable to changing requirements, hence should be designed with generic requirements in mind. A component framework addresses changing requirements by providing a generic software architecture for a family of applications, and a set of components that can be configured and composed in a variety of ways.

Object-oriented languages and systems support the development of component frameworks to some degree, but suffer from a number of limitations. Object-oriented languages support both "black-box" and "white-box" components. The former are fully encapsulated and can be used in arbitrary contexts, whereas the latter may introduce implementation dependencies between components and their clients: subclasses, for example, may depend on implementation details of superclasses they inherit from, thus violating encapsulation.

Object-oriented languages also typically force one to view all kinds of components as objects, whether this model is appropriate or not. A cooperation pattern encapsulating a readers–writers synchronization policy, for example, would be a perfectly reasonable component, but does not make much sense to represent as an object.

Finally, object-oriented systems tend to hide application architecture rather than make it explicit and manipulable. This is an obstacle to open systems comprehension and evolution. A composition environment would support open systems development by explicitly representing components and their interfaces, and by managing and guiding the composition activity.

Component-oriented software development is notably distinct from traditional development because it forces a separation between framework development and application development. These two activities are interdependent, since a component framework should drive application development, while at the same time, experiences with application development influence the iterative design of frameworks. Composition environments will provide tools needed to support these two activities, but they do not tell us what methods we should use to develop and apply software components. Most of the well-known object-oriented methods do not say anything about framework development or reuse. This is where we can expect to see the most significant advances in the near future (Reenskaug *et al.*, 1996).

REFERENCES

Aksit, M., Bosch, J., van der Sterren, W. and Bergmans, L. (1994) Real-Time Specification Inheritance Anomalies and Real-Time Filters. In *Proceedings ECOOP'94*, M. Tokoro and R. Pareschi (eds). Bologna, Italy, LNCS 821, Springer-Verlag, pp. 386–407.

Bracha, G. (1992) The Programming Language Jigsaw: Mixins, Modularity and Multiple Inheritance. Ph.D. thesis, Department of Computer Science, University of Utah.

Briot, J.-P. (1996) An Experiment in Classification and Specialization of Synchronization Schemes. In LNCS, vol. 1049. Springer-Verlag, pp. 227–249.

Briot, J.-P. and Gerraoui, R. (1996) *A Classification of Various Approaches for Object-Based Parallel and Distributed Programming*. Technical Report, Ecole Polytechnique Federale de Lausanne & University of Tokyo.

Casais, E. (1995) Managing Class Evolution in Object-Oriented Systems. In *Object-Oriented Software Composition*, O. Nierstrasz and D. Tsichritzis (eds). Prentice-Hall, pp. 201–244.

Cruz, J.C. and Tichelaar, S. (1996) A Coordination Component Framework for Open Systems. Working Paper, IAM, University of Bern.

Demeyer, S. (1996) ZYPHER Tailorability as a link from Object-Oriented Software Engineering to Open Hypermedia. Ph.D. thesis, Vrije Universiteit Brussel Departement Informatica.

Ellis, M.A. and Stroustrup, B. (1990) *The Annotated C++ Reference Manual*. Addison-Wesley.

Gamma, E., Helm, R., Johnson, R. and Vlissides, J. (1995) *Design Patterns*. Addison-Wesley, Reading, MA.

Goldberg, A. and Rubina, K.S. (1995) *Succeeding With Objects: Decision Frameworks for Project Management*. Addison-Wesley, Reading, Mass.

Gosling, J. and McGilton, H. (1995) *The Java Language Environment*. Sun Microsystems Computer Company.

Helm, R., Holland, I.M. and Gangopadhyay, D. (1990) Contracts: Specifying Behavioural Compositions in Object-Oriented Systems. *Proceedings OOPSLA/ECOOP '90, ACM SIGPLAN Notices*, **25**(10), 169–180.

Kafura, D.G. and Lee, K.H. (1989) Inheritance in Actor Based Concurrent Object-Oriented Languages. In *Proceedings ECOOP '89*, S. Cook, (ed.). Nottingham, Cambridge University Press, pp. 131–145.

Kiczales, G. (1997) Aspect-Oriented Programming: A Position Paper From the Xerox PARC Aspect-Oriented Programming Project. In *Special Issues in Object-Oriented Programming*, Max Muehlhauser (ed.). Heidelberg: dpunkt, verl. für digitale Technologie. (See also: http://www.parc.xerox.com/spl/projects/aop/position.html.)

Konstantas, D. (1995) Interoperation of Object-Oriented Applications. In *Object-Oriented Software Composition*, O. Nierstrasz and D. Tsichritzis (eds). Prentice-Hall, pp. 69–95.

Lamping, J. (1993) Typing the Specialization Interface. In *Proceedings OOPSLA 93, ACM SIGPLAN Notices*, **28**(10), 201–214.

Lavender, R.G. and Schmidt, D.C. (1995) Active Object: an Object Behavioral Pattern for Concurrent Programming. In *Proceedings Pattern Languages of Programs*, J.O. Coplien (ed.).

Lischner, R. (1996) Secrets of Delphi 2. The Waite Group Press.

Madsen, O.L., Møller-Pedersen, B. and Nygaard, K. (1993) *Object-Oriented Programming in the Beta Programming Language*. Addison-Wesley, Reading, Mass.

Matsuoka, S. and Yonezawa, A. (1993) Analysis of Inheritance Anomaly in Object-Oriented Concurrent Programming Languages. In *Research Directions in Concurrent Object-Oriented Programming*, G. Agha, P. Wegner and A. Yonezawa (eds). MIT Press, Cambridge, Mass., pp. 107–150.

McAffer, J. (1995) Meta-level Programming with CodA. In *Proceedings ECOOP '95*, W. Olthoff (ed.). LNCS 952, Aarhus, Denmark, Springer-Verlag, pp. 190–214.

McHale, C. (1994) Synchronisation in Concurrent, Object-oriented Languages: Expressive Power, Genericity and Inheritance. Ph.D. dissertation, Department of Computer Science, Trinity College, Dublin.

Meijler, T.D. (1993) User-level Integration of Data and Operation Resources by means of a Self-descriptive Data Model. Ph.D. thesis, Erasmus University Rotterdam.

Meijler, T.D. and Engel, R. (1996) Making Design Patterns explicit in FACE, a Framework Adaptive Composition Environment. In *EuroPLoP preliminary Conference Proceedings*.

Meijler, T.D. Demeyer, S. and Engel, R., Class Composition in FACE, a Framework Adaptive Composition Environment. In *Special Issues in Object-Oriented Programming*, Max Muehlhauser (ed). Heidelberg: dpunkt, verl. für digitate Technologie.

Mey, V.de. (1995) Visual Composition of Software Applications. In *Object-Oriented Software Composition*, O. Nierstrasz and D. Tsichritzis (eds). Prentice-Hall, pp. 275–303.

Meyer, B. (1986) Genericity versus Inheritance. *Proceedings OOPSLA '86, ACM SIGPLAN Notices*, **21**(11), 391–405.

Meyer, B. (1992) *Eiffel: The Language*. Prentice-Hall.

Microsoft (1993) *Visual Basic Programmer's Guide*, Microsoft Corporation.

Musser, D.R. and Saini, A. (1996) *STL Tutorial and Reference Guide*. Addison-Wesley.

Nierstrasz, O. (1992) A Tour of Hybrid — A Language for Programming with Active Objects. In *Advances in Object-Oriented Software Engineering*, D. Mandrioli and B. Meyer (eds). Prentice-Hall, pp. 167–182.

Nierstrasz, O. (1993) Composing Active Objects. In *Research Directions in Concurrent Object-Oriented Programming*, G. Agha, P. Wegner and A. Yonezawa (eds). MIT Press, Cambridge, Mass., pp. 151–171.

Nierstrasz, O. (1995) Regular Types for Active Objects. In *Object-Oriented Software Composition*, O. Nierstrasz and D. Tsichritzis (eds). Prentice-Hall, pp. 99–121.

Nierstrasz, O. and L Dami, L. (1995) Component-Oriented Software Technology. In *Object-Oriented Software Composition*, O. Nierstrasz and D. Tsichritzis (eds). Prentice-Hall, pp. 3–28.

Nierstrasz, O., Gibbs S. and Tsichritzis, D. (1992) Component-Oriented Software Development. *Communications of the ACM*, **35**(9), 160–165.

Paepcke, A. (1988) PCLOS: A Flexible Implementation of CLOS Persistence. In *Proceedings ECOOP'88*, S. Gjessing and K. Nygaard (eds). LNCS 322, Oslo. Springer-Verlag, pp. 374–389.

Papathomas, M. (1995) Concurrency in Object-Oriented Programming Languages. In *Object-Oriented Software Composition*, O. Nierstrasz and D. Tsichritzis (eds). Prentice-Hall, pp. 31–68.

Pintado, X. (1995) Gluons and the Cooperation between Software Components. In *Object-Oriented Software Composition*, O. Nierstrasz and D. Tsichritzis (eds). Prentice-Hall, pp. 321–349.

Reenskaug, T., Wold P. and Lehne, O.A. (1996) *Working With Objects*. Manning Publications,

Shaw, M. and Garlan, D. (1996) *Software Architecture: Perspectives on an Emerging Discipline*. Prentice-Hall.

Sheth, A.P. and Larson, J.A. (1990) Federated Database Systems for Managing Distributed Heterogeneous, and Autonomous Databases. *ACM Computing Surveys*, **22**(3), 183–236.

Stroud, R.J and Wu, Z. (1995) Using Metaobject Protocols to Implement Atomic Data Types. In *Proceedings ECOOP'95*, W. Olthoff, (ed.). LNCS 952, Aarhus, Denmark, Springer-Verlag, pp. 168–189.

Tsichritzis, D. (1989) Object-Oriented Development for Open Systems. In *Information Processing 89 (Proceedings IFIP '89)*, San Francisco. North-Holland, pp. 1033–1040.

Udell, J. (1994) Componentware. *Byte*, **19**(5), 46–56.

Ungar, D. and Smith, R.B. (1987) Self: The Power of Simplicity. In *Proceedings OOPSLA '87, ACM SIGPLAN Notices*, **22**(12), 227–242.

Wegner, P. (1987) Dimensions of Object-Based Language Design. In *Proceedings OOPSLA '87, ACM SIGPLAN Notices*, **22**(12), 168–182.

Part II

Architectures and Language Paradigms

Supporting Cooperation in Enterprise-Scale Distributed Object Systems

**Frank Manola, Dimitrios Georgakopoulos, Sandra Heiler,
Benjamin Hurwitz, Gail Mitchell and Farshad Nayeri**
GTE Laboratories Incorporated, Waltham, MA, USA

Abstract

Many business and government organizations are planning the development of enterprise-wide, open distributed computing architectures to support their operational information processing requirements, using distributed object middleware technology, such as the Object Management Group's (OMG's) CORBA, as a basic infrastructure. Such architectures require component interoperability and cooperation at multiple levels of abstraction. Initially, the focus of most industry work within OMG was on the lower levels, such as basic object messaging and object service capabilities. However, as agreements have been reached at these levels, attention is shifting to higher-level requirements, such as agreements on the meanings of key business concepts which are needed to support *semantic interoperability*. At the same time, the focus of much cooperative information systems (CIS) research has been on the higher-level requirements, sometimes without making clear connections to industry developments in enterprise architectures. These industry developments are defining the architectures in which CIS research results would need to function in enterprise-scale cooperative systems. This chapter describes a number of industry trends in the development of enterprise-wide distributed object systems that reflect the need for higher levels of cooperation. The chapter also indicates relationships between these trends and areas of CIS research, to make the point that CIS research could usefully build on, and more directly affect, open, commercially-available software technology such as that reflected in OMG's specifications.

Cooperative Information Systems
Trends and Directions
ISBN 0-12-544910-0

I INTRODUCTION

Many business and government organizations are attempting to move from mainframe-based "islands of automation" toward open, enterprise-wide distributed computing environments to support their operational requirements. A typical target architecture of such development is shown in Figure 1. In this architecture, the software is distributed and (for the most part) object-oriented. Components are grouped in three layers, which constitute *logical* groupings of objects (objects in different layers do not necessarily reside on different hardware platforms). Client programs directly serve end users, and consist either of stand-alone applications (word processors, spreadsheets) or presentation interfaces to shared organizational applications. Shared applications, and in fact all operations within the architecture, are controlled by objects representing shared business abstractions (customers, products), together with business rules representing business process definitions, grouped in the next layer. These business objects and processes integrate access to large-scale databases (both new and legacy) and legacy applications, grouped in the third layer. All components communicate via common object messaging middleware. The architecture supports integrated management of objects representing both business abstractions and elements of the enterprise and computing infrastructure (network elements, software, plant

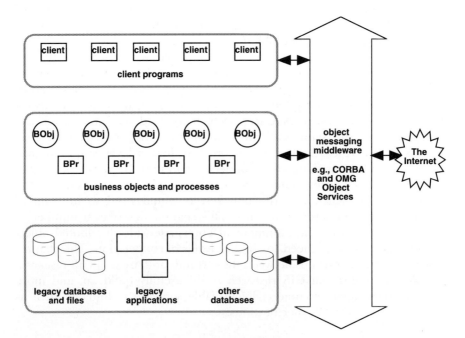

Figure I. Enterprise information system architecture.

facilities). Applications are constructed from reusable components, and users interact with the system via compound document and graphical interfaces. An additional characteristic of these architectures which is becoming increasingly prevalent is the provision of interfaces to the Internet and the use of Internet technology within the architecture to establish enterprise *intranets*.

The use of objects in such architectures reflects the fact that advanced software development increasingly involves the use of object technology. This includes the use of object-oriented programming languages, class libraries and application development frameworks, application integration technology such as Microsoft's OLE, and distributed object middleware, such as the Common Object Request Broker Architecture (CORBA) technology developed by the Object Management Group (OMG, 1995a), and similar technology being developed by Microsoft and others. It also involves the use of object analysis and design methodologies and associated tools.

This use of object technology is driven by a number of factors, including:

1 the desire to build software from reusable components;
2 the desire for software to more directly and more completely reflect business concepts, rather than information technology concepts;
3 the need to support business processes that involve legacy information systems;
4 the inclusion of object concepts and facilities in key software products by major software vendors.

The first two factors reflect requirements for business systems to be rapidly and cheaply developed or adapted to reflect changes in the business environment, such as new services, altered internal business processes, or altered customer, supplier, or business partner relationships. Object technology provides mechanisms, such as encapsulation and inheritance, that have the potential to support more rapid and flexible software development, higher levels of reuse and the definition of software artefacts that more directly model business concepts.

The third factor reflects a situation faced by many large organizations, in which a key issue is not just the development of new software, but the coordination of existing software that supports key business processes and human activities. Mechanisms provided by object technology[1] can help encapsulate existing systems, and unify them into higher-level processes.

The fourth factor is particularly important. It reflects the fact that, as commercial software vendors incorporate object concepts in key products,

---

[1]Particularly *distributed* object technology, since these multiple systems are effectively distributed, and any attempt to integrate them will necessarily involve aspects of distributed technology.

it will become more and more difficult to *avoid* using object technology.[2] This is illustrated by the rapid pace at which object technology is being included in software such as DBMSs (including relational DBMSs) and other middleware, and client/server development environments. Due to this factor, organizations may be influenced to begin adopting object technology before they would ordinarily consider doing so.

Enterprise-scale distributed architectures must support component interoperability and cooperation at multiple levels of abstraction. Obvious levels include the physical level (e.g., agreements on data representations or data translation rules), and the object model level (e.g., agreements on whether OLE- or CORBA-based technology will be used to provide basic distributed object messaging). Much discussion of interoperability and object technology involves these levels. However, there are also requirements for higher levels of agreement. For example, there is a need for agreements at the level of *semantic* interoperability (agreements on shared terminology and meanings), so that the interoperations enabled by the lower levels actually "make sense". Design of large-scale business systems is increasingly based on definitions of *business objects*. These attempt to reflect organization-wide agreements on the meanings of key business concepts and rules, such as what a "customer" is, and how bills are computed. Still other agreements are required at the level of *intelligent* interoperability, or *cooperation*, so that components can divide up the work required to accomplish a given task, and cooperate in performing it. These involve such things as definitions of higher-level task descriptions, and higher-level communication and coordination mechanisms for use by more "intelligent" components.

Supporting increased interoperability in such architectures involves not only the use of standards reflecting these agreements, but also making more aspects of the architecture explicit as *metadata*, so that standards can be applied to them, and so that intelligent components can make decisions on the basis of that metadata. These techniques apply (in different ways) to all levels (from physical to semantic). For example, standards can be applied at the level of object interface specifications (as in the use of OMG's CORBA IDL), and also at the higher level of standard *ontologies* for various application domains or industries (Heiler, 1995).

Applying these techniques also requires software architectures and frameworks that enable these approaches to be properly applied and organized. The OMG's CORBA architecture, and related technology, provides a promising basis for the development of enterprise-wide computing architectures, since it provides key functionality, and is based on open specifications supported by a wide variety of vendors. This openness, and the associated ability to buy software from multiple vendors that will nevertheless work

---

[2] For example, it will be increasingly difficult to avoid using OLE in doing serious development for Microsoft platforms.

together, is a key requirement in enterprise software architectures, as businesses direct development efforts away from basic infrastructure software, and toward software that directly supports distinct business functions.

Initially, the focus of most industry work within OMG was directed to lower level technology, such as the distributed programming capabilities provided by CORBA technology, and Object Services such as transaction and persistence services. However, such capabilities, while crucial, are far from sufficient for enterprise application development. As agreements have been reached at these lower levels, attention is shifting to higher-level requirements. At the same time, the focus of much cooperative information systems (CIS) research has been on higher-level requirements, such as shared semantics, and knowledge-based components that can determine how to cooperate on the basis of explicit descriptions of component requirements and capabilities. Such research has sometimes failed to establish clear connections with industry developments in distributed computing architectures such as CORBA (sometimes redeveloping the same facilities rather than basing their higher-level work on these industry infrastructures), and the additional object structuring mechanisms being developed in the context of such architectures. However, these industry developments will define the environments in which CIS research results will need to function in operational enterprise-scale cooperative systems. Moreover, the lack of such connections means that the requirements of higher-level CIS components may not be adequately reflected in commercially available distributed object infrastructures on which enterprises will wish to base their systems.

This chapter describes a number of industry trends in the development of enterprise-wide distributed object systems that reflect the need for higher levels of interoperability and cooperation, in order to place in perspective various aspects of OMG technology, some of the technology still to be specified, and related OMG and product development activities. The chapter also indicates relationships between these trends and areas of CIS research, to reinforce the point that CIS research could usefully build on, and more directly affect, open, commercially-available software technology, such as that reflected in OMG's specifications. The structure of the rest of this chapter is as follows. Section 2 provides a brief review of OMG's Object Management Architecture (OMA). The section notes that the OMA's CORBA and Object Service specifications are intended to provide a general technology base for building distributed object systems, and shows that additional levels of organization are necessary to fully use this technology in an enterprise computing environment. Section 3 discusses such additional object organizational concepts as *business objects*, *tiered architectures*, and *application frameworks*, and how they represent and facilitate additional levels of cooperation among software components. Section 4 discusses additional technologies, specifically *workflows and extended transactions*, *Internet technology*, and *computational reflection*, and how they provide additional support for cooperative mechanisms in building enterprise systems. Section 5 provides some concluding remarks.

2 DISTRIBUTED OBJECT ARCHITECTURES, CORBA AND CORBASERVICES

There is increasing agreement that modelling a distributed system as a distributed collection of interacting *objects* provides the appropriate framework for use in integrating *heterogeneous, autonomous*, and *distributed* (HAD) computing resources. Objects form a natural model for a distributed system because, like objects, distributed components can only communicate with each other using messages addressed to well-defined interfaces, and components are assumed to have their own locally-defined procedures enabling them to respond to messages sent them. Objects accommodate the heterogeneous aspects of such systems because messages sent to distributed components depend only on the component interfaces, not on the internals of the components. Objects accommodate the autonomous aspects of such systems because components may change independently and transparently, provided their interfaces are maintained. These characteristics allow objects to be used both in the development of new components, and for encapsulating access to legacy components. In addition, because object-oriented implementations bundle data with related operations in modular units, the use of objects supports fine-grained tuning of the computing architecture by moving objects to appropriate nodes of the network.[3]

The OMG is an industry consortium with the goal of developing an object-oriented architecture, with corresponding specifications (Soley, 1995; OMG, 1995a–c) for distributed application integration. Commercial software based on OMG specifications is becoming increasingly available[4] Details of OMG's technology can be found in publications such as Mowbray and Zahavi (1995), Ben-Naton (1995) and Orfali *et al.* (1996). The OMG's OMA (Soley, 1995) defines a particular, generalized, distributed object architecture.

The OMA includes a Reference Model which identifies and character-izes the components, interfaces and protocols that make up the architecture (Figure 2). The Reference Model includes the following major elements:

- The *Object Request Broker* (ORB) is an object-messaging backplane that enables distributed objects to transparently send and receive requests and responses.
- *Object Services* is a collection of services (interfaces and objects) that support basic functions for using and implementing objects, and are likely

---

[3]This is becoming increasingly apparent with the development of Internet *applet* technology, such as Sun's Java, and Microsoft's ActiveX.
[4]For example, a CORBA implementation is now included in the Netscape Communicator Web client.

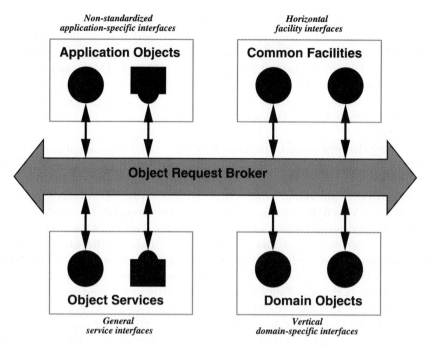

Figure 2.   The OMG object management architecture (OMA).

to be used in any object-based program. Current Object Services include support for queries, transactions, events etc.

- *Common Facilities* is a collection of services that provide end-user-oriented capabilities useful across many application domains. For example, OMG recently adopted a compound document facility. Other planned facilities include workflow, scripting and information storage and retrieval facilities, as well as facilities relating to business objects (discussed in Section 3.1).
- *Domain Objects* provide services that are likely to be used only in specific, vertical application domains, such as telecommunications or manufacturing.
- *Application Objects* are built specifically for a particular end-user application.

The Object Services, Common Facilities, Domain Objects and Application Objects in the OMA correspond to different *categories* of objects which can interoperate via the ORB. The purpose of categorizing objects in this way is to guide OMG's strategy for developing interface specifications. For example, the more fundamental, implementation-oriented specifications (such as the ORB and Object Services) require more vendor participation in their definition, while the more application- or user-oriented specifications require more end-user participation in their definition. Moreover, OMG is primarily in the business of defining object *interfaces*. It does not, except indirectly, define object *implementations*. Hence, from OMG's perspective, the categories in the diagram are primarily categories of *interfaces*, rather than categories of *objects*. OMG specifications define a language for defining object interfaces, called the CORBA *Interface Definition Language* (CORBA IDL)[5]. OMG also defines specific object interfaces using CORBA IDL when defining object interfaces in the various categories.

The ORB in the OMA is defined by the CORBA specifications (OMG, 1995a). As software, the ORB may consist of a single software component, or multiple cooperating (and possibly heterogeneous) software components. Architecturally speaking, the ORB is primarily an object message dispatcher. An ORB does not insist that its "objects" be implemented in an object-oriented programming language. The CORBA architecture describes interfaces for connecting code and data to the ORB to form *object implementations*, whose interfaces are described using CORBA IDL. The ORB then provides facilities so that object operations can be invoked by clients. It is this flexibility that enables ORBs to be used in connecting legacy systems and data together as components in enterprise computing architectures. The CORBA specifications also include the definition of an Internet Inter-ORB Protocol (IIOP), which allows ORBs from different vendors to interoperate.

While the ORB concept is frequently viewed as being relevant only for distributed implementations, its functionality for message dispatching between different environments can be just as relevant in local implementations. For example, IBM's SOM (Orfali *et al.*, 1996) effectively defines an ORB intended to support message dispatching between (local) objects written in different programming languages, rather than to support distribution.

A distributed enterprise object system must provide functionality beyond that of simply delivering messages between objects. OMG's *Object Services* have been defined to address some of these requirements. Object Services provide the next level of structure above the basic object messaging facilities provided by CORBA. The services define specific types of objects (or interfaces) and relationships between them in order to support higher-level facilities. Object Services currently defined by OMG include, among others:

- concurrency control service;
- event notification service;
- persistent object service;
- naming service;

---

[5]CORBA IDL has nearly completed processing toward becoming an ISO standard for specifying object interfaces within the ISO Open Distributed Processing Reference Model (ISO/IEC/JTC1/SC21/WG7,1995).

- life cycle services;
- query service;
- relationship service;
- transaction service;
- collections service;
- trader service.

The OMG has also issued Requests for Proposal (RFPs) for a number of additional services, including:

- interface type versioning service;
- messaging service.

Taken together, OMG Object Services provide services for ORB-accessible objects similar to those that an Object DBMS (ODBMS) provides for objects in an object database (queries, transactions, etc.). The Object Services, together with the basic connectivity provided by the ORB, turn the collection of network-accessible objects into a unified *shared object space*, accessible by any ORB client application. Managing the collection of ORB-accessible objects thus becomes a generalized form of "object database management", with the ORB being part of the internal implementation of what is effectively an ODBMS (Figure 3). Viewed in this way, the OMA

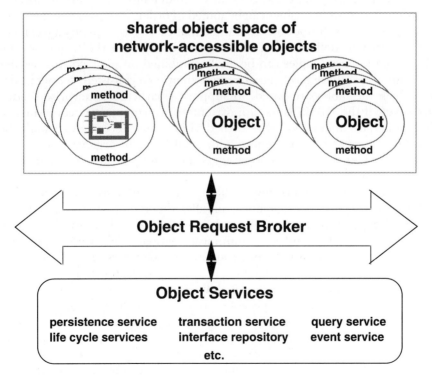

Figure 3.   OMA used to create an ODBMS.

provides a powerful object-oriented infrastructure for the development of general-purpose applications, just as an enterprise database and its associated DBMS provide such an infrastructure for the development of general-purpose enterprise applications. A commercial example of this concept is IBM's Network Centric Computing (IBM Corporation, 1995), which views the network of computing resources as a single computing entity that is responsible for supplying generalized services.

This analogy between an OMA-based distributed object system and a DBMS illustrates key requirements in building cooperative information systems (CISs). A DBMS provides more than simply a place to store individual pieces of persistent data. The value added by a DBMS is that it also provides additional processing capabilities, such as query and transaction processing, that enable the data it manages to be used collectively and cooperatively in dealing with complex problems. Moreover, a DBMS by itself provides a set of very powerful services, but imposes no particular organization on the databases it supports. For example, a relational DBMS will support any collection of tables that users might wish to define, but, aside from requiring that the tables conform to the relational model, it imposes no particular structure on those tables. It does not define how to use the tables to support a given application or set of applications. It does not guarantee that there has been any agreement on primary or foreign key definitions, so that tables can be joined in order to recover relationships among the tables. It does not guarantee that there has been any agreement on the domain definitions of the non-key columns in the tables, so that data from different tables can be easily combined or analysed. It does not guarantee that there has been any agreement on a consistent set of entities on which the tables are based, to support a particular enterprise model. However, if the DBMS is to support enterprise computing requirements, it is generally understood that such decisions and agreements should be reached. These decisions impose additional levels of organization on the database tables, so that they work together to support an identified set of requirements.

These requirements for additional levels of agreement, and for additional processing capabilities, parallel the requirements in building CISs. CISs require additional levels of agreement beyond the simple ability to access data and to communicate between software components, such as agreements on data and cooperation semantics, in order to allow these resources to work together in solving complex tasks. CISs also require higher-level processing capabilities, such as mediator components, to help implement this cooperation. It is not accidental that many CIS examples involve heterogeneous database integration, or that Papazoglou *et al.* (1992) use distributed query processing as an example of cooperative processing, since the database context frequently illustrates both the data agreements and the additional processing components required in cooperative processing.

The same requirements hold true in distributed object architectures. An architecture providing only ORB functionality can play a valuable role in supporting arbitrary collections of objects (the Internet plays a similar role in supporting a world-wide collection of HAD services). However, if the architecture is to support enterprise computing requirements, additional levels of organization and processing support must also be provided. OMG Object Services add DBMS-like capabilities to the architecture, and this provides a powerful basis for supporting more complex requirements. However, as the discussion above indicates, additional levels are needed. These additional levels are where OMG's Common Facilities, Application and Domain Objects, as well as still higher level concepts, come into play. The next section discusses some of these concepts. Moreover, these requirements are independent of whether the distributed object architecture is based on OMG's definitions, or other technology such as the distributed version of Microsoft's COM (Orfali *et al.*, 1995), NeXT's Enterprise Objects Framework (NeXT,1995), or the Open Software Foundation's (OSF) Distributed Computing Environment (DCE) (Nicol *et al.*, 1993). The Internet (especially when considered in the context of its commercial uses) illustrates these same points.

Much CIS research today involves adding semantic agreements and corresponding processing components to integrate heterogeneous DBMSs and processing components. Such research should increasingly consider adding these same elements to OMG-based distributed object architectures. The infrastructure provided by these architectures provides an ideal base for the addition of additional levels of organization and agreements, and higher level components, required to support cooperative processing. In addition, such architectures provide a means to more directly inject higher-level CIS capabilities into commercial software that is increasingly being used in operational enterprise systems. Singh and Gisi (1995) is an example of research illustrating this direction.

3 THE NEED FOR HIGHER-LEVEL OBJECT ORGANIZATIONS

Enterprise computing systems are expensive, complex and critical to the functioning of the enterprise. Hence, in building such systems, a clear overall architectural direction is important to guide the selection of hardware and software components, the making of design decisions and overall development strategy. A clear direction is particularly important in building an *open* architecture, in which products from multiple vendors will have to interoperate, and in building a scaleable *distributed* architecture, in which additional design choices about component location, replication etc., must be made.

The previous section identified an analogy between a CORBA-based distributed object system and a DBMS, and identified the need for additional levels of object organization beyond ORB-based messaging and object services in order to support higher-levels of interoperability and cooperative processing requirements. Several higher level object organizational principles that support increased levels of cooperation among software components are receiving a great deal of attention in the context of enterprise computing architectures. This section discusses these ideas, shows how they are related to OMG's OMA, and describes how they support cooperative processing requirements.

3.1 Business Objects

All business software essentially models a business process, such as filling a customer order. However, while much work has been done in the past on conceptual modelling approaches to describe the real world being represented by software, the structure of the software itself usually did not reflect the actual structure of the enterprise being modelled. Object-oriented software, on the other hand, can be designed so that each software object represents a real element of the business, such as a customer, invoice, or order-entry function.

An increasingly important idea in the development of enterprise computing architectures is the definition of *business objects* directly representing the conceptual model of the enterprise. These business objects play a central role in capturing the semantics of actual business entities and processes, in a way that is understandable by the business in general (not just the information technology staff). For example, enterprise-wide business rules and policy definitions can be centrally located within the business objects. The business objects can then serve as an organizational base for other parts of the architecture. For example, by defining applications in terms of these business objects, enterprise-wide definitions and behaviours can be enforced for all applications. In addition, the potential exists for rapidly changing the software, by direct manipulation of business objects, to implement changes in business processes made necessary by changes in the actual business environment.

Obtaining agreement within an enterprise on a consistent set of business object definitions constitutes one of the higher levels of agreement necessary for enhanced levels of interoperation and cooperation in an enterprise distributed object system. Obtaining agreements *between* enterprises on such business object definitions is also necessary to enable electronic commerce, such as the connection of one enterprise's purchase order system to another enterprise's order entry system.

It might be supposed that it would be straightforward to design general business concepts such as "customer" and "invoice" within an enterprise. Then, since numerous applications within the enterprise involve these concepts, a great deal of reuse should be achieved. However, in practice this is not being realized. It has proven relatively difficult to design reusable business objects, e.g., to define a model of a customer that can be used throughout an enterprise. For example, the definition of "customer" can vary widely among applications, so numerous specializations of the concept often exist. In many respects, this is similar to the problem that was encountered in developing database technology's original vision of a single, corporate-wide database: instead, numerous application-specific databases have become the norm.

Building a reusable enterprise-wide business model is even more difficult when, as with more and more businesses, software is purchased rather than developed internally. When using commercial software, the buyer is constrained by the business concepts built into the software. In addition, unless an integrated software suite is bought from a single vendor, the buyer must attempt to integrate the separate business models assumed by the various purchased packages. (Of course, there are also the usual lower-level interoperability problems of software developed using different programming languages, different interapplication communication mechanisms etc.)

This illustrates that a number of different types of agreements must be reached in order to support the development of reusable business objects:

- agreements on domain-specific business objects and ontologies to provide the basis for describing the concepts of a specific business area (such as accounting);
- agreements on generic, cross-domain business objects to provide the basis for interoperation among the various domain areas within a specific business as well as interoperation between businesses;
- agreements on lower-level details of how such business objects should interoperate, e.g., on data formats, significant processing events, and messages to be interchanged in various circumstances.

If it is possible to reach such agreements, they can be directly reflected in the business object definitions. It is obviously desirable to reach such agreements, and to directly base business object definitions on them, to the maximum possible extent. At the same time, it is necessary to be prepared to deal with situations where such agreements cannot be or have not been reached, such as cooperation between companies using dissimilar definitions. Higher levels of CIS technology can be used to enhance the business object concept to deal with such situations. For example, business objects can be provided with explicit self-descriptions, which can be used by "mediators" or similar components to resolve semantic and other differences (Singh and Gisi, 1995).

The OMG's Business Object Domain Task Force (BODTF) is one group that is attempting to address the issues of obtaining the kinds of agreements mentioned above[6]. The BODTF's work is based on the idea of

---

[6]The business object concept is not a strictly OMG idea.

business objects as self-contained and independently developed *application components* (encapsulated units of functionality) which can be purchased from different vendors and used in different combinations at different times. These interoperable business objects would be usable by application domain developers and, eventually, by end users, for provisioning their own business solutions. To achieve this, there will need to be standards for the interoperability of business objects, the existence of a marketplace (suppliers and consumers) for reusable business objects, and standardization of facilities to hide underlying software technology complexities from business object developers.

The BODTF is explicitly addressing two specific requirements: (i) industry and cross-industry models for business objects; (ii) the ability for application developers to build and deploy business objects that will interoperate in ways that make sense for the users, but that may not have been foreseen by the developers. The BODTF has issued a Request for Proposal (RFP) (OMG, 1996) calling for technology submissions to support two related OMG Common Facilities:

- *Common Business Objects* (CBOs): objects representing business semantics (such as the concept of a "purchase") that can be shown to be common across most businesses.
- the *Business Object Facility*: the infrastructure (application architecture, services etc.) required to support business objects operating as cooperative application components in a distributed object environment.

OMG CBOs are intended to be both design-time and run-time constructs, and to map directly onto design/analysis concepts such as "customer", "invoice", "insurance claim" etc.

The Business Object Facility is the technological infrastructure necessary to support "plug and play" business application components. This infrastructure must provide the semantics to support both CBOs and business objects specific to an enterprise. The Business Object Facility is intended to hide complexity so that CBOs can be implemented by, for example, the average business application developer. Figure 4 (OMG, 1996) shows the intended relationship of CBOs and the Business Object Facility to OMG's CORBA, Object Services and Object Facilities. It also shows how, based on the CBOs, business objects can be specialized to meet the needs of specific domains and enterprises.

The concept of a business object does not prescribe any particular notation for specifying the behaviour of such objects or of business processes involving them. Many different machine-interpretable notations could be used, with their details hidden behind object interfaces. Workflows (discussed in Section 4.1) represent a particularly important approach to specifying business processes.

The BODTF views business objects as examples of the larger-granularity objects that are sometimes referred to as *components*. Some

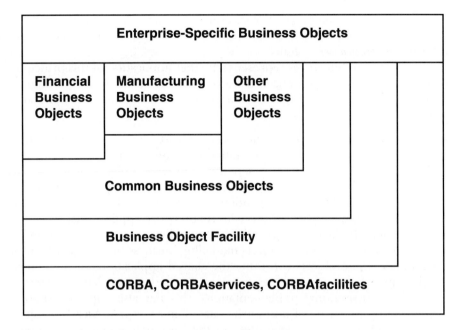

Figure 4.   Business object architecture (OMG, 1996).

recent articles have tended to play down "object technology", and to play up "component technology". If "object technology" refers only to very-small-granularity infrastructure objects and current object-oriented programming technology, it is certainly true that "components" (generally larger units that have application significance and can be readily composed) are more important than objects. However, there is a close connection between object technology and the ability to construct components. Discussion citing the relative importance of "components" vs. "objects" is more a comment on what entities are of significance in enterprise computing than a comment on whether object technology should be used to model and implement them.

3.2 Multiple-Tier Architectures

The identification of business objects is a step in the direction of a more explicit representation of enterprise semantics in enterprise computing systems. The business object concept is being carried into the architecture of enterprise systems in the form of *three-tier client/server architectures*. These architectures involve the division of the system's components into functional *layers* or *tiers*, based on the different levels of abstraction that they represent, or the different functional concerns they address. Under this categorization, a conventional, centralized system is considered a *one-tier* architecture, while the original "client/server" systems, which locate data at a central point and move application functions to distributed workstations, are considered *two-tier* systems.

Three-tier architectures represent a further application of this principle of functional separation. The architecture discussed at the beginning of Section 1 (and shown in Figure 1) was a three-tier architecture. Generally speaking, in a three-tier architecture:

- Tier 3 consists of client software. In a "purist" three-tier architecture, the clients implement only presentation functions. Such *thin clients* invoke shared application services by sending messages to objects in tier 2. In more conventional implementations, the clients also support application-specific functions (either conventional stand-alone applications such as word processors, or parts of specialized enterprise applications). Such *fat clients* resemble those in conventional 2-tier client/server architectures.
- Tier 2 consists of business objects modelling business functions and business logic; these objects constitute the shared applications of the enterprise, and invoke functions at tier 1 to access data and legacy systems. In more conventional implementations, this tier also supports shared applications that are not necessarily part of an enterprise business object model. This tier, which separates out the basic definitions of the enterprise's business operations, constitutes the primary distinguishing characteristic of the architecture.
- Tier 1 consists of database servers, which manage data integrity and access, together with legacy systems.
- All tiers are connected through distributed object messaging middleware, such as the CORBA ORB. In addition to this middleware, and the DBMSs in tier 1, other shared services such as transaction and workflow services are incorporated in the architecture.
- The tiers in the architecture are *logical*, not necessarily physical. While the tiers are often implemented on separate workstations or servers (in particular, using separate *application servers* at tier 2), this is not a requirement.

If OMG's CORBA and CORBAservices are used as middleware, integration of the Internet with the CORBA-based distributed object architecture could be provided by OMG's Internet-based IIOP protocol, as in Netscape Communications' Open Network Environment (ONE) (Netscape, 1996).

The following advantages are typically cited for three-tier architectures:

- The business object layer provides a model that more closely corresponds to meaningful concepts in the enterprise. This allows management to more easily understand and validate concepts and processes, and allows the system to more precisely represent the actual processes of the business. The business objects also support the coherent structuring of the architecture by providing a framework to which the details of databases, applications and presentation functions can be mapped.

- The three tiers separate issues of presentation logic, application logic and business processes, and data access. Applications and business processes can be changed more easily, since application logic is not intertwined with presentation and data access logic. Moreover, application logic can potentially reside on separate servers. This simplifies updates to applications, since the updates can be localized to these servers, rather than having to synchronize updates to the more numerous clients distributed throughout the architecture.
- Key services can be replicated on multiple servers to improve availability reliability, and performance. The number of servers can be tuned based on the number of users, with the messaging middleware routing requests to these servers based on load and availability, thus improving scalability of the architecture.
- Business objects can encapsulate the details of data access. Clients and applications are then dependent only on the attributes of business objects, rather than, for example, on the details of how data is arranged in database tables[7]. This insulates clients from changes to database structures, and allows heterogeneous data sources to be easily integrated into the architecture.

The three-tier architecture is considered to be particularly appropriate for large-scale business information systems, which require robustness and scalability. At the moment, large organizations typically have many independently developed centralized and two-tier systems that need to interoperate. This generally involves the development of bridge or adapter components between them. As the number of systems that need to interoperate increases, the complexity of the resulting architecture explodes. One of the motivations for the three-tier approach is the need to migrate these separately developed systems into a unified architecture in which the various individual components can interoperate, and which scales better than the use of pairwise adapters.

A number of commercial products, e.g., SAP R/3 and (Forte 1994), support three-tier architectures. Three-tier architectures do not require object technology, while the use of object technology does not necessarily entail any particular division of an architecture into tiers. However, developments such as IBM's Open Blueprint (IBM Corporation, 1995) and NeXT's Enterprise Objects Framework (NeXT, 1995) clearly suggest that object technology is particularly well-adapted to supporting three-tier architectures. Using an object-oriented implementation, the division into tiers conceptually groups the objects by the roles they play. The objects can be assigned to hardware platforms based on physical requirements. This

---

[7]An often-heard piece of advice in constructing large-scale enterprise systems is to avoid embedding SQL in client applications, in order to avoid the need to modify the applications when database structures change. To a great extent, this reflects a perceived inadequacy of the view facilities in commercial DBMS products.

application partitioning capability is supported by some existing products. For example, Forte provides facilities for the logical design of objects, and, as a separate step, the targeting of the implemented objects to specified platforms (with a choice of inter-object communication mechanisms). Multiple partitioning schemes using the same logical objects can be supported. This could allow, for example, a three-tier application (with selected corporate data) to be hosted on an individual laptop for use by a mobile worker, and hosted on multiple machine types in a larger-scale environment.

Three-tier architectures raise a number of implementation issues. For example, most of today's commercial tools are designed for the "fat client" form of application, and most commercial software products tend to have this organization as well. Also, as with any layered architecture, careful design is needed to avoid performance problems associated with the division into multiple layers. The implementation of the business object tier requires particularly careful design, since it stands between the clients and their access to data. The interaction of Internet/intranet technologies with these architectures raises other issues. For example, Internet resources cannot necessarily be conveniently organized into tiers. On the other hand, mobile object technologies such as Java and ActiveX provide the potential for more flexible organizations of objects into tiers or other groupings that suit enterprise requirements.

Looking at the objects in the architecture at a more detailed level, additional types of objects will exist within the general groupings of objects represented by the tiers. For example, the middle tier will often have objects implementing mappings to the databases and legacy systems in tier 1, as well as objects representing business abstractions. This flexibility allows the implementation of each tier to freely use whatever configuration of components is required to support that tier. For example, ODBMS vendors suggest that ODBMSs be used as application caches in the middle tier of these architectures. This configuration might be ruled out if the physical configuration had to exactly match the logical configuration.

Continuing the database analogy introduced in Section 2, the three-tier architecture reflects issues similar to those which prompted the development of the ANSI/SPARC three-schema DBMS architecture (Tsichritzis and Klug, 1977). Like the three-tier architecture, this DBMS architecture identified separate descriptions of a database at the *internal* (physical data organization), *conceptual* (enterprise model, or meaning), and *external* (presentation to users) levels, in order to represent the separate concerns of these levels of abstraction. In the three-tier architecture, the business objects play the role of the conceptual schema in defining the core semantics of the enterprise. By organizing the entire system in terms of a common layer of shared business objects, this organization facilitates cooperation by reducing semantic mismatches.

3.3 Application Frameworks

Previous sections have emphasized the need for additional object-structuring concepts at higher levels of abstraction than those often considered in simple distributed programming. However, additional object structuring is also necessary at *lower* levels of abstraction. In particular, Section 3.1, in discussing OMG's Business Object Facility, noted that one of the levels of agreement necessary to construct reusable business objects was agreements on lower-level details of how such business objects should interoperate, e.g., on data formats, significant processing events, and messages to be interchanged in various circumstances. Such agreements are necessary because without them, even if two objects were semantically compatible they would be unable to interoperate.

OMG (1996) uses the analogy of the boards in a computer system: each board provides some useful function and is a component of the whole system. Before standard computer bus architectures, boards were all different, each manufacturer had its own, and there was no open market in such components. Once the *standards and infrastructure* were in place for this type of component the marketplace flourished. Components often require standards for interaction at fine levels of detail. Just being able to wire boards together is insufficient; agreements on timing, voltages, and protocols must all exist for these components to work together. Application components have a similar need for infrastructure and standards, such as the OMG's Business Object Facility, to allow them to cooperate.

These sorts of agreements among objects are those that typically characterize an *object framework*. Gamma *et al.* (1995) describe a *framework* as a set of cooperating classes that make up a reusable design for a specific class of software, such as graphical editors, compilers, or financial modelling applications. MacApp (Apple, 1989) and Taligent's (1995) Common Point Application System are commercial examples of frameworks. A framework is generally customized to a particular application by creating application-specific subclasses of abstract classes from the framework.

Gamma *et al.* (1995) note that a framework defines the overall architecture of the application (or a specific part of it), including the overall structure, its partitioning into classes and objects, the key responsibilities of those classes and objects, how they cooperate, and the thread of control. A framework predetermines these aspects of a design so that the application developer can concentrate on the specifics of the application. In addition, because the patterns of interoperation between participating objects and object classes are predefined, and the enabling assumptions are built into the participants, specialized subclasses (assuming they do not change these assumptions, or that new assumptions are not introduced) are guaranteed to be able to cooperate.

A framework captures the design decisions that are common to its application domain. Frameworks thus emphasize *design reuse* over *code reuse*, though a framework will usually include concrete subclasses that can be used immediately. Larger object-oriented applications can use a *collection* of cooperating frameworks. For example, an accounting application might use the combination of an accounting-specific framework, a user interface framework, and a persistent storage framework. Taligent's (1995) Common Point Application System defines a collection of frameworks that can be used in this way. When frameworks are used properly, most of the design and code in an application will come from, or be influenced by, the frameworks it uses.

OMG appears to expect that, in order to provide functionality of direct interest to end users in particular application domains, application frameworks will be built in terms of objects that provide application, domain, facility, and service interfaces from the categories of interfaces shown in Figure 2. In particular, the OMG Business Object Facility is intended to be a generalized framework so that independent vendors can create objects conforming to the framework that are guaranteed to work together. Such work on application frameworks reflects an attempt to address the problem of how the technologies represented by OMG services, facilities, etc., can be coherently used in building end-user applications.

Use of frameworks is becoming increasingly common and important. Frameworks emphasize the fact that the range of lower-level agreements that must exist to support advanced forms of interoperability (such as "plug and play" among components purchased from independent software vendors) must generally be based on a unified design approach, together with consistent standards.

4 ADDITIONAL ARCHITECTURAL CONSIDERATIONS

Several additional technologies are gaining importance in enterprise distributed computing architectures. These include technology supporting workflows and extended transactions, Internet technology, and reflective capabilities. These technologies reflect the increasingly general requirements, and forms of computation, to be found in enterprise computing. They also represent technologies that either can contribute toward, or must be taken into account in, the development of higher levels of cooperation in enterprise computing systems.

4.1 Workflows and Extended Transactions

In order to fully support the implementation of business processes, particularly when they are modelled in terms of the higher-level business object abstractions discussed in Section 3, enterprise distributed computing systems must provide support for higher-level *process* semantics. Workflow and extended transaction facilities represent important elements of this support.

A *workflow* is a set of tasks (or activities) that cooperate to implement a business process. A workflow model can be used to design automated or semi-automated implementations for business processes within an enterprise, or across multiple enterprises. While workflows are sometimes thought to involve only automated routing of documents between people, extensions of workflow technology, employing event−condition−action (ECA) rules and other techniques, can be used to define complex interactions among software components. Such workflow technology allows the integration of new software, legacy software and human interactions within a given process, and is increasingly being used in support of business processes in enterprise computing systems. An overview of workflow technology, including these extensions, is given in Georgakopoulos *et al.* (1995).

Figure 5 shows several telecommunications workflows (Georgako-poulos, *et al.* 1995). For example, the new service provisioning workflow defines the process that takes place when a telephone company customer requests new service. Task T0 involves an operator collecting information from the customer. When sufficient data has been collected, task T1 is performed to: (a) verify whether the customer-provided information is accurate; (b) create a service order record. On completion of T1, tasks T2, T3 and T4 are initiated. These represent alternative activities to allocate the necessary equipment to provide a circuit from the customer location to the appropriate telephone switch. Only one of these activities should be allowed to complete, as each would result in a completed circuit. T2 attempts to provide a connection by using existing facilities. However, this will not be possible if the necessary facilities are not available. T3 and T4 represent alternative ways to provide a connection by the physical installation of new facilities, and involve producing the alternative installation instructions for field personnel. T5 represents the

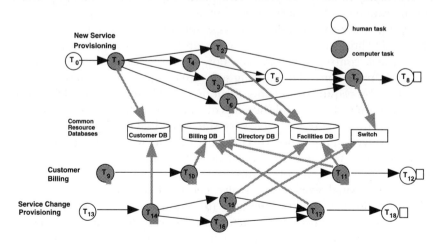

Figure 5.   Telecommunication workflows (Georgakopoulos *et al.*, 1995).

manual work for facility installation based on those instructions, and is completed when the persons involved report completion of the installation. Task T6 involves changing the telephone directory, while T7 updates the switch to activate service and generate billing information. Finally, task T8 involves a customer service representative calling to inform the customer that service has been established, and verifying that the service meets the customer's requirements. In addition to defining the individual tasks involved, the workflow specifies the task dependencies, e.g., that T1 starts after completion of T0, and that T2, T3, T4 and T6 can be performed concurrently after T1 is completed. As the figure indicates, a number of the tasks involve accessing shared databases.

From a computational point of view, a workflow is a higher-level behavioural specification. In a distributed object system, workflows resemble object-oriented applications in that behaviour is defined by messages between objects. In a workflow, however, the objects typically have larger granularity; they correspond to parts of a business process, and may be implemented by human rather than computational processes.

Georgakopoulos, *et al.* (1995) identify distributed object management (DOM) as a key infrastructure technology which must be combined with the capabilities of current commercial workflow management systems to fully support enterprise requirements for workflow technology. DOM technology supports the interoperability and integration of HAD systems and applications involved in business processes, allowing the workflow system to cope with replacement, migration and evolution of HAD systems or changes in their functionality and data. In addition, an object model facilitates managing complexity within the workflow system. Miller *et al.* (1996) discusses the use of CORBA-based technology in implementing several different architectures for workflow management systems. CORBA is seen as particularly valuable due to its cross-platform, non-proprietary approach, and the range of object services it provides.

Supporting the high-level process semantics captured by workflows requires facilities to specify the objects and tasks involved in a business process, task control flow and data flow dependencies, and exceptions. If workflows are to control interacting software components, supporting these semantics also requires capturing the *transactional* aspects of workflows, i.e., the logical units of work and the units of consistency and recovery (either as viewed by end users of the process or the individual component systems or objects involved in the process). This is because the work of the concurrently executing tasks in a workflow must be synchronized at various points in order to satisfy the goals of the process.

Transactional workflows involve coordinated execution of multiple tasks that: (a) may involve humans; (b) require access to HAD systems; (c) support selective use of transactional properties (e.g., atomicity, consistency, isolation and/or durability) for individual tasks or entire workflows. Selective use of transactional properties is required to allow the specialized functionality required by each workflow (e.g., allow task cooperation and support complex workflow structures). The traditional transactions supported by DBMSs[8] and TP monitors do not permit selective use of transactional properties to allow specialized functionality (e.g., to allow tasks to cooperate in complex ways rather than isolating them from each other). As a result, extending or relaxing the transaction models provided by these components is needed to support workflow functionality requirements.

The need to support higher degrees of task cooperation and extended transaction semantics is illustrated by the "canonical" travel reservation example used in many papers on extended transactions (see, e.g., Elmagarmid, 1992). In this example, making a travel reservation requires dealing with the separate reservations systems of airlines, hotels and car rental agencies, and making sure that either a single reservation is made with each, or no reservations are made. However, in this case, conventional ACID transactions are unnecessary, since the independent reservation systems involved deal with compensating actions (reservation changes) and asynchronous activities as a matter of course. Such systems, and their users, have more relaxed expectations of synchronization than are found in ordinary serialized transactions. A workflow mechanism dealing with such systems must reflect these expectations. Cooperating agents in a CIS may similarly not require the strict separation imposed by conventional transactions.

In order to support the full generality of workflow transactional requirements, Georgakopoulos *et al.* (1995) identify *customized transaction management* (CTM) technology as being another key technology in supporting workflow requirements. CTM ensures the correctness and reliability of applications that implement business processes, while permitting the functionality required by the semantics of each particular process (e.g., isolation, coordination, or cooperation among tasks). In addition, CTM copes with changes in the correctness and reliability requirements of the process, and the correctness and reliability guarantees that the HAD systems that may be involved in the process actually provide. Technology to support CTM is still primarily in the research stage. An example of technology to support CTM is the Transaction Specification and Management Environment (TSME) of Georgakopoulos *et al.* (1994). The TSME involves the use of declarative specifications of transaction models in addition to rules. The use of such declarative specifications is important because complex transactional requirements are not always easily specified in workflow rule notations. In addition, the declarative specifications allow the requirements of autonomously developed components to be checked for consistency.

---

[8] Object DBMSs have typically supported extensions to traditional transaction services, including support for some forms of task cooperation, but are limited in the types of cooperation they can directly support.

In general, facilities such as workflows and extended transactions can be considered as enhancements to the behavioural semantics of higher-level object abstractions. This reflects the suggestion in Wegner (1989) that objects and transactions form two complementary structuring mechanisms for concurrent systems. In this view, objects partition the system state into encapsulated components with behaviour determined by sets of applicable operations. Transactions partition system actions into sequences with specified access to shared objects during the complete duration of their execution. Hence, a transaction may be viewed as a *temporal object* in that it defines an atomic action (in terms of a collection of more primitive operations) bounded in time. Additional research is required to further integrate object and transaction concepts.

Fully supporting the behavioural semantics of enterprise business processes defined using workflows and extended transactions also requires enhancements at lower levels of the architecture. One such enhancement is support for enhanced messaging capabilities between objects. The CORBA specifications already support simple asynchronous messaging capabilities, in the form of the *deferred synchronous* and *one-way* messaging options. Similarly, the CORBA IIOP contains specific request and reply messages which can be sent asynchronously by clients and servers. This provides a basic foundation for supporting various forms of either synchronous or asynchronous messaging. In addition, the CORBA *Event Service* supports a decoupled communication model between objects, by introducing an *event channel* as an intermediate object between *suppliers* (objects that produce event data) and *consumers* (objects that process event data).

OMG is also developing further enhancements to its messaging capabilities to support business processes. For example, OMG has issued a Request for Proposal (RFP) for a Messaging Service to support more complex (but still basic) synchronous and asynchronous object interactions. The RFP identifies a number of services that must be supported, including such things as simple synchronous and asynchronous requests, queued deferred transactions, confirmation delivery, transactional message semantics and message priorities. Such facilities are not only important in general enterprise computing, but also provide necessary lower level support for the more complex interactions that must take place between fully cooperating components (e.g., using languages such as KQML[9] (Clark and Skarmeas, this volume; Singh and Gisi, 1995)) when they are used in enterprise systems.

4.2 Integration of Internet Technology

The Internet is becoming an increasingly important factor in planning for enterprise distributed computing environments. For example, companies

[9]Singh and Gisi (1995) note that KQML is being evaluated by OMG.

are providing information via World Wide Web pages, as well as customer access via the Internet to such enterprise computing services as on-line ordering or order/service tracking facilities. Companies are also using Internet technology to create private "intranets", providing access to enterprise data (and, potentially, services) from throughout the enterprise in a way that is convenient and avoids proprietary network technology. Following this trend, software vendors are developing software to allow Web browsers to act as user interfaces to enterprise computing systems. For example, products are being developed to allow Web browsers to act as clients in workflow or general client/server systems (such as SAP R/3). Products are also being developed that link mainframes to Web pages (e.g., translating conventional terminal sessions into HTML pages).

Businesses perceive a number of advantages in using the Web in enterprise computing. For example, Web browser software is widely available for most client platforms, and is cheaper than most alternative client applications. Also, Web pages generally work reasonably well with a variety of browsers, and maintenance is simpler since the browser is the only piece of distributed software to be managed. An architecture in which a Web browser forms the universal client is a special case of the "thin client" client/server architecture discussed in Section 3.2.

There is a close relationship between aspects of Internet technology (particularly the Web) and large-scale distributed object architectures. In particular, the Web's HTTP protocol is somewhat "object-oriented", allowing "objects" identified by URLs to support an extensible set of methods (even though the GET method is the one most frequently used). A number of activities are underway toward further integrating Internet and object technologies. Examples include Sun's Java technology, CORBA's IIOP, and Netscape's ONE (Netscape (1996)). In addition, the World Wide Web Consortium (W3C)[10] is investigating the relationship between the Web and object technology (and in particular the transition of HTTP to a full distributed object system), the OMG has established an Internet Special Interest Group, and OMG and W3C have exchanged membership. Microsoft also is developing technology for integrating OLE and the Web, and has submitted its Distributed Component Object Model specification to the Internet Engineering Task Force. Commercial software addressing the integration of Internet and CORBA technologies is also rapidly being developed. For example, both Visigenic and Sun have announced products that provide interfaces between Java programs and CORBA-based networks.

IBM's Network Centric Computing concept (IBM Corporation, 1995) is an example of how a distributed enterprise computing architecture (IBM's Open Blueprint) can be extended to include the Internet. This

---

[10]See URL http://www.w3.org.

integration of Internet and object technologies is based on the following enhancements:

- the addition of a Web browser to other presentation services provided;
- the addition of HTTP support to the RPC and messaging services;
- support for URLs as "object" identifiers;
- support for Internet security protocols;
- enhancements to messaging services, relational databases and transaction monitors to allow access by the Web browser.

Internet and CORBA technologies are also related in their need for higher-level services and cooperative facilities as they are applied in more complex applications. For example, the World Wide Web, by itself, provides only a form of object messaging service (HTTP) and a simple (but increasingly extensible) client facility (browsers). As the uses to which the Web is put become more complex, more attention is being directed toward providing services that enhance the usability of the basic Web capabilities. For example, search engines (query support) are becoming indispensable tools, and agent technology adds more intelligence to the searching process. Similarly, extended facilities to support transactions over the Web are being investigated.

As with distributed object systems, these Internet capabilities must be further extended to support higher levels of interoperability and cooperation. CIS technology in particular will play a major role in allowing the Internet to serve as the basis for virtual enterprises and other visions of the future (see, e.g., National Research Council, 1994; Tapscott, 1996), by allowing the heterogeneous, autonomous and distributed resources of the Internet to cooperate in providing useful services to enterprises and others. For example, the Internet illustrates the potential semantic inconsistencies that can exist when a world-wide collection of objects must interoperate, and thus serves as a driver for the development of CIS technologies to address these issues.

The Internet is also important in illustrating the design characteristics that must be kept in mind in developing enterprise distributed object environments. For example, the Internet illustrates that large-scale distributed systems will, in the general case, involve a mixture of the tight coupling between objects found in key corporate applications (such as customer service) and a more dynamic location and coupling of resources (e.g., identifying Internet resources for use in a shorter-term project or report). By the same token, unlike current CORBA-based systems in which objects are fixed at either client or server sites, Internet technologies such as Java illustrate the ability to flexibly move complete objects (both code and data) in the network. Although such flexibility raises serious security concerns (which have been widely discussed in the trade press), it also significantly increases the range of design options that exist in developing distributed object systems: objects could potentially be located anywhere, and migrated to new sites as load and other considerations dictate.

4.3 Reflective Capabilities

A key requirement of an enterprise computing architecture is that it be *extensible*, in order to deal with changes over its life cycle. This requires that key *internal* interfaces of the architecture, in addition to application-specific ones, must be made explicit (Manola, 1995). Explicit internal interfaces allow the addition of new services and other capabilities, with minimum impact on existing components. One approach to providing such extensibility is the use of *reflection* (Maes, 1987; Kiczales *et al.*, 1991).

A reflective computational system contains metalevel information which represents its own structural and computational aspects. Such metadata is accessible and modifiable within the system itself and, more importantly, changes made to the metadata affect the actual computations being performed. In an object-oriented reflective system, the system is implemented as a set of explicit objects (*metaobjects*) that exist at run-time. The operations of these metaobjects constitute a *metaobject protocol* (Kiczales *et al.*, 1991). These metaobjects can be overridden or extended dynamically to change the behaviour of the system.

Fully reflective programming languages (the CLOS metaobject protocol is an example) are relatively unusual, although some reflective capability, e.g., run-time access to type information, is increasingly common, particularly in object-oriented programming languages. However, most systems (architectures), in addition to computation about the external problem domain, include some instances of reflective computation. For example, recording performance statistics, recording information for debugging purposes, interface-related computation (e.g., tracking mouse position), control-related computation (determining what process to execute next), self-optimization, self-modification (e.g., response to failures by bypassing failed components) and self-activation (monitors or demons) are all instances of reflective computation. However, these systems do not necessarily have a reflective architecture, designed with the intent of allowing basic aspects of the system's behaviour to be dynamically changed. Further extensions of the reflective capabilities of system architectures can be expected to become more common, in order to support the extensibility and tuning of such system characteristics.

Reflection can also play an important role in supporting other aspects of enterprise computing systems. For example, reflection implemented by metaobjects is used in IBM's SOM to support interoperation among the object models of multiple programming languages (Orfali *et al.*, 1996) Reflection can also be used to integrate existing software and data components into an architecture. For example, (Edmond and Papazoglou, this volume) describe the use of reflection to integrate heterogeneous legacy components in cooperative information systems. Singh and Gisi (1995) describe the use of metalevel information, in the form of a second, declarative interface added to conventional objects (CORBA objects are used as an example), to support facilitator-based coordinated interoperation among the objects. Reflection can also be used to allow the system to be governed by business policies, or to add services such as object persistence or transactions. In such cases, ordinary message processing is interrupted at the metaobject level, and the message diverted for additional processing by other components (e.g., to move the object between disc and main memory in supporting object persistence). As noted in Section 1, metalevel information, possibly represented in the form of objects, is also crucial in providing the information necessary to support cooperation at higher levels of abstraction, from information about differences in data formats, to differences in the meanings of terms or concepts used in different systems. A reflective architecture provides the means for this metalevel information to be consulted at appropriate points in a computation, so that it can govern the operations of interacting components to achieve the required degrees of cooperation. Manola (1993) surveys a number of reflective object-oriented implementations, and describes the use of reflection in supporting various services in distributed object systems.

A reflective capability can be obtained by standardizing interfaces to lower-level components. The OMG has standardized a number of interfaces to lower-level implementation details of its architecture, e.g., internal ORB interfaces and the IIOP. Additional work is being done on such interfaces in the context of work on defining standard interfaces for server-side object implementations, so as to allow object implementations to be portable between ORBs implemented by different vendors. In addition, ORB implementations generally define vendor-specific internal interfaces that allow user-defined customizations to be added to various aspects of ORB processing. Capturing these and other such details in terms of a coherent collection of standard object interfaces would provide the beginnings of a fully reflective CORBA architecture.

5 CONCLUDING REMARKS

OMG technology, and particularly CORBA, provides a promising basis for the development of enterprise-wide computing architectures. However, the effort necessary to reach agreement on the lower-level aspects of CORBA technology has sometimes diverted attention from the additional levels of agreement (and associated architectural components) that must exist in order for it to be effectively used in the development of enterprise computing systems. In the development of the CORBA architecture, and associated Object Services, the necessary infrastructure has been developed to provide a solid basis for these higher levels of agreement. This chapter has attempted to outline what some of these higher levels might entail in the context of a CORBA-based architecture, with particular emphasis on higher-level object organizations, and some of the activities (both within OMG and elsewhere) that are addressing these issues. The combination of such approaches as tiered architectures, business objects and workflows creates an infrastructure which provides a necessary foundation for the inclusion of the "intelligent" components that support even higher levels of cooperation. Moreover, having agreements in place at the levels discussed in this chapter allows such "intelligent" components to be applied to problems actually requiring some degree of "intelligence", rather than simply compensating for the lack of lower-level agreements.

Reaching the numerous agreements that must be in place to support interoperability in large-scale business systems can be a time-consuming process, as illustrated by the work of the OMG. However, achieving agreement among the numerous parties participating in these activities is necessary if fully open, as opposed to proprietary, solutions are to be obtained. Ideally, work must progress in parallel at multiple levels, from implementation to semantic, and among both platform-oriented and application-domain-specific groups, in order to reach the necessary agreements in a timely manner. Merging the work of the CIS research community with these activities would provide the basis for the more rapid introduction of higher-level CIS capabilities into operational enterprise computing systems.

REFERENCES

Apple (1989) *Macintosh Programmers Workshop Pascal 3.0 Reference*. Apple Computer, Inc., Cupertino, CA.

Ben-Naton, R. (1995) *CORBA: A Guide to the Common Object Request Broker Architecture*. McGraw-Hill, New York.

Edmond, D. and Papazoglou, M. (1997) Reflection is the Essence of Cooperation, this volume.

Elmagarmid, A.K. (ed.). (1992) *Database Transaction Models for Advanced Applications*. Morgan Kaufmann, San Mateo, CA.

Forte (1994) *A Technical Introduction to Forte*. Digital/Forte Software Products, Oakland, CA.

Gamma, E., Helm, R., Johnson, R. and Vlissides, J. (1995) *Design Patterns: Elements of Reusable Object-Oriented Software*. Addison-Wesley, Reading, MA.

Georgakopoulos, D., Hornick, M., Krychniak, P. and Manola, F. (1994) Specification and management of extended transactions in a programmable transaction environment. In *Proceedings Tenth International Conference on Data Engineering*. IEEE Computer Society, Houston, TX.

Georgakopoulos, D., Hornick, M. and Sheth, A. (1995) An overview of workflow management: from process modeling to workflow automation infrastructure. *Distributed and Parallel Databases*, 3(2), 119–153.

Heiler, S. (1995) Semantic interoperability. *ACM Computing Surveys* 27(2), 271–273.

IBM Corporation (1995) Network centric computing (NCC) and the open blueprint. White Paper, http://www.software.ibm.com/openblue/OPENBLUE.HTM.

ISO/IEC JTC1/SC21/WG7 (1995) *Reference Model of Open Distributed Processing, Part 1, Overview*. ITU-T X.901, ISO/IEC 10746.1.

Kiczales, G., des Rivieres, J. and Bobrow, D.G. (1991) *The Art of the Metaobject Protocol*. MIT Press, Cambridge, MA.

Maes, P. (1987) Concepts and experiments in computational reflection. In *OOPSLA '87 Conference Proceedings*, N. Meyrowtiz. (ed). ACM.

Manola, F. (1993) Metaobject protocol concepts for a 'RISC' object model. TR-0244-12-93-165, GTE Laboratories Incorporated, (available from ftp.gte.com, directory pub/dom).

Manola, F. (1995) Interoperability Issues in Large-Scale Distributed Object Systems. *ACM Computing Surveys*, **27**(2), 268–270.

Miller, J.A., Sheth, A.P., Kochut, K.J. and Wang, X. (1996) CORBA-Based Run-Time Architectures for Workflow Management Systems. *Journal of Database Management, Special Issue on Multidatabases*, **7**(1), 16–27.

Mowbray, T.J. and Zahavi, R. (1995) *The Essential CORBA: Systems Integration Using Distributed Objects*. Wiley, New York.

Netscape (1996) The Netscape ONE development environment vision and product roadmap. White Paper, Netscape Communications Corp.

NeXT (1995) Architecting for change with the enterprise objects framework and portable distributed objects. White Paper, NeXT Computer, Inc., http:/www.next.com/OpenStep/Products/PDO/ArchForChange/Arch.html.

National Research Council (1994) *Realizing the Information Future: The Internet and Beyond*. National Academy Press.

Nicol, J., Wilkes, C.T. and Manola, F. (1993) Object orientation in heterogeneous distributed computing systems. *IEEE Computer*, Special Issue on Heterogeneous Processing.

OMG (1995a) *The Common Object Request Broker: Architecture and Specification*. Revision 2, Object Management Group.

OMG (1995b) *CORBAservices: Common Object Services Specification*. Revised Edition, OMG Document Number 95-3-31. Object Management Group.

OMG (1995c) *CORBAfacilities: Common Facilities Architecture*. Revision 4.0, Object Management Group.

OMG (1996) *Common Facilities RFP-4: Common Business Objects and Business Object Facility*. OMG TC Document CF/96-01-04, Object Management Group.

Orfali, R., Harkey, D. and Edwards, J. (1996) *The Essential Distributed Objects Survival Guide*. John Wiley & Sons, Inc., New York.

Papazoglou, M.P., Laufmann, S.C. and Sellis, T.K. (1992) An Organizational Framework for Cooperating Intelligent Information Systems. *International Journal of Intelligent and Cooperative Information Systems*, **1**(1), 169–202.

Singh, N. and Gisi, M. (1995) Coordinating distributed objects with declarative interfaces. Stanford University Logic Group.

Soley, R. (ed.). (1995) *Object Management Architecture Guide*. Third edition, Wiley.

Taligent, Inc. (1995) *The Power of Frameworks*. Addison-Wesley.

Tapscott, D. (1996) *The Digital Economy: Promise and Peril in the Age of Networked Intelligence*. McGraw-Hill.

Tsichritzis, D. and Klug, A. (eds). (1977) *The ANSI/X3/SPARC DBMS Framework: Report of the Study Group on Database Management Systems*. AFIPS Press, Montvale, NJ.

Wegner, P. (1989) Granularity of Modules in Object-Based Concurrent Systems. In *Proceedings, ACM SIGPLAN Workshop on Object-Based Concurrent Programming*. G. Agha, P. Wegner and A. Yonezawa (eds). *SIGPLAN NOTICES*, **24**(4).

A Harness Language for Cooperative Information Systems

Keith L. Clark and Nikolaos Skarmeas
Imperial College, London, UK

Abstract

In this chapter we introduce a high-level process-based programming language, AprilQ, and we illustrate its use for building distributed and cooperative information systems over the Internet. The language is a macro-implemented extension of the distributed symbolic programming language April.

Each AprilQ process has a knowledge base (KB) comprising a set of *extensional* relations, defined by sets of records, and a collection of *view functions*. The view functions can be recursively defined. Each process can query its own KB. It can also query the KB of any other process with which it is acquainted, and update the KB of any other process for which it has update permission. The other processes can be located anywhere on the Internet. The queries are expressed in a high-level query language which is a hybrid of Prolog and SQL syntax. A reply to a query is normally a set of answers, but it can be a handle that is then used to retrieve the answers one at a time, giving lazy evaluation of the query. A process can import relations from another process, or a database server. A query condition for an imported relation is expressed in the same way as for a local relation of a process, so another process querying such a hybrid KB need not know which relations are local or imported. So, using imported relations, an AprilQ process can act as a transparent interface to a distributed and persistent information system spread over the Internet.

There remains the question of how information sources become acquainted. For this purpose KQML (Finin *et al.*, 1996) style advertise, subscribe and recommend messages can be used in conjunction with intermediary brokering agents. We show how such a KQML cooperation layer can be constructed using AprilQ.

Cooperative Information Systems
Trends and Directions
ISBN 0-12-544910-0

I INTRODUCTION

McCabe and Clark (1995) introduced the distributed symbolic programming language April (**A**gent **P**rocess **I**mplementation **L**anguage) and showed how it could be used to build simple agent-based applications. A growing trend in implementing cooperative information systems is to use agents as the interface components between component information systems. The agents are effectively intelligent processes distributed over a network that can communicate symbolic data (Edmond *et al.*, 1997). The April language provides all the features needed to implement such an agent-based harness language and has been successfully used for this purpose (Papazoglou *et al.*, 1992).

Specifically, April has pattern match primitives for accessing and manipulating sets of records and for generating new sets of records out of nested iterations. For example:

```
setof {for (?X,bill) in child_of do
        for (X,?A) in age_of do
            if X in male then elemis (X,A)}
```

can be used to construct a new set/relation comprising the set of pairs (X,A) where X is a male child of `bill` and A is its age. (The annotation ? signals a fresh unbound variable.) Since the language is higher order, these collect expressions can be wrapped up as function closures. The function closures can then be used either as the definiens of "view" functions, or as the "code" of queries that can be communicated between processes.

However, the interprocess message format and internal process data representation facilities of April are general purpose and not specifically tailored to the task of building agent-based cooperative information systems. Ideally, each harness agent should be viewed as storing data or metadata in the form of relations, either extensionally or intensionally defined, and the inter-agent communication language should allow the communication of high-level query expressions such as can be expressed in Prolog or SQL. This is what our AprilQ macro-implemented extension of April provides. The Q signifies the high-level query and relation definition facility that AprilQ adds to April. As an example, in AprilQ, we can denote the set comprising the male children of `bill` as:

```
{all of (X,A) where child_of(?X,bill) and age_of(X,?A) and male(X)}
```

This is actually macro-expanded into something very similar to the above `setof` expression.

April was designed at the outset, as part of the EC-funded IMAGINE (Haugeneder, 1994) project on multi-agent systems, as an extensible language. Like Prolog it has a extensible operator precedence syntax. In addition, it has a powerful macro-definition facility. The macros are sets of recursive rewrite rules that operate on the operator parse tree of the program. Using macros we can write complex, and

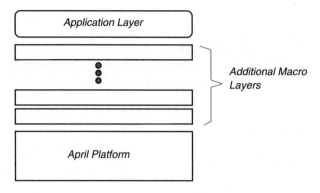

Figure 1.   The layered approach.

context-sensitive, compile-time transformations of the program. With a combination of extra operators and macros one can readily implement sophisticated extensions of the language to support particular classes of applications (Skarmeas, 1997). This is the macro-layer approach to application development (Figure 1).

Recently, the use of April has been significantly enhanced by the implementation of a companion database system, called AdB (McCabe, 1996). This can be used for persistent storage of any April, hence any AprilQ, data value. In implementing AprilQ we have transparently integrated April and AdB making the use of AdB much more high level. Any of the extensional relations of an AprilQ process can be declared as external or persistent, and linked with such an AdB database. In AprilQ the relation is queried in the same way, no matter whether it is stored as a set of records held in a state variable of an AprilQ process, or whether it is stored as an indexed sequence of records in an AdB data file.

The key features of AprilQ are:

- In addition to the usual April process state variables, an AprilQ process can record state information in records of one or more extensional relations. These relations can be queried using high-level logic query expressions that are a hybrid of Prolog and SQL.
- The extensional relations of a process can be augmented by the definition of view functions whose definiens are AprilQ query expressions. These view functions can be recursive. They can return sets for values, in which case they are functions computing virtual relations, or they return *true* or *false*, and are query expressed tests. Together, the extensional relations and view functions constitute a local *knowledge base* for the process.
- Any of the extensional relations of a process's knowledge base can be optionally declared as `foreign`, `external` or `persistent`. A foreign relation is an extensional relation of another process that can be queried as though it was a local relation. An external relation is one that resides on

some AdB database. The relation fetch function of AprilQ will automatically generate the required query messages to be sent to the exporting process, or the AdB database server, should a foreign or external relation need to be accessed during a query evaluation. A persistent relation is one that will be fetched from the designated AdB database when the relation is declared inside an AprilQ process. Thereafter it is held as a local (in memory) relation of the process. All persistent relations of a process are backed up onto the AdB database from which they were fetched when the process executes the sync_adb macro call. These features allow an AprilQ process to act as an interface process to a distributed and persistent information system.

• An AprilQ process can also query the knowledge base of any other process for which it has the *handle* identity. Any query can also specify, by a simple annotation, that one or more subqueries are to be evaluated against the knowledge bases of other processes. That is, any query can be a *distributed* query. A view function can also invoke a distributed query, so it can be a "view" onto a distributed database.

• A query to another process (a remote query) can be synchronous, with the query being effectively a remote function call. Alternatively, it can be asynchronous, explicitly sent as a message using the asynchronous message send of April. The query answer can then be picked up at a later stage when the process needs the answer. Whilst waiting for the answer to an asynchronous query sent to a process P the querying process can optionally open itself to queries sent to it from P. This allows cooperative answering of a query.

• A query can request all or some specified number of answers to a query expression. Alternatively, it can request lazy, stream evaluation of the query expression. In this case, the immediate reply to the query is the handle of a forked and suspended query evaluation process that will compute and return the sequence of answers, one at a time, on demand.

• Finally, the extensional relations of an AprilQ process can be updated using either Prolog style assert and retract statements, or using an elaboration of the SQL relation update statement. This updates designated fields of some subset of the records of a relation (the subset being selected by an arbitrary query), in one atomic operation.

1.1 Structure of the Chapter

In the next section we will briefly review the April language and illustrate its use by defining a procedure which, when forked as a publically named process, can be used a very simple KQML (Kuoka and Harade, 1995) style broker agent. It will allow information agents to advertise the relations about which they hold information, and other agents to discover the identities of agents holding information about a particular relation. It uses the KQML performatives advertise, subscribe and recommend; but it uses a much simplified message syntax. All the agents are assumed to use the same ontology of relation names.

We then introduce AprilQ by recasting this program in AprilQ syntax and by showing how we immediately get much more powerful brokerage facilities.

This is followed by a more general review of the AprilQ features with an illustration of how it can be used as a harness language for a distributed database system in which single relations can be split vertically and horizontally across the Internet. Using a combination of view functions and imported relations, we can provide a single AprilQ access process for such a distributed database system.

We will then return to the issue of open agent-controlled information systems and the use of brokerage agents to allow agents to locate appropriate information sources. We show how we can significantly elaborate the introductory broker agent program so that it offers more of the KQML brokerage facilities.

2 REVIEW OF THE APRIL LANGUAGE

April is a process-based distributed symbolic programming language in which process forking is cheap (a single April invocation, which is one Unix process, can readily handle 10 000 April processes). Complex symbolic messages can be passed between processes irrespective of their location. The messages can be any April data value (number, symbol, string, record of any values, list of any values, function, procedure or pattern closure). The list data structure in April is special because it can be used to represent sets of records (relations). Information stored in these sets of records can be accessed using pattern matching. The sets of records can also be constructed using special operations in the language which have the expressive power of the relational calculus. They can be used to encode information as facts, with quite complex query access to the facts. For example, a process can maintain a list of pairs such as:

```
[(age_of,  [(tom,25),(bill,36),...]),
 (male, [(bill),(tom),...])
 (child_of,[(tom,sarah),(bill,sally),...)]
]
```

where each pair comprises a symbol and an associated list of records as a way of recording the Prolog style facts:

```
male(tom).
male(bill).
...
age_of(tom,25).
```

```
age_of(bill,36).
...
child_of(tom,sarah).
child_of(bill,sally).
...
```

Like an actor (Agha and Hewitt, 1987), each April process has exactly one incoming message queue. It reads messages from the queue by entering a choice statement of alternative guarded commands. Each guarded command is of the form:

```
message_pattern :: test -> action
```

In turn, each message in the message queue is tested against the message patterns/tests of each guarded command of the choice statement. (In an actor, only the first message is tested.) If a message matches the `message_pattern`, and the optional associated `test` is true (this can test values of variables in the pattern, values of state variables of the process or impose conditions that must be satisfied by the sender), the message is removed from the queue and the `action` is executed. Typically, this updates state variables of the process, sends messages to other processes, or forks new processes.

If the end of the message queue is reached with no message pattern/test satisfied, the process suspends until the next message arrives. How long the process suspends can be specified by giving a special *timeout* guarded command at the end of the choice statement. The April message-processing semantics is essentially the same as that of Erlang (Armstrong *et al.*, 1993).

An April invocation runs as a Unix process and all April processes forked within that invocation are time-shared by the April system. They share a single heap for data values. Communication between processes within an April invocation is very fast, it is just a copy of the heap address of the message from the sender process to the message queue of the recipient process. Communication between processes in different invocations of April, whether on the same machine or anywhere on the Internet, is handled by encoding the message as a byte stream and sending it to the target process via special April communication servers. There is one communication server for each Internet host machine. The message is sent using the TCP/IP protocol. The byte encoding of the message, and the use of the communication servers, is transparent to the April application. In the April program the same message send operation is used irrespective of the location of the recipient.

2.1 A Simple Broker Agent as an April Process

We illustrate the basic features of April by giving the program for a process that can act as a simple information broker agent allowing agents to advertise the relations for which they hold facts and for other agents to locate agents holding facts for a specific relation. An agent registers the relations for which it holds records by sending an `advertise` message to the broker. Agents find out about other agents by sending recommend messages to the broker, or by sending a subscribe message. By subscribing with respect to a relation R, an agent will be automatically informed in the future of any other agent that advertises that it holds facts about R.

```
agent_record ::= (handle?agent,symbol[]?relnames);
/* declare a new record type, agent_record, with an agent field
with a value of type handle (ie. an agent/process identity) and a
relnames field which is a list of symbols which will be relation names */

subscription_record ::= (handle?agent,symbol?relname);
/* declare a new record type, subscription_record */

broker(){
    agent_record[]?has_rels:=[];
    subscription_record[]?sub_for:=[];
    /* declare and initialize two (lists of records) state variables
       has_rels and sub_for then enter message processing loop */

    repeat {
      (advertise,symbol[]?rels) -> {
           has_rels := [(sender,rels),..has_rels];
           for (handle?H,symbol?rel) in sub_for :: rel in rels do
              (has_advertised,sender,rel) >> H
      }
      | (subscribe,symbol?rel) -> sub_for := [(sender,rel),.. sub_for]
      | deregister -> has_skills := has_rels reject (sender,?)
      | (remove_sub,symbol?rel) -> sub_for reject (sender,rel)
      | (recommend,symbol?rel) ->
             (answer,rel,
               {has_rels select skill_record?R::rel in relnames}^agent
             ) >> replyto
    } until quit:: sender == creator()
};
```

The program has a typical server agent structure. It starts with the declaration and initialization of local variables that will hold the data on agents that have advertised or subscribed to the broker. The type declaration `agent_record[]?has_rels` means that `has_rels` is a list (or set) of agent records. (In April, a variable is declared by prefixing its first use with a type descriptor as in `type?var_name`. Use of `?` on its own is equivalent to declaring the variable to be of type `any`. A declaration of the form `t[]?v` declares that `v` has type: `list` of values of type `t`.)

The process then enters a `repeat ... until message_pattern` loop to handle the requests for its services. In our case the loop termination message pattern will match a `quit` message providing it is sent from the process that forked the broker program as a process, in the manner we

shall explain below. The receipt of the quit message will also terminate the
process since there is nothing else for the process to do. The assumption is
that the process will not normally be terminated, but will run as a perpetual
server. The test sender == creator() is what ensures that the quit message
comes from the process that forked the broker process. sender is an April
keyword which when used in a message receive test, or in the action associated with a message receipt, denotes the handle of the process that sent
the message. Every April message has an outer wrapper which contains at
least two extra fields. One of these is the sender field, the value of which
is extracted by using the sender keyword. This sender field has its value
inserted by the April communication system and cannot be altered by the
application program. It always denotes the identity of the process from
which the message was sent. The other extra field is a message reply field,
with value extracted by use of the keyword replyto. By default, this will
be set by the communications system to the identity of the sender process,
but it can be explicitly set by the application program. A message can be
sent *as from* another process, the handle of the other process becoming the
value of the replyto field in the outer wrapper.

The body of the message-processing loop comprises a choice statement
of five alternative guarded commands, the | being the separator of the
alternatives.

The first will accept a message of the form (advertise,symbol[]-
?rels). That is, it will accept a message which is a record comprising the
symbol advertise and a second argument which is any list of symbols.
Here, the type of the new variable rels, which is local to this first guarded
command, is symbol[], which is list of symbols. A successful match will result
in this new variable being bound to the list of symbols of the advertise
message (these symbols are the relation names that the sender of the
message wants to advertise). The matched message is also removed from
the message queue of the broker. The action part is now executed. This
first adds a record, comprising the identity of the sender of the received
message and the list of relation names extracted from the message, to the
front of the has_rels list of records. (In April, the operator ,.. has the
same meaning as the Prolog | and the LISP cons.) The advertise method
then iterates over the has_sub list sending a suitable message to any agent
that has a subscription for a relation name that appears in the list of relation
names of the received advertise message. The loop:

```
for (handle?H,symbol?rel) in sub_for :: rel in rels do
        (has_advertised,sender,rel) >> H
```

is a common form of iteration in April. It is an iteration controlled by a
pattern/test. The :: is read as such that.

>> is April's standard message send operator. The transmission is asyn-
chronous, the sender does not block until the message is received. The
standard message send sets the replyto process for the sent message to the

sender of the message. The full message send has the form:

  msg ~~ F >> D

where the ~~ is read as *as from*. This sets the replyto process for the message as the value of F, which must be a handle.

The second guarded command handles subscribe messages with an action that adds a suitable record onto the has_subs list.

The third guarded command deals with a message which just comprises the symbol deregister. The action on receipt is to remove all records with first field the sender of the message from has_rels. This is done using the pattern match reject primitive, which will remove from any list all entries covered by the pattern given as its second argument. Here, the ? in the pattern is a wild card, signifying *any* second component of the record. The keyword any can be used instead of ?.

The fourth guarded command is similar to the third, except that it allows the removal of an individual subscription, rather that all subscriptions, for the sender process of the received message.

The last guarded command deals with a enquiry message which uses the performative recommend and has a second component which is a single symbol acting as a relation name. The action on receipt is to construct a reply message and to send this to the replyto process associated with the recommend message.

The reply message has three components. The third component of the message sent as reply is a list of values that are handles of agents that have registered and given a list of relation names that include the relation name rel of the incoming message. This list of handles is constructed by first selecting from the has_rels all those record entries that include rel in the value of their relnames field, then projecting all these record pairs on their agent field. (^ is the April field project operation on lists of records.) The reply is sent to the replyto process rather than the sender of the message because the sender may have sent the message *as from* another process/agent. select and reject are examples of April's pattern match operators for manipulating lists of records.

2.2 Forking and Using the Broker Agent

An already-running April process C can now fork the above program as a process/agent by executing a statement of the form:

  "broker_agent" public broker;

C will become the creator of the server. This not only launches the execution of the program as a new process, it also gives the process a public name "broker_agent" which will be registered with the April communication server on the host computer on which C is running.

Any other April process, running on the same host, whether or not in the same invocation of April, can communicate with the new process by a message send of the form:

```
message >> handle??"broker_agent"
```

The `handle??` is a type cast that tells the April compiler that the string "broker_agent" is the public name of a process registered on this host.[1]

Any other April process executing in an April invocation running on a different host, *anywhere on the Internet*, can send a message to the new process with a message send of the form:

```
message >> handle??"broker_agent@machine_name"
```

where `machine_name` is the Internet-registered name of the host machine on which the "broker_agent" process is executing. This name is the symbolic name of the machine as used by the telnet and ftp Internet applications. For example, if the process was running on the machine lipo in the Department of Computing at Imperial College, the message send would be:

```
message >> handle??"broker_agent@lipo.doc.ic.ac.uk"
```

This is the *absolute* public name of the process, which will unambiguously resolve to the handle of the process forked with the public name "broker_agent" on this machine.

Note that the same `broker` program could be publicly forked with the same public name, "broker_agent" on any number of hosts. A message send to `handle??"broker_agent"` always gets routed to the locally forked process with that name. It is a relative public name. To send a message to any other "broker_agent" the machine name on which it is running must be appended to this public name.

2.3 A Communication Scenario with the April Broker Agent

Let us suppose that another agent process running on the same host as our newly forked "broker_agent" process now registers with it with a message send:

```
(advertise,[cheap_airfares,packaged_holidays]) >> handle??"broker_agent"
```

where `cheap_fares` and `packaged_holidays` are relations that are known to the community of agents that will link up using this broker agent. Another agent process, perhaps recently forked in another invocation of April on the same machine, can find the handle of this process using the following send/receive sequence:

---

[1]Process handles are not strings; they do not have any literal values. They can only be generated by use of system functions such as `creator()`, keywords such as `replyto` and the `handle??` type caste applied to a string public name. The above type cast will cause the string "broker_agent" to be converted into the appropriate handle at run time.

```
(recommend,cheap_airfares) >> handle??"broker_agent";
{(answer,cheap_airfares,handle[]?Ags) -> .....};
```

In this case, after the message send, the process immediately enters a message receive choice statement which can only accept the one message, the expected reply giving a list of handles of agents who have advertised that they can be queried about the cheap_airfares relation. The process will therefore suspend until this message is put into its message buffer. Alternatively, it could engage in some other actions before reaching the point where it really needs the reply in order to continue. The communication sequence would then be of the form:

```
(recommend,cheap_airfares) >> handle??"broker_agent";
.
. /* other actions */
.
{(answer,cheap_airfares,handle[]?Ags) -> .....};
```

The process could also ensure that the answer came from the "broker_agent" server by a message receive of the form:

```
{(answer, cheap_airfares,handle[]?Ags) ::
                sender==handle??"broker_agent" -> .....};
```

3 THE BROKER PROGRAM IN APRILQ

To introduce the facilities and syntax of AprilQ we will recast the broker program as an AprilQ program.

```
broker(){
    db_initialize;
    /* declare and initialize the invisible state
       variables holding all the relation extensions and view function
       definitions */
    relation has_rels
    schema (handle?agent,symbol[]?relnames)
    initial [];
    relation sub_for
    schema (handle?agent,symbol?relname)
    initial [];
    /* declare has_rels and sub_for as local relations of the
       process with initially empty extensions. */
    recommend(symbol?Rel) is {
        all of handle?A where has_rels(A,symbol[]?Rels) and Rel in Rels
    }
    /* declare recommend as a view function of the process */
    repeat {
```

```
(advertise,symbol[]?rels) -> {
    assert has_rels(sender,rels);
    for handle?H satisfying {sub_for(H,symbol?rel) and rel in rels do}
        (has_advertised,sender,rel) >> H
}
| (subscribe,symbol?rel) -> assert sub_for(sender,rel)
| deregister -> retract_all has_rels(sender,?)
| (remove_sub,symbol?rel) -> retract sub_for(sender,rel)
| query_methods /* macro to add in AprilQ query methods */

} until quit:: sender == creator()
};
```

Notice that the initialization:

```
agent_record[]?has_rels:=[];
```

has been replaced by the relation declaration:

```
relation has_rels
schema  (handle?agent,symbol[]?relnames)
initial [];
```

This does not declare has_rels as a variable of the process. It adds a triple

```
(has_rels,[agent,relnames],[])
```

to a special database variables declared and initialized by the macro call db_initialize. Also, the process has no recommend method. Instead it has a sequence of methods denoted by the macro query_methods that allow any other process to query its database relations has_rels and sub_for, or the relation/set returned by a call to its view function recommend. These queries can use the high-level query syntax of AprilQ; the following is an example query:

```
{all of handle?A where has_rels(A,?)}
```

As it stands, any other process can send a query to the server. However, we could restrict the queries to just those agents who have registered with the broker by using the macro:

```
query_methods restricted_to {all of handle?A where has_rels(A,?)}
```

instead of the unrestricted query_methods.

3.1 A Communication Scenario with the AprilQ Broker

A broker agent with the public name "broker_agent"can be publicly forked as for the April broker program and similar advertise and deregister messages can be sent to the AprilQ version of the broker. The difference is only apparent when we come to querying the information store of the broker.

Any other process, running on the same host as the AprilQ broker, can use a query expression:

```
{all of handle?A where recommend_for(cheap_airfares)(A)}!handle??"broker_agent"
```

The "higher order" predication:

```
recommend_for(cheap_fares)(A)
```

is used to specify that each agent handle A returned by the query should be in the set returned by the function call:

```
recommend_for(cheap_fares)
```

The query expression becomes a query request that blocks until the answer is returned, the answer becoming the value of the expression.

Alternatively, the querier can send an asynchronous **query** message, using a form that gives a label to the query, and then at any future time enter a choice statement to pick up the reply. The querier uses a query send/ pick up reply sequence such as:

```
{ all of handle?A where recommend_for(cheap_airfares)(A)
  label q123 } >> handle??"broker_agent";
  .
  . /* other actions */
  .
handle[]?Ags:=handle[]??get_answer_from(handle??"broker_agent",q123);
```

in which the macro call

```
get_answer_from(handle??"broker_agent",q123)
```

is used when it is time to pick up, and if necessary wait for, the reply from the broker agent to the previously sent query labelled q123.

3.2 More Complex Queries

We are not restricted to sending simple queries that just have a single condition on the visible relation `recommend_for`. A query such as:

```
{all of handle?A where
          recommend(cheap_airfares)(A)
          and recommend(bespoke_holidays)(A)
          and not recommend(package_holidays)(A)}
```

can also be sent, using either the synchronous or asynchronous form of query.

More generally, the query we send can have conditions in it that use relations of any process that accepts remote queries to its knowledge base. For example:

```
{all of handle?A where
          recommend(cheap_airfares)(A)
          and abta_registered(A)!handle??"abta_agent@..."}
```

includes a subquery to another publically named process "abta_agent", on a remote host, to make sure that only the handles of agents that are ABTA registered[2] are returned as answers to the queries.

No extra functionality is required in the broker program to handle this more complex query. The complexity comes in the macro-expansion of the query expression into a set returning function closure that will include code for the remote query. The broker process will not even know that a remote subquery is being executed.

Typically, the "abta_agent" will access the abta_registered relation as an external relation held on some AdB database. It will therefore include a relation declaration such as:

```
relation abta_registered
scheme (handle?agent)
of_type (external,adb1,abta_db)
```

where adb1 is the handle of some invocation of the AdB database server, and abta_db is the name of the set of records which includes those for the abta_registered relation. The abta_agent process will automatically query this AdB database, using the query format that AdB expects, when it is sent a abta_registered subquery.

3.3 Restricting the Number of Answers

A client can also ask for at most N answers, where N is some integer using a query form:

```
N of T where Q
```

This terminates the evaluation of the query Q as soon as the first N solutions have been found, if there are more than N.

If the querying process is not sure how many answers will be needed, a stream of query can be used followed by a one-at-a-time request for answers. The query:

```
handle?QS:= {stream of handle?A where
                A on recommend_for(cheap_airfares)
                and abta_registered(A)!...}
```

will bind QS to the handle of a special answer stream process that will be forked by the stream query method of the "broker_agent" server on receipt of the stream of .. query. The process will find the first answer to the query and then suspend. It returns the first answer to the client when the client executes a next(QS) call on the answer stream handle. It also finds the next answer in anticipation of the next demand. The next call will return the value void when there are no more answers. At any stage

---

[2]ABTA is the UK travel agents association.

the client can terminate the answer stream process with a `kill(QS)` action. This gives the client processes a query functionality similar to the KQML `stream` performative.

3.4 Importing Relations from Other Processes

In the above example, with the remote subquery, the querier has to know which other process holds the definition of the auxiliary relation `abta_registered`. As an alternative, we could declare that relation, and any other skill-certifying relations that a client might want to use, as extensional relations of the `broker` program *imported* from the processes that maintain them. We just add declarations such as:

```
relation abta_registered
schema (handle?agent)
of_type (foreign,handle??"abta_agent@...")
```

to the broker procedure. Now a client process sends the query:

```
{all of handle?A where
            recommend_for(cheap_airfares)(A)
            and abta_registered(A)}
```

treating `abta_registered` as a though it were a local extensional relation of the broker agent. The appropriate subqueries will automatically be sent by the broker to the remote object holding the `abta_registered` relation, which in turn will query its local AdB database.

3.5 Subqueries that Refer Back to the Client — Cooperative Answer Generation

As a last example, let us suppose that the client process that queries the broker agent maintains its own `blacklist` relation of agents that it has had dealings with before with unwelcome consequences. These are agents whose information it does not trust. In that case, it would only like, as answers to one of its new enquiries, agents not on its personal blacklist. To do this, it can send a query of the form:

```
{all of handle?A where
            recommend(....)(A)
            ...... /* any other conditions */
            and not blacklist(A)!Myself}
```

Here the subquery `not blacklist(A)!Myself` will ensure that the sender's `blacklist` relation will be used to filter out the undesirable registered agents. (The `Myself` keyword denotes the handle of the process in which the query is constructed. Use of the more usual `Self` would be interpreted as a reference to the process in which the query will be evaluated.)

Now, this has to be sent as an asynchronous query! If the querier just suspends waiting for the reply it will not be able to answer the subqueries to its `blacklist` relation that will be sent back to it. The query must be sent asynchronously, using the labelled query syntax. A labelled query dispatch:

```
{all of .......} label q154 >> handle??"broker_agent";
```

could be followed, eventually, by the following assignment:

```
handle[]?Ags := interactively_get_answer_from(handle??"broker_agent",q154)
```

This waits for a reply to a labelled query, but whilst waiting the process will answer any number of AprilQ queries sent by the broker agent.

We use the asynchronous labelled query send, followed by an

```
interactively_get_answer_from(...)
```

call, whenever we want to send a query that might result in the sender being queried as part of the query evaluation. Note that this may not even be explicitly expressed in the dispatched query. For example, suppose that we add to the broker agent program the definition of the view function:

```
agreed_recommend(?rel,?ag) is {all of ?A where recommend(rel)(A) and
                                        not blacklist(A)!ag}
```

Then a query:

```
{all of ?A where agreed_recommend(cheap_fares,MySelf)(A)}
```

will indirectly generate queries back to the sender.

3.6 Sending Data in a Query

Returning to the original explicitly cooperative query, because the subqueries that will be sent back by the broker access only the one `blacklist` relation, we can as an alternative embed the extension of this relation in the query. We could use:

```
handle[]?Not_Trusted := {all of handle?A where blacklist(A)}!Self;
handle[]?Ags := {all of handle?A where
                        A on recommend_for(....)
                        ...... /* any other conditions */
                        and not A in Not_Trusted};
```

This embeds the value of the variable `Not_Trusted`, which is global to the query expression, inside the query. Since the query is compiled into a function closure, the value of this variable will not be visible to the broker agent, who will not even know it is embedded in the query.

4 OVERVIEW OF APRILQ

As we have already said, AprilQ is essentially a set of new operators and macros added to the April language.

If we want to have relation definitions as part of the local state of an April process, we simply have to include the macro call db_initialize as a statement in the process. After this, we can declare relations and define intentional view functions.

4.1 Relation Declarations

A process can declare and optionally initialize an extensional relation at any time after the database initialization. The declaration takes the form:

relation *Relation Name*
schema *Schema Description*
of_type *Type Description*
initial *Initial Value*

In the above definition *Relation Name* is a symbol declaring the name of the relation (a set of records), *Schema Description* is a record type which describes the types and the names of the fields of the relation records, *Type Description* is the type of the relation (whether *foreign*, *external* or *persistent* and its location), and finally *Initial Value* is a list of records which is an initial extension of the relation. The of_type and initial fields are optional. If no type is given, the relation is assumed to be local, held within the process as a list of records. If no initial value is given, the relation is initialized to the empty set.

4.2 Relation Update

A process can update its extensional relations using Prolog style assert and retract commands. There are also assert_all and retract_all commands for adding and removing a set of records. In the case of the retract_all the set of records to be removed is denoted by a pattern, as in Prolog.

In addition, an update command allows the selective modification of specific fields of the records of a relation that satisfy some query. The general syntax for the selective update command is:

update *Relation*
with *Field Conditions*
where *Query*
set *Update Assignment*

Relation is the name of the relation to be updated, *Field Conditions* is a simple boolean condition on the field values of the records of *Relation* and *Query* is a general AprilQ query condition that must also be satisfied by these field values. Only the records of *Relation* with field values that satisfy both *Field Conditions* and *Query* will be updated. Which fields will be updated, and expressions giving their new values, is given in the *Update Assignment*.

As an example, suppose that we have a relation declaration:

```
relation salary
schema (symbol?name,symbol?dept,number?value,date?incr_date)
of_type (external,....)
```

The following updates all those records of the `salary` relation that have a value greater than 10 000, increment date field equal to (2,3,93), and where the person named in the name field is recorded as disabled in some social security database. It updates them by adding 10:

```
update salary
with ?N=name : value>10000 and incr_date=(2,3,96)
where disabled(N)!handle??"social_security_agent@..."
set salary:=salary*1.1
```

Access to the social security database is controlled by a publicly named agent called "social_security_agent". This agent will be queried as part of the test for whether a record should be updated.

4.3 Form of Allowed Local Queries

The relations of a process can be queried from within the process using top-level queries that request all solutions, a specified number of solutions, or a stream of solutions.

In addition, a process can query its local database with a statement of the form:

```
Newvars satisfies query_expression
```

It will generate just one set of bindings for `Newvars`, given by the first solution to `query_expression`. In contrast, the iteration:

```
for Newvars satisfying query_expression do .....
```

will execute the loop for each solution of the query.

For more details of the syntax of AprilQ query expressions we refer the reader to Skarmeas and Clark (1997). Essentially they are Prolog style query expressions using `not`, `and`, `or` and `forall` with atomic conditions expressed either as Prolog style

Rel(ArgPatterns)

predications, or as *field conditions*. These have the form:

Vars = Fields from *Rel* : *FieldTest*

This variation is particularly useful when there are a large number of arguments to the relation and only a few of them are involved in the query condition. That is, when, in the Prolog style predication most of the argument patterns would be ?, indicating an unconstrained value.

4.4 View Functions

In addition to the extensional relations, a process can include definitions of set returning view functions, using the form of definition:

$R(A1,..,Ak)$ is {*mode* of $(V1,..,Vn)$ where QE}

where *mode* is: *all*, *stream* or an integer.
    This function is queried using a condition of the form:

$R(E1,..,Ek)(P1,..,Pn)$

where the Ei are argument expressions and the Pi are patterns or values to be used to select from the set of k-tuples that the call $R(E1,..,Ek)$ will return.
    Intentional relations can be recursively defined.

```
descendant_of(symbol?A) is {
      all of (symbol?D) where {
                  child_of(D,A) or
                  child_of(symbol?C,A) and
                  descendant_of(C)(D) }
}
```

defines a "view" function for returning the set of all the descendants of a named individual, accessible by repeated queries to the child_of relation. Note that this can only be used for finding descendants, not ancestors. To do the latter, we need to define the inverse view function:

```
ancestor_of(symbol?D) is {
      all of (symbol?A) where {
                  child_of(D,A) or
                  child_of(D,symbol?P) and
                  ancestor_of(P)(A) }
}
```

    Either of these can be used for checking a pair of individuals, say sam and mary to see if they are in the closure of the child_of relation. We use either the query condition:

```
ancestor_of(mary)(bill)
```

    or the condition:

```
descendant_of(bill)(mary)
```

5 COOPERATION BETWEEN APRILQ SERVERS

The examples presented in the previous sections were fairly simple in the sense that they presented an implementation of a simple client/server inter-action, slightly generalized to allow client and server to cooperate in finding the answers to a client query. In this section, the realization of a more complex scenario is presented. Here, a number of AprilQ servers cooperate with each other, to answer a client query.

In the earlier example, the client used the recommend relation, defined in the broker, to get hold of handles of the information servers that could answer its queries. It then explicitly contacted each one of those to retrieve the information it was interested in.

An alternative "information" architecture is to have the client send a query to a mediator or facilitator agent. Such an agent consults the broker agent, then queries the information servers that it knows have the informa-tion needed to answer the client query. The query forwarding is invisible to the client. What the client sees is a "cloud" of information servers which can be queried for information (Figure 2).

Inside the cloud we could find a number of service providers and servers that cooperate in order to produce the reply to the initial client request. The example that will be used to highlight the implementation of such an infrastructure is based on a ticket reservation system (Figure 3).

The client contacts an agent that acts as a *mediator* between the client and the "cloud". The mediator offers a top-level view of the information that can be provided by the scattered servers inside the cloud. The clients outside the cloud query view functions of the mediator. The view func-tions do all the work of consulting the internal broker agent, querying the internal information sources and marshalling the answers.

An example of such a mediator view function is:

```
ticket_info(?From, ?To, ?MaxFare, ?Date, ?TicketType) is {
```

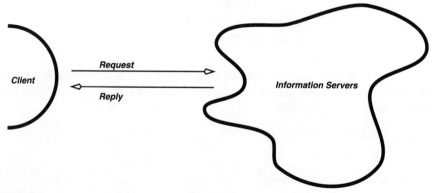

Figure 2.   The cloud view of the client.

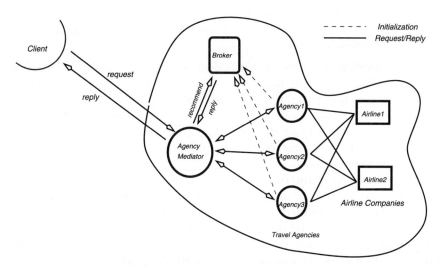

Figure 3.   The internal structure of the cloud.

```
all of (?Flight_no, ?Fare, ?Airline) where {
    recommend(TicketType)(AgencyHandle) ! "broker_agent@..."and
    TicketType(From, To, Date)(Airline, Fare, FlightNo) ! AgencyHandle
    and Fare < MaxFare
    }
};
```

During the evaluation of a call to the `ticket_info` view function, the broker_agent is contacted:

```
recommend(TicketType)(AgencyHandle) ! "broker_agent@..."
```

in order to get the handles of the travel agencies that hold information about the service (TicketType) that the client has requested.[3] Each travel agency registered with the broker with respect to the TicketType service is queried to find flight details and corresponding fares, with remote subquery:

```
TicketType(From, To, Date)(Airline, Fare, FlightNo) ! AgencyHandle
```

All the answers to this remote subquery that have a fare less than the maximum MaxFare specified by the client are returned as answers to the client's query. An example query is:

```
(symbol,number,symbol)[]?Tickets :=
        all of (symbol?FlightNo, number?Fare, symbol?Airline) where {
```

---

[3] In fact, TicketType is the name of a view function of the travel agency and From, To and Date are input arguments to this view function. But the outside client does not need to know this. It only needs to know that the mediator offers the view function ticket_info, one argument of which can be the name of a type of ticket.

```
(FlightNo, Fare, Airline) on
     ticket_info(london, athens, 150, 10_10_96,cheap_airfares)
} ! "agency_mediator@..."
```

The internal structure of the "cloud" can change dynamically. New servers can join and old ones can withdraw from the "cloud". Their existence is mapped by an entry in the broker_agent database. Since the addresses of the servers are retrieved at the time of the execution of the query, the scenario is quite dynamic. Each client query will be evaluated with respect to the configuration of the infrastructure at the time that the query is received.

The above, from the distributed database perspective, can be seen as an example of horizontal fragmentation. A set of tables (cheap_airfares) are horizontally fragmented and distributed in a number of servers (travel agencies in our case). The integration of those tables is achieved by using the AprilQ remote query mechanism and the information stored in the broker can be viewed as information about the fragmentation.

Figure 3 illustrates vertical fragmentation of the cheap_airfares relation, as implemented by the following view function held in each travel agency:

```
cheap_airfares(?From, ?To, ?Date) is {
   all of (?Airline, ?Fare, ?FlightNo) where {
      cheap_tickets(Airline, FlightNo, From, To, Date) and
      airline(Airline, ?AirlineHandle) and
      cheap_ticket_deal(FlightNo, Date, ?Fare) ! AirlineHandle
   }
}
```

The relations cheap_tickets and airline are local to the travel agency. The first relation records the cheap fare deals it has made with different airlines on particular flights. The second is a database of handles for the automated reservation agents of these airlines. It is the analogue of the telephone database of a normal travel agent. Of the triple of values returned by a call on this view function, the Airline and FlightNo components are obtained by querying the local cheap_tickets relation. The Fare field is obtained by a remote subquery to the airline agent for the Airline. The three fields are thus composed from queries to different databases.

6 INTERNETING APRILQ

The above example allows only clients that can send April (and more specifically AprilQ) messages to the "cloud". This restriction limits the usefulness of the application to processes that can be interfaced to April. To overcome this limitation, we have built a prototype distributed information server (Paktzis, 1996) that allows clients to pose queries in a number of popular

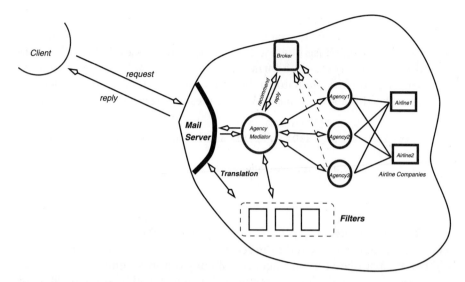

Figure 4.   The internal structure of the cloud (revised).

Internet protocols using standard communication languages (like KQML). For example, it allows a client to submit a query as a KQML string message given as the content of an email message. The internal structure of the information cloud is now as depicted in Figure 4.

When an email message arrives, it is picked up by a communication server (mail server in the specific example), which processes it and forwards it to the mediator. The processing of the email message involves translating it from a sequence of ASCII characters (the typical format of an email message) to an April record. If the message is in KQML format, it is also translated into an April record reflecting the essential structure of KQML message. For example, the KQML message (expressed as a string):

```
"(ask
      :sender MessageSender
      :receiver "agency_mediator@..."
      :reply-with TransID
      :language AprilQ
      :content "all of (symbol?FlightNo, number?Fare, symbol?Airline) where {
               (FlightNo, Fare, Airline) on
                        ticket_info(london, athens, 150, 10_10_96, cheap_airfares)}"
)"
```

is translated into the April record:

```
(ask, [
      (sender, MessageSender),
      (receiver, "agency_mediator@..."),
      (language, AprilQ),
      (content, all of (symbol?FlightNo, number?Fare, symbol?Airline) where {
               (FlightNo, Fare, Airline) on
                        ticket_info(london, athens, 150, 10_10_96, cheap_airfares)})
])
```

To achieve the translation, the communication server makes use of one or more of a set of message filter processes that are now included in the infrastructure. Those filters are stand-alone processes that can translate to and from various message formats.

In order for the mediator to be able to deal with an incoming KQML messages like the above, it has to have a message receive method such as:

```
(ask, (symbol,any)[]?Fields) -> {
    if (language, AprilQ) in Fields and (content, query?Q) in Fields
    then {
        (query_answer, eval_query(Q)) >> replyto}
    }
  }
}
```

The query_answer reply will be sent back to the email server for this will be the replyto process for the received April message. The email server will reverse translate the message. It will embed it in an email message and send to it the original client, MessageSender, which will be some mailbox of an email server. The content of this email will be a KQML reply message. It will look like:

```
"(reply
  :in-reply-to TransID
  :language "AprilQ"
  :sender agency_mediator
  :receiver MessageSender
  :content < List of Answers >
)"
```

The above infrastructure can be easily augmented. Since filters and communication servers are standalone processes, new processes supporting a variety of Internet protocols and communication languages can be easily added without affecting the operation of the rest of the system.

7 SUMMARY AND RELATED WORK

In this chapter a harness language for the construction of cooperative information systems was presented. AprilQ processes, storing metadata and view functions are attached to each information source and interact with each other using high-level queries. An example scenario of a ticket reservation system, which demonstrated how a cooperative information system can be built, was presented. This example was extended to support KQML-based communication, making the system more open. A more detailed description of AprilQ and of further extensions to it is included in Skarmeas (1997).

A current trend of cooperative information systems is the use of object and/or agent technology for the integration of heterogeneous information systems. A framework developed following this trend is the ROK (reflective object knowledge) framework (Edmond *et al.*, 1995, 1997). In the context of this framework an object approach is used to record meta-level information about heterogeneous information sources. This information can be used to construct agent interfaces to pre-existing information and legacy systems which communicate with each other to achieve some shared goals. Although for part of the implementation of ROK, the April language has been used, an alternative option would be to use the high-level and persistence features of AprilQ to enhance the expressiveness and declarativenes of the system.

In Skarmeas and Clark (1997) an alternative approach for integrating distributed information systems is presented. It introduces the concept of a message board. Information sources can advertise preferences for messages to the message board and this will route messages based on these preferences. The preferences are active patterns implemented using the April higher order features.

In O'Hare and Jennings (1996) a number of issues related to the field of distributed artificial intelligence (DAI) in general and agent systems in particular are presented. In Kandzia and Klusch (1997) there is a collection of papers on how DAI and databases can be combined.

An alternative software platform that has been used for the development of cooperative systems is the OMG (CORBA) architecture (Soley, 1995; Orfali, Harkey and Edwards 1995). This architecture offers the middleware, which distributed objects can use to exchange messages transparently. Part of this architecture is the *object request broker* (ORB) which allows the transparent exchange of requests and responses between objects. CORBA is a generic architecture intended for the implementation of client/server interaction regardless of the application domain and the implementation language of the application. It is more low level than AprilQ. In AprilQ the communication between processes is accomplished by the April platform (as opposed to the ORB part of CORBA), and its features are more expressive and declarative than CORBA, (although recently there have been attempts to apply CORBA on semantically rich domains (Manola *et al*, this volume) such as business models etc.). However, AprilQ is not a rival system of CORBA. Both could co-exist, and CORBA could be used to allow applications and services to inter-operate with AprilQ processes.

Finally, a good introduction to issues related to distributed databases and how relation tables can be fragmented and allocated to several distributed servers is Ceri and Pelagatti (1985).

REFERENCES

Agha, G. and Hewitt, C. (1987) Concurrent Programming using Actors. In *Object Oriented Concurrent Programming*, A. Yonezawa and M. Tokoro (eds). MIT.

Armstrong, J., Virding, R. and Williams, M. (1993) *Concurrent Programming in Erlang*. Prentice-Hall.

Ceri, S. and Pelagatti, G. (1985) *Distributed Database: Principles and Systems*. McGraw-Hill.

Edmond, D., Papazoglou, M.P. and Tari, Z. (1995) ROK: A reflective model for distributed object management. In *Research Issues in Data Engineering — Distributed Object Management (RIDE-DOM'95)*. IEEE-CS Press, pp. 34–41.

Edmond, D., Papazoglou, M. and Bartlet, A. (1997) Distributed object reification and control. Technical report, School of Information Systems, Queensland University of Technology, Brisbane, Australia.

Finin, T. Fritzon, R., McKay, D., McEntire, R. (1994) KQML as an agent communication language. *Proceedings Third International Conference on Knowledge Management*. ACM Press. pp. 456–463.

Haugeneder, H. (ed). (1994) *IMAGINE Final Project Report*. Siemens, Munich, Germany.

Kandzia, P. and Klusch, M. (1997) *Proceedings of the 1st International Workshop in Cooperative Information Agents — DAI meets Database Systems*, Germany, Lecture Notes, Springer–Verlag (to appear).

Kuoka, D. and Harada, H. (1995) On using KQML for matchmaking. In *ICMAS Proceedings 1995*, V. Lesser (ed.). AAAI Press. pp. 239–245.

McCabe, F. (1996) *AdB Reference Manual*. Technical report, Fujitsu Laboratories Ltd., Japan.

McCabe, F.G. and Clark, K. (1995) April — Agent PRocess Interaction Language. *Intelligent Agents: ECAI-94 Workshop on Agent Theories, Architectures and Languages*, pp. 324–340.

O'Hare, G.M.P. and Jennings, N.R. (1996) *Foundations of Distributed Artificial Intelligence*. John Wiley & Sons.

Orfali, R., Harkey, D. and Edwards, J. (1995) *Essential Distributed Objects Survival Guide*. Wiley.

Paktzis, T. (1996) Interfacing Mediation Services between KQML and April through E-mail. Technical report, MSc thesis, Imperial College, Department of Computing.

Papazoglou, M., Laufmann, S.C. and Sellis, T.K. (1992) An Organizational Framework for Cooperative Intelligent Information Systems. *International Journal of Intelligent and Cooperative Information Systems*, **1**(1), 169–202.

Skarmeas, N. (1997) *Agents as objects with knowledge base state*. PhD thesis, Imperial College, Department of Computing, London.

Skarmeas, N. and Clark, K. (1996) AprilQ: A database extension to April. Technical report, Imperial College, London, UK.

Skarmeas, N. and Clark, K.L. (1997) Intelligent routing based on active patterns as the basis for the integration of distributed information systems. Technical report, Imperial College, Department of Computing, London.

Soley, R. (ed). (1995) *Object Management Architecture Guide*, Third edition. Wiley.

Part III

Use of Metadata and Ontologies for Information Sharing

Semantic Heterogeneity in Global Information Systems: the Role of Metadata, Context and Ontologies

Vipul Kashyap[a] and Amit Sheth[b]

[a]MCC, Austin, TX, USA and [b]University of Georgia, Athens, GA, USA

Abstract

Semantic heterogeneity has been identified as one of the most critical and toughest problems when dealing with interoperability and cooperation among multiple databases. It was earlier studied in the context of exchanging, sharing and integrating data, especially during the schema/view analysis phase of schema or view integration, or when writing a view or query using a multi-database language. With the advent of global interconnectivity, we now need to deal with more heterogeneous information resources consisting of a variety of digital data, and the scale of the problem has changed from a few databases to millions of information resources, thus making it more important than ever to address this problem. It is also recognized that the problem has only become harder and that simplistic solutions involving only representational or structural components of data will not work in general.

In this chapter, we explore approaches to tackle the semantic heterogeneity problem in the context of global information systems (GIS) which are systems geared to handle information requests on the global information infrastructure (GII). These approaches are based on the capture and representation of metadata, contexts and ontologies. In order to handle *information overload*, it would be advantageous to abstract out the representational details of the underlying data and capture the information content by using *domain-specific metadata*. The next important step is that of understanding the context of the query, using metadata to construct the context and identifying the relevant data in that context. Another critical issue that arises here is that of *different vocabularies* used to characterize similar information. We present an approach to deal with this problem at

Cooperative Information Systems
Trends and Directions
ISBN 0-12-544910-0

the metadata/context level by using terms from *domain specific ontologies* to construct metadata/context. We deal with semantic heterogeneity at this level and propose an approach using *terminological relationships* to achieve semantic interoperability.

I INTRODUCTION

Many organizations face the challenge of interoperating among multiple independently developed database systems to perform critical functions. Three of the best known approaches to deal with multiple databases are tightly coupled federation, loosely coupled federation, and interdependent data management (Sheth and Larson, 1990; Sheth, 1991). A critical task in creating a tightly coupled federation is that of schema integration (e.g., Dayal and Hwang, 1984). A critical task in accessing data in a loosely coupled federation (Litwin and Abdellatif, 1986; Heimbigner and McLeod, 1985) is to define a view over multiple databases or to define a query using a multi-database language. The problem of semantic heterogeneity is the **identification of semantically related objects in different databases and the resolution of schematic differences among them** (Sheth and Kashyap, 1992) and is common to all the above approaches.

However, with global interconnectivity we now need to deal with more heterogeneous information resources consisting of a variety of digital data. Huge amounts of digital data in a variety of structured (e.g. relational databases), semi-structured (e.g. e-mail messages) and unstructured (e.g. image data) formats have been collected and stored in thousands of autonomous repositories and CD-ROMs. Affordable multimedia systems allow creation of multimedia data and support access and presentation of such data. These digital repositories are increasingly being made available on the fast-evolving GII of which the World Wide Web (Berners-Lee *et al.*, 1992) ("the web") is an oft-cited and popular example. A GIS now has to deal with millions of information resources (as opposed to a few databases in a multi-database federation), and simplistic solutions involving only representational or structural components of data will not work in general.

In this chapter we explore an approach that uses **metadata, context** and **ontologies** to handle the semantic heterogeneity problem in a GIS. The key aspects of this approach are (Figure 1):

- Use of metadata to capture the **information content** of the data in the underlying repositories. Intensional descriptions constructed from metadata and termed as *metadata contexts (m-contexts)* are used to abstract from the structure and organization of the individual repositories.
- Terms (concepts, roles) in domain-specific ontologies are used to characterize contextual descriptions called *conceptual contexts (c-contexts)*. The c-contexts capture pieces of **domain knowledge** that describe the data

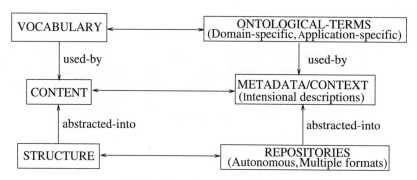

Figure 1. Key aspects of our approach.

in the underlying repositories. Semantic interoperability is achieved by using terminological relationships between terms across ontologies.

The key objective of our approach should be to reduce the problem of knowing the contents and the structure of each of the huge number of information repositories to the significantly smaller problem of knowing the contents of the domain-specific ontologies, which a user familiar with the domain is likely to know or easily understand (Kashyap, 1997). In this chapter we demonstrate the need for techniques that go beyond the structural and representational components of data and focus on the application of those techniques to structured databases.

Different types of metadata may be stored in the system (e.g., indices, schema information). The Rufus (Shoens *et al.*, 1993) and the InfoHarness (Shklar *et al.*, 1995) systems use automatically generated metadata to access and retrieve heterogeneous information independent of type, representation and location. In Section 2, we discuss the different kinds of metadata and present an informal classification. We identify and propose domain-specific metadata as the key for solving the semantic heterogeneity problem (Kashyap *et al.*, 1995).

Section 3 discusses the construction of c-contexts from domain-specific ontologies and their representation in a formalism that can be easily mapped (Kashyap and Sheth, 1996) to a description logic (DL) expression. Issues of language and ontology involved in the above are also discussed. These c-contexts are used to represent extra knowledge about the information content of the database which may not be represented in the schema of the database. A user query can also be represented as a c-context. *Schema correspondences* (Kashyap and Sheth, 1996) that capture the associations between c-contexts and the underlying data are also discussed.

The key to interoperability is vocabulary sharing among the intensional m-context and c-context descriptions associated with the various databases. Different concepts may be used to design contextual descriptions for different databases. We assume the existence of application and domain specific ontologies describing the information content of the various databases from which contextual expressions may be constructed. In fact, ontologies are viewed in our approach as a special case of *domain-specific metadata*. In Section 4 we present an approach for semantic interoperability using terminological relationships across ontologies. We discuss the OBSERVER prototype (Mena *et al.*, 1996a) which demonstrates the use of **synonym** relationships to achieve semantic interoperability. Extensions of the above using **hyponym** (specialization) and *hypernym* (generalization) relationships (Mena *et al.*, 1996 a,b) are also discussed. Section 5 presents future and ongoing work and our conclusions.

2 WHAT IS METADATA?

Metadata in its most general sense is defined as data or information about data. For structured databases, the most common example of metadata is the schema of the database. However, with the proliferation of various types of multimedia data on the GII, we shall refer to an expanded notion of metadata of which the schema of structured databases is a (small) part. We use metadata to store derived properties of media useful in information access or retrieval. They may describe or be a summary of the information content of the data described in an intensional manner. They may also be used to represent properties of or relationships between individual objects of heterogeneous types and media. Figure 1 illustrates the key aspects of our approach for addressing the problem of information on the GII. Metadata is the pivotal idea on which both the components depend. The function of the metadata descriptions is two-fold:

- To enable the abstraction of representational details such as the format and organization of data, and capture the information content of the underlying data **independent of representational details**. This represents the first step in reduction of the information overload as intensional metadata descriptions are in general an order of magnitude less in size than the underlying data.
- To enable representation of **domain knowledge** describing the information domain to which the underlying data belongs. This knowledge may then be used to make inferences about the underlying data. This helps in reducing the information overload as the inferences may be used to determine the *relevance* of the underlying data without accessing the data.

2.1 A Classification of Metadata

We now present a classification of the various types of metadata used by various researchers to capture the information content represented in the various types of digital data (Table 1). The types of metadata that play a key role in enabling **semantic interoperability** are also identified.

Table I. Metadata for digital media.

Metadata	Media type	Metadata type
Q-Features (Jain and Hampapuram, 1994)	Image, video	Domain specific
R-Features (Jain and Hampapuram, 1994)	Image, video	Domain independent
R-Features (Jain and Hampapuram, 1994)	Image, video	Content independent
Impression vector (Kiyoki et al., 1994)	Image	Content descriptive
NDVI, spatial registration (Anderson and Stonebraker, 1994)	Image	Domain specific
Speech feature index (Glavitsch et al., 1994)	Audio	Direct content-based
Topic change indices (Chen et al., 1994)	Audio	Direct content-based
Document vectors (Deerwester et al., 1990)	Text	Direct content-based
Inverted indices (Kahle and Medlar, 1991)	Text	Direct content-based
Content classification metadata (Bohm and Rakow, 1994)	Multimedia	Domain specific
Document composition metadata (Bohm and Rakow, 1994)	Multimedia	Domain independent
Metadata templates (Ordille and Miller, 1993)	Media independent	Domain specific
Land-cover, relief (Sheth and Kashyap, 1996)	Media independent	Domain specific
Parent–child relationships (Shklar et al., 1995)	Text	Domain independent
Contexts (Sciore et al., 1992; Kashyap and Sheth, 1994a)	Structured databases	Domain specific
Concepts from Cyc (Collet et al., 1991)	Structured databases	Domain specific
User's data attributes (Shoens et al., 1993)	Text, structured databases	Domain specific
Domain specific ontologies (Mena et al., 1996b)	Media-independent	Domain specific

- **Content-independent metadata.** This type of metadata captures information that does not depend on the content of the document with which it is associated. Examples of this type of metadata are location, modification-date of a document and type-of-sensor used to record a photographic image. There is no information content captured by these metadata but these might still be useful for retrieval of documents from their actual physical locations and for checking whether the information is current or not.
- **Content-dependent metadata.** This type of metadata depends on the content of the document it is associated with. Examples of content-dependent metadata are size of a document, max-colours, number-of-rows, number-of-columns of an image. Content-dependent metadata can be further sub-divided as follows:

  Direct content-based metadata. This type of metadata is based directly on the contents of a document. A popular example of this is full-text indices based on the text of the documents. Inverted tree and document vectors are examples of this type of metadata.

  Content-descriptive metadata. This type of metadata describes the contents of a document without direct utilization of the contents of the document. An example of this type of metadata is textual annotations describing the contents of an image. This type of metadata comes in two flavours:

  Domain-independent metadata. These metadata capture information present in the document independent of the application or subject domain of the information. Examples of these are the C/C++ parse trees and HTML/SGML document type definitions.

  Domain-specific metadata. Metadata of this type is described in a manner specific to the application or subject domain of information. Issues of vocabulary become very important in this case as the terms have to be chosen in a domain-specific manner. Examples of such metadata are relief, land-cover from the GIS domain and area, population from the Census domain. In the case of structured data, the database schema is an example of such metadata. Another interesting example is domain specific ontologies, terms from which may be used as vocabulary to construct metadata specific to that domain.

2.2 Metadata: a Means for Capturing Information Content

In this section we discuss the information content captured by the various types of metadata enumerated in the previous section. We shall also identify the level corresponding to Figure 1 at which this metadata may be used.

- **Content-independent information.** This type of information is captured by content-independent metadata and helps in the encapsulation of information into units of interest and may be represented as objects in a data model.

- **Capturing representational information.** This type of information is typically captured by content-dependent metadata described in the previous section. This, along with domain-independent metadata (which primarily captures structural organization of the data) enables interoperability via navigational and browsing approaches which depend on representational details of the data.

- **Capturing information content.** Information content is typically captured to various degrees by various types of content-dependent metadata. Direct content-based metadata lies in a grey area in the sense that it is not entirely divorced from the representational details. However, the metadata which helps abstract out representational details and capture information meaningful to a particular application or subject domain is domain specific metadata.

- **Vocabulary for information content characterization.** Domain-specific metadata can be constructed from terms in a domain-specific ontology or concept libraries describing information in an application or subject domain. Thus we view ontologies as metadata which themselves can be viewed as a vocabulary of terms for construction of more domain-specific metadata descriptions. Semantic interoperability at the vocabulary level is achieved with the help of terminological relationships.

The above discussion suggests that domain-specific metadata capture information which is more meaningful with respect to a specific application or a domain. The information captured by the other types of metadata primarily reflect the format and organization of the underlying data. This leads us to propose domain-specific metadata as the most appropriate for dealing with issues related to semantic heterogeneity.

2.3 Constructing Intensional Descriptions from Domain-Specific Metadata

Domain-specific metadata can be used to construct intensional descriptions which capture the information content of the underlying data. As discussed earlier, these descriptions are used for abstraction of representational details or for representing domain knowledge on which inferences can be performed. Based on the desired goal, the intensional descriptions may be categorized as *m-contexts* and *c-contexts*.

2.3.1 Metadata Contexts (m-contexts)

These descriptions primarily serve to abstract the representational details such as format and organization of data. Typically they are boolean combinations of metadata items, where each metadata item captures some piece of information content in the underlying data. The terms used to construct these metadata are typically obtained from ontologies or vocabularies which do not support complex relationships between the various terms, e.g., definition of a term using other terms. Hence each metadata item is independently mapped to the underlying data. At run time, when metadata corresponding to a query are evaluated, the mappings are computed independently and the results are combined to satisfy the boolean combinations. An example of this type of metadata and how they may be used to interoperate across multimedia data (Sheth and Kashyap, 1996) is briefly described below.

Example. Consider a decision support query across multiple data repositories possibly representing data in multiple media:

> Get all regions having a population greater then 500, area greater
> than 50 acres having an urban land-cover and moderate relief.

The m-context can be represented as:

> (**AND** region (population > 500) (area > 50) (= land-cover "urban")
> (= relief "moderate"))

- Each of the attributes population, area, land-cover and relief capture information about regions stored in the underlying data. The attributes population and area capture information stored in structured data whereas land-cover and relief capture information stored in image data.
- The attributes population and area are computed independently and consist of SQL queries which select the appropriate regions satisfying population and area constraints from the census data.
- The attributes land-cover and relief are also computed independently and consist of image processing routines to analyse geological maps and select appropriate regions satisfying land-cover and relief constraints.
- The final answer is the intersection of the regions returned after computing the different metadata and reflects the semantics of the boolean operator **AND** used to construct the m-context.

2.3.2 Conceptual Contexts (c-contexts)

The representation of m-contexts is the first step in abstracting representational details and capturing information content. The information captured in the m-contexts, however, is *data sensitive*. An alternative perspective to capturing information content is to capture information that is *application sensitive*. Conceptual contexts primarily serve to capture *domain knowledge* and help impose a conceptual semantic view on the underlying data. C-contexts are constructed from terms (concepts, roles) in domain specific ontologies. They are more rich in information as compared to m-contexts and constructed when terms are chosen from ontologies that support complex relationships between terms. These relationships are typically used in ontological inferences that are performed before evaluating c-contexts. The relationships typically are definitions of a term based on other terms in the ontology and domain/range constraints on metadata attributes. Ontological inferences may be used to determine relevance of the underlying data.

Example. Consider the m-context discussed in the earlier section. Suppose the ontology from which the metadata description is constructed supports complex relationships. Furthermore, let:

CrowdedRegion ≡ (**AND** region (population > 200))

Inferences supported by the ontology enable determination that the regions required by the query metadata discussed earlier are instances of CrowdedRegion. Thus the metadata description can be rewritten as:

(**AND** CrowdedRegion(population > 500)(area > 50)
(= land-cover"urban")(= relief"moderate"))

Thus when the mappings corresponding to the metadata are computed only those repositories are consulted which are known to contain information about **CrowdedRegion**. C-contexts may be considered to be a more sophisticated version of m-contexts, where ontological inferences are performed before the mappings are computed.

In the rest of the chapter, we focus on the structured data and the use of c-contexts constructed from domain-specific ontologies to capture the information content. The relationships between terms in the ontologies enable the representation of extra knowledge not represented in the database schema. We shall also discuss the cases where c-contexts may be constructed from different domain specific ontologies and how ontological inferences may enable semantic interoperation based on terminological relationships.

3 CONSTRUCTING C-CONTEXTS FROM ONTOLOGICAL TERMS

In Figure 1, we have identified metadata as the pivotal idea on which our approaches to address the information overload problem in the GII are based. In the previous section we discussed the various types of metadata and identified domain-specific metadata as the most appropriate type for handling semantic heterogeneity. One approach to construct metadata that captures meaningful information with respect to an application domain is to use terms from domain-specific ontologies that support complex interrelationships between various terms. We have discussed such metadata descriptions called **c-contexts** in the previous section and illustrated with the help of an example how ontological inferences may be useful to determine relevance of information present in the underlying data. This, along with the abstraction of representational details enabled by the metadata descriptions, helps to deal with the information overload on the GII. In this section we present a discussion of issues related to the representation and use of c-contexts.

We discuss the inadequacies of purely structural and mapping-based methods in representing object relationships and discuss the advantages of representing c-contexts. We shall discuss how c-contexts may be partially represented and explain informally the semantics of the partial representation by expressing them in a description logic formalism. We discuss operations for automatic ways of comparing and manipulating c-contexts and illustrate with the help of examples how they may be used to achieve interoperation across information sources. A brief discussion of issues relating to the language for representing c-contexts and the ontologies from which the c-contexts may be constructed is also given. The c-contexts shall be referred to as contexts unless otherwise specified in the rest of this chapter.

3.1 Rationale for Context Representation

In characterizing the similarity between objects based on the semantics associated with them we have to consider the real-world semantics (RWS) of an object. It is not possible to completely define what an object denotes or means in the model world (Sheth and Gala, 1989). We propose the **context** of an object as the primary vehicle to capture the RWS of the object. We argue for the need for representing context by showing the inadequacy of purely structural representations. We also discuss the computational benefits of representing context.

3.1.1 Inadequacy of Purely Structural Representations

It has been suggested by Sheth and Gala (1989), Sheth and Kashyap (1993) and Fankhauser *et al.* (1991) that the ability to represent the structure of an object does not help capture the real-world semantics of the object. It is not possible to provide a structural and hence a mathematical definition of the complex notion of real-world semantics. In Larson *et al.*, (1989), a one-to-one mapping is assumed between the attribute definition and the attribute's real-world semantics. They define an attribute in terms of fixed descriptors such as **Uniqueness, Lower/Upper Bound, Domain, Scale** etc. which are used to generate mappings between two attributes. They are also used to determine the equivalence of attributes. However, what they establish is the structural equivalence of these attributes; they are not sufficient to determine the semantic equivalence of the attributes.

Consider two attributes, **person-name** and **department-name**. We may be able to define a mapping between the value domains of these two attributes, but we know that they are not semantically equivalent. In order to be able to capture this lack of equivalence, we propose the mappings between the domains of the attributes be made with respect to (*wrt*) a context. We define two objects to be semantically equivalent if it is possible to define mappings *wrt* all known and coherent contexts, and the definition contexts of the objects should be coherent *wrt* each other. Definition contexts and the notion of coherence are discussed later in this section. Since the definition contexts of **person-name** and **department-name** are not coherent (one identifies an animate and the other identifies an inanimate object), they are not defined to be equivalent.

3.1.2 Computational Benefits of Representing Context

Shoham (1991) has discussed the computational benefits that might accrue in modelling and representing context in AI and knowledge-based systems. We believe that some of those reasons are very relevant in the presence of information overload in the GII and are as follows:

- **Economy of representation.** In a manner akin to database views, contexts can act as a focusing mechanism when accessing the component databases on the GII. They can provide a **semantic summary** of the information in a database or group of databases and may be able to capture semantic information not expressed in database schema(s). Thus unnecessary details can be abstracted from the user.

- **Economy of reasoning.** Instead of reasoning with the information present in the database as a whole, reasoning can be performed with the context associated with a database or a group of databases. This approach has been used in Kashyap and Sheth (1994a) for information resource discovery and query processing in multi-databases.

- **Managing inconsistent information.** In the GII, where databases are designed and developed independently, it is not uncommon to have information in one database inconsistent with information in another. As long as information is consistent within the context of the query of the user, inconsistency in information from different databases may be allowed. This has been discussed with the help of an example in Kashyap and Sheth (1996).

- **Flexible semantics.** An important consequence of associating abstractions/mappings with the context is that the same two objects can be related to each other differently in two different contexts. Two objects might be semantically closer to each other in one context as compared to the other.

3.2 A Partial Context Representation

There have been attempts to represent the similarity between objects in different databases. As argued in the previous section, any representation of context that can be described by a fixed set of descriptors is not appropriate. In our approach, the descriptors, called meta-attributes or contextual coordinates, are not fixed but are dynamically chosen to model the characteristics of the application domain in question. It is not possible *a priori* to determine all possible contextual coordinates which would completely characterize the semantics of the application domain. This leads to a **partial** representation of context as a collection of contextual coordinates as:

Context $= \langle (C_1, \text{Expr}_1)(C_2, \text{Expr}_2) \ldots (C_k, \text{Expr}_k) \rangle$

- C_i, $1 \le i \le k$, is a contextual coordinate denoting an aspect of a context.
- C_i may model some characteristic of the subject domain and may be obtained from a domain specific ontology (discussed later in this section).
- C_i may model an implicit assumption in the design of a database.
- C_i may or may not be associated with an attribute A_j of an object O in the database.

We shall now explain the meaning of the symbols C_i and Expr_i by using examples and by enumerating the corresponding description logic (DL) expressions (Brachman and Scmolze, 1985; Borgida *et al.*, 1989; Achilles *et al.*, 1991; MacGregor, 1987: von Luck *et al.*, 1987). Using DL expressions, it is possible to define primitive classes and in addition specify classes using intensional descriptions phrased in terms of necessary and sufficient properties that must be satisfied by their instances. The intensional descriptions may be used to express the collection of constraints that make up a c-context. Using the terminology of DL systems, each term may be modelled as either a **concept** or a **role**. Also, each C_i roughly corresponds to a role and each Expr_i roughly corresponds to fillers for the role. In our case Expr_i might be a term, c-context or a term associated with a c-context. The DL expressions corresponding to the c-contexts are summarized and the operators used in a DL are informally described in Appendix A. We shall use the following example and terminology to explain how c-contexts may capture information in the databases using terms from a domain ontology. Consider the following database objects:

EMPLOYEE(SS#, Name, Salary Type, Dept, Affiliation)
PUBLICATION(Id, Title, Journal)
HAS-PUBLICATION(SS#, Id)

We shall now illustrate with examples how information content in these database objects can be captured with the help of terms organized as c-contexts in a domain specific ontology. For each object O, attribute A and datavalue V, in the database we assume the following:

- term(O)[1] and term(A) are terms corresponding to the database object O and attribute A at the intensional level.
- instance(V) is the instance corresponding to the datavalue V in the database. The datavalue might be a key or an object identifier.
- Ext(Term) denotes the set of instances corresponding to the term in the ontology.

---

[1] The predicate term should have one more identifying the ontology that is being used, as a database might contain information in more than one information domain. However, we can assume WLOG that one ontology is being used to capture the information in this database.

Based on the above we can identify the following:

term(EMPLOYEE) = EmplConcept, term(PUBLICATION) = PublConcept,
term(EMPLOYEE.Dept) = employer, term(PUBLICATION.Id) = article,
term(EMPLOYEE.Affiliation) = affiliation,
term(HAS-PUBLICATION) = HasPublConcept,
term(HAS-PUBLICATION.article) = article,
term(HAS-PUBLICATION.author) = author

The value $Expr_i$ of a contextual coordinate C_i can be represented in the following manner:

- $Expr_i$ can be a variable. It is used as a place holder to elicit answers from the databases and impose constraints on them.

Example. Suppose we are interested in people who are authors and who hold a post. We can represent the query context C_Q (a special type of c-context that captures the constraints on the metadata in a query) as follows:

$C_Q = \langle(\text{author}, X) (\text{designee}, X)\rangle$

The same thing can be expressed in a DL as follows:

$C_Q = [\text{author}]$ for (**SAME – AS** author designee)

The terms author and designee are obtained from a domain-specific ontology. It may be noted here that we use variables in a very restricted manner for the specific purpose of retrieving the relevant properties of the selected objects. They are used only at the highest level of nesting though the c-contexts can have an arbitrary level of nesting (since each $Expr_i$ can be a c-context or a term associated with a c-context) and hence we do not need to perform any complex nested unifications.

- $Expr_i$ can be a set.

  — The set may be an enumeration of terms from a domain-specific ontology.
  — The set may be defined as the extension of an object or as elements from the domain of a type defined in the database.
  — The set may be defined by posing constraints on pre-existing sets.

Example. Suppose we want to represent the following assumptions implicit in the design of the object EMPLOYEE in a database:

  — An employee either works for a department (defined by the datatype **Deptypes**) or is doing a dissertation in some department.
  — All articles written by an employee are represented in the object PUBLICATION in the database.

We can represent these assumptions as:

$C_{def}(\text{EMPLOYEE}) = \langle(\text{employer}, [\textbf{Deptypes} \cup \{\text{restypes}\}])$
$(\text{article}, \text{PUBLICATION})\rangle$

Let term(**Deptypes**) = DeptConcept and
    instance(restypes) = researcher ⇒
C_{def}(EMPLOYEE) = ⟨(employer, [Ext(DeptConcept) ∪ {restypes}])
    (article, PublConcept)⟩

The same thing can be expressed in a DL as follows:

C_{def}(EMPLOYEE) = (**AND** EmplConcept(**ALL** article PublConcept)
                         (**ALL** employer
    (**OR** DeptConcept (**ONE-OF** researcher))))

- Expr$_i$ can be a variable associated with a c-context.

  — The c-context can be used to express constraints that would apply to the set, type or object the variable X would unify with.
  — As discussed earlier, the function of the variable is restricted for the purposes of retrieval and shall not be present at deeper levels of nesting.

Example. Suppose we want all the articles whose titles contain the substring "abortion" in them. This can be expressed in the following query context:

C_Q = ⟨(article, X∘⟨(title, {y|substring(y) = "abortion"})⟩)⟩
    = ⟨(article, X∘Context)⟩

where ∘ denotes association of a c-context with a variable X.
Let us assume that there is a concept AbortionString in the ontology which is subsumed by the concept String where
Ext(AbortionString) = {y|substring(y) = "abortion"}
Context =< (title, AbortionString)⟩
Association of a variable and a c-context ensures that the answer satisfies the constraints expressed in the c-context. The same thing can be expressed in a DL as follows:

C_Q = [article] for (**ALL** article (**ALL** title AbortionString))

- Expr$_i$ can be a set, type or an object associated with a c-context.

  — This is called the association context and is defined later in this section.
  — This may be used to express semantic dependencies between objects that may not be modelled in the database.

Example. Suppose we want to represent information relating publications to employees in a database. Let PUBLICATION and EMPLOYEE be objects in a database. The definition context of HAS-PUBLICATION can be defined as:

C_{def}(HAS-PUBLICATION) = ⟨(article, PUBLICATION)
                              (author,
                                EMPLOYEE∘
                                ⟨(affiliation, {research})⟩)⟩

where research is a term from the ontology and corresponds to a datavalue in the domain of the attribute EMPLOYEE. Affiliation in the database $\Rightarrow$

C_{def}(HAS-PUBLICATION) = ⟨(article, PublConcept)
(author, EmplConcept∘Context)⟩

where ∘ denotes association of a c-context with an object EMPLOYEE, and

Context = ⟨(affiliation, {research})⟩

Association of a c-context with an object is similar to defining a view on the object extensions such that only those instances satisfying the constraints defined in the c-context are exported to the federation. The same thing can be expressed in a DL as follows:

C_{def}(HAS-PUBLICATION) = (**AND** HasPublConcept
(**ALL** article PublConcept)
(**ALL** author (**AND** EmplConcept
(**ALL** affiliation(**ONE-OF**
research)))))

Note that the relationships between EMPLOYEE, PUBLICATION and HAS-PUBLICATION is information represented in the c-context that is not modelled in the database schema.

3.3 Reasoning about and Manipulation of Contexts

We have proposed a partial representation of context in the previous section. This can be used to abstract out the information content of the underlying data and help reduce the information overload in the GII. The next step is to use these representations meaningfully to enable a GIS to focus on relevant information and to correlate information from the various information sources on the GII. In order to achieve this, the following need to be precisely defined (Kashyap and Sheth, 1996):

- **Specificity.** The most common relationship between contexts is the "specificity" relationship. Given two contexts $Context_1$ and $Context_2$, $Context_1 \leq Context_2$ iff $Context_1$ is at least as specific as $Context_2$.
- **Organization in a lattice structure.** It is possible that two contexts may not be comparable to each other, i.e. it may not be possible to decide whether one is more specific than the other. Thus, the specificity relationship gives us a partial order. The following useful operations on the context lattice can be defined:

    overlap($Cntxt_1$, $Cntxt_2$). This is the common set of contextual attributes present in the contextual descriptions.
    coherent($Cntxt_1$, $Cntxt_2$). This operator determines whether the constraints determined by the values of the contextual coordinates are consistent.

Example. Let

Cntxt$_1 = \langle$(salary, $\{x|x \leq 10000\})\rangle$

Cntxt$_2 = \langle$(salary, $\{x|x > 10000\})\rangle$

Thus, coherent(Cntxt$_1$, Cntxt$_2$) = FALSE

greatest lower bound (glb) of two contexts. The contexts can be organized in a special kind of lattice structure called a *meet semi-lattice* in which every pair of contexts has a greatest lower bound. Intuitively the *glb* computes the conjunction of constraints expressed in the contextual descriptions.

3.3.1 Semantics of the glb Operation

We now specify the semantics of the *glb* operation discussed above. The corresponding DL operations are identified in Appendix A. In the next section we shall use the *glb* operations to perform inferences on the information content represented in the underlying databases. Consider two c-contexts represented as follows:

Context$_1 = \langle(C_1, \text{Expr}_1)\dots(C_k, \text{Expr}_k)\rangle$

Context$_2 = \langle(C'_1, \text{Expr}'_1)\dots(C'_m, \text{Expr}'_m)\rangle$

The rules determining **glb(Expr$_i$, Expr$'_j$)** are:

- **Variable.** glb(Expr, X) = Expr where Expr$_i$ = Expr and Expr$'_j$ = X
- **Sets.** glb(Set$_i$, Set$_j$) = Set$_i \cap$ Set$_j$ where Expr$_i$ = Set$_i$ and Expr$'_j$ = Set$_j$
- **Terms.** glb(Term$_1$, Term$_2$) can be determined by the subsumption relationships in the domain specific ontology. It is the most specific term(s) in the ontology which is subsumed by both Term$_1$ and Term$_2$.
- **Association Contexts.** These are rules concerning the glb of values of contextual coordinates when an association context is involved.
  - glb(Expr$_i$∘Context$_i$, Expr$'_j$) = glb(Expr$_i$, Expr$'_j$)∘Context$_i$
  - glb(Expr$_i$∘Context$_i$, Expr$'_j$∘Context$_j$)
    = glb(Expr$_i$, Expr$'_j$)∘glb (Context$_i$, Context$_j$)

The greatest lower bound of the contexts **glb(Context$_1$, Context$_2$)** can now be defined as:

- glb(Context$_1$, $\langle\rangle$) = Context$_1$...(1)
  The **glb** of a context and an empty context is the context itself.
- glb(glb($\langle(C_i, \text{Expr}_i)\rangle$, Context$_1$),
        Context$_2$) = glb($\langle(C_i, \text{Expr}_i)\rangle$, glb(Context$_1$, Context$_2$))
            if C$_i \notin$ Context$_2$...(2)
  If a contextual coordinate is in only one of the two contexts, then it is present unchanged in the **glb** of the contexts.
- glb(glb($\langle(C'_i, \text{Expr}'_i)\rangle$, Context$_2$), Context$_1$) = glb($\langle(C'_i, \text{Expr}'_i)\rangle$,
        glb(Context$_2$, Context$_1$)) if $C'_i \notin$ Context$_1$...(3)
  If a contextual coordinate is in only one of the two contexts, then it is present unchanged in the **glb** of the contexts.

- $glb(glb(\langle (C_i, Expr_i) \rangle, Context_1), glb(\langle (C_i, Expr_i') \rangle, Context_2))$
  $= glb(\langle (C_i, glb(Expr_i, Expr_i')) \rangle, glb(Context_1, Context_2))\ldots (4)$
  If a contextual coordinate is present in both contexts, then the **glb** of the associated values is computed.

An alternative and equivalent representation of a c-context (expressed using the glb operation) is very useful when there is a need to carry out inferences on the context and information associated with it.

$$Cntxt = \langle (C_1, Expr_1)(C_2, Expr_2)\ldots(C_k, Expr_k) \rangle$$
$$= glb(\langle (C_1, Expr_1) \rangle,$$
$$glb(\langle (C_2, Expr_2) \rangle, \ldots, glb(\langle (C_k, Expr_k) \rangle, \langle \rangle)\ldots))\ldots (5)$$

3.3.2 Inferences Using Contextual Descriptions

We now illustrate how reasoning with contextual descriptions can help enable semantic interoperability across different databases on the GII. The interoperability is achieved *wrt* the query which is represented as a context and known as the query context C_Q. The definition contexts of the various objects in the underlying databases enable the (partial) capture and representation of the information content in the databases. The query context is compared with the definition contexts and this can be easily implemented by using the glb operation defined above.

However, a critical assumption made in the examples illustrated below is that the **query and definition contexts are constructed from a common ontology.** This is an unacceptable assumption from the point of view of scalability in the context of a GIS. One way of enhancing the scalability is to support the use of pre-existing and independently developed (often *ad-hoc*) domain ontologies. This requires mechanisms for comparing terms across ontologies at run-time, which is the subject of discussion of the next section. Issues of language to represent the contextual descriptions and ontologies are discussed later in this section.

Consider the following query:

Get all authors that have written articles related to the topic of abortion

The query context C_Q corresponding to the above query can be written as:

$$C_Q = \langle (author, X)(article, Y \circ \langle (title, \{x|substring(x) = \text{``abortion''}\}) \rangle) \rangle$$

Also, consider the definition context of the database object HAS-PUBLICATION as described earlier.

$C_{def}(\text{HAS-PUBLICATION})$
$= \langle (author, EmplConcept \circ \langle (affiliation, \{research\}) \rangle)$
$(article, PublConcept) \rangle$

The greatest lower bound of C_Q and $C_{def}(\text{HAS-PUBLICATION})$ can be computed as follows and is illustrated in Figure 2.

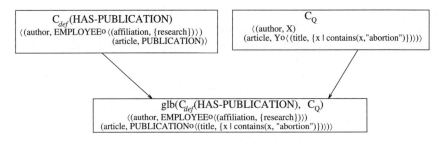

Figure 2.   Comparison of contextual descriptions: incorporating a constraint from the query.

glb(C_Q, C_{def}(HAS-PUBLICATION))
= glb(glb($\langle$(article, PUBLICATION)$\rangle$, Context$_{1,2}$),
             glb($\langle$(article, Y∘$\langle$(title, {x|substring(x) = "abortion"})$\rangle$)$\rangle$,
                                                                       Context$_{2,2}$))   ... (5)
where Context$_{1,2}$ = $\langle$(author, EMPLOYEE∘$\langle$(affiliation, {research})$\rangle$)$\rangle$
and Context$_{2,2}$ = $\langle$(author, X)$\rangle$
= glb($\langle$(article, glb(PUBLICATION, X∘$\langle$
             (title, {x|substring(x) = "abortion"})$\rangle$)$\rangle$),
                                              glb(Context$_{1,2}$, Context$_{2,2}$))   ... (4)
= glb($\langle$(article, glb(PUBLICATION, X)∘$\langle$
             (title, {x|substring(x) = "abortion"})$\rangle$)$\rangle$,
         $\langle$(author, glb(EMPLOYEE,Y)∘$\langle$(affiliation, {research})$\rangle$)$\rangle$)
                                                          ... (association contexts)
= $\langle$(article, PUBLICATION∘$\langle$(title, {x|substring(x) = "abortion"})$\rangle$)
         (author, EMPLOYEE∘$\langle$(affiliation, {research})$\rangle$)$\rangle$
                                              ... (glb of variable and expression)

This example illustrates how constraints in a query can be applied to information in a database to determine the relevant answers. The constraint in the query, requiring the article titles to contain the word "abortion", is incorporated in the contextual descriptions describing the information content of the database and propagated to the object PUBLICATION. The modified contextual description thus characterizes only those instances of the object PUBLICATION that contain the word "abortion" in their titles. It also results in identifying authors as those employees affiliated as researchers to the organization.

Another interesting use of contextual descriptions is to rule out the possibility of a database having information relevant to a query. Suppose we are interested in all authors having a salary > \$200 000. Suppose all the faculty members in the university database are represented as having a salary ≤ \$150 000. Consider the following contextual descriptions.

C_{def} (EMPLOYEE) = $\langle$(salary, {x|x ≤ \$150 000})$\rangle$
C_Q = $\langle$(author, X)(salary, {x|x > \$200 000})$\rangle$

$\text{glb}(C_{def}(\text{EMPLOYEE}), C_Q) \Rightarrow \text{inconsistent}(x \leq \$150\,000, x > \$200\,000)$
$\Rightarrow$ The database is not relevant for the query Q.

3.4 Mapping Contextual Descriptions to the Database Schema

As discussed earlier, the contextual descriptions serve to abstract out the underlying representational details and capture the information content. However once the relevant high-level contextual descriptions have been identified, there is a need to retrieve the relevant data and display it to the user. In Kashyap and Sheth (1996), we propose a uniform formalism used to map contextual descriptions to underlying data. Work on mapping intensional descriptions to SQL queries is reported in Borgida and Brachman (1993). Collet *et al.* (1991) have used articulation axioms to relate object classes in databases to concepts in the Cyc ontology. Our approach is similar to the above but we have also defined an algebra in Kashyap and Sheth (1995) to keep track of the changes in the mappings when the associated contextual descriptions change.

Each information system exports a global object O_G corresponding to the objects O it manages to the GIS. The objects O_G are obtained by applying the constraints in the definition context $C_{def}(O)$ to the object O. The user sees only the exported objects. The contextual coordinates C_i of the $C_{def}(O)$ act as the attributes of O_G. The exported objects O_G are associated with the objects and types defined in the database. This association might be implemented in different ways by various component systems. We use schema correspondences defined as follows to express these associations (Figure 3):

$\text{schCor}(O_G, O) = \langle O_G, \{C_i | C_i \in C_{def}(O)\}, O, \text{attr}(O), M \rangle$

- O_G is the exported GIS object of an object O or type T defined in the database.

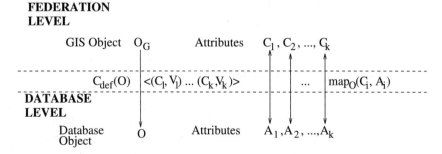

Figure 3.   Schema correspondences: mapping contextual expressions to underlying data.

- The attributes of the object O_G are the contextual coordinates of the definition context $C_{def}(O)$.
- The mapping operation **map$_O$(C$_i$,A$_i$)** stores the association between contextual coordinate C_i and attribute A_i of object O whenever there exists one.
- The mapping M between O_G and O can be evaluated using the projection rules discussed below.

3.4.1 Projection Rules for Mapping c-contexts to Database Objects

We now briefly describe a set of *projection rules* that help map a contextual expression to underlying database objects. A detailed and formal specification of the rules is presented in Kashyap and Sheth (1996).

- **Rule 1.** The *empty context rule* deals with the case when the definition context of a database object is empty, i.e., there are no extra constraints imposed on the object when it is exported to the GII.
- **Rule 2.** The *simple sets rule* deals with the case when the definition context has simple sets of terms from the ontology associated with each contextual coordinate. The constraints applied are of the form $\langle(\mathsf{C}_i, \mathsf{S}_i)\rangle$, where C_i is a contextual coordinate and S_i is a simple set of terms from the ontology corresponding to datavalues in the database. Also each contextual coordinate is associated with an attribute of the given object in the database. This is a special case of *Rule 3*.
- **Rule 3.** The *simple constraint rule* specifies the application of one constraint in the associated c-context to the underlying database objects. The constraint applied is of the form $\langle(\mathsf{C}_i, \mathsf{Expr}_i)\rangle$, where C_i is a contextual coordinate and Expr$_i$ is the value of the contextual coordinate. Thus the constraints in a c-context can be iteratively and simple constraint rule specifies *one iteration*. This rule handles the case where Expr$_i$ is a set of symbols in the ontology corresponding to data values in the database. The contextual coordinate C_i might be associated with:
  - An attribute A_j of the database object O whose definition context is defined by the given c-context.
  - An attribute A_k of another database object O'. In this case a join expression is needed to get a mapping from the contextual coordinate C_i to the attribute A_k.
- **Rule 4.** The *context conditioning rule* deals with the case where a database object is associated with a **conditioning context** other than its own definition context. This happens in cases where there is a query context seeking information related to the database object or when a database object is associated with another database object *wrt* an **association context**. This involves computing the greatest lower bound of the definition context and the conditioning context and may involve inferences *wrt* the domain specific ontology. It might invoke *Rule 3* for iteratively applying the various constraints.

- **Rule 5.** This rule deals with a special case of *Rule 3* where the value of contextual coordinate may either be a term or a term associated with a c-context constructed from terms in the ontology. This is the case where the definition context of an object O makes explicit an association between the different database objects corresponding to the ontological terms.

We now discuss two examples which illustrate how extra information may be represented using contextual expressions.

3.4.2 Representing Relationships Between Objects

We illustrate a case where the definition context of the object HAS-PUBLICATION captures its relationships with another database object EMPLOYEE in an intensional manner. These relationships are *not stored* in the database and mapping the contextual description results in *extra information* being associated with the GIS object HAS-PUBLICATION$_G$. A naive user will ordinarily not be aware of this relationship. The detailed mapping of this relationship is computed by using the projection rules described in the previous section. The detailed computation is illustrated in (Kashyap and Sheth, 1996).

Example. Consider the objects EMPLOYEE, PUBLICATION and HAS-PUBLICATION defined earlier. The definition context of HAS-PUBLICATION as defined earlier is:

C_{def}(HAS-PUBLICATION)
= ⟨(author,EMPLOYEE∘⟨(affiliation, {research})⟩))
  (article, PUBLICATION)⟩

This represents a semantic relationship between the objects which states that:

Only employees affiliated as researchers have publications and they are stored in the object PUBLICATION

This relationship is reflected in the HAS-PUBLICATION object when it is exported to the GII. The instances of HAS-PUBLICATION that are exported are given by the following SQL-like expression:

HAS-PUBLICATION$_G$ = Join((SS# = SS#), Select(Affiliation ∈ {research}, EMPLOYEE), Join((Id = Id), PUBLICATION,HAS-PUBLICATION))

Thus only those instances are exported to the GII that satisfy the constraints specified in the contextual descriptions. The user does not have to keep track or know the relationships between the various objects in the database.

3.4.3 Using Terminological Relationships in Ontology to Represent Extra Information

In this section, we illustrate an example in which terminological relationships obtained from an ontology are used to represent *extra information.* In the example illustrated below, the contextual coordinate *researchInfo* is a composition of two contextual coordinates (*researchArea* and *journalTitle*) and is obtained from the ontology of the domain. This is then used to correlate information between the objects PUBLICATION and JOURNAL. However, the contextual coordinate researchArea has not been modelled for the object PUBLICATION. Thus, this results in *extra information* about the relevant journals and research areas being associated with the object PUBLICATION, even though no information about research areas is modelled for PUBLICATION.

Example. Consider a database containing the following objects:

PUBLICATION(Id, Title, Journal), (as defined earlier)   where
C_{def}(PUBLICATION)
= ⟨(researchInfo,JOURNAL∘((researchArea,Deptypes)
                                    (journalTitle,JournalTypes)))⟩
JOURNAL(Title, Area), where C_{def}(JOURNAL) = ⟨⟩

The mapping expression is given as follows (see (Kashyap and Sheth 1996) for details):

PUBLICATION$_G$
= Join((researchArea = Area) ∧ (Title = Journal), PUBLICATION,
     Select((Area ∈ Deptypes) ∧ (Title ∈ JournalTypes), JOURNAL))

- Only journals belonging to the research areas corresponding to the departments are selected:

  (Select((Area ∈ Deptypes) ∧ (Title ∈ JournalTypes), JOURNAL))

- The join condition (Title = Journal) ensures that only those articles which are from the research areas corresponding to the departments are exported to the GIS:

  (Join((researchArea = Area) ∧ (Title = Journal), PUBLICATION, Select(...)))

- This is achieved even though the attribute Area is not modelled for PUBLICATION. Thus there is extra information in terms of association of Deptypes with PUBLICATION through the join condition.

3.5 Issues of Language and Ontology in Context Representation

In this section we discuss the issues of a language in which the explicit context representation discussed in Section 3.2 can be best expressed. Besides, as discussed earlier, we use terms from domain-specific ontologies as vocabulary to characterize domain-specific information. We also discuss in this section issues of ontology, i.e. the vocabulary used by the language to represent the contexts.

3.5.1 Language for Context Representation

In Section 3.2 we have represented context as a collection of contextual coordinates and their values. The values themselves may have contexts associated with them. In this section, we enumerate the properties desired of a language to express the context representation.

- The language should be declarative in nature as the context will typically be used to express constraints on objects in an intensional manner. Besides, the declarative nature of the language will make it easier to perform inferences on the context.
- The language should be able to express the context as a collection of contextual coordinates, each describing a specific aspect of information present in the database or requested by a query.
- The language should have primitives (for determining the subtype of two types, pattern matching etc.) in the model world, which might be useful in comparing and manipulating context representations.
- The language should have primitives to perform navigation in the ontology to identify the abstractions related to the ontological objects in the query context or the definition contexts of objects in the databases.

3.5.2 The Ontology Problem

The choice of the contextual coordinates (C_is) and the values assigned to them (V_is) is very important in constructing the contexts. There should be *ontological commitments* that imply agreements about the ontological objects used between the users and the information system designers. In our case this corresponds to an agreement on the terms and the values used for the contextual coordinates by both a user in formulating the query context, and a database administrator for formulating the definition and association contexts. In the example in Section 3.2, we defined C_{def}(EMPLOYEE) by making use of symbols like **employer, affiliation** from the ontology for contextual coordinates, and **research, teaching**, etc. for the values of the contextual coordinates.

We assume that each database has available to it an ontology corresponding to a specific domain. The definition and association contexts of the objects take their terms and values from this ontology. However in designing the definition contexts and the query context, the issues of combining the various ontologies arise. We now enumerate various approaches one might take in building ontologies for a GIS comprising numerous information sources. Other than the ontological commitment, a critical issue in designing ontologies is the **scalability** of the ontology as more information sources enter the federation. Two approaches are discussed next.

The Common Ontology Approach

One approach has been to build an extensive global ontology. A notable example of global ontology is Cyc (Lenat and Guha, 1990) consisting of

around 30 000 objects. In Cyc, the mapping between each individual information resource and global ontology is accomplished by a set of *articulation
axioms* which are used to map the entities of an information resource to the
concepts (such as frames and slots) in Cyc's existing ontology (Collet *et al.*,
1991).

    Another approach has been to exploit the semantics of a single
problem domain (e.g., transportation planning) (Arens *et al.* 1993). The
domain model is a declarative description of the objects and activities
possible in the application domain as viewed by a typical user. The user
formulates queries using terms from the application domain.

Reuse of Existing Ontologies/Classifications

We expect that there will be numerous information systems participating
in the GIS. In this context, it is unrealistic to expect any one existing
ontology or classification to suffice. We believe that the reuse of various
existing classifications such as ISBN classification for publications, botan-
ical classification for plants is a very attractive alternative. An example of
such a classification is illustrated in Figure 4. These ontologies can then
be combined in different ways and made available to the GIS. However

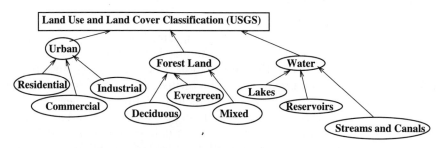

A classification using a generalization hierarchy

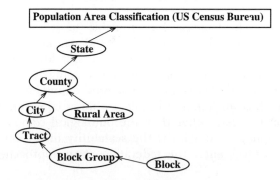

A classification using an aggregation hierarchy

Figure 4. Examples of generalization and aggregation hierarchies for ontology
construction.

these existing classifications/ontologies have been designed independently and with different perspectives on the real world. Hence reuse of existing ontologies gives rise to issues of combining them in a consistent manner:

- A critical issue in combining the various ontologies is determining the overlap between them. One possibility is to define the "intersection" and "mutual exclusion" points between the various ontologies (Wiederhold 1994).
- Another approach has been adopted in McLeod and Si (1995). The types determined to be similar by a sharing advisor are classified into a collection called *concept*. A concept hierarchy is thus generated based on the superconcept−subconcept relationship. These types may be from different databases and their similarity or dissimilarity is based on heuristics with user input as required.

4 SEMANTIC INTEROPERABILITY USING TERMINOLOGICAL RELATIONSHIPS

In the previous section we illustrated with examples how terms from domain-specific ontologies can be used to construct c-contexts that capture/describe the information content of the underlying data repositories. We also discussed with the examples of how definitions of terms based on other terms within an ontology may be used to determine relevance of the underlying data to a query without actual data access. As regards to describing the information content in the underlying data, we have illustrated how c-contexts with the help of terminological relationships in an ontology can help represent extra information not captured in the database schema.

Domain-specific ontologies are thus an essential component of our approach to tackle the semantic heterogeneity and information overload problem on the GII. An alternative use of domain-specific ontologies for sharing information is presented in Kahng and McLeod (this volume). Before we proceed further, an interesting distinction must be made between the ontologies themselves and the c-contexts constructed by using terms from the ontologies.

- Ontologies are typically designed to capture knowledge about a significant domain of information and can be used to describe information in a large number of data repositories. However, **data-sensitive** constraints are typically not represented in an ontology. Suppose a **medical ontology** has a concept called **Doctor** defined within it. A large number of databases in the Houston area may contain information only about doctors in Houston. This can be overcome suitably defining a c-context and imposing constraints on the concept **Doctor** to define another concept called **HoustonDoctor**. Thus c-contexts are more **data sensitive** than ontologies.

- C-contexts can also be more **application sensitive** than ontologies. Suppose a user wants to request information on the GII that involves concepts represented in different ontologies and also obeys constraints not defined in any ontology. A user can construct a c-context which could possibly map into multiple ontologies before being mapped to the underlying data.

The issue of making c-contexts *application sensitive* may involve the ability to interoperate across multiple ontologies. In the previous section, we made an implicit assumption of a common ontology behind the construction of the contextual expressions which is a very unacceptable assumption. In this section we discuss the issues involved when c-contexts may be translated to terms from different domain-specific ontologies. We discuss how **semantic interoperability** may be achieved by interoperation across these domain-specific ontologies.

We first discuss an architecture for interontology interoperation and identify the components for mapping the c-contexts to the underlying data and also for translating them across various ontologies. In the previous section we have illustrated how contextual expressions may be represented using DL expressions and how various operations on the c-contexts have corresponding DL operations. In this section we shall use DL expressions to represent c-contexts and discuss, with the help of examples, approaches to achieve interontology interoperation using terminological relationships like **synonyms, hyponyms** and **hypernyms**. We shall conclude by identifying other different types of terminological relationships that might be used to perform interontology interoperation.

4.1 An Architecture for Interontology Interoperation

We now discuss our work in the OBSERVER[2] (Mena *et al.*, 1996a,b) system and describe its architecture for enabling interoperation across various independent pre-existing ontologies based on terminological relationships between terms in different ontologies.

Query processor. This component takes as input a DL expression corresponding to a query context C_Q using terms from a chosen *user ontology*. It then navigates other component ontologies of the GIS and translates terms in the user query into the component ontologies using the terminological relationships stored and managed by the *interontology relationships manager (IRM)*. The user query may be either partially or completely translated at a given ontology. The query processor is responsible for combining the partial translations from different ontologies into a full translation in which all constraints in the user query are translated and the semantics of the query are preserved. The query

---

[2]*Ontology-Based System Enhanced with Relationships for Vocabulary hEterogeneity Resolution*

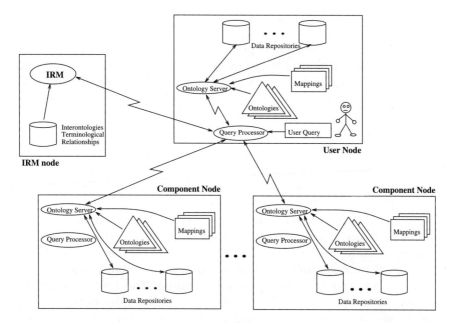

Figure 5. OBSERVER: an architecture to support interoperation across ontologies.

processor may also convert partial translations into lossy full translations by using similar but non-equivalent terms and compute the resulting loss of information.

Ontology server. The ontology server provides information about ontologies to the query processor. It provides the definitions of the terms in the ontology and helps perform ontological inferences on the c-contexts based on the complex relationships between various terms. The ontology server also retrieves data underlying the terms in the ontology. It is responsible for evaluating the mappings of the c-contexts to the underlying data and retrieving the data that satisfies the constraints in the user query.

Interontology relationships manager (IRM). Terminological relationships relating the terms in various ontologies are represented in a declarative manner in an independent repository. At present the terminological relationships that we deal with in the OBSERVER system are synonyms, hyponyms and hypernyms. The repository also includes information about transformer functions which can transform values (or role-fillers) from a domain in one ontology to another.

Ontologies. Each ontology is a set of terms of interest in a particular information domain, expressed using DLs in our work. They are organized as a lattice and may be considered as semantically rich metadata capturing the information content of the underlying data repositories. The various ontologies used in OBSERVER are illustrated in Appendix B.

4.1.1 Scalability and the IRM

As discussed earlier, relationships between terms across ontologies that capture the overlapping of domains are stored in a repository managed by the IRM. The IRM is the critical component which supports ontology-based interoperation. It enhances the **scalability** of the query processing strategy because:

• There is no longer a need for designing a common global ontology containing all the relevant terms in the GIS. A lot of time and energy for the development of an ontology specific for your needs can be saved as "similar" ontologies are available and can be suitably adapted by defining the appropriate terminological relationships.

• An interesting point to be noted is that only the "minimal" relationships between terms in two ontologies need to be stored. For example, if a concept A subsumes another concept B in a particular ontology and a concept C from another ontology is a hypernym of both A and B, then only one of these relationships need be stored. This leads to much less information that needs to be stored when compared to all the concepts in the global ontology. We do not need to store other ontological information related to the definitions of concepts and the domain and ranges of roles in the IRM. The main assumption behind the IRM is that **the number of relationships between terms across ontologies is an order of magnitude smaller than the number of all the terms relevant to the system.**

• The extensions of semantically similar terms in different ontologies can be combined in an appropriate manner based on the terminological relationship between them. This is in contrast to the case of the global ontology where complex mappings corresponding to each term would need to be computed at all the repositories.

4.2 Use of Synonyms for Interontology Interoperation in OBSERVER

We now discuss a query processing approach that involves the reuse of pre-existing ontologies and the use of synonyms between terms in different ontologies for interoperation. The query processor performs the following important steps:

1. Translation of terms in the query into terms in each component ontology. The query processor obtains information from the IRM (discussed in Section 4.1) and the ontology server.

2. Combining the partial translations in such a way that the semantics of the user query is preserved.

3. Accessing the ontology server to obtain the data under the component ontology that satisfy the translated query. This basically amounts to the

evaluation of the mappings of the contextual expressions to the underlying database schema and has been discussed in the previous section.
4. Correlation of the objects retrieved from the various data reposit-
ories/ontologies.

We illustrate steps 1, 2 and 4 using an example in Mena *et al.* (1996b).
A detailed discussion of the query processing strategy is described in the
same paper. Consider the following query:

'Get the titles, authors, documents and the number of pages of doctoral theses
dealing with "metadata" and that have been published at least once.'

Let us assume that there are four ontologies (described in detail in Mena
et al. (1996b)) as discussed below:

- **Stanford-II.** This ontology is a subset of the Bibliographic Data ontology
  (Gruber, 1994) developed as a part of the ARPA Knowledge Sharing
  Effort (http://www-ksl.stanford.edu/knowledge-sharing). It corresponds
  to the sub-tree under the concept "reference" of the Bibliographic Data
  ontology and is illustrated in Appendix B (Figure B4).
- **Stanford-I.** This ontology is also a subset of the Bibliographic Data
  ontology and corresponds to the rest of the ontology. It is illustrated
  in Appendix B (Figure B3).
- **WN.** This ontology was built by reusing a part of the WordNet 1.5
  ontology (Miller, 1995). The concepts in the WN ontology are a subset
  of terms in the hyponym tree of the noun "print-media". It is illustrated
  in Appendix B (Figure B2).
- **LSDIS.** This ontology is a local "home-grown" ontology which represents
  our view of our Lab's publications and is illustrated in Appendix B
  (Figure B1).

The query can be constructed from the concepts in Stanford-II
(denoted as the user ontology) and represented in a DL as follows:

[title author document pages] for (**AND** doctoral-thesis-ref (**FILLS** keywords
"metadata") (**ATLEAST** 1 publisher))

We now enumerate the translations of the query into the ontologies
discussed above and identify the translated and non-translated parts:

- **Stanford-II.** The query always represents a full translation into the user
  ontology.
- **Stanford-I.** There is a **partial translation** of the query at this ontology.

   Translated Part [title author NULL number-of-pages] for
                        (**AND** doctoral-thesis (**ATLEAST** 1 publisher))
   Non-translated Part (**FILLS** keywords "metadata")

- **WN.** Terms in the query are substituted by their definitions in the ontology from which they are chosen (Stanford-II) to obtain a complete translation into WN.

doctoral-thesis-ref ≡ (**AND** thesis-ref (**FILLS** type-of-work "doctoral"))
thesis-ref ≡ (**AND** publication-ref (**FILLS** type-of-work "thesis"))
Translated Part [name creator NULL pages] for (**AND** print-media
        (**FILLS** content "thesis" "doctoral") (**ATLEAST** 1 publisher)
        (**FILLS** general-topics "metadata"))

- **LSDIS.** There is a **partial translation** at this ontology where the value of the role-filler of the role keywords is transformed by the transformer function between the roles keywords (Stanford-II) and subject (LSDIS).

Translated Part [title authors location-document NULL] for
        (**AND** publications (**FILLS** type "doctoral" "thesis")
        (**FILLS** subject "METADATA"))
Non-translated Part (**ATLEAST** 1 publisher)

Consider the partial translations of the user query at the ontologies Stanford-I and LSDIS. As the intersection of the non-translated parts of the partial translations into Stanford-I and LSDIS is empty, then the intersection of both partial answers must satisfy all the constraints in the query. Intuitively:

- From Stanford-I, doctoral theses about any subject that have been published at least once will be retrieved.
- From LSDIS, documents about metadata that may not have been published will be retrieved.
- The intersection of the above will be those documents classified as doctoral theses about metadata and have been published at least once, which is exactly the user query.

After obtaining the corresponding data for each ontology involved in the user query, that data must be combined to give an answer to the user. For each answer (represented as a relation), the query processor will transform the values in the format of the user ontology by invoking the appropriate transformer functions obtained from the IRM. After this initial step, the different partial answers can be correlated since all of them are expressed in the language of the user ontology. The correlation plan corresponding to the translations illustrated above is:

User_Query_Objects = Objects('[self title author document pages] for
        (**AND** doctoral-thesis-ref (**FILLS** keywords "metadata")
        (**ATLEAST** 1 publisher))')
Stanford-II_Objects = Objects('[self title author document pages] for
        (**AND** doctoral-thesis-ref (**FILLS** keywords "metadata")
        (**ATLEAST** 1 publisher))', Stanford-II)

Stanford-I_Objects = Objects('[self title author NULL number-of-pages] for(**AND** doctoral-thesis (**ATLEAST** 1 publisher))', Stanford-I)

WN_Objects = Objects('[self name creator NULL pages] for (**AND** print-media (**FILLS** content "thesis" content "doctoral") (**FILLS** general-topics "metadata"))', WN)

LSDIS_Objects = Objects('[self title authors location-document NULL] for (**AND** publications (**FILLS** type "doctoral" "thesis") (**FILLS** subject "METADATA")', LSDIS))

Based on the combination of partial translations the data retrieved from the repositories underlying the ontologies can be combined as follows:

User_Query_Objects = Stanford-II_Objects ∪ WN_Objects ∪ [Stanford-I_Objects ∩ LSDIS_Objects]

4.3 Using Hyponyms and Hypernyms for Interontology Interoperation

Synonym relationships between terms in independent developed ontologies are very infrequent. On the contrary, and real examples confirm it, hierarchical relationships like hyponyms and hypernyms are found more frequently. The substitution of a term by its hypernyms or hyponyms changes the semantics of the query. We try to translate the non-translated terms in the user ontology into terms (which are not its synonyms) in a target component ontology.

We substitute a non-translated term by the intersection of its immediate parents or the union of its immediate children. The loss of information is measured in both cases and translation with less loss of information is chosen. This method is applied recursively until a full translation of the non-translated term is obtained. Using hyponym and hypernym relationships as described above can result in several possible translations of a non-translated term into a target ontology. Very simple intuitive measures depending on the extensions of the terms in the underlying ontologies may help in choosing the translations and minimizing the loss of information.

In order to obtain the immediate parents and children of a term in the target ontology, two different kinds of relationships related to the conflicting term must be used:

1. Synonyms, hyponyms and hypernyms between terms in the user and target ontology.
2. Synonyms, hyponyms and hypernyms in the user ontology.

The first three types of relationships are stored in the IRM repository. The second are relationships between terms in the same ontology; synonyms are equivalent terms, hyponyms are those terms subsumed by

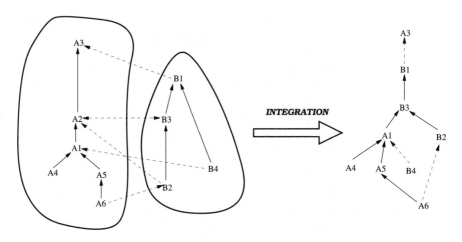

Figure 6.   Integrating two ontologies.

the non-translated term and hypernyms are those terms that subsume the conflicting term.

The task of getting the immediate parents/children is not easy to perform. To obtain the parents/children within the user ontology, the corresponding functions (e.g., subsumption) of the DL systems can be used. But we must combine that answer with the immediate parents/children in the target ontology. Taking into account that some relationships stored in the IRM can be redundant (they were independently defined by different ontologies administrators) such a task can be quite difficult. We would need a DL system dealing with "distributed" ontologies.

In Figure 6, we show two ontologies with some relationships between them (arrows are hyponyms relationships, double arrows are synonyms, and dashed lines are interontology relationships) and with the integrated ontology (synonyms are grouped into one term) on the right. We can see that obtaining the immediate parents is not evident; for instance to get the immediate parents of B4 we must deduce that A1 is a child of B1. There are also redundant relationships like the one between A2 and B2.

To work with the above relationships in a homogeneous way, an approach is to integrate the user and the target ontologies, and to use the deductive power of the DL system to obtain the immediate parents/children of a term in the target ontology (Blanco *et al.*, 1994b). The properties between terms in the different ontologies are exactly the interontology relationships stored in the IRM, so no intervention of the user is needed. Although some of the previous relationships can be redundant, the DL system will classify the terms in the right place in the ontology. To know if the resulting terms of the integrated ontology are **primitive** or **defined** (depending on A and B) the rules described in (Blanco *et al.*, (1994a) can be used.

4.4 Using Other Relationships for Interontology Interoperation

In the previous sections we discussed an approach for interontology interoperation using synonym relationships in the OBSERVER system and extensions for using hyponyms and hypernyms. Different types of terminological relationships have been suggested for capturing overlaps between ontologies. Hammer and McLeod (1993) have suggested a set of relationship descriptors to capture relationships between terms across different (locally developed) ontologies. A set of terminological relationships has been proposed in Miller (1995). An interesting set of relationships that we are planning to explore in the future are the knowledge transmutation operators defined in Michalski (1993). An interesting relationship that measures overlap between terms in ontologies has been used for dynamic classification and is discussed in Kahng and McLeod (this volume).

5 CONCLUSIONS

We have discussed in this chapter the implications of the exponential growth of the information on the GII on the semantic heterogeneity problem and explored new techniques to enable a solution to the same. Information overload which arises as a consequence of the heterogeneity of the digital data and media types is identified as the first problem. We explored an approach whereby metadata descriptions are used to abstract out the representational details and characterize the information content. An informal classification of the various types of metadata used to handle the wide variety of digital data was presented in Section 2. The amount of information content captured by each is identified and domain-specific metadata are identified as critical to the semantic heterogeneity problem.

We then discussed how approaches dependent on representational or structural components are inadequate and argue the need for representation of contextual expressions in Section 3. We discussed the representation of these expressions using description logics and proposed operations to reason with contextual expressions. We showed how extra information that may not be represented in the database schema may be represented using contextual descriptions. Reasoning with the contextual descriptions also helps determine the *relevance* of information stored in the underlying data. We illustrated how contextual expressions may be constructed from domain-specific ontologies and how terminological relationships between concepts in an ontology enable representation of extra information.

We have recognized the problem of vocabulary sharing as the most critical problem in construction of contextual descriptions. We proposed approaches to tackle the semantic heterogeneity (as opposed to representational heterogeneity) at the metadata/context level in Section 4. An architecture for scalable semantic interoperability across ontologies was proposed.

We illustrated interontology interoperation enabled by utilizing terminological relationships like **synonyms, hypernyms** and **hyponyms**.

We have thus explored various approaches based on metadata, context and ontologies which we believe are important and provide the required capabilities to handle the semantic heterogeneity problem in the context of the GII. This research is a part of the InfoQuilt project within the theme of **Enabling Infocosm** (Kashyap and Sheth, 1994b; Ferguson, 1995) at the Large Scale Distributed Information Systems Laboratory (http://lsdis.cs.uga.edu/) at the University of Georgia. Some of the interesting research topics that are being investigated further in this theme are as follows:

- Use of domain-specific metadata to enable correlation of information across image and structured data. A future extension of this project will be to look into use of metadata standards such as FGDC, OGIS and domain-specific ontologies to describe multimedia data.
- Extending the OBSERVER system to enable support for **hyponyms** and **hypernyms**.
- Measures to characterize the loss of information incurred when a term is replaced by expressions with differing semantics. These measures are being developed and experimented within extended OBSERVER system.
- Providing a metadata-based reference link ⟨A MREF...⟩ as an alternative to the physical reference link ⟨A HREF...⟩. This is being implemented as an extension to HTML on the web (Sheth and Kashyap, 1996). This enables the publisher of an HTML document to specify domain-specific metadata which are then mapped to the underlying multimedia data by the enhanced server. This would enable a higher-level metadata based metastructure over the current web infrastructure.

ACKNOWLEDGEMENTS

OBSERVER is a joint project carried out with Eduardo Mena and Arrantza Illarramendi.

REFERENCES

Achilles, E., Hollunder, B., Laux, A. and Mohren, J. (1991) KRIS: Knowledge Representation and Inference System. Technical Report D-91-14, DFKI Kaiserslautern-Saarbrucken.

Anderson, J. and Stonebraker, M. (1994) Sequoia 2000 metadata schema for satellite images. In *SIGMOD Record, Special Issue on Metadata for Digital Media*, **23**(4).

Arens, Y., Chee, C., Hsu, C. and Knoblock, C. (1993) Retrieving and integrating data from multiple information sources. *International Journal of Intelligent and Cooperative Information systems*, **2**(2).

Berners-Lee, T. *et al.*, (1992) World-Wide Web: the information universe. *Electronic Networking: Research, Applications and Policy*, **1**(2).

Blanco, J.M., Illarramendi, A. and Goñi. A. (1994a) Building a federated database system: an approach using a knowledge based system. *International Journal of Intelligent and Cooperative Information Systems*, **3**(4) 415–455.

Blanco, J., Illarramendi, A., Goñi, A. and Perez, J. (1994b) Using a terminological system to integrate relational databases. In *Information Systems Design and Hyper-media* Cepadues-Editions.

Bohm, K. and Rakow, T. (1994) Metadata for multimedia documents. In *SIGMOD Record, Special Issue on Metadata for Digital Media*, W. Klaus and A. Sheth (eds). **23**(4).

Borgida, A. and Brachman, R. (1993) Loading data into description reasoners. In *Proceedings of 1993 ACM SIGMOD.*

Borgida, A., Brachman, R., McGuinness, D. and Resnick, L. (1989) CLASSIC: a structure data model for objects. In *Proceedings of ACM SIGMOD-89.*

Brachman, R. and Scmolze, J. (1985) An overview of the KL-ONE knowledge representation system. *Cognitive Science*, **9**(2).

Chen, F., Hearst, M., Kupiec, J., Pederson, J. and Wilcox, L. (1994) Metadata for Mixed-Media Access. In *SIGMOD Record, Special Issue on Metadata for Digital Media*, W. Klaus and A. Sheth (eds). **23**(4).

Collet, C., Huhns, M. and Shen, W. (1991) Resource Integration using a Large Knowledge Base in Carnot. *IEEE Computer.*

Dayal, U. and Hwang, H. (1984) View Definition and Generalization for Database Integration of a Multidatabase System. *IEEE Transactions on Software Engineering*, **10**(6).

Deerwester, S., Dumais, S., Furnas, G., Landauer, T. and Hashman, R. (1990) Indexing by Latent Semantic Indexing. *Journal of the American Society for Information Science*, **41**(6).

Fankhauser, P., Kracker, M. and Neuhold, E. (1991) Semantic vs. Structural Resemblance of Classes. In *SIGMOD Record, Special Issue on Semantic Issues in Multi-databases*, A. Sheth (ed). **20**(4).

Ferguson, C. (1995) Into the infocosm. *Computerworld Leadership Series*, **1**(6).

Glavitsch, U., Schauble, P. and Wechsler, M. (1994) Metadata for Integrating Speech Documents in a Text Retrieval System. In *SIGMOD Record, Special Issue on Metadata for Digital Media*, W. Klaus and A. Sheth (eds). **23**(4).

Gruber, T. (1994) Theory BIBLIOGRAPHIC-DATA. http://www-ksl.stanford.edu/ knowledge-sharing/ontologies/html/bibliographic-data/index.html.

Hammer, J. and McLeod, D. (1993) An approach to resolving Semantic Heterogeneity in the Federation of Autonomous, heterogeneous, Database Systems. *International Journal of Intelligent and Cooperative Information Systems.*

Heimbigner, D., McLeod, D. (1985) A federated architecture for Information Systems. *ACM Transactions on Office Information Systems*, **3**(3).

Jain, R. and Hampapuram, A. (1994) Representations of Video Databases. In *SIGMOD Record, Special Issue on Metadata for Digital Media*, W. Klaus and A. Sheth (eds). **23**(4).

Kahle, B. and Medlar, A. (1991) An Information System for Corporate Users: Wide Area Information Servers. *Connexions — The Interoperability Report*, **5**(11).

Kashyap, V. (1997) Information Brokering over Heterogeneous Digital Data: a Metadata-based Approach. PhD Thesis, Department of Computer Science, Rutgers University, October.

Kashyap, V. and Sheth, A. (1994a) Semantics-based Information Brokering. In *Proceedings of the third International Conference on Information and Knowledge Management (CIKM).*

Kashyap, V. and Sheth, A. (1994b) Semantics-based Information Brokering: A step towards realizing the Infocosm. Technical Report DCS-TR-307, Department of Computer Science, Rutgers University.

Kashyap, V. and Sheth, A. (1995) Schematic and Semantic Similarities between Database Objects: A Context-based Approach. Technical Report TR-CS-95-001,

LSDIS Lab, University of Georgia. Available at http://lsdis.cs.uga.edu/~amit/66-context-algebra.ps. (An abridged version appears as Kashyap and Sheth (1996).)

Kashyap, V. and Sheth, A. (1996) Schematic and Semantic Similarities between Database Objects: a Context-based Approach. *The VLDB Journal*, **5**(4), 276–304.

Kashyap, V., Shah, K. and Sheth, A. (1995) Metadata for building the MultiMedia path quilt. In *MultiMedia Database Systems: Issues and Research Directions*, S. Jajodia and V. Subrahmanian (eds). Springer-Verlag.

Kiyoki, Y., Kitagawa, T. and Hayama, T. (1994) A meta-database System for Semantic Image Search by a Mathematical Model of Meaning. In *SIGMOD Record, Special Issue on Metadata for Digital Media*, W. Klaus and A. Sheth (eds). **23**(4).

Klaus, W. and Sheth, A. (1994) Metadata for digital media. *SIGMOD Record, Special Issue on Metadata for Digital Media*, Klaus, W. and A. Sheth (eds), **23**(4).

Larson, J., Navathe, S. and Elmasri, R. (1989) A Theory of Attribute Equivalence in Databases with Application to Schema Integration. *IEEE Transactions on Software Engineering*, **15**(4).

Lenat, D. and Guha, R.V. (1990) *Building Large Knowledge Based Systems: Representation and Inference in the Cyc Project*. Addison-Wesley Publishing Company.

Litwin, W. and Abdellatif, A. (1986) Multidatabase Interoperability. *IEEE Computer*, **19**(12).

MacGregor, R. (1987) A deductive pattern matcher. In *Proceedings AAAI-87*.

McLeod, D. and Si, A. (1995) The Design and Experimental Evaluation of an Information Discovery Mechanism for Networks of Autonomous Database Systems. In *Proceedings of the 11th IEEE Conference on Data Engineering*.

Mena, E., Kashyap, V., Illarramendi, A. and Sheth, A. (1996a) Managing Multiple Information Sources through Ontologies: Relationship between Vocabulary Heterogeneity and Loss of Information. In *Proceedings of the workshop on Knowledge Representation meets Databases in conjunction with European Conference on Artificial Intelligence*.

Mena, E., Kashyap, V., Sheth, A. and Illarramendi, A. (1996b) OBSERVER: an approach for query processing in global information systems based on interoperation across pre-existing ontologies. In *Proceedings of the First IFCIS International Conference on Cooperative Information Systems (Coop IS '96)*.

Michalski, R. (1993) Inferential Theory of Learning as Conceptual Basis for Multistrategy Learning. *Machine Learning*, **11**(2/3).

Miller, G. (1995) WordNet: a lexical database for English. *Communications of the ACM*, **38**(11).

Ordille, J. and Miller, B. (1993) Distributed Active Catalogs and Meta-Data Caching in Descriptive Name Services. In *Proceedings of the 13th International Conference on Distributed Computing Systems*.

Sciore, E., Siegel, M. and Rosenthal, A. (1992) Context Interchange using Meta-Attributes. In *Proceedings of the CIKM*.

Sheth, A. (1991) Federated Database Systems for managing Distributed, Heterogeneous, and Autonomous Databases. In *Tutorial Notes—the 17th VLDB Conference*.

Sheth, A. and Gala, S. (1989) Attribute relationships: an impediment in automating Schema Integration. In *Proceedings of the NSF Workshop on Heterogeneous Databases*.

Sheth, A. and Kashyap, V. (1993) So Far (Schematically), yet So Near (Semantically). In *Proceedings of the IFIP TC2/WG2.6 Conference on Semantics of Interoperable Database Systems, DS-5*, 1992. *IFIP Transactions* A-25, North Holland.

Sheth, A. and Kashyap, V. (1996) Media-independent Correlation of Information. What? How? In *Proceedings of the First IEEE Metadata Conference*. http://lsdis.cs.uga.edu/~kashyap/IEEE paper.

Sheth, A. and Larson, J. (1990) Federated Database Systems for managing Distributed, Heterogeneous and Autonomous Databases. *ACM Computing Surveys*, **22**(3).

Shklar, L., Sheth, A., Kashyap, V. and Shah, K. (1995) Infoharness: Use of Auto-
    matically Generated Metadata for Search and Retrieval of Heterogeneous Infor-
    mation. In *Proceedings of CAiSE '95*. Lecture Notes in Computer Science 932,
    Springer-Verlag.
Shoens, K., Luniewski, A., Schwartz, P., Stamos, J. and Thomas, J. (1993) The
    Rufus System: Information Organization for Semi-Structured Data. In
    Proceedings of the 19th VLDB Conference.
Shoham, Y. (1991) Varieties of Context.
von Luck, K., Nebel, B., Peltason, C. and Schmiedel, A. (1987) The anatomy of the
    BACK system. Technical Report KIT Report 41, Technical University of Berlin,
    Berlin.
Wiederhold, G. (1994) Interoperation, Mediation and Ontologies. In *FGCS Work-
    shop on Heterogeneous Cooperative Knowledge-Bases*.

A REPRESENTING C-CONTEXTS USING A DL

In the following we assume the representation of a c-context (Section 3.2)
as follows:

c-context $= \langle (C_1, \text{Expr}_1) \ldots (C_k, \text{Expr}_k) \rangle$

As discussed earlier, the terms used to construct the c-context are used from
domain specific ontologies. The terms C_i denoting the contextual coordinates are represented using **roles** in a DL. The values of the contextual
coordinates are expressions which might consist of terms from the ontologies associated with c-contexts. Both the c-contexts and the values of the
contextual are represented using **concept descriptions** in a DL.

A.1 An Informal Explanation of DL Operators

We now describe informally the DL operators which the c-contexts may
map to. It may be noted that some DL systems may not support all the
operators listed below:

• **Anything.** This is a special concept used in a DL to denote the universal
  concept, i.e., all concepts are subsumed by Anything and all instances are
  members of Anything.
• **Nothing.** This is a special concept used in a DL to denote the empty
  concept, i.e., it is subsumed by all concepts and no instance is a member
  of Nothing.
• **Primitive concepts.** These are primitive concepts which have been predefined in the system and have only necessary conditions for their existence.
• **(AND ⟨concept⟩⟨concept⟩).** This operator delimits the set of all instances
  in the intersection of the sub-concepts.
• **(OR ⟨concept⟩⟨concept⟩).** This operator delimits the set of all instances
  in the union of the sub-concepts.
• **(ALL ⟨role⟩⟨concept⟩).** This operator delimits all instances that have fillers
  for ⟨role⟩ that belong to ⟨concept⟩.

- **(ONE-OF ⟨set⟩).** This operator enumerates the instances of a concept as a set.
- **(SAME-AS ⟨role-chain⟩⟨role-chain⟩).** This operator describes instances that are restricted to have the same filler for the two chains of roles given to it as arguments.
- **(FILLS ⟨role⟩⟨value⟩).** This operator is used to characterize instances having one of their fillers for ⟨role⟩ as ⟨value⟩.
- **(ATLEAST k ⟨role⟩).** This operator is used to characterize instances having at least k values for ⟨role⟩.
- **(ATMOST k ⟨role⟩).** This operator is used to characterize instances having at most k values for ⟨role⟩.

A.2 The DL Expressions Corresponding to c-contexts

Let the c-context be the definition context of an object O in the database.

$$C_{def}(O) = \langle (C_1, \text{Expr}_1) \ldots (C_k, \text{Expr}_k) \rangle$$
$$\Rightarrow (\textbf{AND } \text{term}(O)(\textbf{ALL } C_1 \text{Expr}_1) \ldots (\textbf{ALL} C_1 \text{Expr}_1))$$

The various possibilities corresponding to Expr_i are:

- **Variable** $\langle (C_i, X) \rangle \Rightarrow [C_i]$ for **Anything**.

  $\langle (C_i, X)(C_j, X) \rangle \Rightarrow [C_i]$for(**SAME-AS** $C_i C_j$)

  It should be noted here that since variables are used only for the specific purpose of retrieval, they are not found at deeper levels of nesting in c-context expression. Hence $[C_i]$ for **DL-expression** is not used as a concept-forming expression.
- **Sets.** $C_{def}(O) = \langle (C_i, \{a_1, \ldots, a_n\}) \rangle \Rightarrow$
  (**AND** term(O) (**ALL** C_i (**ONE-OF** $a_1 \ldots a_n$)))
- **Terms.** $C_{def}(O) = \langle (C_i, \text{term}(O_1)) \rangle \Rightarrow (\textbf{AND } \text{term}(O) (\textbf{ALL } C_1 \text{term}(O_1)))$
- **Term ∘ c-context.** $C_{def}(O) = \langle (C_i \text{ term}(O_i) \circ \text{c-context}) \rangle$
  $\Rightarrow (\textbf{AND } \text{term}(O) (\textbf{ALL } C_i (\textbf{AND } \text{term } (O_i)\text{Expr(c-context)})))$
  where Expr(c-context) denotes the DL expression corresponding to the c-context. c-context in this case is an association context and an association is expressed using the **AND** operator in a DL.
- **Variable ∘ c-context** $\langle (C_i, X \circ \text{c-context}) \rangle$
  $\Rightarrow [C_i]$ for (**ALL** C_i Expr(c-context))

A.3 Using the AND operation in DLs for glb of c-contexts

We now describe how the **AND** operator in DLs corresponds to the **glb** of two contexts. The operations for glb of two Expr_i's are as follows:

- **Variable:** $\text{glb}(\text{Expr}_i, X) = \text{Expr}_i \Rightarrow (\textbf{AND } \text{Expr}_i \textbf{ Anything}) = \text{Expr}_i$.
- **Sets:** $\text{glb}(S_1, S_2) = S_1 \cap S_2$
  $\Rightarrow (\textbf{AND } (\textbf{ONE-OF}\{ii\})(\textbf{ONE-OF } \{jj\})) = (\textbf{ONE-OF } \{ii\} \cap \{jj\})$

- **Terms:** $\text{glb}(\text{Term}_1, \text{Term}_2) = (\textbf{AND}\ \text{Term}_1\ \text{Term}_2)$
  The **AND** operator defines a new concept which can be named and used.
- **Association Contexts:** The rules concerning the glb values of the contextual coordinates when an association context is involved can be expressed in a DL as follows:

  - $\text{glb}(A_1 \circ \text{Cntxt}_1, A_2) = \text{glb}(A_1, A_2) \circ \text{Cntxt}_1$
    $\Rightarrow (\textbf{AND}\ (\textbf{AND}\ A_1 \text{Expr}(\text{Cntxt}_1))\ A_2))$
    $= (\textbf{AND}\ (\textbf{AND}\ A_1 A_2)\text{Expr}(\text{Cntxt}_1))$
  - $\text{glb}(A_1 \circ \text{Cntxt}_1, A_2 \circ \text{Cntxt}_2) = \text{glb}(A_1, A_2) \circ \text{glb}(\text{Cntxt}_1, \text{Cntxt}_2)$
    $\Rightarrow (\textbf{AND}\ (\textbf{AND}\ A_1 \text{Expr}(\text{Cntxt}_1))\ (\textbf{AND} A_j\ \text{Expr}(\text{Cntxt}_2)))$
    $= (\textbf{AND}\ (\textbf{AND}\ A_1 A_2)(\textbf{AND}\ \text{Expr}(\text{Cntxt}_1)\ \text{Expr}(\text{Cntxt}_2)))$

The greatest lower bound of the contexts **glb(Cntxt₁, Cntxt₂)** can now be defined as:

- $\text{glb}(\text{Cntxt}_1, \langle\rangle) = \text{Cntxt}_1$
  $\Rightarrow (\textbf{AND}\ \text{Expr}(\text{Cntxt}_1)\ (\textbf{AND}\ ())) = (\textbf{AND}\ \text{Expr}(\text{Cntxt}_1)\ \text{ANYTHING})$
  $= \text{Expr}(\text{Cntxt}_1)$
- $\text{glb}(\text{glb}(\langle(C_{1,i}, \text{Expr}_{1,i})\rangle, \text{Cntxt}_1), \text{Cntxt}_2)$
  $= \text{glb}(\langle(C_{1,i}, \text{Expr}_{1,i})\rangle, \text{glb}(\text{Cntxt}_1, \text{Cntxt}_2))$ if $C_{1,i} \notin \text{Cntxt}_2$
  $\Rightarrow (\textbf{AND}\ (\textbf{AND}\ (\textbf{ALL} C_{1,i} \text{Expr}_{1,i})\ \text{Expr}(\text{Cntxt}_1))\ \text{Expr}(\text{Cntxt}_2))$
  $= (\textbf{AND}\ (\textbf{ALL}\ C_{1,i} \text{Expr}_{1,i})\ \text{Expr}(\text{Cntxt}_1)\ \text{Expr}(\text{Cntxt}_2))$
- $\text{glb}(\text{glb}(\langle(C_{2,i}, \text{Expr}_{2,i})\rangle, \text{Cntxt}_2), \text{Cntxt}_1)$
  $= \text{glb}(\langle(C_{2,i}, \text{Expr}_{2,i})\rangle, \text{glb}(\text{Cntxt}_2, \text{Cntxt}_1)) \text{if} C_{2,i} \notin \text{Cntxt}_1$
  $\Rightarrow (\textbf{AND}\ (\textbf{AND}\ (\textbf{ALL} C_{2,i}\ \text{Expr}_{2,i})\ \text{Expr}(\text{Cntxt}_2))\ \text{Expr}(\text{Cntxt}_1))$
  $= (\textbf{AND}\ (\textbf{ALL} C_{2,i}\ \text{Expr}_{2,i})\ \text{Expr}(\text{Cntxt}_2)\ \text{Expr}(\text{Cntxt}_1))$
- $\text{glb}(\text{glb}(\langle(C_i, \text{Expr}_{1,i})\rangle, \text{Cntxt}_1), \text{glb}(\langle(C_i, \text{Expr}_{2,i})\rangle, \text{Cntxt}_2))$
  $= \text{glb}(\langle(C_i, \text{glb}(\text{Expr}_{1,i}, \text{Expr}_{2,i}))\rangle, \text{glb}(\text{Cntxt}_1, \text{Cntxt}_2))$
  $\Rightarrow (\textbf{AND}\ (\textbf{AND}(\textbf{ALL}\ C_i\ \text{Expr}_{1,i})\ \text{Expr}(\text{Cntxt}_1))$
  $(\textbf{AND}\ (\textbf{ALL}\ C_i\ \text{Expr}(\text{Cntxt}_2)))$
  $= (\textbf{AND}\ (\textbf{ALL}\ C_i(\textbf{AND}\ \text{Expr}_{1,i}\ \text{Expr}_{2,i}))\ \text{Expr}(\text{Cntxt}_1)\ \text{Expr}(\text{Cntxt}_2))$

B THE ONTOLOGIES USED IN THE OBSERVER SYSTEM

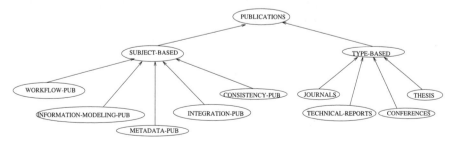

Figure B1.   The LSDIS ontology.

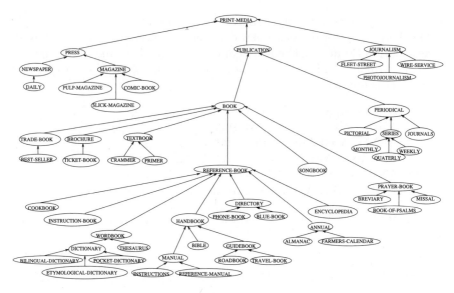

Figure B2. WN: a subset of the WordNet 1.5 ontology.

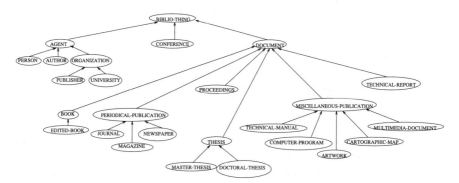

Figure B3. Stanford-I: a subset of the Bibliographic Data ontology.

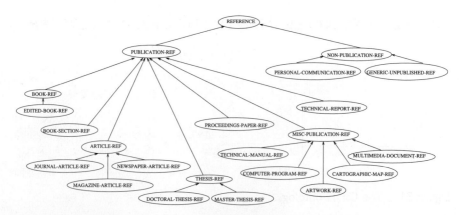

Figure B.4. Stanford-II: a subset of the Bibliographic Data ontology.

Dynamic Classificational Ontologies: Mediation of Information Sharing in Cooperative Federated Database Systems

Jonghyun Kahng and Dennis McLeod
University of Southern California, Los Angeles, CA, USA

Abstract

A Cooperative Federated Database System (CFDBS) is an information sharing environment in which units of information to be shared are substantially structured, and participants are actively involved in information sharing activities. In this chapter, we focus on the problem of building a common ontology for the purpose of information sharing in the CFDBS context. We introduce the concept and mechanism of the *Dynamic Classificational Ontology* (DCO), which is a collection of concepts and interrelationships to describe and classify information units exported by participating information providers: a DCO contains top-level knowledge about exported information units, along with knowledge for classification. By contrast with fixed hierarchical classifications, the DCO builds domain-specific, dynamically changing classification schemes. Information providers contribute to the DCO when information units are exported, and the current knowledge in the DCO is in turn utilized to assist information sharing activities. We will show that, at the cost of information providers' cooperative efforts, this approach supports effective information sharing in the CFDBS environment.

I INTRODUCTION

With the rapid growth of computer communication networks over the last decade, a vast amount of information of diverse structure and modality has become available on the networks. We consider this environment from the viewpoint of a *Cooperative Federated Database System* (CFDBS) (Heimbigner

Cooperative Information Systems
Trends and Directions
ISBN 0-12-544910-0

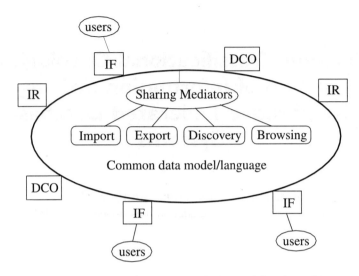

Figure 1.   Top-level view of a Cooperative Federated Database System.

and McLeod, 1985); here, units of information to be shared are substantially structured and participants are actively involved in information sharing activities.

A CFDBS consists of a number of autonomous *Information Frameworks* (IFs) and *Information Repositories* (IRs), as well as one or more *Dynamic Classificational Ontologies* (DCOs) (Figure 1). IRs are major sources of information, while IFs are principally portals to IRs and other IFs (since an IR is a special kind of IF, in the following, IF will stand for both IFs and IRs unless otherwise mentioned). A DCO is a common ontology (a collection of concepts and their relationships to describe information units) which serves the basis of mutual "understanding" among participating IFs. Information is shared via mediators provided to support import (folding remote information into local environments), export (registering information to share), discovery (searching for relevant information) and browsing (navigating through information sources). Participants in the CFDBS communicate through an agreed common data model and language.

Information sharing in the CFDBS faces a number of challenging problems due to the large volume of information and the rich structure of information units. Our approach is to dynamically build a common ontology, which is used by participants to describe and interpret information that they share. An emphasis of our approach is based on the observation that it is extremely difficult to reach a total agreement on an ontology if the number of participants is large, and that the ontology should be allowed to change dynamically as the CFDBS evolves.

In this chapter, we present the concept and mechanism of the DCO which addresses problems of the common ontology, and illustrate how the

DCO facilitates information sharing activities. In order to reduce the size of the DCO, it contains a small amount of high-level metaknowledge on exported information. Specifically, it contains a collection of concepts and their relationships that is to be used for classification of exported information. We rely on classification because it is an effective scheme for organizing a large amount of information. Further, some relationships in the DCO are not pre-determined, but computed based on exported information. Such relationships typically involve interrelated concepts which are useful for describing or classifying other concepts (for example, relationships among a set of subjects). An advantage of this approach is that participants are not required to agree on those relationships in advance. Another advantage is that those relationships are allowed to change as the usage of involved concepts changes.

The remainder of this chapter is organized as follows. Section 2 describes the spectrum of heterogeneity present in the CFDBS environment. Section 3 examines issues associated with the common ontology for resolution of semantic heterogeneity, and reviews related research. Section 4 discusses the role of classification as an information organization scheme, and discusses the representation of classification. Section 5 describes the DCO in detail, while Section 6 shows how the knowledge in the DCO is utilized for the mediation of information sharing activities, in particular, export and discovery. Section 7 concludes this chapter.

2 HETEROGENEITY

A key aspect of the CFDBS is heterogeneity of information at two levels of abstraction:

1. *Data model heterogeneity.* Information systems may use different collections of structures, constraints and operations (i.e., different data models) to describe and manipulate data. For example, an information system may use a DBMS that supports object-based data modelling and an OSQL; another may store data in a collection of HTML documents and access them through http; and yet another may use a UNIX file system with various file management tools.
2. *Semantic heterogeneity.* Information systems may agree on a data model, but they may have independent specifications of data. This exhibits a wide spectrum of heterogeneity because most data models offer many different ways to describe the same or similar information.

2.1 Data Model Heterogeneity

Apparently, there are two alternatives to resolve data model heterogeneity. The first is to translate between every distinct pair of data models; and the second is to adopt a common data model, and to translate between each data model and the common one. In the CFDBS, in which the number of distinct data models is expected to be large, the second alternative is more cost effective and scalable. This follows from a simple calculation of the number of necessary translations: $O(n^2)$ vs. $O(n)$ where n is the number of distinct data models. The price to pay for this alternative is that participating information systems should agree on a common data model. However, the cost of adopting a common data model can be well justified by its benefits. In fact, nearly all proposed systems for database interoperation assume some common data model (Arens *et al.*, 1993; Garcia-Molina *et al.*, 1995; Hammer and McLeod, 1993; Levy *et al.*, 1996; Mena *et al.*, 1996; Sciore *et al.*, 1992).

There is a tradeoff in choosing a common data model. Simple data models reduce the degree of potential semantic heterogeneity and the maintenance cost, but they limit the capability of information sharing; and the opposite applies to semantically rich data models. A good example can be drawn from the recently exploding World-Wide Web (WWW). Although it provides a great opportunity for people around the world to initiate information sharing, it comes with some intrinsic drawbacks. First of all, its data model is too simple to effectively describe diverse information. The simplicity, of course, has two sides. It is the simplicity in part that has made WWW so rapidly accepted in the Internet community. The simplicity would be acceptable as far as information to be shared remains simple. This, however, is not the case because people are now becoming more and more keen to share diverse information, both structured and unstructured, using WWW.

In the CFDBS, it is essential to adopt a data model that is more expressive than simple hypertext or flat files/tables, for example, because the CFDBS is to share information with diverse structure. An advantage of semantically rich models is that no information is lost when translation is done from less expressive models. It is also essential to have operations (query and manipulation languages) that are expressive enough to meet various demands and yet primitive enough to understand easily. An object-based data model might be a good choice because it is easy to understand (compared to richer models such as those of the KL-ONE family which are more popular in the AI community), it allows effective data modelling in various application domains, and translation from other popular models is reasonably feasible. However, the query language for object-based data models needs improvement. Currently, variations of OSQL are the most prevalent languages for object-based models, but they fail to take advantage of object-oriented concepts such as inheritance. This is mainly because OSQL has its origin in SQL for relational models. Another drawback of OSQL is that users need quite a lot of training before effectively using it. A language that allows users to navigate through databases comfortably without formulating complicated queries would make information sharing in the CFDBS much more effective.

2.2 Semantic Heterogeneity

As object-based models, relational models and some extensions of them have been widely adopted as a common data model in federated database environments, taxonomies of semantic heterogeneity that is allowed in such models have been extensively studied for the last decade (Kent, 1989; Kim, 1993; McLeod, 1992; Sheth and Kashyap, 1992). For the purpose of illustration, two university databases described in an object-based data model are shown in Figure 2. We summarize incompatibilities between objects resulting from the semantic heterogeneity:

- *Category.* Two objects from different information sources are under compatible categories if they represent the same or similar real world entities. Specifically, they may have equivalence, subconcept/superconcept, or partially overlapping relationships. For example, Employees in (a) and People in (b) are equivalent because they both represent employees of the universities; Persons in (a) is a superconcept of People in (b) because the former represents a more general category of human beings than the latter; and Students in (a) and People in (b) may be partially overlapping because some students may be employees as well. On the other hand, Courses in (a) and People in (b) are under incompatible categories.
- *Structure.* Two objects of a compatible category may have different structures. For example, Employees in (a) and People in (b) have quite different structures: People has an attribute birthday, but Employees does not; the attribute phone-nos of Employees is equivalent to combination of the attributes work-phone and home-phone of People. Another common example of structural incompatibility is that an attribute in one database is an object in another.
- *Unit.* Two objects under a compatible category with a compatible structure may use different units. Salary in (a) and (b) gives an example of this

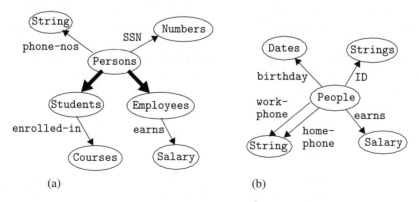

(a)　　　　　　　　　　　(b)

Figure 2. Examples of semantic heterogeneity: (a) personnel database of a university in the USA; (b) employee database of a university in France.

incompatibility, assuming that the former is given in dollars whereas the latter is given in francs. Quality grades are another frequently encountered example. A grade may be measured on the scale of A, B, C etc. Or, it may be measured on the scale of 1 to 10, for instance.

Other incompatibilities orthogonal to those above include:

- *Terminology*. Synonyms and homonyms cause terminological incompatibilities. The attributes `SSN` of `Employees` and `ID` of `People` are an example of synonyms.
- *Universe of discourse*. Semantics of data is often hidden in the context. For example, the currencies used in (a) and (b) are presumably dollar and franc, respectively, considering their locations.

Resolution of semantic heterogeneity is at the centre of interoperation in the CFDBS. Because of the difficulty of the problem, however, decades of research have been able to provide only primitive solutions to the problem, and there is little consensus on how to go beyond them. Among the first three incompatibility problems, we focus on the first one because locating relevant (i.e., categorically compatible) objects alone, setting aside their structural and unitary compatibilities, is a challenge in the CFDBS environment, and because resolution of the first should precede that of the others.

A common approach to semantic heterogeneity resolution is to adopt a common ontology as a basis for mutual understanding. This introduces another level of agreement among participants in addition to an agreed common data model. The remainder of this chapter is focused on this approach.

3 COMMON ONTOLOGY

An ontology is a collection of concepts and interconnections to describe information units. In particular, the common ontology in the CFDBS is to describe information exported from information sources. Figure 3 shows a generic architecture for information sharing in the CFDBS. Information to be exported is first extracted from information sources and then translated from local data models to a common data model. Semantic heterogeneity among the exported information is resolved by mapping it into a common ontology. In other words, the common ontology is used to describe the exported information. Information sharing is facilitated by mediators provided for export, import, discovery etc. There are several issues in working with a common ontology:

- *Contents*. A common ontology could be as simple as a collection of concepts whose relationships are unspecified, or as complicated as a complete collection of concepts and their relationships that is enough to unambiguously describe all the exported information (like an integrated schema,

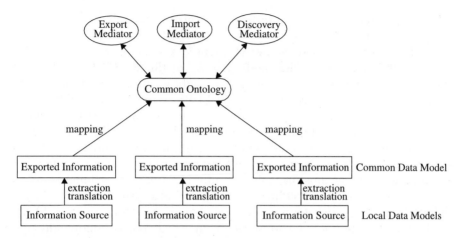

Figure 3.   Information sharing in the CFDBS.

for instance). Since neither of these two extremes are practical, most proposed systems adopt a common ontology that lies between the two. The contents of the common ontology strongly depends on the kinds of semantic heterogeneity that are to be resolved.

- *Mapping.* Exported information needs to be mapped to (or described by) the common ontology. This process is typically the most labour-intensive and time-consuming one, and is mostly carried out by domain experts. Thus, semi-automatic tools to assist this process would be very useful.
- *Relevance.* Similarity/difference between two information units from different information sources or relevance of exported information to a given request needs to be determined at some point of information sharing activities.
- *Maintenance.* Building a common ontology in the first place before any information sharing occurs is a challenging problem. Further, it is very helpful to allow evolution of the common ontology.

The problem of the common ontology has been addressed either implicitly or explicitly in several different contexts, including database interoperation, information retrieval and Internet resource discovery.

3.1 Database Interoperation

Early studies in database interoperation paid attention to tightly-coupled federated database systems in which the common ontology is an integrated database schema (Batini *et al.*, 1986; Sheth and Larson, 1990). The focus of these systems is to build a database schema that supersedes all component database schemas and to define mappings between the integrated schema and component schemas. A number of techniques have been proposed for this purpose. Extensions of existing relational or object-based data models to improve capability of disambiguating semantic mismatches among information units from different information sources have been also proposed. Some AI-oriented systems (Arens *et al.*, 1993; Levy, 1996) use richer data models, those of the KL-ONE family, and focus on efficient query processing. This tightly coupled approach is not suitable for large systems such as the CFDBS. First, it is very difficult to construct an integrated schema if there are more than a few information sources. Second, a complete resolution needs to take care of detailed semantic conflicts, which could very well result in undesired complications. Third, evolving the system is difficult because every change in individual information sources must be reflected into the integrated schema.

Because of these difficulties, a more practical approach for the CFDBS is loosely coupled federated systems (Heimbigner and McLeod, 1985; Sheth and Larson, 1990; Wiederhold, 1992), in which the common ontology provides partial information about participating information sources. The choice of the common ontology in this approach strongly influences the functionality and capability of the system. Examples of proposed common ontologies include: a set of meta-attributes (Sciore *et al.*, 1992); a network of terms (Fankhauser and Neuhold, 1992); concept hierarchies (Yu *et al.*, 1991); summary schema hierarchies (Bright *et al.*, 1994); a set of canonical terms and transformer functions (Mena *et al.*, 1996); and a collection of concepts and relationship descriptors (Hammer and McLeod, 1993). Most of these systems emphasize relevance computation (or query processing) with a given common ontology and the mappings; others are concerned with mappings/relationships to a given common ontology. A common drawback of these systems is that they do not deal with the problem of building and evolving the common ontology: the common ontology is defined in advance and more or less fixed.

3.2 Information Retrieval

Traditional information retrieval systems are concerned with instance level (vs. type/class level) information, since the type of information to share is documents with well-known properties such as title, authors, subjects etc. As in database interoperation, common ontologies play an important role in these systems. In particular, the focus is measuring relevance of two documents or relevance of documents to a given request.

The simplest approach is to rely on keyword matching. That is, keywords are extracted from each document either manually or automatically, and two documents are compared based on the extracted keywords (Salton, 1989). The common ontology in this case is implicitly all words in a natural language with relationships among words nearly ignored. This can be improved by introducing synonyms or by replacing extracted keywords with their stems, but it is still too primitive to be useful in a more cooperative environments such as the CFDBS.

Another common approach is to take a collection of pre-classified subjects (Sammet and Ralston, 1982) (a common ontology) and to assign a few of them to each document. While the pre-defined classification does include relationships between subjects, it has several undesirable features. First, it is hierarchical for the most part. That is, it contains only subsumption relations between subjects. Although cross-references between related subjects are often a part of the classification, they are not enough to represent overlapping relationships among subjects. Second, it tends to be static. Revision of the classification requires much time and effort. Consequently, it fails to accommodate dynamically changing usage of subjects. Third, it is typically huge and hard to understand because it usually covers all disciplines and because it contains many artificial terms which are not commonly used in documents. These features make it difficult to apply this approach to the CFDBS environment.

An active area of research in information retrieval is to build term relationships from existing documents. Developed techniques include thesaurus-group generation (Chamis, 1988; Salton, 1989), concept networks for concept retrieval (vs. keyword retrieval) (Chen and Lynch, 1992) and latent semantic indexing by singular value decomposition (Deerwester et al., 1990). They basically rely on statistical analysis of term occurrence patterns in documents. This research is related to our approach, although our mechanism, assumptions and context are quite different.

3.3 Internet Resource Discovery

It is interesting to observe that Internet resource discovery tools have followed in the footsteps of information retrieval systems. A number of systems based on keywords have been developed and are in use today. As expected, however, searching is not as efficient as desired due to their limitations: precision of search results is so low that users need to spend much time to sort out retrieved information. To remedy such problems, some of recent systems took the approach of classification. Yahoo (http://www.-yahoo.com/), for example, takes a hierarchical classification of subjects, and classifies URL objects by those subjects, which is reminiscent of subject classification used in many library systems. Another one is Harvest (Bowman et al., 1994), in which each broker specializes in a certain category such as technical reports, PC software etc. It effectively divides the WWW space into several categories, and searching is carried out under each category. This is useful when users know which category of objects is relevant to their interests.

In summary, a common ontology plays an important role in information sharing in the CFDBS environment. Many proposed systems adopt a common ontology as the basis of information sharing, but methodologies to construct and evolve the common ontology require more investigation.

4 CLASSIFICATION

Studies in cognitive science have shown that classification is the most basic scheme that humans use for organizing information and making inferences (Cagne *et al.*, 1993). Categories of objects have features that help identification of the categories, and objects are recognized by associating them with categories. For example, some children distinguish cats from dogs by the feature that cats have whiskers. In principle, all objects in the universe could be placed into a single classification tree. However, that is not the way humans picture the universe. Instead, there are categories at a certain level of generality (basic-level categories) on which people agree the most. When people were asked to list all the features of objects in categories such as trees, fish, birds, chairs and cars, there was a high level of agreement among people with respect to the common features of those objects. Agreement is less prominent for superordinate categories such as plants, animals, furniture, and vehicles, as well as for subordinate categories such as robin, chicken, sedans, trucks etc. Further studies showed that basic-level categories are the first ones learned by small children. An implication of these results is that classification is an effective method to organize a large amount of information and it is natural to classify objects in two steps: the first is to classify objects into basic-level categories; the second is to further classify objects in individual categories as necessary.

Following these research findings, our approach to constructing a common ontology is based on classification. That is, the common ontology will contain interrelated concepts that are just enough to classify exported information. In particular, the classification is organized around basic-level categories that are specific to the application domain. If independent information systems are in similar application domains, they are likely to agree on basic-level categories, regardless of their underlying data models and physical data structures. For example, most university databases will include information about courses, students, faculty, staff and libraries at the top level. The agreement on basic-level categories would be very helpful for information sharing in the environment of a large-scale CFDBS.

Classification, in fact, has played an important role in information management. Most of popular information management systems, such as relational/object-based database management systems (DBMSs), WWW and hierarchical file systems, provide constructs for classification. Some of them facilitate the two-step classification scheme that was mentioned above. To explore the representation of classification in the common ontology, we will examine each data model in turn.

In relational and object-based DBMSs, objects to be modelled are first classified into tables or classes. In the latter, objects in a class can be further classified into subclasses, resulting in class hierarchies. Classification mechanisms directly supported by the systems stop here. But, for a large amount of information, it is useful to classify objects in individual tables or classes. The systems provide an indirect mechanism for that: objects in a table or

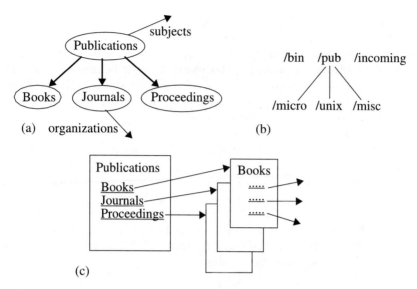

Figure 4. Classifications: (a) a library database; (b) an anonymous ftp site; (c) a web site.

a class are implicitly classified by their attribute values. Figure 4(a) shows a fragment of a library system. In this example, publications are broken down into three subclasses, where all four classes can be regarded as basic-level categories. In addition to the class hierarchy, publications are implicitly classified by subjects, that is, they can be grouped by the same or related subjects. Likewise, journals are classified by affiliated organizations as well as subjects.

Hierarchical file systems are supported in virtually all modern operating systems. A primary use of such file systems has traditionally been the management of personal files, such as documents and programs. Since computer communication networks became widely available, the file systems have been used as the primary storage of information by Internet resource sharing tools such as WWW, Gopher and anonymous ftp: they are now an important information organization tool. In hierarchical file systems, a directory can be used as a class of objects, and files in the directory can be regarded as objects in that class. If the number of files in a directory becomes large, they can be broken into subdirectories, resulting in a finer classification of objects. Figure 4(b) shows a top-level directory structure of a typical anonymous ftp site. Many anonymous ftp sites have similar directory names and structure in the first one or two levels of directory trees; those directories tend to represent basic-level categories.

WWW is an interesting invention for various reasons. It is basically a network of URL objects. A main strength of WWW is that it supports diverse kinds of URL objects including HTML documents, images, video objects and audio objects. It also provides gateways to Gopher, network news and anonymous ftp sites. Its capability to organize information, on the other hand, is primitive. It is even more primitive than hierarchical file systems in the sense that it does not support any second-order modelling primitive which can be used for classification. That is, there is no notion of "type", "class" or "directory" as a collection of similar objects. Consequently, classification of objects is totally up to the person who manages information (see Figure 4(c), for example).

From these observations, relational and object-based data models are good candidates for the representation of classification. However, note that tables or class hierarchies with attributes (commonly referred to as a database schema) are insufficient to describe the two-step classification. For example, publications are implicitly classified by their subjects (Figure 4(a)), but that classification would not be very useful if subjects are not well understood. That is, understanding relationships among subjects would be necessary to make that classification meaningful. The common ontology in our approach addresses this problem.

5 DYNAMIC CLASSIFICATIONAL ONTOLOGY

Information sharing in the CFDBS is centred upon common ontologies, termed *Dynamic Classificational Ontologies* (DCOs). The CFDBS environment is characterized by a large amount of information with diverse semantic heterogeneity. Resolving semantic heterogeneity and setting up an interoperative environment is therefore an extremely difficult and typically costly task. To assist this task, the DCO keeps a small amount of meta-information on concepts (information units) exported from IFs: a DCO maintains a common ontology to describe and classify exported concepts.

If the number of participating IFs is more than a handful, it is very difficult to draw a total agreement on a common ontology. Among other difficulties, it is common in the CFDBS environment that certain concepts, such as "interoperability", are loosely defined but frequently used. Moreover, usage of concepts will keep changing as the CFDBS evolves. It would therefore be impractical to make precise definitions of all concepts in advance and enforce them. To address these problems, the DCO dynamically develops a common ontology which accommodates different understanding of concepts and their relationships in different IFs. Further, evolution of the common ontology is based on the input from individual IFs: the common ontology is maintained by their collaboration. This reduces the central coordination and the cost of setting up a cooperative environment.

A DCO consists of a *base ontology* and a *derived ontology*. The base ontology contains an ontology to describe and classify concepts exported by IFs, and the derived ontology contains an additional ontology to help classification of exported concepts in finer grains. The former is typically static, which is maintained by a DCO administrator; and the latter is dynamic,

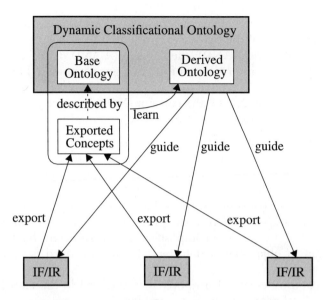

Figure 5.   Information flow in a CFDBS.

which is computed based on the base ontology and the population of exported concepts. Figure 5 shows the flow of information among the DCO and the IFs in a CFDBS. As we see here, export is a part of a learning cycle: it adds knowledge to the DCO while being guided by the knowledge in the current DCO.

5.1 Classificational Object-Based Data Model

Knowledge in the DCO is represented by the *Classificational Object-based Data Model* (CODM). The basic unit of information in this model is the *concept*; concepts are grouped into *classes*. A class may have one or more *properties*. A collection of classes and their properties is termed a *schema*. Looking ahead, Figure 6(a) shows an example of the schema. The CODM supports generalization/ specialization, and inheritance of properties from superclasses to subclasses (Cardenas and McLeod, 1990).

In addition, the CODM supports conceptual relationships between concepts and concept operators, which is useful for dynamic classification. A concept is essentially a representative of a set of real-world entities. Two concepts are *disjoint* if the two sets of entities that they represent are disjoint. One concept is a *superconcept/subconcept* of the other if the set of entities represented by the former is a superset/subset of that represented by the latter. Two concepts are *overlapping*, otherwise. A concept operator takes one or more concepts and produces a new concept. There are three concept operators:

1. *Conceptual union* (OR): The concept (*A* OR *B*) represents a set of entities that is the union of the two sets represented by concepts *A* and *B*.
2. *Conceptual intersection* (AND): the concept (*A* AND *B*) represents a set of entities that is the intersection of the two sets represented by concepts *A* and *B*.
3. *Conceptual negation* (NOT): the concept (NOT *A*) represents a set of entities that is the complement of the set represented by *A*.

A concept is a *composite concept* if it can be decomposed into other concepts and concepts operators. Otherwise, it is a *simple concept*.

A property is a mapping from a class to another class (a *value class*): that is, a property assigns to each concept of a given class a *value* which is composed from concepts of the value class. A property is *single-valued*, *multi-valued* or *composite-valued* if the property value takes a simple concept, a set of simple concepts or a composite concept, respectively. The first two are common in object-based data models, but the third is unique to the CODM.

The composite-valued property is introduced in the CODM because the multi-valued property generates ambiguities in some cases. To illustrate this point, consider the following examples, where pairs of subjects are given to describe some research articles:

- {AI, knowledge-representation}: if the article is about knowledge representation techniques in AI, it probably means (AI AND knowledge-representation). That is, it covers the overlapping area of AI and knowledge representation.
- {object-based-data-model, relational-data-model}: if the article introduces and compares the two models, (object-based-data-model OR relational-data-model) might be a better expression.
- {database, network}: if the article is a survey of database technology, and a part of the article covers network-related materials, ((database AND network) OR (database AND (NOT network))) might well represent its intention, meaning that both network-related and not network-related materials are covered in the article.

The ambiguities are present because subjects are not independent of each other. In general, a property may be defined as composite-valued when concepts of its value class are interrelated with each other.

5.2 Base Ontology

A base ontology consists of a schema in the CODM and concepts of selected classes. Figure 6(a) shows an example of the schema. Classes in the base ontology represent (basic-level) categories of concepts, and properties represent relationships between such categories. Every concept in the base ontology has two required properties: `owner` is the owner of the concept (see below), and `time-of-entry` is the time when the concept was recorded.

Figure 6(b) describes a concept DBNETLAB (for convenience, a concept will be identified by a textual string) of the class Research-Lab, where its property names and values are given (e.g., owner: usc-database-if indicates that the value of the property owner is the concept usc-database-if).

The owner of a concept is either the DCO or an IF. Concepts owned by the DCO (e.g., concepts of Organization, Subject, Hobby) are a part of the base ontology. Concepts of other classes (e.g., Research-Lab, Text, Time) are exported by IFs and owned by them. Only the owner of a concept may remove or change it. Concepts owned by the DCO along with the schema are used to describe exported concepts. For example, Figure 6(b) shows that the concept of the class Research-Lab was exported by the IF usc-database-if, and the values of its property institutions were chosen from concepts of the class Organization which are owned by the DCO.

The ownership of concepts depends on, in part, how much information is going to be managed by the DCO. For instance, Organization could be owned by IFs or by the DCO. If the DCO is planned to rigorously follow up information about organizations in any detail, the latter might be a good choice. In this case, the base ontology should include most of known organizations so that exported concepts may refer to them. On the other hand, Organization could be owned by IFs if, for instance, only the names of organizations are to be kept in the DCO.

Another (more critical) reason for the DCO to own and manage some concepts is to assist classification. In Figure 6, research labs are implicitly

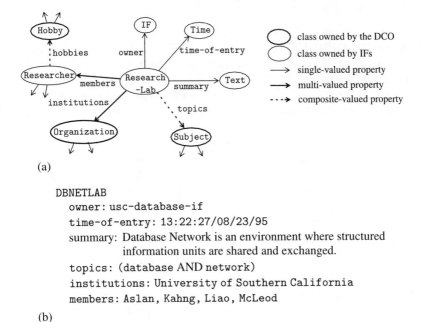

(a)

```
DBNETLAB
    owner: usc-database-if
    time-of-entry: 13:22:27/08/23/95
    summary: Database Network is an environment where structured
             information units are shared and exchanged.
    topics: (database AND network)
    institutions: University of Southern California
    members: Aslan, Kahng, Liao, McLeod
```

(b)

Figure 6.   A base ontology: (a) the schema; (b) A concept of Research-Lab.

classified by their topics (as well as by any other properties). This classification could be however ambiguous because subjects are interrelated with each other and the relationships tend to be non-objective. It is therefore necessary to understand conceptual relationships among subjects in order to make the classification useful. To deal with this problem, topics is defined as a composite-valued property and concepts of Subject are owned by the DCO in our example. Conceptual relationships among subjects are determined by statistical analyses, which will be discussed next.

5.3 Derived Ontology

A derived ontology records information about conceptual relationships. Specifically, if concepts of a class is owned by the DCO and the class is the value class of a composite-valued property, conceptual relationships among those concepts enter the derived ontology. We will first discuss how composite concepts can be interpreted since they are the main source of information, and then describe how to derive conceptual relationships from them.

5.3.1 Interpretations of Composite Concepts

Suppose that simple concepts $C_1, C_2, \ldots, C_N$ of a class are owned by the DCO. A composite concept C composed from these concepts can be interpreted in two different ways:

1. *Open interpretation*: C can be interpreted as $(C$ AND $(C_{S1}$ OR (NOT $C_{S1}))$ AND $(C_{S2}$ OR (NOT $C_{S2}))$ AND $\ldots$ AND $(C_{Sm}$ OR (NOT $C_{Sm})))$, where $C_{S1}, C_{S2}, \ldots, C_{Sm}$ are simple concepts that do not appear in C. For example, (database AND network) means (database AND network AND (artificial-intelligence OR (NOT artificial-intelligence)) AND (operating-systems OR (NOT operating-systems)) $\ldots$). In other words, a composite concept may or may not be related to the concepts that are not explicitly mentioned in it.
2. *Closed interpretation*: C can be interpreted as $(C$ AND (NOT $C_{S1})$ AND (NOT $C_{S2})$ AND $\ldots$ AND (NOT $C_{Sm}))$, where $C_{S1}, C_{S2}, \ldots, C_{Sm}$ are simple concepts that do not appear in C. For example, (database AND network) means (database AND network AND (NOT artificial-intelligence) AND (NOT operating-systems) $\ldots$). In this case, a composite concept is not related to the concepts that are not explicitly mentioned in it.

A composite concept given by a user might need different interpretations depending on his/her intention. If a user is searching for some information, and the composite concept is provided as a specification of desired information, the open interpretation is probably a better one. That is, the user may not care whether the information that he/she wants is also related to other information or not. On the other hand, if a user is asked to describe some information by a composite concept as precisely as possible, the closed interpretation may be closer to his/her intention. This is because the user would try not to leave out any of relevant concepts.

The open interpretation is safer, while the closed one is more informative. If the user is not forced to adhere to either of the two interpretations, it is most likely that he/she will produce composite concepts whose interpretation falls somewhere between the two. The DCO takes the closed interpretation for composite concepts given by exporters. We will later show how the DCO can help them to progressively formulate informative composite concepts that are subject to the closed interpretation.

5.3.2 Conceptual Relationships

The population of exported concepts is the basis for the derivation of conceptual relationships. We first define the frequency of composite concepts:

Definition. For a composite concept C of a class Q, and a composite-valued property p whose value class is Q, the *frequency* of C is the number of super-concepts of C among the values of p.

For the example in Figure 6(a), if some values of topics are (database AND network), (database OR network), ((database OR information-retrieval) AND network), each of them counts toward the frequency of a concept (database AND network) since all of them are its superconcepts.

As in mining association rules (Agrawal *et al.*, 1993), we introduce a variable to indicate the significance of statistical data:

Definition. A *minimal support* is the frequency such that any frequency below it is considered as statistically insignificant.

Thus, if the minimal support is 10 and the frequency of (database AND complexity-theory) is less than 10, then there is not enough data to determine whether database and complexity-theory are related.

We introduce another variable, the *tolerance factor*, to indicate confidence of derived conceptual relationships. Conceptual relationships are defined with the tolerance factor.

Definitions. Suppose that concepts C_1, C_2, and (C_1 AND C_2) have frequencies f_1, f_2, and f_3, respectively (see Figure 7(a)), and t is the tolerance factor. When f_3 is larger than the minimal support,

- C_1 and C_2 are disjoint concepts within a tolerance factor t, if both f_3/f_1 and f_3/f_2 are smaller than t.
- C_1 is a subconcept of C_2 within t ($C_1 < C_2$) or C_2 is a superconcept of C_1 within t ($C_2 > C_1$), if f_3/f_1 is larger than $(1 - t)$.
- C_1 and C_2 are equivalent concepts within t ($C_1 = C_2$), if C_1 is a subconcept of C_2 within t and vice versa.
- C_1 and C_2 are overlapping concepts within t, otherwise.

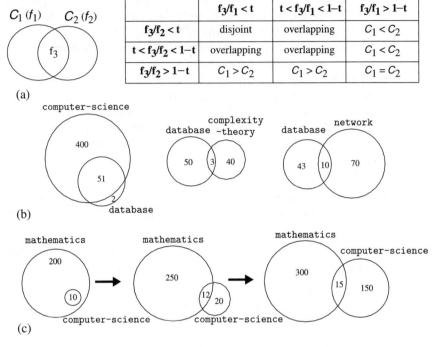

Figure 7. Conceptual relationships: (a) definitions; (b) examples; (c) evolutions.

When f_3 is smaller than the minimal support, C_1 and C_2 are considered as disjoint concepts.

Conceptual relationships between C_1 and C_2 are summarized in the table in Figure 7(a). The tolerance factor represents statistical variations. There are two main causes for such variations: the first is simply that IFs may make mistakes at the time of export, and the second is that different IFs may have somewhat different understanding of involved concepts.

Conceptual relationships among two or more concepts can be best illustrated by diagrams as in Figure 7(b); this figure shows some relationships among concepts of Subject. Numbers in the figure indicate frequencies of the concepts: there are currently 400, 51, 2 research labs whose topics include (computer-science AND (NOT database)), (computer-science AND database), ((NOT computer-science) AND database), respectively, and so on. Assuming a tolerance factor of 10%, the figure shows that database is a subconcept of computer-science; database and complexity-theory are disjoint concepts; and database and network are overlapping concepts. Figure 7(c) shows how conceptual relationships may evolve. In the example, computer-science began as a part of mathematics, and has grown out of it so that the two are now more or less separate disciplines.

The derived ontology is not fixed, but dynamically changes as the population of exported concepts grows. Compared to using fixed conceptual relationships such as pre-defined hierarchical classifications, this approach has several advantages: the derived ontology can be progressively built up, it may change as usage of concepts changes, and it will shape up in a way to reflect domain-specific usage of concepts. It is important to note that the aim of dynamically building the derived ontology is not to derive exact conceptual relationships, but to evolve a collection of reasonably agreeable conceptual relationships.

6 MEDIATORS FOR INFORMATION SHARING

We will discuss in this section how the knowledge in the DCO is used by mediators provided for information sharing. First of all, the derived ontology depends heavily on information provided by IFs, and it might be unrealistic to expect IFs to provide precise description of information to export from the beginning. We will show how the DCO can help them progressively formulate their descriptions. We will then discuss discovery: in the presence of abundant information, one of critical problems is to sort out information that is relevant. It is therefore essential to measure relevance of available information to a given discovery request. We will show how to do that with the help of the DCO.

6.1 Export Mediator

An IF exports a concept by submitting an entry using the schema of the base ontology as a template. The entry should include the name of the class to which the concept belongs, along with values for its properties. Figure 8 shows an example. If the value of a property is concepts owned by the IF, it is accepted as entered (e.g., `members: McLeod, McNeill`). On the other hand, if it is owned by the DCO, it should be composed from existing concepts of the value class (e.g., `institutions: University of Southern California`). In particular, if the property is composite-valued (e.g., `topics, hobbies`), the IF is allowed and encouraged to refine the value as precisely as possible with the help of the DCO.

CLASS: `Research-Lab`
`owner: usc-bp-if`
`time-of-entry: 09:12:35/09/15/95`
summary: The lab have been developing neuroscience databases that contain
information about related literature and experimental data.
`topics: (discovery AND scientific-db)`
`institutions: University of Southern California`
`members: McLeod, McNeill`

Figure 8.   An entry for export.

The export mediator utilizes the knowledge in the DCO to help IFs formulate the description of concepts that they export, especially when the description involves composite-valued properties and concepts owned by the DCO. It applies the following strategies to achieve this goal with minimal interaction with IFs.

Strategy 1. For a composite concept (as the value of a composite-valued property) given by the IF, concepts that are overlapping with it are retrieved from the DCO, and presented to the IF so that the composite concept may be modified, restricted, or extended with them.

This is a rather straightforward strategy of utilizing conceptual relationships. Lines 1−3 in Figure 9 show that `application`, `heterogeneous-db`, `data-model`, `language` etc. turned out to be overlapping with the given composite concept (`discovery AND scientific-database`), and the IF added three of them to the composite concept.

Strategy 2. Among the overlapping concepts found by Strategy 1, only the concepts that are not subconcepts of others are presented to the IF in order to enable the IF to refine the composite concept from the top level to lower ones in progressive steps.

This strategy reduces the number of related concepts to present to the IF so that it is not overwhelmed by a large number of concepts to choose from. Concepts that are left out will be further explored later only if

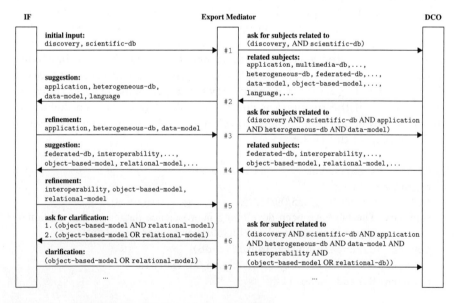

Figure 9.   Description of topics of a research lab.

their superconcepts are determined to be relevant by the IF. Lines 3 and 4 in Figure 9 show that subconcepts of `data-model` (i.e., `object-based-model` and `relational-model`) are presented to the IF in the second round because `data-model` was selected by the IF in the previous round.

Strategy 3. If two concepts A and B given by the IF are disjoint, the IF is asked to choose either (A AND B) or (A OR B).

It is useful to distinguish between (A AND B) and (A OR B) in order to improve accuracy of the derived ontology. The list of concepts given by the IF is by default regarded as a conceptual intersection of those concepts. If A and B are disjoint, (A AND B) is a non-existing composite concept (i.e., its frequency is insignificant), and it may not be what the IF intended. Lines 5–7 demonstrate this strategy. In this example, `object-based-model` and `relational-model` are assumed to be disjoint in the current DCO. If the IF insists that the previously given input is correct, it provides a basis for the composite concept (`object-based-model` AND `relational-model`) to develop and for the conceptual relationship between `object-based-model` and `relational-model` to change in the DCO.

6.2 Discovery Mediator

An IF submits a discovery request using the schema of the base ontology as a template, as for export. The request includes the class name of the concepts in which the IF is interested. It may also specify some or all property values of the concepts (see Figure 10). As in export, the discovery request can be first validated and refined with the help of the DCO. This will make the discovery request precise so that the precision and recall of retrieved results will be high.

Once the request for discovery is constructed, the next step is to retrieve relevant ones from exported concepts. Critical in this step is to measure relevance of exported concepts to the discovery request. For that purpose, we introduce a *relevance factor* (RF) which measures the relevance using the knowledge in the DCO. The RF is first computed for each property, and the final RF is the product of all those RFs. Retrieved concepts

```
CLASS: Research-Lab
owner: *
time-of-entry: *
summary: *
topics: ((database OR network) AND information-retrieval)
institutions: *
members: McLeod, Smith
```

Figure 10. A discovery request.

will be listed with corresponding RFs in the decreasing order of the RF. In the following definition of the RF, we will use examples of the discovery request shown in Figure 10 and the exported concept DBNETLAB shown in Figure 6(b).

For the property whose value is not specified in the discovery request such as owner and institutions,

$$RF = I$$

For a single-valued or multi-valued property,

$$RF = \frac{\#|D \cap O|}{\#|D \cup O|}$$

where D is the set of the property values in the discovery request, O is that of the exported concept, and $\#|S|$ is the cardinality of the set S. For example, the RF for members is

$$RF = \frac{\#|\{\text{McLeod, Smith}\} \cap \{\text{Aslan, Kahng, Liao, McLeod}\}|}{\#|\{\text{McLeod, Smith}\} \cup \{\text{Aslan, Kahng, Liao, McLeod}\}|} = \frac{I}{5}$$

For a composite-valued property,

$$RF = \frac{\#|D \text{ AND } O|}{\#|D \text{ OR } O|}$$

where D is the property value in the discovery request, O is that of the exported concept, and $\#|C|$ is the frequency of the concept C. For example, assuming conceptual relationships given in Figure 11, the RF for topics is

$$RF = \frac{4}{4 + 10 + 9 + 8} = \frac{4}{31}$$

The final RF for the above examples is

$$RF = \frac{I}{5} \times \frac{4}{31} = \frac{4}{155}$$

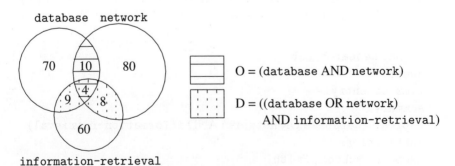

Figure 11.   Conceptual relationships among concepts of Subject.

To illustrate advantages of the RF over relevance measurements in conventional information retrieval systems, suppose that $D = (A \text{ AND } B)$ and $O = A$ for some composite-valued property in the above notation, and compare the RF with Radecki's coefficient which measures similarity between two boolean expressions (Radecki, 1982). It takes the same form as the RF for composite-valued properties, but the interpretation of $\#|C|$ is different: C is first converted into a disjunctive normal form $C = (C_1 \text{ OR } C_2 \text{ OR } \dots C_n)$ such that each C_i contains all the terms that appear in C, and then $\#|C| = n$. For our example, Radecki's coefficient is

$$\frac{\#|D \text{ AND } O|}{\#|D \text{ OR } O|} = \frac{\#|A \text{ AND } B|}{\#|A|} = \frac{\#|A \text{ AND } B|}{\#|(A \text{ AND } B) \text{ OR } (A \text{ AND } (\text{NOT } B))|} = \frac{1}{2}$$

regardless of how the two concepts A and B are related. In contrast, the RF is

- 1, if A is a subconcept of B (i.e., $(A \text{ AND } B) = A$).
- 0, if A and B are disjoint concepts (i.e., $(A \text{ AND } B)$ does not exist).
- between 0 and 1, depending on how much A and B overlap with each other.

That is, the RF results in more meaningful relevance measurements by taking advantage of the knowledge in the DCO on generality of concepts as well as relationships among them.

7 CONCLUSIONS

We introduced the Dynamic Classificational Ontology (DCO) for mediation of information sharing in the Cooperative Federated Database System environment. In the presence of a large amount of heterogeneous information, it is beneficial to reduce the central coordination and distribute the maintenance cost. To this end, the DCO keeps only a small amount of meta-information, specifically, a common ontology to describe and classify information exported by participating IFs; and it is maintained by their cooperative efforts. The Classificational Object-based Data Model was introduced as a model that facilitates two-step classification: concepts are classified into classes of basic-level categories, and concepts of each class can be further classified by their property values. While relying on partial agreement among participating IFs, the DCO is progressively established, and dynamically adapts to changing usages of concepts.

We have developed an experimental prototype of the DCO, and applied it to document search problems in Medline (a medical information retrieval system provided by the Norris Medical Library at USC) in the context of the USC Brain Project (http://www-hbp.usc.edu/). We have developed a data mining algorithm that is advantageous for library systems with deep hierarchies of terms such as Medline. Preliminary results indicates that the precision and recall of document searches in Medline can be significantly improved by the interactive query refinement and the relevance measurement which are supported by the DCO. We are currently extending the system to support browsing and pattern discovery based on the knowledge accumulated in the DCO.

ACKNOWLEDGEMENT

This research has been funded in part by NIMH under grant no. 5P01MD/DA52194-02, and in part by the Integrated Media Systems Center, a National Science Foundation Engineering Research Center with additional support from the Annenberg Center for Communication at the University of Southern California and the California Trade and Commerce Agency.

REFERENCES

Agrawal, R., Imielinski, T. and Swami, A. (1993) Data mining: a performance perspective. *IEEE Transactions on Knowledge and Data Engineering*, **5**(6), 914–925.

Arens, Y., Chee, C.Y., Hsu, C.-N. and Knoblock, C.A. (1993) Retrieving and integrating data from multiple information sources. *International Journal of Intelligent and Cooperative Information Systems*, **2**(2), 127–158.

Batini, C., Lenzerini, M. and Navathe, S.B. (1986) A comparative analysis of methodologies for database schema integration. *ACM Computing Surveys*, **18**(4), 323–364.

Bowman, C.M., Danzig, P.B., Hardy, D.R., Manber, U. and Schwartz, M.F. (1994) The Harvest information discovery and access system. In *Proceedings of the Second International World Wide Web Conference*, Chicago, Illinois, pp. 763–771.

Bright, M.W., Hurson, A.R. and Pakzad, S. (1994) Automated resolution of semantic heterogeneity in multidatabases. *ACM Transactions on Database Systems*, **19**(2), 212–253.

Cagne, E.D., Walker Yekovich, C. and Yekovich, F.R. (1993) *The Cognitive Psychology of School Learning*. HarperCollins College Publishers, New York.

Cardenas, A.F. and McLeod, D. (1990) *Research Foundations in Object-Oriented and Semantic Database Systems*. Prentice Hall, Englewood Cliffs, NJ.

Chamis, A.Y. (1988) Selection of online databases using switching vocabularies. *Journal of the American Society for Information Science*, **39**(3).

Chen, H. and Lynch, K.J. (1992) Automatic construction of networks of concepts characterizing document databases. *IEEE Transactions on Systems, Man, and Cybernetics*, **22**(5), 885–902.

Deerwester, S., Dumais, S.T., Furnas, G.W., Landauer, T.K. and Harshman, R. (1990) Indexing by latent semantic analysis. *Journal of the American Society for Information Science*, **41**(6), 391–407.

Fankhauser, P. and Neuhold, E.J. (1992) Knowledge based integration of heterogeneous databases. In *Proceedings of the IFIP WG2.6 Database Semantics Conference on Interoperable Database Systems (DS-5)*, Lorne, Victoria, Australia, pp. 155–175.

Garcia-Molina, H., Hammer, J., Ireland, K., Papakonstantinou, Y., Ullman, J. and Widom, J. (1995) Integrating and accessing heterogeneous information sources in TSIMMIS. In *Proceedings of the AAAI Symposium on Information Gathering*, Stanford, California, pp. 61–64.

Hammer, J. and McLeod, D. (1993) An approach to resolving semantic heterogeneity in a federation of autonomous, heterogeneous database systems. *International Journal of Intelligent and Cooperative Information Systems*, **2**(1), 51–83.

Heimbigner, D. and McLeod, D. (1985) A federated architecture for information management. *ACM Transactions on Office Information Systems*, **3**(3), 253–278.

Kent, W. (1989) The many forms of a single fact. In *Proceedings of the IEEE COMPCON Spring '89*, pp. 438–443.

Kim, W., Choi, I., Gala, S. and Scheevel, M. (1993) On resolving schematic heterogeneity in multidatabase systems. *Distributed and Parallel Databases*, **1**(3), 251–279.

Levy, A.Y., Rajaraman, A. and Ordille, J.J. (1996) Querying heterogeneous information sources using source descriptions. In *Proceedings of the International Conference on Very Large Data Bases*, pp. 251–262.

McLeod, D. (1992) The Remote-Exchange approach to semantic heterogeneity in federated database systems. In *Proceedings of the Second Far-East Workshop on Future Database Systems*, Kyoto, Japan, pp. 38–43.

Mena, E., Kashyap, V., Sheth, A. and Illarramendi, A. (1996) OBSERVER: an approach for query processing in global information systems based on interoperation across pre-existing ontologies. In *Proceedings of the First IFCIS International Conference on Cooperative Information Systems*, Brussels, Belgium, pp. 14–25.

Radecki, T. (1982) Similarity measures for boolean search request formulation. *Journal of the American Society for Information Retrieval*, **33**(1), 8–17.

Salton, G. (1989) *Automatic Text Processing*. Addison-Wesley, Reading, MA.

Sammet, J.E. and Ralston, A. (1982) The new (1982) computing reviews classification systems—final version. *Communications of the ACM*, **25**(1), 13–25.

Sciore, E., Seigel, M. and Rosenthal, A. (1992) Context interchange using meta-attributes. In *Proceedings of the First International Conference on Information and Knowledge Management*, Baltimore, Maryland, pp. 377–386.

Sheth, A. and Kashyap, V. (1992) So far (schematically) yet so near (semantically). In *Proceedings of the IFIP WG2.6 Database Semantics Conference on Interoperable Database Systems (DS-5)*, Lorne, Victoria, Australia, pp. 283–312.

Sheth, A. and Larson, J. (1990) Federated database systems for managing distributed, heterogeneous, and autonomous databases. *ACM Computing Surveys*, **22**(3), 183–236.

Wiederhold, G. (1992) Mediators in the architecture of future information systems. *IEEE Computer*, **25**(3), 38–49.

Yu, C., Sun, W., Dao, S. and Keirsey, D. (1991) Determining relationships among attributes for interoperability of multi-database systems. In *Proceedings of the First International Workshop on Interoperability in Multidatabase Systems*, Kyoto, Japan, pp. 251–257.

Part IV

Communication, Cooperation and the Exchange of Knowledge

Dealing with Semantic Heterogeneity by Generalization-Based Data Mining Techniques

Jiawei Han[a], Raymond T. Ng[b], Yongjian Fu[c] and Son K. Dao[d]
[a]Simon Fraser University, Burnaby, British Columbia, Canada;
[b]University of British Columbia, Vancouver, British Columbia, Canada;
[c]University of Missouri—Rolla, Rolla, MO, USA; [d]Hughes Research Laboratories, Malibu, CA, USA

Abstract

Data mining, or knowledge discovery from databases, may play an important role in the construction of cooperative information systems. A major challenge for building cooperative information systems is the semantic heterogeneity problem. Methods for schema analysis, transformation and integration have been investigated for providing a good tool to handle this problem. However, schema level analysis may sometimes be too general to solve the problem. Data-level analysis, i.e., the analysis of database contents, should be taken into serious consideration. Data mining provides a powerful tool to view database contents at a high abstraction level and transform low-level heterogeneous data into high-level homogeneous information. We discuss the necessity of data mining in cooperative information systems and study the methods for construction and maintenance of multiple-layer databases and intelligent query answering using generalization-based data mining techniques.

I INTRODUCTION

The study of heterogeneous databases, or cooperative database systems, has been an active research area for the past decade. Most studies focus on issues such as architectural design, schema translation, schema integration and transaction control (Elmagarmid and Pu, 1990; Schek, 1993). As the name implies, a key challenge of heterogeneous databases is how to deal with the semantic heterogeneity presented by the multiple autonomous databases.

Cooperative Information Systems
Trends and Directions
ISBN 0-12-544910-0

Techniques for schema analysis, translation, and integration attempt to solve the semantic heterogeneity problem at the schema level. That is to say, the solution to the problem is based on finding schemas (e.g., federated schemas in Sheth and Larson, 1990) that all databases involved can agree upon and can relate (i.e., translate) to.

However, based on our observation, schema-level analysis may only touch one aspect of the semantic heterogeneity problem. Many heterogeneous databases, even being analysed and transformed into federated schemas, may still have problems communicating with each other effectively. A deeper-level analysis of semantic heterogeneity, called *data-level analysis*, i.e., the analysis of database contents, should be taken into consideration.

Consider a simple example where the heterogeneous databases are university databases. A graduate admission office receives thousands of applications regularly from all over the world. The schema-level transformation and analysis may help transform different schemas of student transcripts into one federated schema, such as,

grading (name, student_id, semester, year, course_num, department, university, ..., grade)

which paves the way for information exchange among different databases. Nevertheless, one may still have a difficult time comparing the applicants (i.e., comparing the "so-transformed" data) based on the federated schema. This is because different universities may have quite different standards in course offering and course grading. In many cases, it is necessary to perform a deeper-level analysis, i.e., the analysis of database contents, to solve the semantic heterogeneity problem.

The diversity of data and the difficulty of understanding the meaning of the data poses great challenges to cooperating multiple databases based on their information contents (Dao and Perry, 1995). It is difficult to communicate among databases based on the low-level heterogeneous database contents, such as concrete course or grade information in a university database. However, their corresponding high-level concepts, such as general course information or grade distribution, could be less heterogeneous and easier to communicate. Thus generalization of low-level data to relatively high-level concepts may help communicate among different databases despite the existence of semantic heterogeneity of concrete database contents.

In the university example, although different universities many offer courses with very different names and contents, those courses can be classified according to their contents, subjects and levels. For example, a course "CMPT354 database systems I" could be viewed, based on different concept "granularities", as "database systems course, introductory_level", "DB course", "CS course", "applied_science_course" etc. Similarly, *grade* assignment, though diverse at different universities, such as letter grades vs. percentage grades etc., can be transformed into relatively homogeneous high-level concepts. Notice that one may specify some data transformation functions between the local schemas of the databases and the federated schema by domain-specific experts. For example, percentage grades can be converted into letter grades based on some conversion formula specified by experts (e.g., B corresponds to the range of [68%, 79%]) and vice versa. However, conversion formulas may not always be possible. It is often desirable to express grades in the federated schema in terms of top-2%, next-8%, top-one-third etc., which will create a basis for people from one university to understand the transcripts from another. In this case, there is no simple conversion formula that can be set up without taking the distribution of grades into consideration, whereas the distribution of grades can be obtained by performing data-level analysis against the database using some data analysis techniques. Especially, a generalization technique that transforms low-level diverse data into relatively high-level, commonly sharable information will be valuable for such analysis.

The above analysis demonstrates why, apart from schema-level analysis, data-level analysis, i.e., the analysis of database contents, is valuable for solving the semantic heterogeneity problem. Many techniques in data mining (Fayyard *et al.*, 1996) provide powerful means to view database contents at a *high concept level* (i.e., a *high level of abstraction*) and to transform low-level heterogeneous data into high-level homogeneous information. In this chapter, we study the relationships between data mining and cooperative heterogeneous databases. The data mining methods discussed in this chapter are confined to those for data generalization, summarization and characterization (Han *et al.*, 1993; Dao and Perry, 1995; Han *et al.*, 1996a) and methods for the construction of *multiple-layer databases*. We also explore its potential for supporting heterogeneous databases.

The chapter is organized as follows. In Section 2, the concept of a multiple-layer database (MLDB) is introduced. The techniques for generalizing different kinds of data are presented in Section 3. The construction and maintenance of an MLDB is studied in Section 4. Query answering in MLDBs is presented in Section 5. Finally, the potential of MLDBs for supporting heterogeneous databases is discussed in Section 6.

2 A MULTIPLE-LAYER DATABASE

To facilitate our discussion, we assume that the database to be studied is constructed based on an extended-relational data model with the capabilities to store and handle different kinds of complex data, such as structured or unstructured data, hypertext, spatial or multimedia data etc. It is straightforward to extend our study to other data models, such as object-oriented, deductive etc. Intuitively, an MLDB is a database composed of several layers of information, with the lowest layer corresponding to the primitive information stored in a conventional database, and with higher layers storing more general information extracted from lower layers. More formally, an MLDB can be defined as follows:

Definition 1. *A* multiple-layer database *consists of four major components*: ⟨S, H, C, D⟩

1. **S:** a database schema, *which contains the meta-information about the multiple-layer database structures*;
2. **H:** a set of concept hierarchies;
3. **C:** a set of integrity constraints;
4. **D:** a set of database relations, *which consists of all the relations (primitive or generalized) in the multiple-layer database.*   □

The first component, **a database schema,** outlines the overall database structure of an MLDB. It stores general information such as types, ranges, and data statistics about the relations at different layers, their relationships and their associated attributes. More specifically, it describes which higher-layer relation is generalized from which lower-layer relation(s) and how the generalization is performed. Therefore, it presents a route map for schema browsing and database content browsing and for assistance of cooperative query answering and query optimization. More details will be given later.

The second component, **a set of concept hierarchies,** provides a set of predefined concept hierarchies to assist the system to generalize lower-layer relations to high-layer ones and map queries to appropriate layers for processing.

The third component, **a set of integrity constraints,** consists of a set of integrity constraints to ensure the consistency of an MLDB.

The fourth component, **a set of database relations,** stores data relations, in which some of them are **primitive** (i.e., **layer-0**) relations, whereas others are higher layer ones, obtained by generalization.

Example 1. A real-estate database is taken as a running example to see how multiple-layer databases can be constructed to facilitate the analysis and understanding of database contents, and hence the information exchange among heterogeneous databases. Suppose the database contains the following four data relations:

1. *house (house_id, address, construction_date, constructor(...), owner (name, ...), living_room (length, width), bed_room_1 (...), ..., surrounding_map, layout, picture, video, listing_price).*
2. *buyer (name, id_#, birth_date, education, income, work_address, home_address, spouse, children (...), phone, ...).*
3. *sales (house, buyer, agent, contract_date, sell_price, mortgage (...), ..., notes).*
4. *agent (...).*

These relations are layer-0 relations in the MLDB. Suppose the database contains the concept hierarchies for *geographic locations, occupations, income ranges* etc. An MLDB can be constructed as follows.

First, the relation *house* can be generalized to a higher-layer relation *house'*. The generalization can be performed, for example, as follows: (1) transform the *house construction date* to *years_old*, e.g., from "*Sept. 10, 1980*" to 16; (2) preserve the *owner's name* but remove other information associated with the *owner*; (3) compute the *total floor area* of all the rooms and the *number of rooms* but remove the detailed specification for each room; (4) remove some attributes: *surrounding_map, layout, video* etc. The generalized relation *house'* can be considered as the layer-1 information of the house, whose schema is presented as follows:

house' (house_id, address, years_old, owner_name, floor_area, #_of_rooms, ..., picture, listing_price).

Secondly, further generalization on *house'* can be performed to produce an even higher layer relation *house"*. For example, generalization may be performed as follows: (1) remove the attributes *house_id, owner, house_picture* etc.; (2) generalize the *address* to *areas*, such as *north_burnaby, east_vancouver*, etc.; (3) generalize *years_old* to *year_range* etc.; (4) transform *#_of_rooms* and other associated information into *category*, such as *5-bedroom house, 3-bedroom town-house* etc.; (5) merge identical tuples in the relation and store the total *count* of such merged tuples. The generalized relation *house"* could be as follows.

house" (area, year_range, floor_area_range, category, ..., price_range, count).

Similarly, *buyer* can be generalized to *buyer', buyer"* etc., which forms multiple layers of a *buyer* relation. Multiple layers can also be formed in a similar way for the relations, *sales* and *agent*.

A high-layer relation can also be formed by joining two or more primitive or generalized relations. For example, *buyer_sales'* can be produced by generalization on the join of *buyer'* and *sales'* as long as it follows the regulation(s) for the construction of MLDBs (to be presented in the next section). Similarly, one may join several relations at different layers to form new higher-layer relations. For instance, the relation *house_sales_buyer'* in Figure 1 is defined by a three-way join among *house', sales'* and *buyer'*. This shows that multiple relations at different generalization levels can participate in a join.

A possible overall MLDB structure, i.e., the schema of an MLDB, is presented in Figure 1.

Queries can be answered efficiently and intelligently using the MLDB. For example, a user may ask for information about the houses with the price range between $250k and $300k. The query can be answered indirectly by first using *house"*, which may return "*none in West Vancouver, 10% in East*

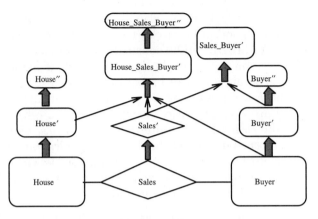

Figure 1.   The route map of a real-estate DB.

Vancouver, 15% in South Burnaby, etc.". Such an answer may help the user form more accurate queries to search for houses in specific regions.   □

3 GENERALIZATION OF DIFFERENT KINDS OF DATA

An MLDB is constructed by generalization of the layer-0 (original) database. Since a database may contain different kinds of data, it is important to examine the method for generalization of each kind of data, including unstructured and structured values, spatial and multimedia data etc.

3.1 Generalization of Simple Non-numerical Values

Simple (containing no internal structures) numerical and nonnumerical data are the most commonly used attribute values in databases. Generalization of non-numerical values may rely on the available concept hierarchies specified by domain experts or users or implicitly stored in the database. Concept hierarchies represent necessary background knowledge which directs the generalization process. Different levels of concepts are often organized into a taxonomy of concepts. The concept taxonomy can be partially ordered according to a general-to-specific ordering. The most general concept is the null description (described by "**any**"), and the most specific concepts correspond to the specific values of attributes in the database. Using a concept hierarchy, the primitive data can be expressed in terms of generalized concepts in a higher layer.

A conceptual hierarchy could be given by users or experts, stored or partially stored as data in a database, specified by some generalization meta-rules, such as deleting the street number from a street address etc., being derived from the knowledge stored elsewhere, or being computed by applying some rules or algorithms, such as deriving *"British Columbia*

⇒ *Western Canada*" from a geographic map stored in a spatial database etc. Moreover, it can be defined on a single attribute or on a set of related attributes, and it can be in the shape of a balanced tree, a lattice or a general DAG. Furthermore, a given concept hierarchy can be adjusted dynamically based on the analysis of the statistical distribution of the relevant data sets (Han and Fu, 1994).

3.2 Generalization of Simple Numerical Values

Generalization of numerical attributes can be performed similarly but in a more automatic way by the examination of data distribution characteristics (Agarwal *et al.*, 1992; Fisher, 1987; de Ville, 1990). In many cases, it may not require any predefined concept hierarchies. For example, the household income of buyers can be clustered into several groups, such as {*below*30K, 30K−50K, 50K−70K, *over* 70K}, according to a relatively uniform data distribution criteria or using some statistical cluster analysis tools. Appropriate names can be assigned to the generalized numerical ranges, such as {*low_income*, *mid_range*, *mid_high*, *high*} by users or experts to convey more semantic meaning.

In the past 30 years, cluster analysis has been widely applied to many areas such as medicine (classification of diseases), chemistry (grouping of compounds), social studies (classification of statistical findings) and so on. The main goal is to identify structures or *clusters* present in the data. Existing clustering algorithms can be classified into two main categories: *hierarchical* methods and *partitioning* methods. Hierarchical methods are either agglomerative or divisive. Given n objects to be clustered, agglomerative methods begin with n clusters (i.e., all objects are apart). In each step, two clusters are chosen and merged. This process continues until all objects are clustered into one group. On the other hand, divisive methods begin by putting all objects in one cluster. In each step, a cluster is chosen and split up into two. This process continues until n clusters are produced. While hierarchical methods have been successfully applied to many biological applications (e.g., for producing taxonomies of animals and plants (Kaufman and Rousseeuw, 1990), hierarchical methods are not useful in grouping simple numerical values into ranges.

In contrast, given the number k of partitions to be found, a partitioning method tries to find the best k partitions[1] of the n objects. It is very often the case that the k clusters found by a partitioning method are of higher quality (i.e., more similar) than the k clusters produced by a hierarchical method. Because of this property, developing partitioning methods has been one of the main focuses of cluster analysis research. Indeed, many partitioning methods have been developed, some based on k-means, some

---

[1] Partitions here are defined in the usual way: each object is assigned to exactly one group.

on k-medoid, some on fuzzy analysis, etc. See Kaufman and Rousseeuw (1990) for a more detailed comparison of these methods. Also see Ng and Han (1994) for the CLARANS clustering algorithm designed specifically for data mining. CLARANS and other recently developed database-oriented partitioning methods, such as Ester *et al.* (1995) and Zhang *et al.* (1996), are directly applicable to clustering numerical values into groups.

3.3 Generalization of Structured Data

A set-valued attribute may be of homogeneous or heterogeneous types. Typically, set-valued data can be generalized in two ways: (1) generalization of each value in a set into its corresponding higher-level concepts, or (2) derivation of the general behaviour of a set, such as the number of elements in the set, the types or value ranges in the set, the weighted average for numerical data etc. Moreover, the generalization can be performed by applying different generalization operators to explore alternative generalization paths. In this case, the result of generalization is a heterogeneous set.

For example, the *hobby* of a person is a set-valued attribute which contains a set of values, such as {*tennis, hockey, chess, violin, nintendo*}, which can be generalized into a set of high-level concepts, such as {*sports, music, video_games*}, or into 5 (the number of hobbies in the set), or both etc.

Set-valued attributes are simple structure-valued attributes. In general, a structure-valued attribute may contain sets, tuples, lists, trees, records etc. and their combinations. Furthermore, one structure can be nested in another structure at any level. Similar to the generalization of set-valued attributes, a general structure-valued attribute can be generalized in several ways, such as; (1) generalize each attribute in the structure while maintaining the shape of the structure; (2) flatten the structure and generalize the flattened structure; (3) remove the low-level structures or summarize the low-level structures by high-level concepts or aggregation; (4) return the type or an overview of the structure.

3.4 Aggregation and Approximation as a Means of Generalization

Besides concept tree ascension (i.e., replacing concepts by their corresponding higher-level concepts in a concept hierarchy) and structured data summarization, aggregation and approximation (Shum and Muntz, 1988) should be considered as an important means of generalization, which is especially useful for generalization of attributes with large sets of values, complex structures, spatial or multimedia data etc.

Take spatial data as an example. It is desirable to generalize detailed geographic points into clustered regions, such as business, residential, industry or agricultural areas, according to the land usage. Such generalization often requires the merge of a set of geographic areas by spatial operations, such as spatial union or spatial clustering algorithms. Approximation is an important technique in such generalization. In spatial merge, it is necessary not only to merge the regions of similar types within the same general class but also to ignore some scattered regions with different types if they are unimportant to the study. For example, different pieces of land for different purposes of agricultural usage, such as vegetables, grain, fruits etc. can be merged into one large piece of land by spatial merge. However, such agricultural land may contain highways, houses, small stores etc. If a majority of land is used for agriculture, the scattered spots for other purposes can be ignored, and the whole region can be claimed as an agricultural area by approximation. The spatial operators, such as *spatial_union, spatial_overlapping, spatial_intersection* etc., which merge scattered small regions into large, clustered regions can be considered as generalization operators in spatial aggregation and approximation.

3.5 Generalization of Multimedia Data

A multimedia database may contain complex text, graphics, images, maps, voice, music and other forms of audio/video information. Such multimedia data are typically stored as sequences of bytes with variable lengths, and segments of data are linked together for easy reference. Generalization of multimedia data can be performed by recognition and extraction of the essential features and/or general patterns of such data.

For an image, the size, shape and colour of the contained objects and/or their proportional distributions in the image can be extracted by aggregation and/or approximation. For a segment of music, its melody can be summarized based on the approximate patterns that repeatedly occur in the segment and its style can be summarized based on its tone, tempo, major musical instruments played etc. For an article, its abstract or general organization such as the table of contents, the subject and index terms frequently occurring in the article etc. may serve as generalization results. In general, it is a challenging task to generalize multimedia data to extract the interesting knowledge implicitly stored in the data. Further research should be devoted to this issue.

4 BUILDING AND MAINTAINING MLDBS

4.1 Key-Preserving vs. Key-Altering Generalizations

With attribute generalization techniques available, the next important question is how to selectively perform appropriate generalizations to form useful layers of databases. In principle, there could be a large number of combinations of possible generalizations by selecting different sets of attributes to generalize and selecting the levels for the attributes to reach in the generalization. However, in practice, a few layers containing most frequently referenced attributes and patterns will be sufficient to balance the implementation efficiency and practical usage.

Frequently used attributes and patterns should be determined before generation of new layers of an MLDB by the analysis of the statistics of query history or by receiving instructions from users or experts. It is wise to remove rarely used attributes but retain frequently referenced ones in a higher layer. Similar guidelines apply when generalizing attributes to a more general concept level. For example, users may like the age of a house to be expressed by *ranges* (of the years since construction) such as {*below_5*, 6_15, 16_30, *over_30*} instead of the exact *construction date* etc.

Note that finding frequently used attributes amounts to detailed book-keeping and thresholding. For instance, the MLDB administrator may decide that there would be three layers for a particular relation, and all attributes are divided into three classes. The first class consists of attributes that are in the top-10% in terms of frequencies of accesses. The second class consists of attributes that are in the top-30%, and the third class consists of all attributes. Then the highest layer only includes attributes in the first class, the intermediate layer only attributes in the second class, and the bottom layer all attributes.

A new layer could be formed by performing generalization on one relation or on one or more joins of several relations based on the selected or frequently used attributes and patterns. Generalization is performed by removing a set of less-interested attributes, substituting the concepts in one or a set of attributes by their corresponding higher-level concepts (Han *et al.*, 1993; Han and Fu, 1996), performing aggregation or approximation on certain attributes etc.

Since most joins of several relations are performed on their key and/or foreign key attributes, whereas generalization may remove or generalize the key or foreign key attributes of a data relation, it is important to distinguish the following two classes of generalizations:

1. **key-preserving generalization**, in which all the key or foreign key values are preserved.
2. **key-altering generalization**, in which some key or foreign key values are generalized, and thus altered. The generalized keys should be marked explicitly since they usually cannot be used as join attributes at generating subsequent layers.

It is crucial to identify altered keys since if the altered keys were used as join attributes for joining different relations, it may generate incorrect information. This can be observed in the following example.

Example 2. Suppose one would like to find the relationships between the ages of the houses sold and the household income level of the house buyers. Let the relations *house'* and *buyer'* contain the following tuples:

house' (945_Austin, ..., 35 (*years_old*), ...).
house' (58_Austin, ..., 4 (*years_old*), ...).
buyer' (945_Austin, mark_lee, 30_40k (*income*), ...).
buyer' (58_Austin, tim_akl, 60_70k (*income*), ...).

Their further generalization may result in the relations *house''* and *buyer''* containing the following tuples:

house'' (Austin, ..., over_30 (*years_old*), ...).
house'' (Austin, ..., below_5 (*years_old*), ...).
buyer'' (Austin, 30_40k (*income*), ...).
buyer'' (Austin, 60_70k (*income*), ...).

If the join is performed between *house'* and *buyer'*, it still produces the correct generalized information *house_buyer'*, which contains two tuples

house_buyer' (945_Austin, 35, mark_lee, 30_40k, ...).
house_buyer' (58_Austin, 4, tim_akl, 60_70k, ...).

and further generalization can still be performed on such a joined relation.

However, if join is performed on the altered keys between *house''* and *buyer''*, four tuples will be generated, which is obviously incorrect:

house_buyer'' (Austin, over_30, 30_40k, ...).
house_buyer'' (Austin, over_30, 60_70k, ...).
house_buyer'' (Austin, below_5, 30_40k, ...).
house_buyer'' (Austin, below_5, 60_70k, ...).

Clearly, joins on generalized attributes may produce more tuples than on original ones since different values in the attribute may have been generalized to identical values at a high layer.   □

Notice that join on generalized attributes, though undesirable in most cases, could be useful if a join is to link the tuples with *approximately* the same attribute values together. For example, for bus transfer, the bus stops within two street blocks may be considered "approximately the same" location. Such kind of join is called an **approximate join** to be distinguished from the **precise join**. In this chapter, the term *join* refers to *precise join* only. This restriction leads to the following regulation.

Regulation 1. (Join in MLDB). Join in an MLDB cannot be performed on the generalized attributes.

Based on this regulation, if the join in an MLDB is performed on the generalized attributes, it is called **information-loss join** (since the information could be lost by such a join). Otherwise, it is called **information-preserving join**.

4.2 An MLDB Construction Algorithm

Based on the previous discussion, the construction of an MLDB can be summarized into the following algorithm, which is similar to attribute-oriented generalization in knowledge discovery in databases (Han *et al.*, 1993; Han and Fu, 1996).

Algorithm 1. Construction of an MLDB.

  Input: a relational database, a set of concept hierarchies, and a set of frequently referenced attributes and frequently used query patterns.
Output: a multiple-layer database.

Method. An MLDB is constructed in the following steps.

1. Determine the multiple layers of the database based on the frequently referenced attributes and frequently used query patterns.
2. Starting with the most specific layer, generalize the relation step-by-step (using the given concept hierarchies) to form multiple-layer relations (according to the layers determined in Step 1).
3. Merge identical tuples in each generalized relation and update the *count* of the generalized tuple.
4. Construct a new schema by recording all the primitive and generalized relations, their relationships and the generalization paths.   □

Rationale of Algorithm 1. Step 1 indicates that the layers of an MLDB should be determined based on the frequently referenced attributes and frequently used query patterns. This is reasonable since to ensure the elegance and efficiency of an MLDB, only a small number of layers should be constructed, which should provide maximum benefits to the frequently accessed query patterns. Obviously, the frequently referenced attributes should be preserved in higher layers, and the frequently referenced concept levels of these attributes should be considered as the candidate concept levels in the construction of higher layers. Steps 2 and 3 are performed in a way similar to attribute-oriented induction, studied previously (Han *et al.*, 1993; Han and Fu 1996). Step 4 constructs a new schema which records a route map and the generalization paths for database browsing and cooperative query answering, which will be discussed in detail below.
                                                                         □

4.3 Schema: a Route Map and a Set of Generalization Paths

Since an MLDB schema provides a route map, i.e., a general structure of the MLDB for query answering and database browsing, it is important to construct a concise and information-rich schema. Besides the schema information stored in a conventional relational database system, an MLDB schema should store two more important pieces of information.

1. A **route map**, which outlines the relationships among the relations at different layers of the database. For example, it shows which higher-layer relation is generalized from one or a set of lower-layer relations.
2. A set of **generalization paths**, each of which shows *how* a higher-layer relation is generalized from one or a set of lower-layer relations.

Similar to many extended relational databases, a *route map* can be represented by an extended E−R (entity−relationship) diagram (Teorey *et al.*, 1986), in which the entities and relationships at layer-0 (the original database) can be represented in a conventional E−R diagram (Silberschatz *et al.*, 1997); whereas generalization is represented by a double-line arrow pointed from the generalizing entity (or relationship) to the generalized entity (or relationship). For example, *house′* is a higher-layer entity generalized from a lower-layer entity *house*, as shown in Figure 1. Similarly, *sales_buyer′* is a higher-layer relationship, obtained by generalizing the join of *sales′* and *buyer′*. It is represented as a generalization from a relationship obtained by joining one entity and one relationship in the route map (Figure 1). Since an extended E−R database can be easily mapped into an extended relational one (Silberschatz *et al.*, 1997), our discussion assumes such mappings and still adopts the terminologies from an extended relational model.

A *generalization path* is created for each high-layer relation to represent how the relation is obtained in the generalization. Such a high-layer relation is possibly obtained by removing a set of infrequently used attributes, preserving some attributes and/or generalizing the remaining set of attributes. Since attribute removing and preserving can be obviously observed from a relational schema, the generalization path needs only to register how a set of attributes are generalized. A generalization path consists of a set of entries, each of which contains three components: ⟨old_attr(s), new_attr(s), rules⟩, which tells how one or a set of old attributes is generalized into a set of new (generalized) attributes by applying some generalization rule(s), such as generalizing to which concept levels of a concept hierarchy, applying which aggregation operations etc. If an existing hierarchy is adjusted or a new hierarchy is created in the formation of a new layer, such a hierarchy should also be registered in the *hierarchy* component of an MLDB.

4.4 Maintenance of MLDBs

Since an MLDB is constructed from extracting extra layers from an existing database by generalization, an MLDB will take more disc space than its corresponding single-layer database. However, since a higher-layer database is usually much smaller than the original database, query processing is expected to be more efficient if done in a higher database layer. The rapid progress of computer hardware technology has reduced the cost of disc space dramatically in the last decade. Therefore, it could be beneficial to trade disc space for intelligent and fast query answering.

In response to the updates to the original relations, the corresponding higher layers should be updated accordingly to keep the MLDB consistent. Incremental update algorithms can be used to minimize the cost of update propagation. Here we examine how to propagate incremental database updates at insertion, deletion and update of tuples in an original relation.

When a new tuple t is inserted into a relation R, t should be generalized to t' according to the route map and be inserted into its corresponding higher layer. Such an insertion will be propagated to higher layers accordingly. However, if the generalized tuple t' is equivalent to an existing tuple in this layer, it needs only to increment the count of the existing tuple, and further propagations to higher layers will be confined to count increment as well. The deletion of a tuple from a data relation can be performed similarly.

When a tuple in a relation is updated, one can check whether the change may affect any of its high layers. If not, do nothing. Otherwise, the algorithm will be similar to the deletion of an old tuple followed by the insertion of a new one.

Although an MLDB consists of multiple layers, database updates should always be performed at the primitive database (i.e., layer-0) and the updates are then propagated to their corresponding higher layers. This is because a higher layer represents more general information, and it is impossible to transform a more general value to a more specific one, such as from *age* to *birth-date* (but it is possible in the reverse direction by applying appropriate generalization rules).

5 QUERY ANSWERING IN AN MLDB

A query may involve concepts matching different layers. Moreover, one may expect that the query be answered *directly* by strictly following the request, or *intelligently* by providing some generalized, neighbourhood or associated answers.

In this section, we first examine the mechanisms for *direct* answering of queries in an MLDB and then extend the results to *cooperative* query answering.

5.1 Direct Query Answering

Direct query answering refers to answering queries by strictly following query specifications without providing (extra) associative information in the answers. Rigorously speaking, if all the provided and inquired information of a query are at the primitive concept level, a query can be answered directly by searching the primitive layer without exploring higher layers. However, a cooperative system should provide users with flexibility of expressing query constants and inquiries at a relatively high concept level. Such "high-level" queries can be answered directly in an MLDB.

At first glance, it seems to be easy to process such high-level queries by simply matching the constants and enquiries in the query to a corresponding layer and then directly processing the query in this layer. However, there could be dozens of attributes in a relation and each attribute may have several concept levels. It is impossible and often undesirable to construct all the possible generalized relations whose different attributes are at different concept levels. In practice, only a small number of all the possible layers will be stored in an MLDB based on the analysis of the frequently referenced query patterns. This implies that transformations often need to be performed on some query constants to map them to a concept level corresponding to that of an existing layer database.

In principle, a high-level query constant is defined in a concept hierarchy, based on which the high-level constant can be mapped to primitive level concepts. For example, *"great vancouver area"* can be mapped to all of its composite regions, and *"big house"* can be mapped to *"total_floor_area $\geq$ 3000(sq. ft.)"*, etc. Thus, a query can always be transformed into a primitive level query and be processed in a layer-0 database. However, to increase processing efficiency and present high-level (and more meaningful) answers, our goal is to process a query in the highest possible layer, *consistent* with all of the query constants and enquiries.

Definition 2. A database layer L is **consistent** on an attribute A_i with a query q if the constants of attribute A_i in query q can absorb (i.e., level-wise no lower than) the concept(s) (level) of the attribute in the layer.

For example, if the query constant in query q for the attribute *"floor_area"* is *"big"*, whereas the concept level for *"floor_area"* in layer L is the same as *"big"*, or lower, such as "3000_4999", "over_5000", etc., then layer L is consistent with query q on the attribute *"floor_area"*.

Definition 3. The **watermark** of a (nonjoin) attribute A_i for query q is the topmost database layer which is consistent with the concept level of query constants/enquiries of attribute A_i in query q.

Lemma 1. *All the layers lower than the watermark of an attribute A_i for query q must be consistent with the values of attribute A_i in query q.*

This lemma is a property immediately following from Definitions 2 and 3.

We first examine the case that a query references only one generalized relation and all the high-level query constants are nonnumerical values.

Proposition 1. *If a query q references only one generalized relation and no other relations, and all the high-level query constants are nominal (non-numerical) values, the highest possible layer consistent with the query should be the lowest watermark of all the participant attributes of q in the route map of the MLDB.*

Rationale. Suppose layer L is the lowest watermark of all the participant attributes of q in the route map of the MLDB. Since a layer no higher than the watermark of attribute A_i must be consistent with the corresponding query constant/enquiry on attribute A_i, L must be consistent with all the constants and enquiries of all the participant attributes of query q. Furthermore, since a watermark for an attribute is the highest possible database layer for such an attribute, the layer so derived must be the highest possible layer that is consistent with all the participating attributes in the query.
□

Next, we examine the case of queries involving join(s) of two or more relations. If such a join or its lower layer is already stored in the MLDB by an information-preserving join, the judgement should be the same as the case for single relations. However, if no such a join has been performed and stored as a new layer in the MLDB, the watermark of such a join attribute must be the highest database layer in which generalization has not been performed on this attribute (i.e., on which the information-preserving join can be performed). This is because join cannot be performed on the generalized attributes according to Regulation 1.

Definition 4. The watermark of a join attribute A_i for query q is the topmost database layer which is consistent with the concept level of query constants/enquiries of attribute A_i in query q and in which the information-preserving join can be performed on A_i.

Thus, we have the following proposition.

Proposition 2. *If a query q involves join(s) of two or more relations, and all the high-level query constants are nominal (non-numerical) constants, the highest possible layer consistent with the query should be the lowest watermark of all the participant attributes (including the join attributes) of q in the route map of the MLDB.*

Rationale. Based on the definition of the watermark of a join attribute in a query, and the similar reasoning in the rationale for Proposition 1, it naturally leads to the assertion for a query involving one join. By induction, one can easily show that the proposition holds for queries involving more than one join.
□

Example 3. Suppose the query on the real-estate MLDB is to describe the relationship between *house* and *sales* with the following given information: *located in north-vancouver, 3-bedroom house, and sold in the summer of 1993.* Moreover, suppose the route map of an MLDB corresponding to this query is shown in Figure 2.

The query involves a join of *sales* and *house* and the provided query constants are all at the levels high enough to match those in *house″* and *sales″*. However, a join cannot be performed at these two high-layer relations since the join attributes of *house″* and *sales″* have been generalized (with their

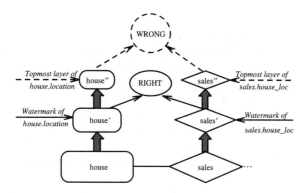

Figure 2. Perform joins at the appropriate layers.

join keys altered). The watermarks of the join attributes, *house.location* and *sales.house_loc*, are one layer lower than their topmost layers.

If there exists a relation such as *house_sales* in the MLDB, which represents the join between the two relations and/or their further generalizations, the query can be processed within such a layer. Otherwise (as shown in Figure 2), join must be performed on the highest joinable layers (which should be *house'* and *sales'*, as shown in Figure 2). Then further generalization can be performed on this joined relation to form appropriate answers.

□

Finally, we examine the determination of the highest possible database layers if the query contains numeric attributes. If the value in a numeric attribute in the query is expressed as a generalized constant, such as "*expensive*", or the specified range in the query has an exact match with some (generalized) range in a concept hierarchy, such as "$300–400 k", the numeric value can be treated the same as a nonnumeric concept. Otherwise, we have two choices: (1) set the watermark of the attribute to the highest layer in which such numeric attributes have not been generalized; (2) relax the requirement of the preciseness of the query answering. In the latter case, the appropriate layer is first determined by non-numeric attributes. A coverage test is then performed to see whether the generalized range is entirely covered by the range provided in the query. For the entirely covered (generalized) ranges, the precision of the answer remains the same. However, for that which only partially covers a range, the answer should be associated with certain probability (e.g., by assuming that the data are relatively uniformly distributed within the generalized range), or be associated with a necessary explanation to clarify that the answer may not match the exact query condition but cover the entire generalized range.

Example 4. Suppose the query on the real-estate database is to describe the big houses in North Vancouver ranging in price from $280 k to

$350 k. Since the query is to *describe* houses (not to find exact houses), the enquired portion can be considered at a high layer, matching any layers located by its query constants. To find the layer of its query constants, we have *"floor_area = big"*, *"address = north-vancouver"*, and *"price_range = $280 k–$350 k"*. The watermarks of the first two are at the layer *house"*, whereas the third one is a range value. Suppose in the layer *house"*, the generalized tuples may have ranges like $250 k–$300 k, $300 k–$350 k etc., which do not exactly match the range $280 k–$350 k. Still, the query can be processed at this layer, with the information within the range $300 k–$350 k returned without additional explanation, but with the information within the range $250 k–$300 k returned, associated with an explanation that the returned information is for the range of $250 k–$300 k instead of $280 k–$300 k to avoid misunderstanding.   ☐

5.2 Cooperative Query Answering

Since an MLDB stores general database information in higher layers, many techniques investigated in previous research into cooperative query answering in (single-layer) databases (Imielinski, 1987; Cuppens and Demolombe, 1991; Chu and Chen, 1992; Gaasterland, 1993; Han *et al.*, 1996b) can be extended effectively to cooperative query answering in MLDBs.

The following reasoning may convince us that an MLDB may greatly facilitate cooperative query answering.

Many cooperative query answering techniques need certain kinds of generalization (Chu and Chen, 1992; Gaasterland *et al.*, 1992), whereas different kinds of frequently used generalizations are performed and stored in the high layers of an MLDB. Also, they often need to compare the "neighbourhood" information (Cuppens and Demolombe, 1991; Chu and Chen, 1992). The generalized neighbourhood tuples are usually stored in the same high-layer relations, ready for comparison and investigation. Moreover, they often need to summarize answer-related information, associated with data statistics or certain aggregations (Chu and Chen, 1992; Witteman and Kunst, 1993). Interestingly, a higher-layer relation not only presents the generalized tuples but also the *counts* of the identical tuples or other computed aggregation values (such as sum, average etc.). Such high-level information with counts conveys important information for data summarization and statistical data investigation.

Furthermore, since the layer selection in the construction of an MLDB is based on the study of the frequently referenced attributes and frequently used query patterns, the MLDB itself embodies rich information about the history of the most regular query patterns and also implies the potential intent of the database users. It forms a rich source for query intent analysis and plays the role of confining the cooperative answers to frequently referenced patterns automatically.

Finally, an MLDB constructs a set of layers step-by-step, from most specific data to more general information. It facilitates progressive query refinement, from general information browsing to specific data retrieval. Such a process represents a top-down information searching process, which matches the human reasoning and learning process naturally, thus providing a cooperative process for step-by-step information exploration (Vrbsky and Liu, 1991; Wolf, 1993).

Example 5. A query like *"what kind of houses can be bought with $300k in the Vancouver area?"* can be answered using an MLDB efficiently and effectively. Here we examine several ways to answer this query using the MLDB constructed in Example 1.

1. **Relaxation of query conditions using concept hierarchies and/or high-layer relations.** Instead of answering the query using *"house_price = $300k"*, the condition can be relaxed to *about $300k*, that is, the price range covering $300k in a high-layer relation, such as *house"*, can be used for query answering. This kind of relaxation can be done by mapping query constants up or down using concept hierarchies, and once the query is mapped to a level that fits a corresponding database layer, it can be processed within the layer.

2. **Generalized answers with summarized statistics.** Instead of printing thousands of houses within this price range, it searches through the top-layer *house* relation, such as *house"*, and prints the generalized answer, such as "20% 20−30 years-old, medium-sized, 3-bedroom house in East Vancouver, ...". With the availability of MLDBs, such generalized answers can be obtained directly from a high-layer DB by summarization of the answers (such as presenting percentage, general view etc.) at a high layer.

3. **Comparison with the neighbourhood answers.** Furthermore, the printed general answer can be compared with its neighbourhood answers using the same top-level relation, such as "10% 3-bedroom 20−30-year-old houses in Central Vancouver priced between $250k to $350k, while 30% such houses priced between $350 to $500k, ...". Notice that such comparison information can be presented as concise tables using an existing high-layer relation.

4. **Query answering with associative information.** It is often desirable to provide some "extra" information associated with a set of answers in cooperative query answering. Query answering with associative information can be easily achieved using high-layer data relations. For example, the query can be answered by printing houses with different price ranges (such as $230−280k, $330−380k etc.) as *row extension*, or printing houses in neighbouring cities, printing other interesting features as *column extension*, or printing sales information related to such houses as *table extension*. These can be performed using high-layer relations.

5. **Progressively query refinement or progressive information focusing.** The query can be answered by progressively stepping down the layers to find more detailed information. The top layer is often examined first, with general data and global views presented. Such a presentation often gives a user a better idea on what should be searched further with additional constraints. For example, a user may focus the search on the East Vancouver area after he or she finds a high percentage of the houses within this price range since it is likely that a suitable house can be found within this area. Such a further enquiry may lead the search to lower-layer relations and may also promote users to pose more restricted constraints or refine the original ones. In this case, the route map associated with the MLDB will act as a tour guide to locate related lower-layer relation(s).   □

6 MLDBs FOR HETEROGENEOUS DATABASE SYSTEMS

A major challenge to the interoperability of a heterogeneous database system is the semantic heterogeneity of multiple, autonomous information systems. Since each information system has its own regulations and its own ways to specify its data and rules, it may cause ambiguity and incompatibility problems when interoperating multiple database systems.

The interoperability of multiple information systems should be taken as a major concern in the design and construction of the MLDB for a heterogeneous database system. Although such a heterogeneous system may still allow each component system to have its own independent multiple-layer relations, higher-layer relations with their sub-schemas and concepts shared among different components should be constructed systematically.

The construction of a shared, cooperative MLDB may involve the negotiation and standardization of higher-layer concepts and schemas for multiple components. The result of such negotiation and standardization may lead to an agreement on a minimum information consistent layer, called the *minimum cooperative layer*, in which the schema is a commonly agreed one and each attribute contains (*generalized* or *transformed*) concepts (or values) agreed by every component system. Each component system should specify the rules of mapping from a certain layer of their MLDB to this minimum cooperative layer. Higher layers constructed on top of this minimum cooperative layer will be shared among the components.

According to this architecture, a heterogeneous database system consists of a shared, cooperative MLDB for the whole system; each component may have its own MLDB; and the minimum cooperative layer is the interface layer between the MLDB of the whole system and the component MLDB. Queries on the whole system can be answered by referencing first the MLDB of the system and, when more detailed information is needed, mapping the query from the minimum cooperative layer to the corresponding component MLDB.

Notice that the minimum cooperative layer and the layers above, even constructed for the whole system, may still belong to each component database and be stored in their corresponding sites. Alternatively, they can also be stored in multiple copies, e.g., one copy at each site, if the size of the high-layer relations is not so large, to reduce the cost of network transmission. In either case, if the query involves only frequently asked items or high-level information, the data transmission across the network can be reduced substantially using the architecture of MLDBs.

Moreover, although the MLDB architecture may facilitate query transformation among different sites, cooperative query answering techniques should often be used for answering queries against the shared heterogeneous MLDBs instead of returning the primitive-level data or the data in the nonshared portion of the heterogeneous MLDBs. This is because primitive-level data or non-shared generalized data may carry different data semantics from different component databases which may be misinterpreted or misunderstood by users.

Example 6. Let us examine how to achieve cooperation among heterogeneous university databases for graduate admission, the example illustrated in the introduction section.

Let the federated schema be worked out as follows, based on schema transformation and analysis.

grading(name, student_id, semester, year, course_num, department, university, ..., grade),

Taking the primitive level data in each database as layer-0 database, a layer-1 relation *grading*, viewed as the minimum cooperative layer, can be constructed by generalizing data in a set of shared attributes into concepts which are cooperative in heterogeneous databases. For example, "*semester, year*" can be generalized to *semester* in a form like 932 (i.e., the second semester of 1993). Similarly "*course_num*" can be generalized to some generic, summarative course_information, such as DB1 (first DB course), OS2 (second OS course) etc., and *grades* into grade distributions, such as top-5% etc. Such transformations make database contents exchangeable among different component databases.

The formation of this minimum cooperative layer may involve the negotiation and standardization of higher-layer concepts and schemas among multiple components. Each component system should specify the rules of mapping from a certain layer of their MLDB to this minimum cooperative layer. In this example, rules may work out for each component database on how to transform course numbers, grades etc. to commonly sharable course names, grade distributions etc.

One example of such a transformation is shown in Table 1, which results in a set of layer-1 relations. Notice at this layer, contents of some attributes such as *semester, course_num, department, grade*, etc. have been generalized and transformed into cooperative concepts. However, not every attribute in such a higher-layer relation will have their contents

Table 1.   A set of cooperative layer-1 relations *grading* from multiple university databases.

Name	student_id	semester	course_num	department	university	...	grade
Jane Doe	93350924	932	DB1	BU	SFU	...	top-2%
John Smith	85140298	923	OS2	CS	SFU	...	top-40%
...	...	...	...	...	...	... ...	
Name	student_id	semester	course_num	department	university	...	grade
Sam Carey	941CS0135	953	Java	CS	U.B.C.	...	top-15%
...	...	...	...	...	...	... ...	
Name	student_id	semester	course_num	department	university	...	grade
Tom Hardy	3H702953	951	C++	CIS	OSU	...	top-30%
...	...	...	...	...	...	... ...	

generalized uniformly. For example, values in the attributes *name* and *student_id* remain unchanged. Such treatment at the construction of minimal cooperative layer is important since such retained values will be useful in many applications, such as, evaluation of individual applicants.

Higher layers constructed on top of this minimum cooperative layer will be shared among the components. Such higher layers may provide high-level, generalized views of the database contents.

An interesting point is that when a user at one university poses a query about the applicants from other universities, it is often preferable not to return detailed primitive data but to return data at the minimum cooperative layer or higher. This is because the primitive-level data, such as a course number or a grading system in another university may not be comprehensible to users at a different institution. Therefore, cooperative query answering at different layers discussed in the last sections may become a valuable tool for cooperating heterogeneous information systems.

□

7 CONCLUSIONS

In this chapter, a major challenge for building cooperative information systems — the semantic heterogeneity problem — is analysed, which shows that schema level analysis, though popularly performed in current studies, may not be sufficient to solve the problem, and the data level analysis, i.e., the analysis of database contents, should be explored to ease the semantic heterogeneity problem in cooperative information systems. In particular, a multiple-layer database (MLDB) model is proposed and studied, which is useful in cooperative query answering, database browsing, query optimization, and cooperating heterogeneous databases.

Our study shows that data mining may provide a powerful tool at construction of multiple-layer databases since it facilitates the transformation of low-level heterogeneous data into high-level homogeneous information. Data generalization and layer construction methods have been developed in this study to ensure that new layers can be constructed efficiently, effectively and consistent with the primitive information stored in the database.

The necessity of data mining in cooperative information systems and the techniques for data mining are studied, including the methods for data generalization, summarization and the construction and maintenance of multiple-layer databases. Direct and cooperative query answering in such an MLDB and the methods for cooperating heterogeneous databases are studied with the implementation techniques examined and the benefits and limitations analysed.

Currently, we are further investigating the methods for construction of MLDBs for heterogeneous databases. New techniques, implementations and performance studies for the construction of MLDBs for heterogeneous databases will be reported in the future.

ACKNOWLEDGEMENTS

The research of the first author was supported by the grant NSERC-A3723 from the Natural Science and Engineering Research Council of Canada, the grant NCE:IRIS/PRECARN-HMI-5 from the Networks of Centres of Excellence of Canada, and grants from MPR Teltch Ltd. and Hughes Research Laboratories. The research of the second author was partially supported by the Natural Sciences and Engineering Research Council of Canada under grants OGP0138055.

REFERENCES

Agrawal, R., Ghosh, S., Imielinski, T., Iyer, B. and Swami, A. (1992) An interval classifier for database mining applications. In *Proceedings 18th International Conference on Very Large Data Bases*, Vancouver, Canada, pp. 560–573.

Chu, W.W. and Chen, Q. (1992) Neighborhood and associative query answering. *Journal of Intelligent Information systems*, **1**, 355–382.

Cuppens, F. and Demolombe, R. (1991) Extending answers to neighbor entities in a cooperative answering context. *Decision Support Systems*, **7**, 1–11.

Dao, S. and Perry, B. (1995) Applying a data miner to heterogeneous schema integration. In *Proceedings First International Conference on Knowledge Discovery and Data Mining*, Montreal, Canada, pp. 63–68.

de Ville, B. (1990) Applying statistical knowledge to database analysis and knowledge base construction. In *Proceedings 6th Conference on Artificial Intelligence Applications*, Santa Barbara, CA, pp. 30–36.

Elmagarmid, A. and Pu, C. (eds). (1990) Special issue on heterogeneous databases. *ACM Computing Surveys*, **22**.

Ester, M., Kriegel, H.-P. and Xu. X. (1995) Knowledge discovery in large spatial databases: Focusing techniques for efficient class identification. In *Proceedings,*

J. Han et al.

4th International, Symposium, on Large Spatial Databases (SSD'95), Portland, Maine, pp. 67–82.

Fayyad, U.M., Piatetsky-Shapiro, G., Smyth, P. and R. Uthurusamy. (1996) *Advances in Knowledge Discovery and Data Mining*. AAAI/MIT Press.

Fisher, D. (1987) Improving inference through conceptual clustering. In *Proceedings 1987 AAAI Conferences*, Seattle, Washington, pp. 461–465.

Gaasterland, T. (1993) Restricting query relaxation through user constraints. In *Proceedings 1st International Conference on Cooperative Information Systems*, Toronto, Canada, pp. 359–366.

Gaasterland, T., Godgrey, P. and Minker, J. (1992) Relaxation as a platform for cooperative answering. *Journal of Intelligent Information Systems*, 1, 293–321.

Han, J. and Fu, Y. (1994) Dynamic generation and refinement of concept hierarchies for knowledge discovery in databases. In *Proceedings AAAI'94 Workshop on Knowledge Discovery in Databases (KDD'94)*, Seattle, WA, pp. 157–168.

Han, J. and Fu, Y. (1996) Exploration of the power of attribute-oriented induction in data mining. In *Advances in Knowledge Discovery and Data Mining*, U.M. Fayyad, G. Piatetsky-Shapiro, P. Smyth and R. Uthurusamy (eds). AAAI/MIT Press, pp. 399–421.

Han, J., Cai, Y. and Cercone, N. (1993) Data-driven discovery of quantitative rules in relational databases. *IEEE Transactions on Knowledge and Data Engineering*, 5, 29–40.

Han, J., Fu, Y., Wang, W., Chiang, J., Gong, W., Koperski, K., Li, D., Lu, Y., Rajan, A., Stefanovic, N., Xia, B. and Zaiane, O.R. (1996a) DBMiner: A system for mining knowledge in large relational databases. In *Proceedings 1996 International Conference on Data Mining and Knowledge Discovery (KDD'96)*, Portland, Oregon, pp. 250–255.

Han, J., Huang, Y., Cercone, N. and Fu, Y. (1996b) Intelligent query answering by knowledge discovery techniques. *IEEE Transactions on Knowledge and Data Engineering*, 8, 373–390.

Imielinski, T. (1987) Intelligent query answering in rule based systems. *Journal of Logic Programming*, 4, 229–257.

Kaufman, L. and Rousseeuw, P.J. (1990) *Finding Groups in Data: an Introduction to Cluster Analysis*. John Wiley & Sons.

Ng, R. and Han, J. (1994) Efficient and effective clustering method for spatial data mining. In *Proceedings 1994 International Conference on Very Large Data Bases*, Santiago, Chile, pp. 144–155.

Schek, H., Sheth, A. and Czejdo, B. (eds). (1993) Interoperability in multidatabase systems. In *Proceedings Third International Workshop on Research Issues in Data Engineering*.

Sheth, A.P. and Larson, J.A. (1990) Federated database systems for managing distributed, heterogeneous, and autonomous database. *ACM Comput. Survey*, 22, 183–236.

Shum, C. and Muntz, R. (1988) An information-theoretic study on aggregate responses. In *Proceedings 14th International Conference on Very Large Data Bases*, Los Angeles, USA, pp. 479–490.

Sibberschatz, A., Korth, H.F. and Sudarshan, S. (1997) *Database Systems Concepts*, 3rd edn. McGraw-Hill.

Teorey, T.J., Yang, D. and Fry, J.P. (1986) A logical design methodology for relational databases using the extended entity-relationship model. *ACM Comput. Survey*, 18, 197–222.

Vrbsky, S.V. and Liu, J.W.S. (1991) An object-oriented query processor that returns monotonically improving answers. In *Proceedings 7th IEEE Conference on Data Engineering*, Kobe, Japan, pp. 472–481.

Wittemann, C. and Kunst, H. (1993) Intelligent assistance in flexible decisions. In *Proceedings 1st International Conference on Cooperative Information Systems*, Toronto, Canada, pp. 377–381.

Wolf, M.F. (1993) Successful integration of databases, knowledge-based systems, and human judgement. In *Proceedings 1st International Conference on Cooperative Information Systems*, Toronto, Canada, pp. 154–162.

Zhang, T., Ramakrishnan, R. and Livny, M. (1996) BIRCH: an efficient data clustering method for very large databases. In *Proceedings 1996 ACM-SIGMOD International Conference on Management of Data*, Montreal, Canada, pp. 103–114.

Reflection is the Essence of Cooperation

David Edmond[a] and Michael P. Papazoglou[b]

[a]Queensland University of Technology, Brisbane, Australia and [b]Tilburg University, The Netherlands

Abstract

The work reported in this chapter uses *operational reflection* as a means of enabling cooperation between pre-existing and autonomous information sources located at a number of remote sites. Each component database system is encapsulated by a layer of metalevel software that knows about that system's functionality and competence, incorporates basic programmable cooperative processing facilities, and provides access to the enclosed system by means of an abstract program interface, regardless of the underlying system's complexity.

I INTRODUCTION

The goal of a dynamic, distributed information network is to enable its *component* information sources (typically autonomous database systems) to be combined into a coherent and complete application, with each component performing a limited range of useful functions. In such situations, the question of how to combine distributed, pre-existing heterogeneous information sources, such as legacy systems, and applications becomes critical. Early approaches to building federated database systems do not scale well, due to the large number and diversity of the internetworked information sources.

The only long-term solution to this problem is to provide a controllable way of integrating legacy systems with each other and with new software. Such concerns are addressed by multi-database and federated database systems which have as their aim the ability to access multiple autonomous databases through querying. The approach taken is to make the multiple autonomous databases usable without a conceptually unified schema in order to preserve autonomy, while supporting global updates. In multi-database systems the focus has mainly been on sharing of distributed

Cooperative Information Systems
Trends and Directions
ISBN 0-12-544910-0

information by means of a common language (Sheth and Larson, 1990). However, such systems are mostly built using *ad hoc* implementations where system-related aspects cut across each other and the final implementation code and cannot be constructed in controlled piecemeal manner.

More recently, technological solutions have been proposed by leveraging distributed object management with wrapping technology (Manola *et al.*, this volume). Distributed object management deals with issues that are inherent in creating single-image, client/server solutions based on objects that work together across machine and network boundaries. Object-wrapping technology provides access to pre-existing information sources through abstract application program interfaces. These hide much of the internal implementation and complexity of the underlying systems. The blending of these two technologies provides object gateways between disparate (networked) information systems, and allows coordinated construction of and access to *interwoven* objects.[1] Such a blend constitutes a typical example of a technology critical for cooperation.

One of the most challenging problems to be addressed by cooperative information systems is the development of an infrastructure that opens up the process of constructing and managing interwoven objects based on dispersed and pre-existing networked information sources. Instead of such activities being totally hidden, we may provide a general policy framework for object construction and management, one that allows particular object control and management policies to be developed and applied in a *controlled* manner. This results in self-describing, dynamic and reconfigurable systems that facilitate the composition (specification and implementation) of a new application system, by drawing upon (and possibly specializing) the functionality of already existing component database systems.

Such cooperative information systems cannot be built by using *ad hoc* solutions and implementation techniques. There are several system-related aspects, such as information combination, distribution, communication and message processing strategies, which constitute what we claim to be the *essence* of cooperation and that need to be carefully considered and expressed in an abstract manner. With traditional interoperable system implementations, system-related aspects fundamentally cut across each other and the final implementation code. Implementation is a process that, almost by its very nature, tends to tangle together various aspects of the original system's requirements and design, resulting in an artefact that is complex yet monolithic, difficult to change and difficult to regulate and reason about. We require that, at certain stages of systems development,

---

[1]Interwoven objects are virtual objects with multiple, and possibly overlapping, subcomponents. Their subcomponents reside in different address spaces and are called *object fragments* or *dispersed objects*. Interwoven objects are packaged as independent pieces of data and code that can be accessed by application clients via method calls which will ultimately have to be routed to their appropriate fragments. All *application objects* used in applications developed in terms of cooperative information systems are interwoven objects.

we are able to isolate and represent relevant system aspects, recognizing that, at the implementation level, these will be coordinated into some total computation. It is our view that what is needed is the ability to work with abstractions that express naturally and directly system aspects (rather than with monolithic modules of executable code) and then combine these into a final meaningful implementation.

Such ideas can benefit tremendously from techniques found in meta-object protocols (Kiczales *et al.*, 1991; Paepcke, 1990) and reflection (Maes, 1987; Honda and Yonezawa, 1988). There, a system provides *two* interfaces to achieve separation and coordination of control: a primary interface that provides the basic functionality, and another that can be used to monitor, reason about and tune the functionality available through the primary interface (Kiczales, 1996). Our approach to building agile (self-describing, dynamic and reconfigurable) cooperative information systems comes from extending the ideas of separation of domain (application) and control knowledge as advocated by meta-object protocols and reflective approaches.

In this chapter we describe reflective techniques that may be used as a way of opening up the general process of interwoven object reification and management. Specifically, we discuss the *ROK* (reflective object knowledge) framework and how it may be used to reveal the process or processes involved in interweaving object fragments and making them available to an application program. We feel that, by separating implementation from domain representation concerns and by revealing the former in a modifiable and object-oriented way, distributed and possibly heterogeneous information sources, such as the so-called *legacy systems* (Brodie 1994), may be used by new applications in a transparent way. Instead of composing new systems from old in an *ad hoc* or "one-off" way, we provide a programmable meta-object space which allows particular composition policies to be applied in a *controlled* and *coordinated* manner. Meta-objects are used to reify dispersed objects and provide them with an execution environment that implements operations on them such as message passing and scheduling.

In Section 2 we discuss the ideas behind reflection, and their manifestation in the concept of a meta-object protocol. In Section 3, we introduce the *ROK* framework and, in particular, the four meta-objects around which it is based. In Section 4, we discuss the use of reflection as a means of building agents from metadata such as that provided by the four meta-objects just discussed. We then describe and demonstrate how these objects work together across machine and network boundaries to create client/server application solutions based on an automatically generated C++ API. We also discuss the *ROK* meta-object support infrastructure. In Section 5, we discuss some of the issues involved in building a prototype of the *ROK* model. In Section 6, we review a number of proposed architectures for generic distributed object management.

2 REFLECTION AND META-OBJECT PROTOCOLS

In human beings, reflection may be characterized as the ability to stand back, take stock and then take action. In an information systems context, it is characterized by self-representation and by the ability to act upon and alter that representation. Reflection makes it possible to reveal a system's implementation without uncovering necessary details. A primary focus of reflection has been to provide a metalevel component that affects the way in which a base-level component, such as the source-code of some program, may be implemented. A reflective computational system contains data that represent both structural and computational aspects of the system itself. Moreover, it is possible to explicitly access and manipulate such representations, from within the system, in order to adjust the behaviour of the system to suit the needs of a particular application. The major characteristics of a reflective system are:

- The clear separation of *domain* knowledge from *control* knowledge (Davis, 1980).
- The *explicit* representation of that control knowledge.

Domain knowledge is *what* a system knows of its domain, and is encoded within the application system. Control knowledge is *how* that knowledge is or should be applied, and is encoded in the metalevel.

Reflection has been particularly successful in object-oriented settings. There, it has been employed as a novel methodology for constructing flexible, large-scale complex systems such as: (1) programming languages (Maes, 1987, 1988; Kiczales *et al.*, 1991; Stemple *et al.*, 1992; Masuhara *et al.*, 1992); (2) the next generation of operating systems, providing them with open-ended and self-extending facilities (Yokote *et al.*, 1991; Yokote, 1992); (3) window systems (Rao, 1991).

In programming languages, reflection has been used to provide an auxiliary interface to the language, one that enables a language's designer(s) to incrementally modify its behaviour and implementation — whether compiled or interpreted. This interface is known as a *meta-object protocol*, and is based on the idea that one can open languages up, allowing users to adjust the design and implementation to suit their particular needs. In a language incorporating such a protocol, the language implementation is itself structured as an object-oriented program.

A meta-object protocol uses object-oriented programming to provide better scope control and extensibility than was possible with previous non-reflective architectures. Every aspect of a language's mapping down onto the base-level substrate, i.e., its compile-time and run-time environments, is controlled by some object or class following a well-defined protocol (Kiczales, 1996). These objects and classes are called meta-objects and metaclasses respectively, as their main concern is the mapping of the syntactic elements of the program rather than the objects in the program's

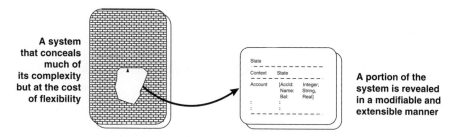

A system that conceals much of its complexity but at the cost of flexibility

State
Context   State
Account   [AccId: Integer;
            Name: String,
            Bal: Real]

A portion of the system is revealed in a modifiable and extensible manner

Figure 1.   Revelation and reflection.

application domain. Programmers can specialize these meta-objects to affect specific aspects of the language implementation.

The concepts behind meta-object protocols may be usefully trans-ferred to cooperating systems. Core cooperative tasks, carried out in an *ad hoc* manner up to now, can be performed using metalevel facilities (Stroud and Wu, 1992). Such core tasks may include transaction scheduling, object communication and method dispatching to remote objects, object synthesis and composition, object migration (which is especially beneficial for mobile computing purposes (Yokote *et al.*, 1991)), distributed object implementa-tion policies, and so on. To address such challenges cooperative information systems should possess the ability to specialize their meta-objects to describe or export the metadata of pre-existing information sources and control distributed message processing activities, and thus combine, override or modify the standard behavior of the systems involved (see Figure 1).

We use the term *operational reflection* to describe that form of reflection whereby we construct a set of interrelated, logically distinct meta-objects. These will contain operational knowledge, such as knowledge of location and processing activities, and control policies related to computational aspects of interwoven data objects. In this way, we can turn interconnected information sources, such as conventional database systems, into a set of cooperating systems. Operational reflection not only allows descriptions of the capabilities of existing information systems and their interrelationships but also facilitates the specification and implementation of a newly composed system, by drawing upon (and specializing) the functionality of already existing systems. Such issues will be raised in the following section.

3 THE *ROK* FRAMEWORK

As already argued, in order to cooperate, a system must be able to *reconsider* or reflect upon previously defined work and its usage, with a view to extending or customizing such work. The goal of system customization corresponds closely to that of *reuse* in an object-oriented setting. To this end, we consider cooperation, and how it may be achieved, in terms of data objects, meta-objects (that possess operational reflection capabilities), classes and inheritance (or reuse of data and computations).

3.1 *ROK* Characteristics

There are two questions of particular importance when considering cooperation:

- How may two or more database systems be unified in a conceptually coherent manner? This problem is made more difficult by any attempt to incorporate further such systems in a controlled and incremental way. We attempt to solve this particular problem by revealing the mappings from conceptual entities to any underlying databases used to provide concrete representations of these entities. By revealing such mappings, and making them extensible, we hope to enable the incorporation of a diverse range of legacy systems in a systematic but flexible way.
- Cooperation is not a passive activity. So, how may two or more, hitherto autonomous, database systems be turned into actively cooperating ones? We attempt to solve this problem by isolating and understanding the factors involved in controlling the interaction of systems. We intend to capture the *essence* of interaction. By this, we mean the way in which individual systems may be driven towards the accomplishment of some shared task, a task that, independently, they would be unable to undertake.

ROK (Edmond *et al.*, 1995) is a framework that addresses these two issues. Its objective is to provide the enabling technology which supports the selective blending of applications, both new and old, into a single system, one capable of flexibly responding to changes in organizational requirements. Using this architecture, legacy software can be encapsulated in objects, retaining its semantics and continuing to serve its users while it gracefully evolves into a fully networked application.

ROK is used to generate, by means of its metalevel protocol, a well-defined API that provides coordinated access to networked autonomous database systems. This high-level API hides implementation details and forms the basis for building new networked applications by mapping its database services onto a collection of networked host database systems (see Figure 2). The *ROK* API resembles CORBA's (OMG, 1995) dynamic invocation APIs in that it allows a client program to dynamically build and invoke requests on application objects. The application program specifies the objects to be invoked, the method to be performed, and the set of parameters through a call within some object-oriented programming language, e.g., C++. Figure 3 depicts an automatically generated *ROK* API for a simple savings bank networked application implemented across two database systems, one called *ATM* and the other called *Assets*. This simple example will be used through this chapter to illustrate the use of the *ROK* metalayer machinery.

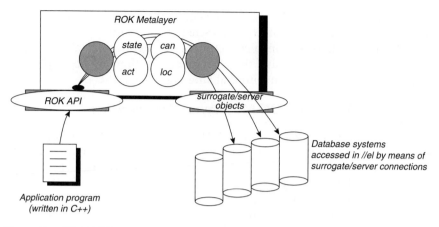

Figure 2.   The *ROK* application environment.

```
class  rokAccount : ROK{        Pointers to meta-objects which are
public:                         inherited from the ROK class.

int    AccId;                   The user key.

char*  seeName();               Observation functions for each of the
float  seeBal();                non-key attributes of the object.
float  seeMinBal();

set    seeAssets();

int    msgDeposit(float amt);   Member functions for each of the methods
int    msgWithdraw(float amt);  associated with the object.

int    msgInterest(float rate);

int    openContext();           Various utilities that need to be called to
int    closeContext();          perform housekeeping functions.
int    establish();
int    disestablish();
};
```

Figure 3.   An automatically generated C++ interface for *ROK* account objects.

Behind the API sits the *ROK metalayer* machinery: a set of specialized meta-objects necessary to achieve coexistence and cooperation of its underlying component database systems. The *ROK* meta-objects provide mechanisms that control the functionality and implementation strategies of a cooperative information system out of its constituent or component database systems. In effect, the meta-object layer acts as a switchboard to direct service calls from application programs which utilize the API, through the appropriate meta-objects, into its underlying database systems. Figure 2 motivates the need for two kinds of programmers: application and systems programmers. Application programmers use the API to develop networked applications, while systems programmers code the *ROK* metalayer in a way that seamlessly unifies a set of exported schema items and services, provided in the form of metadata, from a collection of independent databases. These unified exported services are then provided by the API to application programs for use within conventional languages such as C++.

3.2 The *ROK* Metalayer Components

ROK provides the mechanisms by which application objects transparently make requests to, and receive responses from, autonomous information sources located at a number of remote sites. Each local database system is encapsulated with a layer of metalevel software that: (1) knows about each system's functionality and competence; (2) provides basic cooperative processing facilities. This software comes in the form of a collection of *meta-objects*[2]. These are designed to capture domain and operational knowledge, and to describe, at least in part, remote systems and to monitor task-oriented activities.

Objects in a cooperative information system application must exhibit three main characteristics: representation, location and processing. These provide convenient ways for systems programmers to deal with the relevant aspects of the distributed information infrastructure. Accordingly, each application object in the *ROK* environment is managed by a set of specialized meta-objects which reflect these characteristics and make various cooperative information system functionalities adaptable to a wider range of program behaviour. These meta-objects provide descriptions of information about an object's structure, its behaviour, how it is controlled at run-time and how it is constructed from possibly distributed resources. Every application object has access to four meta-objects. The first two know about the representation of an application object: the *state* meta-object knows about the structure of any associated application object and the *can* meta-object knows about the behaviour of an application object. The third meta-object (*act*) knows about the processing activities in which an object is involved, while the fourth one (*loc*) knows how to locate both the attributes and any executable code associated with an application object. The *ROK* metalayer provides the implementation environment for an application object by coordinating its four separate meta-objects as part of the total computation of an application object. It should be made clear that many application objects may share the same meta-object if, for example, all these objects have the same basic structure and behaviour.

Figure 4 depicts a unified view of an application object representing one particular account for the savings bank application. This object is implemented by the synergy of the four *ROK* meta-objects and corresponds to an instantiation of an object created from the API in Figure 3. In the

---

[2]The term *meta-object* is used only to indicate the relation of such an object to the object it describes. A meta-object is just another object, with structure and behaviour.

```
                    The Account object
  ─────────────────────────────────────────────────────
  [AccId   is 00000507
   Name    is Dave
   Bal     is 500
   MinBal  is 280
   Assets  is { (House, 200 000), (Car, 40 000)}
   ]
```

Figure 4.   An account object instantiated from the *ROK* API.

following we will explain how the *ROK* meta-objects are used to create
and introduce into the environment such interwoven objects and how they
invoke corresponding services on its object fragments.

3.2.1 The state Meta-object

A state meta-object knows the structure of any associated object, naming
each attribute and specifying its type. By its nature, such a meta-object
provides only a static picture of an object.

This meta-object has four attributes (Figure 5):

- *Context* allows us to name a description of an account object.
- The description is in the form of a record type, and is provided by the
  State attribute. This attribute declares that an account object will have five
  attributes AccId, Name, Bal, MinBal and Assets. The MinBal attribute
  represents the minimum balance since the last time interest was paid.
  The *Context* attribute allows the record type to be given a name.

```
                    The state(Account) meta-object
  ─────────────────────────────────────────────────────
  [Context    is Account
   State      is
              ┌──────────────────────────────────────────┐
              │ Attribute  Type                           │
              │ [AccId:  Integer;                         │
              │  Name:    String;                         │
              │  Bal:     Float;                          │
              │  MinBal: Float;                           │
              │  Assets: set [asset:String; worth:Float]] │
              └──────────────────────────────────────────┘
   Invariant is Bal >= MinBal
   Initially  is Bal=0; MinBal=0
   ]
```

Figure 5.   The state meta-object for an account.

- *Invariant* expresses any condition that must be true of the object's state *at all times.*
- *Initially* expresses a condition that must be true on the instantiation of an object with this state.

3.2.2 The can Meta-object

A can meta-object knows about the behaviour of any associated object — it knows what an object *can* do. This object may also be associated with a number of application objects, all of which share the same (outward) behaviour.

Figure 6 shows an example of such an object. Activities described in this meta-object are: (1) depositing money; (2) withdrawing money;

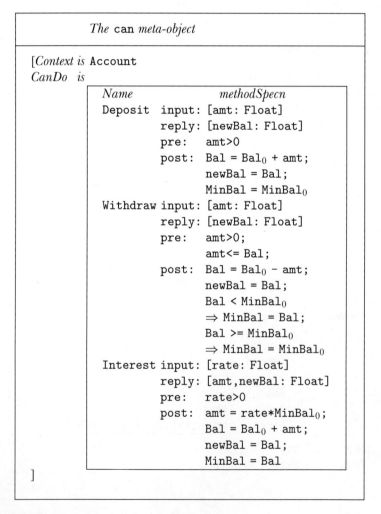

Figure 6. The can meta-object for an account.

(3) applying interest, at some given rate, to the minimum balance since the last occasion on which interest was calculated.

The meta-object has two attributes:

- *Context* allows us to label the behaviour.
- A function-valued attribute *CanDo* describes each individual activity permitted to or by the application object. These activities are described in terms of:
  — the input arguments;
  — any reply that might be forthcoming;
  — pre- and post-conditions.

  For example, the *Withdraw* method has one argument, the amount to be withdrawn. It will reply with the new balance. The method will succeed only if the account has enough to cover the withdrawal. The post-condition requires that if the new balance is less than the previous minimum, then the minimum is reset.

The `can` meta-object allows a system to consider possible behaviour and its consequences upon the object(s) concerned. It also allows a system to investigate alternative ways of achieving some goal. It may be seen that, in this case, there are two ways of increasing the balance of an account — should that be considered desirable.

3.2.3 The `loc` Meta-object

A `loc` meta-object knows how to *locate* attributes and *execute* the methods of an object in local as well as remote address spaces.

As may be seen in Figure 7, this object contains these attributes:

- *Context* enables *ROK* to link the "implementation" described by this particular meta-object to some pre-existing specification.
- *Key* names any attribute or attributes that may be used, within this context, to distinguish one object from another. In the `Account` context, it is the account Id.
- The *Lookup* table indicates how each attribute of the associated application object is materialized. This reification is accomplished by *surrogate* objects. These metalevel objects have specific knowledge of the location of data. It is a form of symbol table (which parallels the Object Naming Service in CORBA (OMG, 1995)), mapping each symbol found in pre- and post-condition code to an object that knows about the symbol:

name	*object*
attribute name	surrogate object id

Any activity relating to the symbol is forwarded to its surrogate object and executes on its corresponding component database system. The `loc` specification in Figure 7 indicates that we are dealing with an interwoven

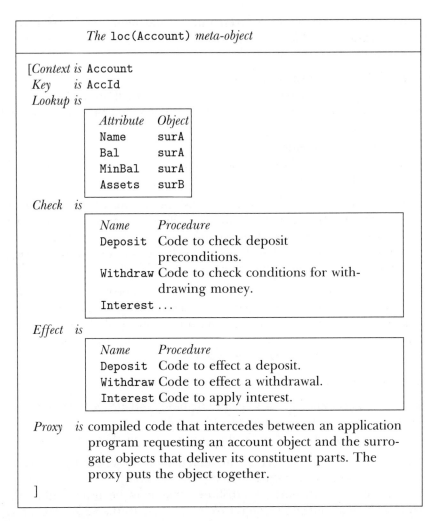

Figure 7.   The `loc` meta-object for an account.

object assembled from two fragments: one from the *ATM* database (comprising the attributes `name, bal, minbal`) and monitored by surrogate `surA`, and the other from the *Assets* database (comprising the attribute `assets`) and monitored by surrogate `surB`.

- The *Check* table contains, for each operation, procedural descriptions of how that operation's preconditions are to be checked:

name	*procedure*
method name	procedural code

The preconditions will be broken into its constituent parts and each part will be handled by the appropriate surrogate.

- The *Effect* table contains, for each method, procedural descriptions of how that method is effected:

name	procedure
method name	procedural code

Again, the *Lookup* table is used to determine the responsibility of each surrogate in effecting the post-condition.

- The *Proxy* attribute contains compiled code. The corresponding source code is constructed from the *Lookup*, *Check* and *Effect* attributes. This code is then compiled and stored here. When executing, it intercedes between the associated act meta-object, acting on behalf of an application program requesting an account object, and the surrogate objects that deliver its constituent parts.

Surrogate and proxy objects are discussed in Section 4.3

3.2.4 The act Meta-object

An act meta-object knows about the *activity* in which some group of objects is involved. It is a task-oriented object that monitors the activities of the collection of objects that constitute *its* domain.

According to this meta-object (Figure 8):

- Every account object will have its own act meta-object. The *Granularity* attribute indicates the granularity of control. It indicates whether the control is to be exercised upon all objects within this context or to each object individually.
- Any outstanding Deposit message is to be processed before any Withdraw one, which, in turn, is to be processed before any Interest message. The *Priority* attribute allows a *sequence* of operations to be created. This sequence determines the order in which messages are processed.

The act(Account) *meta-object*
[*Context*   *is* Account *Granularity is* singular *Priority*   *is* [Deposit, Withdraw, Interest] *Mutex*   *is* { Deposit, Withdraw} *SelfMutex*   *is* { Deposit, Withdraw} *Blocking*   *is* all *Reactive*   *is* none *Periodic*   *is* Interest *SourceCode is* source code that has been generated in line with the control specifications provided in the rest of this object. *Runtime*   *is* executable code compiled from the above.]

Figure 8.   The act meta-object for an account.

- The `Deposit` and `Withdraw` messages are mutually exclusive. The *Mutex* attribute indicates which message types are to be dealt with exclusively.
- Only *one* message of any kind is to be in operation at any one time. The *SelfMutex* attribute indicates any message types that are to be allowed only one thread at a time.
- All messages are blocking, that is, the senders will be forced to wait pending completion of the message. The *Blocking* attribute indicates which message types are to cause the sender to be blocked awaiting some form of reply.
- *No* message is to be triggered automatically, that is, whenever its preconditions are satisfied. The *Reactive* attribute indicates which message types are to be triggered automatically whenever their preconditions are satisfied.
- There is one periodic message — `Interest`. The *Periodic* attribute indicates any messages that are to be triggered periodically.
- The *SourceCode* attribute contains source code that has been generated in line with the control specifications provided in the rest of this object.
- The *Runtime* attribute contains executable code compiled from the above source code.

Once the object has been specified, a procedural version is generated automatically. This is available for inspection and refinement as the `SourceCode` attribute. It is then compiled into a directly executable form, and stored in the `Runtime` attribute. In the subsequent discussion, when we refer to the `act` meta-object, we intend its executable form.

3.2.5 Summary

The combination of these four meta-objects in a computational process: (1) captures application and operational knowledge (describing, at least in part, remote systems); (2) allows task-oriented activities to be monitored. As may be seen in Figure 9, the meta-objects may be divided into two pairs:

- The `state` and `can` meta-objects aim to provide specifications of objects within the same domain. That domain may be part of the application domain, as in the case of the `state` (Account) and `can` (Account) meta-objects. However, the domain may equally be within the metalayer itself.
- The `loc` and `act` meta-objects provide descriptions of the run-time environment in which the application objects may operate, and the placement of the application objects, in the form of mappings from conceptual entities to physical databases.

   In this way, the four meta-objects materialize the interwoven object depicted in Figure 4 and invoke all the necessary operations on its fragments in remote parts of the database network. In essence, we turn interconnected conventional database systems into cooperating knowledge-based systems.

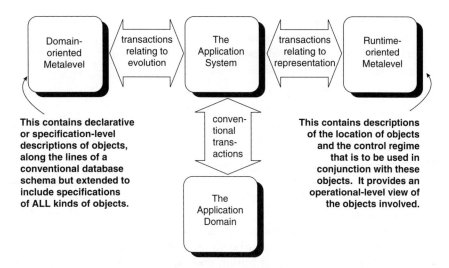

Figure 9.   Dimensions of reflection.

4 COOPERATIVE PROCESSING

In the following we first describe how the metalayer objects work together across machine and network boundaries to create client/server application solutions based on an automatically generated C++ API. We then introduce a simple application program in C++ that invokes the *ROK* API service specifications in Figure 3. Finally, we discuss the *ROK* meta-object support infrastructure.

4.1 Systems Development and Administration

The process required in setting up a *ROK* system can be summarized as follows:

1. *Provide a conceptual description of each application object type.* Each such type is called a *context* and is described, at the conceptual level, by means of a `state` and a `can` meta-object. These descriptions are formed on the basis of exported metadata from component database systems, e.g., data formats and exported services, after applying the appropriate mapping operations (Sheth and Larson, 1990). Such issues will not be considered in this chapter.
2. *Develop a `loc` meta-object from a related pair of `state` and `can` meta-objects.* This step describes the *placement* of each of the attributes of the application object type. It also contains what might be termed *sequential* code, that is, procedural code related to the *semantics* of the situation being modelled by application objects within the current context. This code implements the pre- and post-conditions provided by the corresponding `can` meta-object.

3. *Construct an* `act` *meta-object for each context*. This step is accomplished by instantiating a number of generic control policies, *in conjunction with* the corresponding pair of `state` and `can` meta-objects. For example, a specifier might declare that:

- The `Deposit` and `Withdraw` are never to be processed concurrently, that is, they are to be *mutually exclusive*.
- Any outstanding `Deposit` operation is to be processed before any `Withdraw` operation, that is, one has a higher *priority* than the other.

The results of these policy instantiations are held or gathered into the `act` meta-object — they constitute that object. In this regard, our work may be compared to that of McHale (1995). In that work, he discusses the so-called *inheritance anomaly* in which the mixing of sequential and synchronization code within the body of a method leaves the resulting class as one that is not reusable because of this mix of code that serves two different purposes. His suggestion is that synchronization code should result from the instantiation of *generic synchronization policies*, rather than through conventional inheritance. Our work is similar in this regard. We believe that: (1) the `act` and `loc` meta-objects allow the separation of these two kinds of code; (2) the `act` meta-object is best viewed as one that results from the instantiation of more generic policies.

The `act` and `loc` meta-objects may be viewed as the client and server ends of a pathway between an application (client) program and a number of pre-existing databases (servers). These are used to invoke and route services on objects (fragments of an application object) residing in component database systems across the network.

From a systems development and administration point of view, we can distinguish two complementary roles:

- that of a systems programmer who will need to program/construct the necessary meta-objects and associated support objects;
- that of an applications programmer who will need to write the application programs that use the distributed object infrastructure made available by *ROK*. A C++ interface is provided for this programmer, and is discussed below. This interface is generated automatically, from the `loc` object, by the *ROK* system.

4.2 Developing an Application in C++

The *ROK* API includes a description of any data items and services that a component database system in the network exposes to its client applications. The API separates specification from implementation by routing all service requests, through the *ROK* meta layer, to the appropriate server component databases where they get implemented. In this sense, the *ROK* API provides a direct path between a distributed application — defined by its interfaces — and the code that implements the services which may execute on remote database nodes. Next, we will look at the API generated from the state (Account) and can (Account) meta-objects. The interface is presented in the form of a class specification called rokAccount which is automatically generated. The specification for the rokAccount class is shown in Figure 3.

The rokAccount class may be used by a programmer in a fairly straightforward way. There is no need for the programmer to know anything of the behind-the-scenes activities involved in passing a request from the program to the relevant information sources across the network, and in transmitting data back from there. The following application program shows the class being used in withdrawing money from an account:

```
/* Program that uses the ROK API to enable a Withdraw
      operation to be performed upon a ROK account object.
*/
#include "rokAccount.h"
void main()
{
    rokAccount acct;

    acct.openContext();
    cout << "Account Id? "; cin >> AcctId;
    s.establish();
    cout << s.seeName() << s.seeBal() << "\n";
    float givenAmt;
    cout << "Deposit amount? "; cin >> givenAmt;

    acct.msgWithdraw(givenAmt);
    acct.disestablish();
    acct.closeContext();
}
```

The program enables its user to withdraw a given amount of money from a given account and is materialized from two databases. Five member functions help establish and manipulate the object in question:

- openContext(): this function locates the (compiled) executable code that will deal with any activity surrounding an account. It then forks a process to run this code.
- establish(): this locates the compiled code that will materialize an account record with a given Id. A process accountProxy encapsulating this code is forked. The program then waits for the record to be retrieved from whatever sources are involved.
- msgWithdraw(): a "withdraw" message, and accompanying arguments, is sent to the act(Account) process which will attempt to apply the method involved.

- `disestablish()`: a "quit" signal is sent to the `accountProxy` process. This causes the record to be written out to whatever data resources were used in its materialization. When complete, the process terminates.
- `closeContext()`: this function terminates the `act (Account)` process, or at least disconnects from it.

4.3 The *ROK* Meta-object Support Infrastructure

Next we present the meta-object support infrastructure which interacts with the *ROK* meta layer to materialize and manage application objects. The *ROK* run-time system routes a client request via the meta-object support infrastructure (proxy, surrogate and server objects) to a target object that may reside in a remote address space. A typical application may involve interactions with a variety of local and remote objects, but the support meta-objects make distributed-object interactions to be the same as local object interactions.

4.3.1 Proxy Objects

A *proxy* object is an object (similar to a client stub) that is used to provide network transparency and hide argument-passing details in a distributed processing environment (Shapiro, 1986). A proxy is a piece of code that represents a server object on a client side, i.e., it runs on the same address space as the client. To access the server, the client simply performs a local invocation on the server's proxy. The proxy performs the actual remote invocation (cross-address space procedure call) and returns the result to the client.

In *ROK* a proxy object is the name given to a process that is, effectively, a run-time version of the `loc` meta-object. While the `act` object supervises the use of an object by application programs, the proxy supervises the gathering and dispersal of data from and to the underlying information sources (Figure 10).

An application program is provided with an interface through which the interwoven objects may be regarded as having real existence. All

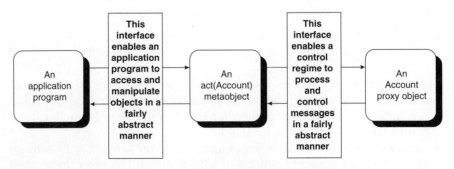

Figure 10.   The use of an intermediary control meta-object.

attempts to use this interface are trapped by the act object and dealt with in accordance with the rules it has been created to enforce. The work involved in applying these rules is not performed directly by the act object. Rather, that object passes on to the proxy object requests such as "check the preconditions for operation X using data D". The proxy masks the complexities of accessing a real target object by managing (marshalling/unmarshalling) the parameters of the invocation, providing location transparency and maintaining state and location information about the target objects (Menon and LeBlanc, 1994). In order to achieve this it needs to interact with other *ROK* support objects.

4.3.2 Surrogate and Server Objects

In general, there two additional kinds of support objects involved in any system developed using the *ROK* model:

- At the client end (see Figure 11) there are *surrogate* objects, as already described. They cache the parts of an object that they help materialize. A *proxy* process will monitor and interact with the appropriate surrogates in order to reference remote objects.
- At the server ends, there are *server* objects. These wrap the server database in an appropriate way. This will depend upon the exact nature of the database and the actions required of that database in response to any request received from a surrogate.

In the example situation described in this chapter, there are two surrogate objects: surA and surB. The interaction between the account proxy and these objects acting on the client side, and the server objects and data resources at the client sites, is shown in Figure 12.

The accountProxy process deals with all requests to access an account object, whether from an application program directly or from the act (Account) object already discussed. All requests received by a proxy object, however, are passed on to the appropriate surrogate object. The proxy merely acts as a single entry-point into a interwoven account object.

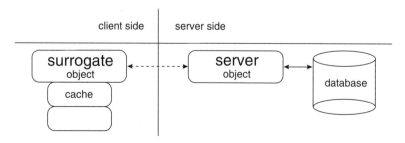

Figure 11.   Surrogate/server objects.

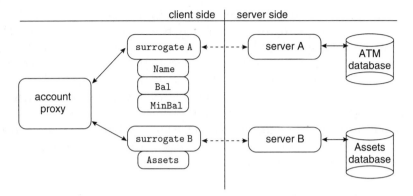

Figure 12.   Coordinating surrogate objects.

4.3.3 Example: Checking Preconditions

To illustrate how the *ROK* metalayer machinery interacts with its support infrastructure, we consider the following scenario where the `act` object requests the proxy to check the precondition for some withdrawal operation performed on fragmented objects (see Figure 13). We assume that the precondition is in conjunctive normal form, that is, it is of the form $P \wedge Q \wedge R \ldots$ The proxy object then farms out responsibility for checking the individual conjuncts to the relevant surrogate — where this is appropriate. These objects will then respond with a `true` or `false` response. The proxy then conjoins these individual responses before replying to the `act` object. For example, suppose that it is a requirement that withdrawals over \$12 000 may only occur if there is sufficient in the account *and* the account-holder has an asset worth that much. The precondition is thus:

$amt \geq Bal \wedge (\exists\ a: Assets\ |\ a.worth \geq amt)$

The first conjunct is submitted to surrogate `surA` (in the *ATM* database) because it has knowledge of the account balance; the second conjunct is

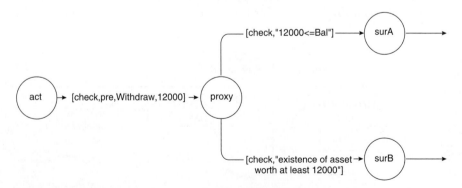

Figure 13.   The passage of a request to check a precondition.

sent to surrogate surB (in the *Assets* database) because it has been created specifically to deal with assets.

Once the act meta-object has been notified, it may choose to pass that notification back to the application program. That decision will depend upon the control regime embodied by the act meta-object. In a conventional interactive environment, control will be passed back to the application program, and the user notified. In a reactive environment, the request to check a precondition may be expressed more in the form of a request to be notified when the precondition is satisfied. Thus the surrogates are continuously monitoring changes in the values of any attributes under their supervision. The form of control required is determined by the specification of the relevant act meta-object.

5 IMPLEMENTATION

In this section, we discuss some of the issues involved in building a prototype of the *ROK* model.

While the model is expected to operate in a distributed or client/server environment, the issues that it raises and the problems that it attempts to solve are *not* ones of distribution, *per se*. Rather, they are ones of reuse, heterogeneity and concurrency. We required a development environment that, while removing from us the load involved in network protocols and marshalling, provided a rich array of types, and expressive process-oriented facilities.

5.1 April

Much of the lower-level work required to animate a *ROK* system is accomplished by means of an agent-programming system known as April (McCabe and Clark, 1994; Clark and Skarmeas, this volume) which, the authors claim, is meant to allow the *implementation* of multi-agent systems. April is a process-oriented symbolic language containing facilities for defining processes, and for allowing processes to communicate with each other. In this section, we discuss how April features are used to implement some aspects of our model. Details of the implementation may be found in Bartlett (1995).

The code section below depicts an example implementation of a surrogate object. It corresponds to surA in Figure 12.

```
// Excerpt of April code for the surA process
string?vName; float?vBal; float?vMinBal;
handle?server_A;
surrogate_A() {
   repeat {
        [APPLY, givenId] -> {
```

```
        [BEGIN, givenId] >> server_A;
    }
    :
    :
    | [FLUSH] -> {
        [END, [vName,vBal,vMinBal]] >> server_A
      }
  } until quit
};
```

The process will respond to several kinds of message, two of which
are illustrated. One requests the name, balance and minimum balance for
a given account, and the other requests that these variables be rewritten to
the ATM database. These alternatives are expressed by means of an April
message receive choice statement which, in general, has the form:

$$\{pattern_1 \rightarrow action_1 | pattern_2 \rightarrow action_2 | \ldots | pattern_n \rightarrow action_n\}$$

The patterns are used to match incoming messages such as [APPLY,
givenId] and [FLUSH] in the above example. If a match is made then
the corresponding action is taken.

The surrogate process will, among other things, materialize its portion
of an account object. It does this in response to an [APPLY, givenId]
message from its proxy. It then passes this on to the server process discussed
above. When a proxy signals that an object is to be dematerialized, a
[FLUSH] message is sent to each surrogate which then in turn sends an END
message with the modified values to its server which are then committed.

The server object/process runs at the site where the database is located.
It retrieves the results from an SQL database, as illustrated in the following
code segment:

```
// Excerpt of April code for the serverA process
string?vName; float?vBal; float?vMinBal;
integer?givenId;

server_A() {
  repeat {
        [BEGIN, givenId] -> {
            EXEC SQL
                BEGIN_TRANSACTION
                SELECT Name, Bal, MinBal
                INTO vName, vBal, vMinBal
                FROM ATM_Accounts
                WHERE AccId = givenId
            END EXEC
            // replyto is the handle of BEGIN message sender
            [vName, vBal, vMinBal] >> replyto;
```

```
        }
      | [END, [vName, vBal, vMinBal]] -> {
           EXEC SQL
                 UPDATE ATM_Accounts
                 SET Name = vName,
                     Bal = vBal,
                     MinBal = vMinBal
                 WHERE AccId = givenId
             END_TRANSACTION
             END EXEC
        }
   } until quit
};
```

5.2 Implementing the `act` **Meta-object**

In the following we discuss briefly on how we implement aspects of the `act`
meta-object as described in Section 3.2.

5.2.1 Granularity

This attribute determines the extent of the control regime specified by an
`act` meta-object. There are two options:

- Each individual object of the nominated context is to be supervised by *its*
  own meta-object. In this case, the granularity is at the *object* level.
- Alternatively, all objects of the nominated context are to be supervised
  by *the same* meta-object. In this case, the granularity is at the *context* level.

5.2.2 Priority

Given a queue of messages waiting to be handled by an object, this attribute
determines the order in which they will be processed.

Consider a simple message receive choice statement like the following:

```
{[Deposit,...]-> action_D
|[Withdraw,...]-> action_W
|[Interest,...]-> action_I}
```

Care must be taken. The above statement, while giving priority to
Deposit over Withdraw and so on, does not do so in the desired way.
Suppose we have the messages W_1,D_2,W_3 in the message buffer. The priority
accorded to the message types requires that the deposit message, D_2, be
processed next. April will take the first of these and attempt to match
it against the three names in the order shown. Thus, W_1 will match the
second pattern and be processed. The second message, D_2, is not granted
the priority required.

This problem may be circumvented (McCabe and Clark, 1994) by testing each of the messages, in turn, to see whether or not it is a Deposit. If it is, then processing commences, otherwise the *next* message is examined. If none matches, that is, there is *no* Deposit message in the queue, then a timeout is forced:

```
{ [Deposit, [amt?Float]] -> {/* deal with deposit */}
| timeout 0 secs ->
  { [Deposit, [amt?Float]] -> {/* deal with deposit */}
  | [Withdraw, [amt?Float]] -> {/* deal with withdraw */}
  | timeout 0 secs ->
    { [Deposit, [amt?Float]] -> {/* deal with deposit */}
    | [Withdraw, [amt?Float]] -> {/* deal with withdraw */}
    | [Interest, [rate?Float]] -> {/* deal with interest */}
    | timeout 0 secs -> { }
    }
  }
}
```

As a result of this timeout, the queue is re-examined, but this time April looks for a Withdraw message. However, because we have commenced a new message receive choice statement, the message queue may have been replenished, and we must, therefore, ensure that, if it is a Deposit, then it still has priority. If this next re-examination also fails, yet another timeout is triggered, and the queue is searched for an Interest message.

5.2.3 Mutual Exclusion

The *Mutex* attribute allows the specification of messages that may *not* run in conjunction.

A message receive guard consists of a message pattern and an optional condition of some kind. These are separated by a :: symbol. Thus, if we know whenever a particular operation is in process, we may guard against any other form of message. Suppose we keep an integer variable ActiveWithdraw that is incremented whenever a Withdraw message is being processed, and decremented when one completes. Suppose also, that there are similar indicators for each kind of message. We may prevent the simultaneous processing of the three message forms by means of the following kind of code:

```
{ [Deposit,...]
    :: ActiveWithdraw==0 && ActiveInterest == 0
    -> { ActiveDeposit++; action_D; ActiveDeposit-- }
| [Withdraw,...]
    :: ActiveWithdraw==0 && ActiveInterest == 0
    -> { ActiveWithdraw++; action_W; ActiveWithdraw--}
| [Interest,...]}
    :: ActiveWithdraw==0 && ActiveInterest == 0
    ->{ ActiveInterest++; action_I; ActiveInterest--}}
```

Segments of code such as this are generated according to the contents of the *Mutex* attribute.

5.2.4 Self-mutual Exclusion

The *SelfMutex* attribute allows the specification of messages that may run in single-thread mode *only*. For example, only one Deposit message may be dealt with at any particular time.

```
{ [Deposit, ...] :: ActiveDeposit ==0 -> action_D
| [Withdraw,...] :: ActiveWithdraw==0 -> action_W
| [Interest,...] :: ActiveInterest==0 -> action_I}
```

Again, code segments are generated using the *SelfMutex* attribute as a specification.

5.2.5 Blocking

An application program interacts with an object by means of that object's act meta-object. The default situation is for the program to wait until any request it has made to be satisfied. In other words, the program is blocked.

6 RELATED WORK

The work reported herein relates to research activities in multi-databases and federated databases, which was briefly summarized at its outset. It also relates to current activities and standards in the area of distributed object management. We summarize these in the remainder of this section.

A number of proposals for generic distributed object management architectures have been developed, such as the Common Object Request Broker Architecture (CORBA) defined by OMG (1995), and the SOM (Danforth and Forman, 1994; Lau, 1994) product family which provide for communications among objects in different processes on the same or different systems.

CORBA was designed to provide a general-purpose infrastructure to enable the use of distributed objects in a wide variety of client/server applications. It provides a number of system services that enables a client to locate and reference an object at run-time. Each server object publishes its interface to an interface repository using CORBA's IDL. The purpose of CORBA's IDL is to allow the (programming) language-independent expression of interfaces, including the complete signatures of methods and the names and types of accessible attributes. The Object Request Broker (ORB) is the component that provides the mechanisms by which interaction between client and server objects is managed. This includes all the responsibilities of a distributed computing system, from locating and referencing of objects to the marshalling of request parameters and result types. The CORBA specification defines object interfaces without regard to implementation.

IBM's SOM technology extends the CORBA specification by supporting object implementation inheritance and polymorphism, providing meta classes that are manipulated as first-order objects, and allowing dynamic addition of methods to a class interface at run-time (Lau, 1994). SOM is a packaging technology and run-time support for the building of language-independent class libraries. To provide language neutrality, SOM defines a runtime API that is based on few external procedures and simple data structures that are required by client processes. This API is used by programmers to create and use SOM objects according to a traditional object-oriented model of computation (Danforth and Forman, 1994). SOM's distributed framework — a set of system SOM classes — allows methods to be invoked (in a transparent way) on SOM objects that exist in different address spaces from the calling program. Distributed SOM conforms to the OMG's basic architecture for CORBA compliant systems by allowing applications to access SOM objects across machine boundaries in a networked environment. DSOM supports transparent, remote access to distributed systems based on the generation of proxy objects that support remote method invocation.

The *ROK* framework shares the same concerns as CORBA and DSOM in that it provides infrastructure support for the management of distributed objects and applications. *ROK* provides the object-enabling infrastructure that supports the development of networked applications that are designed to interoperate with legacy data and software, while CORBA and DSOM concentrate mainly on cross-language mappings. In contrast, the *ROK* framework spans both the system domain as well as the application domain and has as its main objective to automatically generate APIs that provide simple abstractions of the services exported by networked component database systems and transparently handle all inter-component collaborations. It also provides reflective object facilities which allow the separation of control and domain knowledge thus allowing the system to explicitly control and program message passing and communications between objects. This feature leads to extensible implementations and systems and is not available by CORBA or DSOM. Unlike both CORBA and DSOM which rely on centralized interface repositories (or directory facilities) to provide collective information about the server interfaces in the system, the *ROK* framework packages this type of information on a peer object basis allowing thus for a high degree of flexibility.

7 SUMMARY

The aims of the *ROK* framework are, primarily, to reveal the processes involved in assembling an object from distributed components and making it available to an application program. Such revelations are made in a modifiable and object-oriented way, enabling distributed and possibly heterogeneous data and program resources to be used by new applications in a flexible and transparent way.

Having encapsulated one or more legacy systems, having provided them with an abstract functional profile, we may:

- extend this profile, by writing new software that adds new functions;
- build distributed systems using these revamped systems as a foundation.

This framework intends to provide the technology required to revamp existing applications and to incorporate them into networks of application systems, thus allowing the development of large-scale distributed and cooperating information systems. Application programs are developed around automatically generated APIs that provide simple abstractions of the services exported by networked database systems, with the inter-component collaborations being handled transparently. To achieve this, the framework provides reflective facilities which support the separation of control and domain knowledge thus allowing a cooperative information system to explicitly control and program message-passing and synchronization activities between objects across machine and network boundaries. This requires the adaptation and extension of existing approaches in the areas of database, artificial intelligence and distributed systems technologies.

ACKNOWLEDGEMENTS

We would like to thank Dr Frank McCabe and Fujitsu Laboratories Ltd, Japan for kindly allowing us to use April in the development of our system and Mr Adrian Bartlett for prototyping *ROK*.

REFERENCE

Bartlett, A. (1995) Distributed concepts pertaining to the architecture and implementation of the *ROK* model. Technical report, School of Information Systems, QUT.
Brodie, M. (1994) The promise of distributed computing and the challenges of legacy information systems. In *Advances in Object-oriented Database Systems*. A. Dogac, M.T. Özsu, A. Biliris and T. Sellis (eds). Springer-Verlag, Berlin.
Danforth, S. and Forman, I.R. (1994) Reflections on metaclass programming in SOM. In *Proceedings, Conference on Object-oriented Programming Systems, Languages and Applications — OOPSLA'94*, Portland, Oregon.
Davis, R. (1980) Metarules: reasoning about control. *Artificial Intelligence*, **15**, 179–222.
Edmond, D., Papazoglou, M.P. and Tari, Z. (1995) *ROK*: a reflective model for distributed object management. In *RIDE-DOM'95 (Research Issues in Data Engineering — Distributed Object Management)*, M. Tamer Özsu, O. Bukres and M-C. Shan (eds). Taiwan, IEEE-CS Press, pp. 31–41.
Honda, Y. and Yonezawa, A. (1988) Debugging concurrent systems based on object groups. In *Proceedings of ECOOP'88 (European Conference on Object-oriented Programming)*, Oslo, Norway.

Kiczales, G. (1996) Beyond the black box: open implementation. *IEEE Software*, **13**, 8−11.

Kiczales, G., des Rivières, J. and Bobrow, D.G. (1991) *The Art of the Metaobject Protocol*. The MIT Press, Cambridge, Mass.

Lau, C. (1994) *Object-Oriented Programming: Using SOM and DSOM*. Van Nostrand Reinhold, New York.

Maes, P. (1987) Concepts and experiments in computational reflection. In *Proceedings of OOPSLA'87 (Conference on Object-oriented Programming Systems, Languages and Applications)*.

Maes, P. (1988) Computational reflection. *The Knowledge Engineering Review*, **3**(1), 1−19.

Masuhara, H., Matsuoka, S., *et al*. (1992) Object-oriented concurrent reflective languages can be implemented efficiently. In *Proceedings, Conference on Object-oriented Programming, Languages and Applications — OOPSLA'92*.

McCabe, F.G. and Clark, K.L. (1994) Programming in April. Technical report, Department of Computing, Imperial College, London.

McHale, C. (1995) Synchronisation in concurrent object-oriented languages: expressive power, genericity and inheritance. PhD thesis, Trinity College, Dublin.

Menon, S. and LeBlanc, R. (1994) Object replacement using dynamic proxy updates. *Distributed Systems Engineering*, **1**(5).

OMG (1995) CORBAservices: common object services specification. Technical Report 95-3-31, The Object Management Group.

Paepcke, A. (1990) PCLOS: Stress testing CLOS. In *Proceedings, Conference on Object-oriented Programming Systems, Languages and Applications — OOPSLA'90*.

Rao, R. (1991) Implementation reflection in Silica. In *ECOOP'91*, Lecture Notes in Computer Science 512. Springer-Verlag.

Shapiro, M. (1986) Structure and encapsulation in distributed systems: the proxy principle. In *Proceedings, 6th International Conference on Distributed Computing Systems*.

Sheth, A. and Larson, P. (1990) Federated database systems for managing distributed, heterogeneous and autonomous databases. *Computing Surveys*, **22**(3), 183−236.

Stemple, D., Sheard, T. and Fegaras, L. (1992) Linguistic reflection: a bridge from programming to database languages. In *Hawaii Conference on Systems and Sciences*, Koloa.

Stroud, R. and Wu, Z. (1992) Using metaobject protocols to implement atomic data types. In *ECOOP'95: 9th European Conference on Object-Oriented Programming*, LNCS 952. Springer-Verlag.

Yokote, Y. (1992) The Apertos reflective operating system: The concept and its implementation. In *Proceedings, Conference on Object-oriented Programming Systems, Languages and Applications — OOPSLA'92*.

Yokote, Y., *et al*. (1991) Reflective object management in the Muse operating system. In *International Workshop on Object-Orientation in Operating Systems*. (Also in Selected Technical Reports, Sony Computer Science Lab. Inc., May 1992.)

Part V

Modelling Organizations and Systems Requirements

Model-Driven Planning and Design of Cooperative Information Systems

Matthias Jarke, Peter Peters and Manfred A. Jeusfeld
Informatik V, RWTH Aachen, Germany

Abstract

Cooperative information systems (CISs) aim at *continued cooperativity* between user groups through componentized networks of information systems. Change management is therefore a definitional part of CIS. We advocate a conceptual modelling strategy for addressing this task, and illustrate it with experiences gained in WibQuS, a project aimed at CIS support for total quality management in manufacturing organizations. These experiences emphasize the role of metamodels in focusing the change process. Specific metamodels and supporting environments are presented for: cooperative business process modelling in distributed organizations; simulation analysis of short-term and long-term effects of information flow designs; forward and reverse mappings between a distributed system interoperability layer and the information flow model. Models are not just analysed at change time, but also support planned and unplanned information flows at runtime.

I INTRODUCTION

Information systems have traditionally been characterized as hardware/software/people *systems* that maintain data about a specific *subject domain* for one or more *users*, sometimes within a formal organization. The database community has dedicated much work to subject domain modelling (e.g. relational, object-oriented and semantic data models) and efficient systems implementation (e.g. query processing, concurrency control, and recovery).

Relatively less attention has been paid to the usage side, neither at the system level of user interface research nor at the design level of modelling usage by individuals, teams and formal organizations. Recently, this has begun to change due to massive complaints by user organizations that their central needs are not being adequately addressed by information technology.

One of the responses raising to this challenge is the vision of *cooperative information systems* (CISs) (Brodie and Ceri, 1992; Jarke and Ellis, 1993; De Michelis *et al.*, this volume). This vision presents information systems as a communications medium among user groups in and across organizations. On one hand, this brings groupware and organizational research into the information systems field. On the other, it changes conventional database wisdom about the required information modelling, system implementation and integration technologies.

We conceptualize CIS as a layered network of user and system components as sketched in Figure 1. At the *system level*, the old idea of one-time view integration — followed by the integrated design of an integrated system — is replaced by a trend towards componentization (including the "wrapping" of legacy software) into small and easily reconfigurable objects. Coordination between these units is no longer hardcoded in applications but dynamically achieved by workflow mechanisms.

At the *usage level*, we observe very similar phenomena. Formal organizations are being decomposed into small autonomous units with market-oriented rather than hierarchical coordination (Malone *et al.*, 1987). In these federated organizations the units have their own local information systems configuration, either from new or from legacy components. But they may also be customers or suppliers of other units with respect to information services. Thus, in a CIS, we have necessary interactions between user groups (1 in Figure 1), between system components (2), between user groups and system components (3), and — most importantly for us — between user groups *through* system components (4).

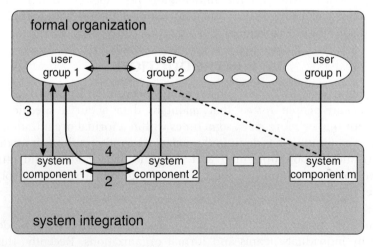

Figure 1.   Static structure of a CIS.

Why is all this happening? The answer — at both levels — is *reactiveness to change* (Heinzl and Srikanth, 1995, Scott-Morton, 1994). Organizations have to react quickly to ever-changing market requirements. System technology has to react quickly to organizational change as well as technical innovation. Hierarchies have turned out to be too clumsy, therefore the trend is towards small largely autonomous units that can react quickly.

CISs are intended to assure this reactiveness to change (often called *agility*) by providing flexible communication mechanisms and rapid feedback between stakeholder groups such as customers, planners, designers, production managers and workers. Under these requirements lack of relevant information is as dangerous as information overload, and schema evolution due to changing user interests is a necessity.

In this chapter, *we argue that cooperativeness and agility are not just requirements in the usage of CIS but also central determinants of the change process itself.* Our main message is that conceptual modelling technology, properly supported and applied, can go a long way in addressing such CIS engineering goals. Specifically, we propose *user-definable meta meta models* as a means of coordination in requirements engineering and systems design for CISs. Elaborating this idea, we demonstrate how conceptual modelling technology can be extended to deal in an integrated manner with problems such as:

- the integration of different terminologies and methodological frameworks through metamodelling and the resulting need for uncovering implicit assumptions about business processes and systems (Klein and Lyytinen, 1992) by the stakeholders in the modelling process;
- the evaluation of different information flow policies through simulation models derived from the metamodels by explaining the effects of local CIS changes on the overall CIS performance;
- the computer-supported mapping of metamodels to database structures, workflow definitions, and monitoring facilities at the operational level and therefore an enhancement the agility of the CIS;
- the use of the conceptual models at runtime as a domain-specific information trader to facilitate intelligent question-answering and workflow coordination.

To ground the discussion, Section 2 presents an example CIS — a prototype environment for life-cycle-wide quality management developed in a German industrial engineering project called WibQuS. In Section 3, we introduce the basics of our conceptual modelling approach which relies heavily on user-definable metamodels to coordinate distributed CIS engineering, and discuss its technical support by the ConceptBase meta data manager. Section 4 describes how the engineering approach applies in the structural design and quantitative evaluation of organizational information flows, while Section 5 discusses the mapping of such designs to the system level. Section 6 lists some limitations and summarizes ongoing work.

2 AN EXAMPLE CIS: THE WibQuS ENVIRONMENT

Total quality management (TQM) is one of several business philosophies that can be associated with the trend of on-going change as a basis of business success. It aims at continuous business process improvement by emphasizing customer orientation throughout, relying on local ideas and improvement initiatives, influencing the organization via cleverly designed feedback cycles. Therefore, the implementation of a TQM system appears as a prototypical example of a (not necessarily fully computerized) CIS.

The question of how to design and implement such CIS was investigated since 1992 by a consortium of five German engineering centres, an organizational science group, and ourselves in a project called WibQuS[1] (Jarke *et al.*, 1993); production data from a "real" product life cycle were provided by a manufacturer of forklifts. Figure 2 shows how the CIS components are instantiated in industrial quality management (Pfeifer, 1993).

The outer circle presents the product life cycle stages. Traditionally, the stages have been associated with different departments or companies,

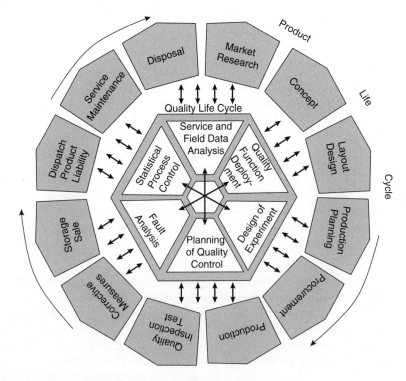

Figure 2.   The quality life cycle as a CIS.

[1] WibQuS is the German abbreviation for "Knowledge-based Systems in Quality Management".

each with their local IT solution. Due to business process orientation, the forward flow of information along the product life cycle is now reasonably under control. However, the feedback loop around the whole cycle takes too much time for companies to stay competitive. The idea of quality management is to introduce smaller feedback cycles that provide selected information about particular quality issues, thus enabling rapid and continuous improvement. This so-called *quality life cycle* can be supported by methods and software tools as shown in the inner part of Figure 2. The six methods in the WibQuS project that form the framework for the CIS are as follows (Pfeifer, 1996):

- *Quality function deployment (QFD).* The QFD method (Hauser and Clausing, 1988; Akao, 1990) is a quality planning method that relates customer wishes to product and process features. In a stepwise team process, customer requirements are related to product features, which in turn are related to production process and quality control features. The process is guided by a multi-matrix structure, the House of Quality (HoQ). In the WibQuS environment, a system called DACAPO supports the knowledge-based structuring of products and their functions in order to prepare the HoQ structure for team sessions. QFD engineers need information about products and processes from all over the company in a compressed manner in order to relate customer wishes to the engineering and technical capabilities of the company.

- *Design of experiments (DoE).* The goal of the DoE (Quentin, 1989; Pfeifer, 1993) is a systematic optimization of processes and products by a set of experiments. The CADOX tool supports the DoE team in the selection of the right experimental design based on the knowledge that already exists about the processes and products (critical quality features, previous experiments, production experience) as well as the possible experiment designs.

- *Computer-aided fault analysis (CAFA).* The CAFA method (Pfeifer *et al.*, 1995) collects and provides cause–effect knowledge about products and processes in order to define corrective actions in case that faulty process behaviour is detected by the SPC. The tool supports knowledge acquisition as well as the detection of appropriate actions by inference over the company's quality management knowledge base.

- *Knowledge-based planning of quality control.* This method deals with the systematic description of structural and functional knowledge of quality control techniques in order to support the engineer in the selection and preparation of the appropriate control technique, plan, and measurement instruments according to the planned product features.

- *Extended statistical process control (XSPC).* Statistical process control (Köppe and Heid, 1989) is one of the earliest quality management methods. It checks the process by analysing a particular feature using statistical samples. XSPC does the same for two correlated features. The XSPC tool supports the selection of the appropriate control chart and the analysis of probably critical process developments.

- *Service and field support (FDE)*. This method supports the service engineer in the efficient collection and goal oriented preparation of quality data gained during customer visits. The FDE tool provides guidance for this data collection. It also supports the definition of service actions and the statistical analysis of data for further use by other methods.

Broadcasting all available quality information produced by these methods will quickly overwhelm and turn off users. The goal of our work in WibQuS was therefore to develop a set of methods and tools for CIS planning and design which would help companies identify possibly useful information flows, help them in structuring the information flows according to the possible interactions in Figure 1, estimate the impact of different information flow designs, and provide different degrees of operational support for planned and unplanned information flows with respect to the chosen design. Since quality management implies continuous change, the interplay of these methods had to be organized to make change as easy as possible.

The consortium of the WibQuS project and the methods represented reflect the issues in CIS for federated organizations very well. At the system level the participating engineering groups had their own software standards, partially existing systems and databases on which the above tools were based so that significant heterogeneity existed. In the WibQuS prototype, interoperability at the implementation level was provided by using SQL as the exchange standard for data; all subsystems had relational databases (of different vendors such as Sybase, Oracle and Informix) to interface with the rest of the environment.

On the organizational level the groups were distributed across Germany so that major geographical distances were involved. The methods to be represented originate from different sub-disciplines and it turned out that the different engineering sub-disciplines had also developed quite different and not always consistent vocabularies and conceptual understandings. Due to the differing complexity of the methods — from complex design support methods to automatable process control tasks — the involved agents, their roles in the methods and the needed tool support differed widely. Furthermore, the degree of computing knowledge varied widely in the teams.

For the following sections, the experiences from this exercise will serve as our main basis for examples. While the users/developers were mostly industrial engineering researchers rather than actual users in companies, and despite the technical limitation to relation-based interoperability, we believe that useful lessons can be learned from these experiences. Moreover, several of the individual analysis and design methods presented below were tested in real-world industrial environments; where appropriate, we shall mention these experiences as well.

3 CONCEPTUAL MODELS AS A BASIS FOR CHANGE MANAGEMENT

3.1 A Basic Change Management Process for CIS

Even if an organization is federated, the user groups must still be coordinated such that they move towards common goals and, more importantly, that adaptation to *changing* goals is always possible. Given that coordination mechanisms should be loose and market-like, how can we create the necessary market infrastructure and force fields that let the organization drift in the direction management and customers want, and still provide services to the users that make working with the CIS effective?

Our solution is based on *conceptual modelling* (Figure 3). It is a generalization of the task−artefact cycle for user interface design (Carroll *et al.*, 1991): you (1) reverse-engineer the rationale from the existing man−machine system into a conceptual model, then (2) analyse a proposed change conceptually, finally (3) implement the agreed change, (4) taking into account the existing legacy context. Then the cycle repeats, *ad infinitum.*

There are different ways to manage this evolution cycle. A commercially most successful approach is ARIS/SAP (Scheer, 1994): you start with an ARIS reference model for the business process in question, and customize it to your specific situation. Each component of the reference model is linked to a parameterized SAP software component. The resulting software system is largely configured by parameter tuning.

Although this approach has become very popular, it has some drawbacks. Obviously, the feasibility depends on the coverage of the reference model and, in particular, on the regularity of the business process itself. In complex cooperative settings that include creative aspects, it either does not cover much of the required information flows, or tends to over-constrain user cooperation.

Structuration theory in organizational behaviour gives one possible explanation for these observations (Orlikowski and Robey, 1991). According

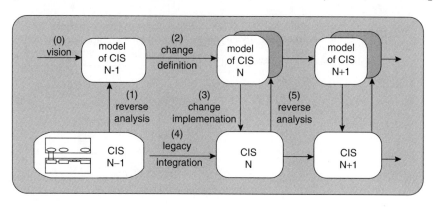

Figure 3.   A model-based evolution process for CISs.

to this theory, organizational structure and organizational change are inextricably linked. If you want a structured operational workflow, a centrally driven reference model adaptation process will work well. If you want a distributed CIS, your design approach also needs to be distributed and cooperative. Moreover, if you want to support organizational change, your models of reality must necessarily reflect the purpose of the change. In Figure 3, the reverse-engineering link therefore goes back to a revised version of the model from which the system was initially constructed. In other words, the cycle actually does *not* start with step (1) but with an initial vision of step (2), the intended change. In previous work, we have expressed this observation by defining requirements engineering as "the process of establishing a vision in the existing technical, cognitive, and social context" (Jarke and Pohl, 1993).

3.2 Metamodelling as a Coordination Strategy

Distributed modelling is a necessity in CISs due to the diversity of knowledge and the autonomy of the network nodes. However, it also makes reconciliation of viewpoints quite a difficult task. To illustrate, Figure 4 shows how designers of two WibQuS applications (WiFEA support

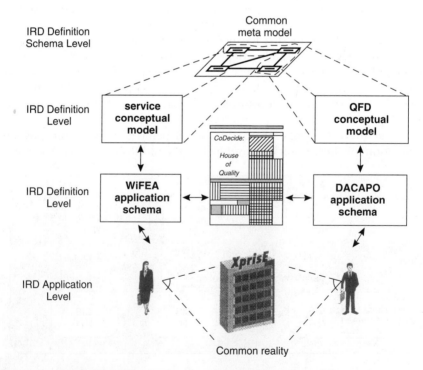

Figure 4.   Integrating different business views with metamodels.

for service technicians and DACAPO for quality function deployment) are coordinated in defining their viewpoints of the same corporate reality — step (1) in Figure 3. They abstract their observations of reality into local application models. These models may differ not only in the notations used but are also influenced by the different knowledge background, and the different interests of the modelers. In other words, viewpoint resolution must happen in all three dimensions of requirements engineering: representation (notations), specification (domain understanding) and agreement (negotiation) (Pohl, 1994).

To indicate how this can be supported by a repository, the left of the figure relates the picture to the levels of the ISO Information Resource Dictionary Standard (ISO/IEC, 1990). In IRDS, the concepts on level $n + 1$ (the defining level) constitute a type system for level n (the defined level). A sub-repository at level $n + 1$ can manage the interaction of subsystems at level n.

In such a multilevel framework, reconciliation can happen in an *ad hoc* manner at the level of the models themselves. In this case, the participating tools are seen purely as drawing tools and practically no computerized support for cross-analysis is possible.

Integrated CASE environments (e.g. the Oracle CASE family) or recently proposed viewpoint resolution mechanisms (Easterbrook and Nuseibeh, 1995) go one step further: they explicitly represent possible relationships between the different notations or domain models controlling the development of each viewpoint, e.g. in the form of consistency rules. The environments then differ in whether they see these rules as strictly to be enforced or as quality control tools to be applied to a "sloppy modelling" process at the user's discretion.

However, in complex heterogeneous environments, the development of such mapping rules is itself a difficult and error-prone process. A number of environments have therefore adopted explicit *metamodels* (actually meta meta models) defining a shared language in which the domain models, notations etc. are represented. Similarities, transformations and consistency checks between notations or domain abstractions can then be defined in terms of this metamodel.

The first metamodels have focused on the integration or generation of *design notations*. Several commercial CASE environments, including PROMOD by Cap debis, include metamodels for the integration of different notations. The MetaEdit+ environment developed at the University of Jyväskylä (Tolvanen and Lyytinen, 1992) allows users to define graphically their own graphical notations, together with referential constraints across such graphics. Enforcement of constraints is strict, as all notations are seen as views on a consistent design database. Notational metamodels can also support runtime tasks such as exploratory search in large networks of heterogeneous databases, where node schemata only become known opportunistically as they are visited for querying (Papazoglou *et al.*, 1995).

Integration via shared *domain metamodels* is a more recent phenomenon. For example, in the medical domain, the Unified Medical Language System (UMLS) (National Library of Medicine, 1994) offers a semantic network structure, metathesaurus and information sources map with the goal of providing uniform access to heterogeneous knowledge sources and aiding their integration. ARIS offers its reference models under a metamodel of event-driven process chains (Scheer, 1994). The most ambitious attempt was probably the Carnot project at MCC (Huhns *et al.*, 1993) which used the "universal" ontology of hundreds of thousands of terms in the CYC knowledge base for IS integration.

However, having a huge ontology in a system does not mean that users share understanding of this ontology. Indeed, given the diversity of aspects on which modeller viewpoints can differ, we believe that no single domain metamodel can be at the same time specific enough to provide actual guidance, and small enough to enable shared understanding and avoid unnecessary modelling overhead. A distinguishing feature of our approach is therefore that the development team can define *their own metamodel*. The metamodel is negotiated by the owners of the notations and then serves as a guidelines for the modelling process, as well as a basis for communication about the coherence of different models. In other words, our user-definable metamodels represent *the shared "vision" of potential problems or solutions which drives the analysis process*.

The ConceptBase system (Jarke *et al.*, 1995) enables this by the unlimited classification hierarchy in its *Telos* language (Mylopoulos *et al.*, 1990) which directly supports modelling the multi-level repository hierarchy shown in the figure. So-called *metaformulas* attached to a metaclass allow you to define deductive rules and integrity constraints that specialize automatically to each class which is an instance of this metaclass. The thus specialized formulas then apply to the instances of these classes. This makes metaformulas robust with respect to notational variations and is a good means for conflict analysis across heterogeneous representations or world views.

The common language defined in the metamodel alone is usually not enough to ensure coherence of distributed modelling since at maximum the formalizable part of a vision can be captured in it. The modelling environment is therefore augmented with additional conflict analysis and negotiation support tools which are defined at the same level as the methods and tools they try to relate. In ConceptBase, they are specialized automatically or configured semi-automatically from two generic instruments defined with the metamodel: query classes and matrix-based visualizations.

Query classes (Staudt *et al.*, 1994) are parameterized and possibly materialized views defined by necessary and sufficient membership constraints similar to description logics (Borgida, 1995). They defer the checking of consistency and completeness of the perspectives generated by parallel development to a moment definable by the teams themselves. Usually, a large number of query classes can be associated with a metamodel and later applied in the negotiations between the modelling teams whose modelling work is based on this metamodel.

CoDecide is a visualization toolkit for conflict analysis (Jarke *et al.*, 1996). A CoDecide tool shows interrelationships between submodels via one or more matrix representations. The toolkit approach allows modellers to quickly develop specialized visualizations for particular kinds of conflicts. Different synchronization styles, ranging from fully shared editing to asynchronous cooperation with partial visibility of mutual views can be supported. A standard example of a conflict visualization interface based on CoDecide is the House of Quality from the QFD method shown in the middle of Figure 4 which offers a comprehensive visualization of the relationships within and between two parties, plus some external context such as versions or competing solutions.

The combination of formal modelling and negotiation management makes ConceptBase a flexible modelling environment for CISs. The models designed cooperatively in the repository architecture implemented in ConceptBase form the starting point for other CIS engineering tools supporting system planning, design and usage tasks, as discussed in the next sections.

4 IDENTIFYING AND PLANNING CIS INFORMATION FLOWS

In this section, we discuss the CIS engineering process at the level of information flows in federated organizations. Here, meta models firstly help to link the analysis step (1) in Figure 3 with the change definition step (2). Secondly, they identify suitable design choices by simulation in the transition from the change definition step (2) to the change implementation step (3). Both activities will be described in the following subsections.

4.1 Cooperative Modelling of Information Flows

There is usually a large conceptual and spatial distance among the different groups involved in CIS design and use. This distance needs to be bridged to some degree before a successful modelling process can start. The modelling process does not aim at generic mutual understanding but has a *specific purpose*. In WibQuS this purpose was the capturing of information flows between the supported methods. Only after some agreement on this purpose has been reached, should distributed modelling start. The formalizable part of this agreement can be coded in a *business process metamodel* that defines a language in which modellers communicate about processes, methods and their interactions.

Our strategy for defining an overall model of information flows to be implemented in the CIS consists of four phases (cf. Figure 6):

1. Joint design of a shared language metamodel as a basis for process definition.
2. Distributed modelling of business processes and information flows within the methods.
3. Integration of the method models.
4. Revision of the shared metamodel based on the gained experiences, followed by optimization of the integrated method models.

The *first phase* involves significant literature studies as well as lengthy negotiations and first experiments with the six modelling teams involved. Starting from the principles of the CRIS methodology (Olle *et al.*, 1991), the business process description consists of **Tasks** and **Objects** consumed and produced by those **Tasks**. Additionally, due to the cooperative nature of the system, it refers to the **Agent** as the responsible performer of a specific **Task** to whom a supporting IS should be adapted. Finally, the concept of **Method** was introduced, because there may be different ways-of-working for a specific task. Methods and tasks form an AND/OR decomposition structure in that a task can be supported by one or several methods while a method consists of a partial order of sub-tasks. Figure 5(a) shows the final version of the WibQuS meta model.

In the *second phase*, each team of engineers developed models of the different methods used along the product life cycle by distributed instantiation of the modelling language making use of the client/server architecture of ConceptBase.

The consistency checks of ConceptBase ensured that the models were in line with the metamodel by strict monitoring of superficial concept correctness via the axioms of the knowledge representation language (here: Telos). The *instantiation principle* avoided modelling errors, since all concepts had to be instances of the defined metamodel. The *naming principles* of ConceptBase avoided that two different concepts with the same

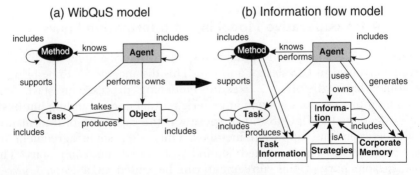

Figure 5.   (a) The WibQuS meta model and (b) its successor, the information flow model.

name were defined. The detection of such inconsistencies led to direct communication between the modelling groups. If a differing meaning of concepts was detected, one of the groups had to change the name. If the same meaning was intended with the same naming, the first interfaces between methods were detected even before the model integration phase had started.

The *third phase* of our strategy, partially overlapping with the second one, concerns negotiations that are intended to ensure coherence between the models. The groups discuss the defined concepts in iterating cycles until a common understanding and agreement about the models is reached (cf. Figure 6). Besides the naming principles described above, ConceptBase offers two techniques for this purpose:

1. *Analysis of formal conflicts such as inconsistency or incompleteness via query classes*. As an example, consider the search for concepts that fulfilled the defined semantics of the modelling language only partially. We were looking for **Objects** that were not taken or produced, **Tasks** where no **Agent** was attached to, and concepts that were not connected to others at all.[2] A simple example for a query class looks as follows:

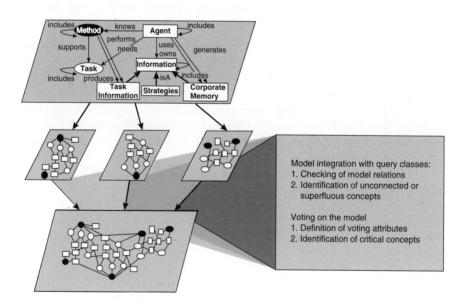

Figure 6. Support of distributed modelling by the modelling language and ConceptBase.

---

[2] In a commercial business process analysis environment based on ConceptBase, about 80 such query classes were identified to uncover analysis errors, differences in opinion, and problems of the business process (Nissen *et al.*, 1996).

```
QueryClass DeadEnd isA ConceptualCategory with
        comment
            explanation :  ''Information provided but not needed''
        constraint
            qr_deadend  : $ exists t1/task (t1 produces this)
                            and not exists t2/task (t2 takes this) $
    end
```

CoDecide was not yet available during the WibQuS modelling process; an example of its use for cooperative business process analysis is given in (Jarke *et al.*, 1996).

2. *Analysis of subjective conflicts through structured annotations.* In the WibQuS project, we initiated a voting on concepts included in the knowledge base under a simple variant of the IBIS model (Conklin and Begemann, 1988). We attached voting attributes to each concept such that modellers could annotate their opinions about the definition (Peters and Jeusfeld, 1994). Table 1 shows the result of the voting, grouped in criticality classes represented by special queries. The results of this classification were given to the groups, who resolved the problems indicated by direct communication. The cycle of voting and discussing was performed until the number of critical concepts was getting small enough to discuss them at a meeting where all groups were represented.

The end result of the modelling process was a set of almost 600 classes which constituted the first formal ontology of the quality cycle in engineering-oriented enterprises. The pen-and-paper analysis and integration of such a complex model in a federated fashion would have been very costly or even impossible to conduct. The meta-modelling approach together with the client/server architecture of ConceptBase enabled quite a fast process which lasted about six months from the first language definition to the integrated model.

The *fourth phase* was a review of this ontology considering the goal of facilitating the planning, design and operation of CIS with high local autonomy. Therefore, the review included theoretical considerations of information flow analysis as well as experiences with the developers themselves (Peters and Jeusfeld, 1994). Two major shortcomings identified during this analysis were:

Table 1.   The results of the voting process.

Number of objects	592
accepted_by	195
rejected_by	2
not_understood_by	13
comment	178
accepted_by and rejected_by	90
accepted_by and not_understood_by	7

1. The interpretation of information flows as inputs and outputs of tasks as in the CRIS model was too simplistic. Firstly, the information exchange needs do not just depend on the task but more on the method by which it is performed. Secondly, there are many important information exchanges between agents, e.g. concerning product quality and improvement opportunities, which cannot be related to specific tasks but can rather be interpreted as materialized *organizational memory*.
2. The models differed widely in their emphasis and degree of detail since no guidelines were available *when to stop modelling*. Some modellers designed the model not as a pure business process model but as a specification of the tools they wanted to build. This over-commitment hindered the integration of the models and led to high overall model complexity.

The first problem led to the refocusing of the language model towards explicit representation of information flow categories, based on the literature about information management and organizational IS in industrial environments (Peters, 1996). The revised metamodel (cf. Figure 5(b)) distinguishes three major groups of information flows within organizations, which are to be implemented and supported differently:

1. *Task information* drives and controls the business processes in organizations (Hammer, 1992; Olle *et al.*, 1991; Scheer 1994). Like, e.g., the structure of a product in manufacturing industries, this information is commonly understood within an organization. Its transfer between departments or tasks is based on standardized formats. The effects of task information are *short term and local*. It results from one department, is transferred to the next, and can initiate a new task. After task execution it is stored in the IS and might become part of the corporate memory.
2. *Corporate memory* about products and processes results from accumulated execution and analysis of business processes (Senge, 1990; Vennix *et al.*, 1994; Harmsen *et al.*, 1994). Capturing this corporate memory can ensure higher quality and efficiency of a process execution (Chen *et al.*, 1992; Fine, 1986; Pentland, 1994). Shared knowledge enables higher productivity and a faster learning curve of the company (Adler and Clark, 1991; Cooprider and Victor, 1993). In contrast to task information, corporate memory cannot be formalized easily. It consists of informal documents like experience collections, stories or rationales (Goldstein, 1993; Ramesh and Sengupta, 1994) and of formal ones like design rules or process models. It needs rich communication support that reduces equivocality[3] and uncertainty in communication (Daft and Lengel, 1986).
3. *Strategies* define a common context according to which tasks are organized and information is interpreted (Hammer, 1992). They consist

---

[3] Equivocality is like uncertainty but with a twist: it evolves in ambiguous or questionable discussion domains.

of a set of visions, policies and goals under which an organization or department operates. Examples are TQM, Just-in-Time (JIT) or Business Process Reengineering (BPR). Strategies result from long-term experiences (Burgelman, 1988) or theories. They are implemented to ensure long-term competitiveness and should influence every part of the organization.

Besides structuring the vast number of objects in the WibQuS knowledge base with respect to usage criteria, the definition of these categories is of major importance for CIS analysis and process support as we will show in the following sections.

With respect to the second problem (when to stop modelling), we argue for a *low modelling depth* of the method model for two reasons:

1. The purpose of the model is the integration of loosely coupled, autonomous methods. Hence, the internal structure of a method is regarded as a black box in terms of integration as long as the necessary information is available to the outside on time.
2. According to Reichwald (1989), QM and design tasks are of medium complexity and planability. Information needs are dependent on the problem and cooperation is flexible but performed with defined partners. In those situations a framework for information exchange is the right level of detail for business process planning.

Therefore, we added a constraint to the method concept:

```
Individual Method in Class with
   attribute
      supports : Task;
      includes : Method;
   constraint
         nondecompose1 : $ forall a,b,c/Method
                           (a includes b) and (a includes c)
                            ==> not (forall x/task_information
                                       (b produces x)
                                    and  (c needs x))
```

The constraint says that a Method a cannot be decomposed in b and c if information exchange takes place only from b to c. A similar constraint was defined for the agent/corporate memory relationship. These constraints ensure that the model is decomposed only as far as information flows to other methods are defined. Applying this modelling rule to the results of the WibQuS modelling process led to a significant reduction of model complexity. For example, in the original model the QFD was described by about 100 concepts. Using the non-decomposition constraint this was reduced to 40.

The example of the revised WibQuS meta model shows, how the selection of the modelling concepts constrains the view of the modellers and influences the model quality. The resulting model of QM methods formed the basis for defining a technical infrastructure of federated information systems. It also offered the basic structure upon which quantitative analyses of data flow and organizational learning could be piggybacked, as discussed in the next subsection.

4.2 Analysing Information Flow Designs by Simulation

The previous subsection showed a strategy for the conceptual design of CIS in a distributed organization. We now describe how these models can be further exploited for an analysis of information flow impact on organizational performance in order to choose among possible change scenarios. Those are to be implemented in step (3) of Figure 3.

The selection of the analysis methods is highly dependent on the information flow category. The analysis of task information is driven by its transaction costs, its timeliness and its completeness. The exchange of corporate memory is analysed to find out its long-term effects on quality, flexibility or personnel qualification[4].

Task information criteria describe short-term, local effects that relate directly to the business process. The analysis of such criteria is usually performed by Petri-net or queuing system simulation (Deiters *et al.*, 1995; Oberweis *et al.*, 1994).

The analysis of *corporate memory* is much harder, because its effects are related to long-term feedback loops within an organization: information has to be accumulated, condensed and then transferred to the organizational units where its effects are supposed to happen. These processes are not related directly to the task workflows and cannot be measured by hard business variables like time and money. The effect of corporate memory is defined by *the way they influence* the variables that produce those time-and-money effects along multiple feedback loops.

In his work on software project dynamics, Abdel-Hamid showed that system dynamics (SD) simulation is well-suited for the analysis of multiple cause–effect feedback loops that describe the productivity behaviour of a software development team performing a specific project (Abdel-Hamid and Madnick, 1991). In the SD technique (Forrester, 1961) the interaction of variables and systems is described as a flow of resources between levels, influenced by the perimeter of valves (rates). This perimeter in turn is determined by the states of variables throughout the system. The philosophy of SD is that people can describe structure and local behaviour of a system well, but fail to predict global behaviour, especially if feedback loops of different length and complexity are part of the system.

Abdel-Hamid developed and validated a set of models for the major factors related to software development productivity and established the

---

[4]We have not yet attempted the impact of strategy information, since the WibQuS had a predefined strategy underlying CIS design, namely TQM.

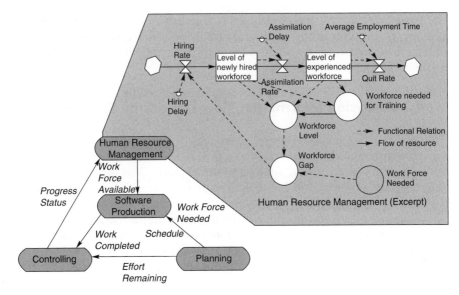

Figure 7. Software development subsystems (adapted from Abdel-Hamid and Madnick, 1991).

feedback loops within and among them (see Figure 7 for a overview of the model structure).

As an example, consider the simulation of a well-known effect called Brook's law: if schedule pressure is detected in the *controlling* submodel the *planning* module is defining the *workforce needed* to meet the schedule. This workforce needed determines the current workforce gap and influences the hiring rate. Addition of new workforce to *newly hired workforce* leads to additional *workforce needed for training*. This reduces the overall workforce available, since newly hired workforce is considered to be of significantly lower availability. The result is a lower productivity and even more schedule pressure.

For the analysis of CIS we generalized the model such that it can represent interacting organizational units with explicit information flow management and error propagation models (Peters, 1996). In addition, information flow planning in CIS requires modelling the *interplay* between the short-term and long-term effects. At the system level, this implies a *heterogeneous simulation* by interoperating discrete (queuing systems) and continuous (system dynamics) simulation techniques. Fishwick recently showed that every quasi-continuous simulation technique can be mapped to a discrete-event technique if the time increment is sufficiently small (Fishwick, 1995). Our MultiSim environment generalizes this idea to a graphical simulation definition and execution environment (Peters *et al.*, 1996).

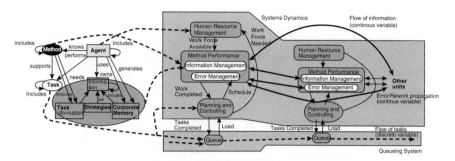

Figure 8.   Mapping of the conceptual to the simulation model.

The kernel of MultiSim is a ConceptBase *repository for simulation techniques*. We developed a definition language for simulation techniques by which simulation languages like SD, Queuing Systems, or Petri-Nets can be modelled and connected. We do not show this metamodel directly but rather the mapping between its major submodels and the WibQuS meta model constructs (Figure 8).

Each *agent* is represented by a *human resource management* model. *Tasks* are represented by *planning and controlling/queue* models. *Methods* are mapped on *method performance* models which describe how manpower made available by human resource management is spent on various parts of a task. The *error management* model analyses the rate by which errors are generated, detected and reworked within a method and the resulting effort in needed manpower. A variable models error propagation between error management models along the business process. The *information management* model describes the amount of work necessary to access, provide and manage the information flows defined in the conceptual model. It also provides the corporate memory as a resource that influences the productivity of other tasks in the model, e.g. training effort, task productivity or error generation.

A first empirical validation of this combined simulation model in a business process re-engineering project for a manufacturing company showed a good match between simulation model and real business dynamics (Peters *et al.*, 1996).

4.3 Coupling Design and Simulation Repository

Figure 9 shows the interplay of metamodels for the design and analysis tasks which are performed in the steps (1) and (2) of the CIS engineering process.

On the right branch, starting from the *WibQuS metamodel*, process models for QM are coordinated using the method models at the second level as reference models. These process models are mapped to a multi-simulation model (left branch) which is itself based on interoperability

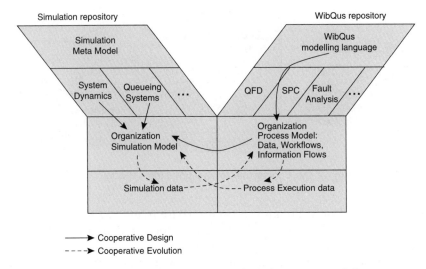

Figure 9.   CIS design and simulation process based on metamodelling.

between different simulation methods defined through a *simulation meta model*. In our special case this is the interaction between System Dynamics and Queuing Systems.

The interplay of simulation and actual process allows on-going evolution of the CIS: on the one hand, the observation of real processes leads to changes of the simulation model which in turn indicate necessary changes of the organizational process structure. On the other hand, experimenting with envisioned changes to the CIS in the simulation model leads to insights about the dynamics of those changes and therefore allows for the selection of appropriate evolution steps.

5 OPERATIONAL SUPPORT FOR CIS INFORMATION FLOWS

The cooperative modelling process identifies *possible information flows* while the multi-simulation approach helps the organization evaluate which of these should be *specifically facilitated*. In this section, we show that such choices can be *implemented* by linking certain views on the conceptual model to the system level, in the WibQuS project a federated network of relational databases. This supports the integration of steps (3) and (4) in Figure 3. The mappings are maintained in a *quality trader* which was implemented by linking ConceptBase to the Sybase OMNI-SQL gateway for distributed execution, and a relational database for maintaining temporary exchange data such as contract status (Peters *et al.*, 1995b).

Three kinds of mappings are derived from the WibQuS meta model. The "owns" link in Figure 5 is mapped to ownership of database nodes. In practical CIS settings, this partitioning is often given and must simply be recorded as a dependency link in the meta database. Section 5.1 shows how the conceptual structure of task and memory information is related to the underlying database schemata; this allows users to make *unplanned information searches* in a browser-based environment (Section 5.2). *Planned information flows* are mapped to stored queries and workflow structures (Section 5.3) which are more efficient to use but more difficult to change than the unplanned ones.

5.1 Mappings Between Concept and System Layer

Task information flows were defined in a subset of Telos that is basically an extended Entity–Relationship language. Many techniques exist how to map such models to efficient relational schemas; the reverse mapping, how to extract conceptual models from existing relational databases, has also been studied. Since both questions are equally relevant in the CIS context, we developed a *symmetric approach* where the mapping in both directions is constrained by the same metamodel (Jeusfeld and Johnen, 1995). In Figure 10, the organization level of Figure 1 is shown to the right, the

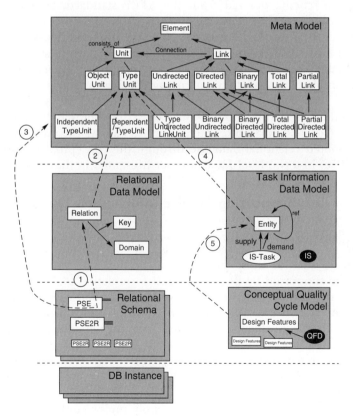

Figure 10.   Metamodel constraining the mapping between concepts and relations.

system level to the left. Steps (1)–(5) sketch how, as an example, reverse modelling is driven by the lowest common ancestor of the metaclasses of which the two concepts that have to be mapped, are instances. Since the expressiveness of both formalisms is not the same, the process is partially interactive (steps 3 and 5): reverse mapping demands a *semantic* enrichment whereas forward mapping demands performance-oriented design choices.

CIS engineering uses neither of these directions alone but demands a sophisticated interleaving. As *organizational model and system implementation co-evolve*, business and system modellers should benefit from each others' work. Typically, system designers know more details, while business modellers have a broader overview. Once a link between the two models has been established, business modellers can apply reverse engineering to elaborate their conceptual task information models, and forward mapping to inform system designers about the usage context.

The main purpose of schema design in CIS is support for intergroup information flows. To interpret the thus exchanged messages, it turns out to be useful to standardize their contents using a shared metamodel of the manufacturing product and process. In WibQuS, this metamodel was a relational schema derived from the STEP standard, augmented with quality attributes. This *product and process model* became part of all exchange schemata of the federated databases. Now, the conceptual task information model for each subsystem must be considered a *view* on this standard model which further complicates the reverse- and forward-engineering task.

A complete methodology for co-engineering organization and system models is still under development. The result is in any case a set of dependencies between the two models that helps in further system evolution (Jeusfeld and Jarke, 1995), but also allows the end user to view the distributed relational database through the conceptual model (Peters *et al.*, 1995a) in a two-level filter-browser presented in the next section.

5.2 Supporting *Ad Hoc* Information Flows

In a distributed environment under ongoing evolution only a limited number of information requests can be supported by predefined mechanisms such as those presented in Section 5.3. The other requests need to be supported by flexible request formulation tools which provide an acceptable compromise between tool flexibility and user friendliness.

At the system level, as it is defined in the WibQuS project, one has to deal with the problems of classical query languages (hard to learn, difficult to use, not adapted to the specific domain), which are even more complicated in federated information systems. First, there are several query languages used in the system. Second, there is no central database schema known by all system members but a number of loosely coupled schemas whose structure and contents are not easily understandable for someone looking for information. The advantages of graphical database browsing and access mechanisms for central databases have been pinpointed in various publications (d' Atri, 1989; Wong and Kuo, 1982; Zhou, 1994). They are at least as striking for federated systems if they exploit the knowledge stored in the model repository, as we will show in this section.

As mentioned before, the model of quality management methods and all schema information are stored in the quality trader repository. This adds up to about a thousand schema objects, and searching the whole repository would be inefficient. Therefore, the browsing environment was structured by separating the method model from the database schema information and by dividing the schema information into PPM (general interest) and private schemas. This led to the browsing window layout shown in Figure 11.

Further, to adjust the search space to the tasks to be supported, we have developed a view concept that restricts the information provided at the windows (Peters *et al.*, 1995a). Agent-oriented, method-oriented, product-oriented, or change-step oriented perspectives serve as filters to prevent "getting lost in hyperspace".

In the upper window, the filtered conceptual model is shown; an exchangeable palette of graphical types facilitates user understanding. The lower window shows the corresponding part of the relational schema. The user can graphically formulate relational queries which are automatically

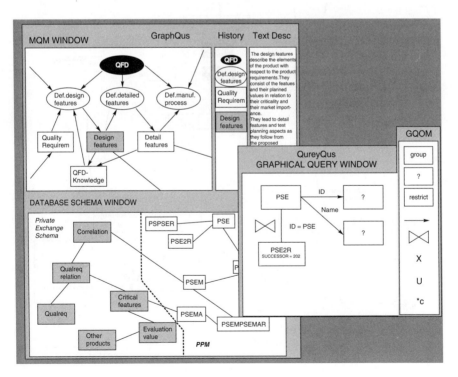

Figure 11.   The information search and access tool.

augmented with the applied filter definitions; location transparency is
provided by the quality trader.

5.3 Supporting Planned Information Flows

Units in a market-like organization interact in customer−supplier relationships. Workflows in WibQuS are therefore modelled in *request−commit−
perform−evaluate cycles* (Medina-Mora *et al.*, 1992) which map task delegation
between agents (Figure 5). The quality trader encodes the necessary data
structures in a special relational schema, shown as an entity−relationship
diagram in the middle of Figure 12. Active communication tasks record
tuples concerning their (order, argument list) and status (negotiation,
commitment, error). The task description can be just a specification for
humans, it can be an executable program, or it can be a parameterized
database query.

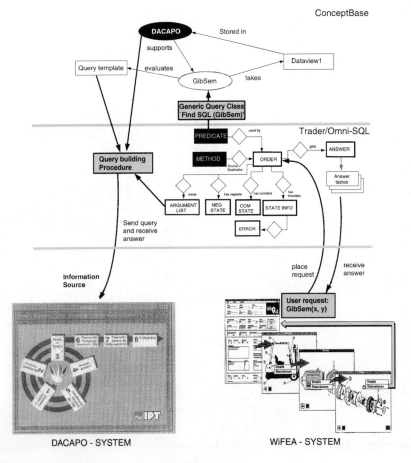

Figure 12.   The order evaluation process.

Figure 12 illustrates the latter case for an interaction between the WiFEA service support tool and the DACAPO quality planning tool in WibQuS. The service person has used her tool to zoom into the details of a forklift to be serviced, and detected some problem. She now wants to know if this problem is a known bug and therefore invokes the standard task GibSem which returns detailed information about a structure element in the product and process model. The task is placed in the order relation and abstracted to a ConceptBase query class which was defined in the conceptual model when fixing GibSem as a standard information flow.

In detail, the process of order evaluation is the following. Placing the **predicate** and the **argument list** in the **order** relation and setting the value of the **comstate** relation to 1 initiates the order evaluation process by the quality trader based on triggers defined on the **comstate** relation:

1. **comstate** = 1: The quality trader checks the **comstate** relation of every system frequently and starts the query evaluation procedure.
2. The quality trader looks up the query represented by the **predicate**. This is done by evaluating the GenericQueryClass "findSQL(**predicate**)" on the repository. Each predicate is represented as an instance of **Task** at repository level 3.
3. The relations which are involved into the query are related to the systems in which they are stored. The quality trader finds those information source(s) using the **stored in** attribute added to the structure of the repository.
4. The query variables in the predefined **query template** are instantiated with the **argument list** and the locations found in step 3.
5. OmniSQL transfers the query into the database dialect(s) of the source(s). **Comstate** = 2.
6. Execution of the (distributed) query.
7. The quality trader collects the answer(s) and transforms it into the dialect of the requesting system. **Comstate** = 3
8. The answer table is sent to the requesting system. **Comstate** = 4.
9. The quality trader documents the querying process for statistical purposes.

ConceptBase now determines that the owner of this information is the quality planning subsystem. The corresponding SQL query is constructed in Omni-SQL and sent to DACAPO's Oracle database. After negotiation, the query is executed there and the resulting tables are made available to the WiFEA database (implemented using Informix). A monitor window of the quality trader allows control of this process from each involved node.

6 SUMMARY AND CONCLUSION

The WibQuS experiences show that many tasks involved in the planning and operation of federated organizations with cooperative information systems can be coordinated by user-definable and repository-supported metamodels. Promising first commercial experience has been gained with several parts of the overall approach though the full combination of techniques in the WibQuS prototype has only been tested with relatively small example datasets.

The metamodelling technology must be sufficiently formal to enable the largely automatic generation of the distributed coordination software. The not-too-complicated semantics of Telos in ConceptBase proved a major plus in this regard. However, our results so far have been limited to the case of heterogeneous relational databases; the follow-up project FoQuS currently investigates the generalization to object-oriented target environments. Even for the relational case, attempts are under way to increase further the degree of methodological and automated support for the co-evolution of organization and system model. Finally, our simulation approach has focused on the organizational impact of information flows alone; in future work, we intend to link this with a system-performance oriented distributed database design environment being developed in our group.

REFERENCES

Abdel-Hamid, T. and Madnick, S. (1991) *Software Project Dynamics*. Prentice Hall, Englewood Cliffs, NJ.

Adler, P. and Clark, K. (1991) Behind the learning curve: a sketch of the learning process. *Management Science*, **37**(3), 267–281.

Akao, Y. (1990) *Quality Function Deployment: Integrating Customer Requirements into Product Design*. Productivity Press, Cambridge.

Borgida, A. (1995) Description logics in data management. *IEEE Transactions on Knowledge and Data Engineering*, **7**(5), 671–682.

Brodie, M. and Ceri, S. (1992) On intelligent and cooperative information systems: a workshop summary. *International Journal of Intelligent and Cooperative Information Systems*, **1**(2), 249–290.

Burgelman, R. (1988) Strategy making as a social learning process: the case of internal corporate venturing. *Interfaces*, **18**(3), 74–85.

Carroll, J., Kellogg, W. and Rosson, M. (1991) The Task-Artifact Cycle. In *Designing Interaction: Psychology at the Human–Computer Interface*, J. Carroll, (ed). Cambridge.

Chen, M., Liou, Y. and Weber, E. (1992) Developing Intelligent Organizations: A Context-Based Approach to Individual and Organization Effectiveness. *Journal of Organizational Computing*, **2**(2), 181–202.

Conklin, J. and Begemann, M. (1988) gibis: a hypertext tool for exploratory policy discussion. *ACM Transactions on Office Information Systems*, **10**, 140–151.

Cooprider, J. and Victor, K. (1993) The Contribution of Shared Knowledge to IS Group Performance. In *14th Conference on Information Systems*, Orlando, Fl., 285–297.

Daft, R. and Lengel, R. (1986) Organizational Information Requirements, Media Richness and Structural Design, *Management Science*, **32**(5), 554–571.

d'Atri, A. (1989) From Browsing to Querying. *IEEE Database Engineering*, **8**, 110–117.

Deiters, W., Gruhn, V. and Striemer, R. (1995) The FUNSOFT Approach to Business Process Management. *Wirtschaftsinformatik*, **37**(5), 459–466.

Easterbrook, S. and Nuseibeh, B. (1995) Managing Inconsistencies in an Evolving Specification. In *2nd IEEE International Symposium on Requirements Engineering*, York, England, pp. 48–56.

Fine, C. (1986) Quality Improvement and Learning in Production Systems. *Management Science*, **32**(10), 1301–1315.

Fishwick, P. (1995) *Simulation Model Design and Execution*. Prentice Hall, Englewood Cliffs, N.J.

Forrester, J. (1961) *Industrial Dynamics*. MIT Press, Cambridge, Mass.

Goldstein, D. (1993) Computer-Based Data and Organizational Learning: The Importance of Managers' Stories. *Journal of Organizational Computing*, **3**(4), 417–441.

Hammer, D.K. (1992) Lean Information Management: The Integrating Power of Information. In *IFIP Transactions: Integration in Production Management Systems*, H.J. Pels and J.C. Wortmann (eds). Elsevier Science Publishers B.V., pp. 147–163.

Harmsen, F., Brinkkemper, S. and Oei, H. (1994) Situational Method Engineering for Information System Project Approaches. In *Methods and Associated Tools for the Information Systems Life Cycle*, Elsevier Science B.V., pp. 169–194.

Hauser, J.R. and Clausing, D. (1988) Wenn die Stimme des Kunden bis in die Produktion vordringen soll. *Harvard Manager*, **4**, 57–70.

Heinzl, A. and Srikanth, R. (1995) Entwicklung der betrieblichen Informationsverarbeitung. *Wirtschaftsinformatik*, **37**(1), 10–17.

Huhns, M., Jacobs, N., Ksiezyk, T., Shen, W.-M., Singh, M. and Cannata, P. (1993) Integrating Enterprise Information Models in Carnot. In *Proceedings of the International Conference on Intelligent and Cooperative Information Systems*, Rotterdam, pp. 32–43.

ISO/IEC (1990) Information Technology — Information Resource Dictionary System (IRDS) — Standard ISO/IEC 10027. Technical report, ISO/IEC International Standard.

Jarke, M. and Ellis, C. (1993) Distributed Cooperation in Integrated Information Systems. *International Journal of Intelligent and Cooperative Information Systems*, **2**(1), 85–103.

Jarke, M. and Pohl, K. (1993) Establishing Visions in Context: Towards a Model of Requirements Process. In *14th Conference on Information Systems*, Orlando, Fl.

Jarke, M., Jeusfeld, M. and Szczurko, P. (1993) Three Aspects of Intelligent Cooperation in the Quality Life Cycle. *International Journal of Intelligent and Cooperative Information Systems*, **2**(4), 355–374.

Jarke, M., Gallersdörfer, R., Jeusfeld, M., Staudt, M. and Eherer, S. (1995) ConceptBase — A Deductive Object Base for Meta Data Management. *Journal of Intelligent Information Systems*, **4**(2).

Jarke, M., Gebhardt, M., Jacobs, S. and Nissen, H. (1996) Conflict Analysis Across Heterogeneous Viewpoints: Formalization and Visualization. In *29th Annual Hawaii Conference on System Sciences*, **3**, 199–208, Wailea, Hawaii.

Jeusfeld, M. and Jarke, M. (1995) Repository Structures for Evolving Federated Database Schemas. In *IFIP Working Conference on Models and Methodologies for Enterprise Integration*, Heron Island, Australia.

Jeusfeld, M. and Johnen, U. (1995) An Executable Meta Model for Re-Engineering of Database Schemes. *International Journal of Cooperative Information Systems*, **4**(2), 237–258.

Klein, H and Lyytinen, K. (1992) Towards a New Understanding of Data Modeling. In *Software Development and Reality Construction*, C. Floyd, H. Zullighoven, R. Budde and R. Keil-Slawik (eds). Springer-Verlag, pp. 203–219.

Köppe, D. and Heid, W. (1989) Möglichkeiten and Grenzen der SPC. *Qualität and Zuverlässigkeit*, **34**(12).

Malone, T., Yates, J. and Benjamin, R. (1987) Electronic Markets and Electronic Hierarchies. *Communication of the ACM*, **30**(6), 484–497.

Medina-Mora, R., Winograd, T., Flores, R. and Flores, C. (1992) The Action Workflow Approach to Workflow Management Technology. In *4th International Conference of Computer-Supported Cooperative Work*, Toronto, Canada, pp. 281–288.

Mylopoulos, J., Borgida, A., Jarke, M. and Koubarakis, M. (1990) Telos: a Language for Representing Knowledge about Information Systems. *ACM Transactions on Informations Systems*, **8**(4), 325–362.

National Library of Medicine (1994) Unified Medical Language System, 5th edn. Technical report, US Department of Health and Human Services.

Nissen, H., Jeusfeld, M., Jarke, M., Zemanek, G. and Huber, H. (1996) Managing Multiple Requirements Perpectives with Meta Models. *IEEE Software*.

Oberweis, A., Scherrer, G. and Stucky, W. (1994) INCOME/STAR: Methodology and Tools for the Development of Distributed Information Systems. *Information Systems*, **19**(8), 643–660.

Olle, T., Hagelstein, J., MacDonald, I., Rolland, C., Sol, H., van Assche, F. and Verrijn-Stuart, A. (1991) *Information Systems Methodologies — A Framework for Understanding*. North-Holland, Amsterdam.

Orlikowski, W. and Robey, D. (1991) Information Technology and the Structuring of Organizations. *Information Systems Research*, **2**, 143–169.

Papazoglou, M., Russell, N. and Edmond, D. (1995) A Semantic-Oriented Translation Protocol for Heterogeneous Federated Database Systems. Technical report, Queensland University of Technology, Australia.

Pentland, B. (1994) Information Systems and Organizational Learning: The Social Epistemology of Organizational Knowledge Systems. Technical report.

Peters, P. (1996) Planning and analysis of information flow in quality management. PhD thesis, RWTH Aachen.

Peters, P. and Jeusfeld, M. (1994) Structuring Information Flow in Quality Management. In *International Conference on Data and Knowledge Systems for Manufacturing and Engineering*, Hong Kong, pp. 258–263.

Peters, P., Löb. U. and Rodriguez Pardo, A. (1995a) A Task-Oriented Graphical Interface to Federated Databases. In *Proceedings of 3rd International Conference of the International Society for Decision Support Systems*, Hong Kong, pp. 223–231.

Peters, P., Szczurko, P., Jarke, M. and Jeusfeld, M. (1995b) A Federated Information System for Quality Management Processes. In *IFIP WG8.1 Working Conference on Information Systems for Decentralized Organizations*, Trondheim, Norway, pp. 100–117.

Peters, P., Mandelbaum, M. and Jarke, M. (1996) Simulation-Based Method Engineering in Federated Organizations. In *Method Engineering 96*, Atlanta, Georgia, pp. 246–262.

Pfeifer, T. (1993) *Quality Management* (in German). Carl Hanser Verlag, München.

Pfeifer, T. (ed). (1996) *Wissensbasierte System in der Qualitätssicherung — Verteiltes Wissen nutzbar machen* (in German). Springer-Verlag, Heidelberg, Berlin, New York.

Pfeifer, T., Grob, R. and Klonaris, P. (1995) Teamgestützte Erfassung von Erfahrungswissen zur Fehleranalyse. In *3. Deutsche Expertensystemtagung*, Kaiserslautern.

Pohl, K. (1994) The Three Dimensions of Requirements Engineering: a Framework and its Applications. *Information Systems*, **19**(3), 243–258.

Quentin, H. (1989) Statistische Versuchsmethodik. *Qualität und Zuverlässigkeit*, **34**(5), 229–232.

Ramesh, B. and Sengupta, K. (1994) Managing Cognitive and Mixed-Motive Conflicts in Concurrent Engineering. *Concurrent Engineering Research and Application*, **2**(3).

Reichwald, R. (1989) Die Entwicklung der Arbeitsteilung unter dem Einfluss von Technologieeinsatz im Industriebetrieb. In *Die Betriebswirtschaft im Spannungsfeld zwischen Generalisierung und Spezialisierung*, W. Kirsch and A. Picot (eds). Gabler Verlag, pp. 300–321.

Scheer, A.-W. (1994) *Business Process Reengineering — Reference Models for Industrial Business Processes*. Springer-Verlag, Berlin, Heidelberg.

Scott-Morton, M. (1994) The 1990s research program: Implications for Management and the Emerging Organization. *Decision Support Systems*, **12**(2), 251–256.

Senge, P. (1990) *The Fifth Discipline: The Art and Practice of the Learning Organization*. Currency, New York.

Staudt, M., Jeusfeld, M. and Jarke, M. (1994) Query by Rule, Class, and Concept. *Journal of Applied Intelligence*, **4**(2).

Tolvanen, J.-P. and Lyytinen, K. (1992) Flexible Method Adaptation in CASE Environments — The Metamodelling Approach. In *Proceedings of the 15th IRIS*, Bjerknes *et al.* (eds). pp. 388–405.

Vennix, J., Andersen, D., Richardson, G. and Rohrbaugh, J. (1994) Model Building for Group decision Support: Issues and Alternatives for Knowledge Elicitation. In *Modeling for Learning Organizations*, J. Morecroft and J. Sterman (eds). Productivity Press.

Wong, H. and Kuo, I. (1982) GUIDE: Graphical User Interface for Database Exploration. In *Proceedings of the 8th Very Large Databases Conference*.

Zhou, J. (1994) GUI to Databases — Survey and Practice. *GI Datenbank Rundbrief*, **13**, 49–51.

From Organization Models to System Requirements: a "Cooperating Agents" Approach

Eric Yu[a], Philippe Du Bois[b], Eric Dubois[b] and John Mylopoulos[a]

[a]University of Toronto, Ontario, Canada and [b]University of Namur, Belgium

Abstract

Increasingly, information systems development occurs in the context of existing systems and established organizational processes. Viewing organizational and system components as *cooperating agents* offers a way of understanding their interrelationships and how these relationships would or should be altered as new systems are introduced. In this chapter, we show how two agent-oriented frameworks can be used in combination during requirements engineering for cooperative information systems. The ALBERT language is used to specify requirements, in terms of states and actions, and information and perception. The i^* framework is used to understand and redesign organizational processes, in terms of strategic relationships and rationales. A small banking example is used to illustrate how the requirements process may iterate between the two levels of modelling and analysis towards a requirements specification.

I INTRODUCTION

Increasingly, information systems development occurs in the context of existing systems and established organizational processes. For example, the development of systems to support a banking-by-phone service would have to take into account existing systems that store and process customer information and account transactions. These systems engage in processes that involve customers and bank employees (managers, tellers, accountants etc.), which together constitute an organizational configuration that makes a banking service possible, and at some desired levels of availability, security and quality of service. *Cooperation* among the many "agents" — whether they be human or computer-based — is crucial in order to attain these organizational goals.

Information systems can be viewed as being *cooperative* to the extent that they contribute to the achievement of organizational goals (de Michelis *et al.*, this volume). In determining requirements for cooperative information systems, it is necessary to have an understanding of the organizational environment and goals, so that the resulting systems (which may be already existing, or to be developed) will work together with human agents to achieve overall goals (such as a phone-banking service that is viable from the customer's and the bank's viewpoints). To support the development of cooperative information systems, we need models and frameworks that recognize that agents in distributed, dynamic organizations typically have limited knowledge about each other, and may have conflicting or complementary goals.

In the past decade, requirements modelling frameworks have been developed to assist in the understanding and specification of systems and their environments (e.g., Bubenko, 1980; Borgida *et al.*, 1985; Dubois *et al.*, 1988). More recently, goal-oriented frameworks for requirements engineering involving multiple agents have been developed (e.g., Feather, 1987; Dubois, 1989; Fickas and Helm, 1992; Dardenne *et al.*, 1993; Bubenko, 1983; Yu, 1995a). In such frameworks, *goals* are either (i) associated with a set of constraints which describe restrictions on the behaviour desired of the system (and that should result from the interleaving of the behaviours of the different system's components) or (ii) associated with organizational and business rules allowing analysis of the rationale underlying a system's architecture. We draw on this line of research to further develop requirements engineering techniques for cooperative systems.

Our contention is that a single conception of *agent* as embedded in a particular modelling framework may not be adequate to deal with the different types of analyses and reasoning that are needed during requirements engineering. Traditionally, requirements are usually taken to be specificational — as prescribing *what* systems should do. However, to understand and characterize the cooperative aspects of multi-agent systems, we need models that can express and help reason about *why* agents do what they do. Languages designed for prescribing agent behaviour are not well-suited for describing competing or complementary interests among agents, or for reasoning about strategic implications, such as those resulting from failure to adhere to prescriptive specifications (Yu, 1997).

In this chapter, we view the requirements engineering effort as consisting of two levels — a specificational level which prescribes *what* agents should do or know, and an "understanding" level which describes *why* agents relate to each other in a certain way, and why they might prefer some other configuration of relationships. Adopting a two-levelled approach allows each level to offer agent concepts that are appropriate for that level of modelling and reasoning. We show how the two levels can work together to achieve better understanding of systems and their organizational environments, and to come up with system requirements.

The ALBERT language[1] (Dubois *et al.*, 1993a; Du Bois, 1995) has been designed for specifying the (primarily functional) requirements of distributed real-time systems. Agents have states and actions. They are constrained in terms of obligations, information and perception. From an ALBERT specification, one can determine whether certain desired properties are satisfied (Du Bois *et al.*, 1997). Agents cooperate by giving each other information about their own state of knowledge. ALBERT offers a higher-level view than earlier requirements languages (such as ERAE (Dubois *et al.*, 1988) or RML (Greenspan, 1984)) through the use of agent-oriented concepts such as knowledge and obligation.

The *i** framework[2] (Yu, 1995a) is used to obtain an understanding about organizational relationships and the rationales behind them. Agents have wants and abilities. They depend on each other for goals to be achieved, tasks to be performed and resources to be furnished. However, within the constraints imposed by these dependencies, agents have freedom of action. A model of *strategic dependencies* among agents can be analysed for opportunities and vulnerabilities. A model of *strategic rationales* can assist in the search for alternative configurations of organizational relationships that can better address the strategic interests of agents, for example, by introducing information systems. *i** offers a more open and strategic conception of agents than other goal-oriented requirements frameworks (e.g., Dardenne *et al.*, 1993).

We use the *i** models to support the generation and evaluation of organizational alternatives, and the ALBERT language to produce a requirements specification document for system development. As organizational requirements change (in the *i** models), they need to be reflected in the functional requirements (the ALBERT specification). Elaboration of the functional requirements may reveal further organizational issues that need to be addressed, resulting in an iterative process of refinement of the organizational and functional requirements. We anticipate that this iterative process would lead to a more systematic and thorough examination of organizational issues and system specifications than if either framework were used on its own.

As a running example in this chapter, we consider a bank whose existing banking systems have been designed with the assumption that customers visit bank branches to conduct their business (i.e., a *customer* gives a transfer request to a *teller*, who validates it by verifying the identity of the customer; if it is OK, the teller transmits the transfer request to the *account handler* subsystem which processes it providing that the balance of

---

[1] ALBERT stands for *Agent-oriented Language for Building and Eliciting Real-Time requirements*.
[2] The name *i** (pronounced *i-star*) refers to the notion of distributed intentionality among cooperative agents.

the customer's account permits it). Within that context, we envisage that the bank wishes to offer "banking-by-phone" as a new service. In order to decide what changes to the banking systems are required, we use i^* to obtain an understanding of the organizational and business environment — for example, that customers would like to be able to transfer funds more quickly and more conveniently, but are also concerned about security. Using means–ends reasoning in i^*, a PIN (personal identification number) code is proposed as a way to address the security goal. At the ALBERT level, one discovers that a PIN code does not offer security if the code is also known to other agents. Returning to the i^* models, we add the organizational requirement that customers be committed to keeping the PIN code confidential. These new requirements lead to changes to system requirements at the ALBERT level, which may in turn have further implications at the organization model level. The example is pedagogical and is meant to be suggestive of the much more complex sets of issues typically found in actual situations.

In Section 2, we briefly review the main features of ALBERT and i^*, using the traditional banking-by-teller arrangement as the example. Section 3 shows how the two levels of modelling work together to obtain system requirements for introducing a banking-by-phone service. In Section 4 we discuss our approach and compare with related work. We conclude in Section 5 with some observations about the implications of our approach, and outline some avenues for future research.

2 FEATURES OF ALBERT AND i^*

In this section, we review the main concepts of ALBERT and i^* and we illustrate their use through the bank case study. The example is necessarily greatly simplified and does not reflect the complexity of real banking. It is only used here to illustrate the basic concepts of our approach.

2.1 Specifying Requirements Using the ALBERT Language

The ALBERT language supports the modelling of functional requirements in terms of a collection (or *society*) of *agents* interacting together in order to provide services necessary for the organization. Each agent is characterized by *actions* that change or maintain its own *state* of knowledge about the external world and/or the states of other agents. Such actions are performed by agents in order to discharge contractual obligations expressed in terms of *internal* and *cooperation* constraints.

In ALBERT, functional requirements are expressed in terms of a set of formal statements. The semantics has been defined in terms of a specific real-time temporal logic enriched with the concept of object and called *AlbertCORE* (Du Bois, 1995).

ALBERT supports the encoding of requirements in both *declarative* and *operational* styles.

In order to enhance readability, a specification is organized into units called *agents*. Logical statements are grouped around agents in order to define the set of admissible behaviours (or *lives*) they may experience. Statements describing an agent are classified into categories, each corresponding to a pattern of property. Such pattern provides guidance in the elicitation and structuring of requirements.[3]

The language[4] is made up of (i) a graphical component in terms of which is *declared* the vocabulary of the application to be considered and (ii) a textual component in terms of which the specification of the admissible behaviours of agents is *constrained* through logical formulas. The "Declarations" and "Constraints" components of the banking-by-teller example are shown in Figures 1 and 2 respectively.

- *Declarations*. The Declarations component consists of a description of the general structure of the composite system in terms of agents as well as of the structure of each individual agent.

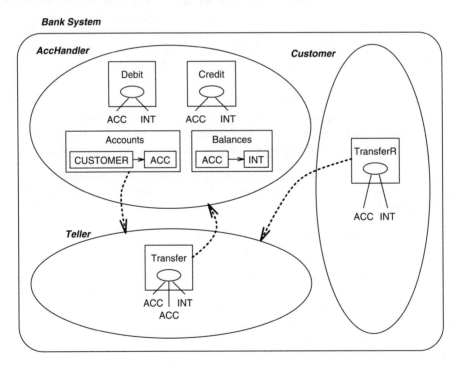

Figure 1.   Structure of the bank system.

---

[3]The usefulness of such patterns was also previously identified in the RML language (Greenspan *et al.*, 1986) built on top of first order logic.
[4]For a detailed presentation of ALBERT, see Du Bois (1995).

A specification consists of a collection of agents. Our small example (see Figure 1) consists of three agents: *AccHandler* (declared as an individual agent), *Customer* and *Teller* (each declared as a class of agents).

The declaration part of an agent consists of the description of its *state* structure (i.e. the memory of the agent) and the list of *actions* which may happen during the life of the agent and which may change the state of the agent. State components (graphically depicted with rectangles) are typed and actions (graphically depicted with ovals) can have typed arguments. Types may vary from simple data types to complex data types (recursively built using predefined type constructors).

In the example (see Figure 1), the state of the *AccHandler* agent is structured into two tables (resp. *Accounts* and *Balances*). The index of the *Balances* table is of type *ACC*(ount) and the elements of type *INT*(eger). The *AccHandler* may perform two kinds of actions: *Credit* and *Debit*. Both have two arguments: the first of type *ACC* and the second of type *INT*.

In addition, the graphical notation also expresses visibility relationships linking agents to the outside. Dotted lines on Figure 1 show how agents make information visible to other agents, e.g., the *Account* table of the *AccHandler* agent is exported to the *Teller* agent; on the contrary, the *Balances* table is shown to no other agents. Dotted lines also show how agents influence each others' behaviour through exportation of actions, e.g., the *AccHandler* agent is influenced by the *Transfer* actions of the *Teller* agent.

- *Constraints*. Constraints are used for pruning the (usually) infinite set of possible lives associated with the agents of a composite system. The life of an agent is (usually) an infinite alternating sequence of changes (occurrences of actions) and states values. An admissible life will respect:

1. *local* constraints related to the internal behaviour of the agent;
2. *cooperation* constraints defining how the agent interacts with other agents.

Local constraints are classified under four headings. The use of two of them is illustrated in the example.

1. **Effects of actions.** The effect of an action is expressed through its functional characterization in terms of a mathematical relationship between successive information states (Figure 2 shows the effects of the *Credit* and *Debit* actions).
2. **Causalities among actions.** Action triggering is usually ensured through ECA (Event–Condition–Action) rules, i.e., at any moment, when an event occurs if a condition on the current state is met, then the action happens. In ALBERT, this rather operational style of specification is supported (see below) but a more declarative style also permits keeping track of action occurrences and of specific causalities among them (Figure 2 illustrates the concept of *process*).

AccHandler

LOCAL CONSTRAINTS

EFFECTS OF ACTIONS

$Credit(a,n)$: $Balances[a] = Balances[a]+n$

┃ The account a is credited with amount n

$Debit(a,n)$: $Balances[a] = Balances[a]-n$

┃ The account a is debited by amount n

CAUSALITY

$tlr.Transfer(a1,a2,n) \xrightarrow{\Diamond \leq 1d} Debit(a1,n); Credit(a2,n)$

┃ A transfer order should be followed within at most 1 day, by the corresponding credit and debit operations.

COOPERATION CONSTRAINTS

ACTION PERCEPTION

ӁӃ ($tlr.Transfer(a,\_,n)$ / $Balances[a]>n-\$2000$)

┃ A transfer order is processed by the AccHandler if and only if the resulting balance of the
┃ customer's account does not reach more than a $2000 overdraft.

STATE INFORMATION

ӁӃ ($Accounts.\ TELLER$ / TRUE)

┃ The Accounts table is always shown to all Tellers.

Customer

COOPERATION CONSTRAINTS

ACTION INFORMATION

ӁӃ ($Transfer(\_,\_,\_)\ TELLER$ / TRUE)

┃ In any situation, the customer sends his/her transfer orders to a Teller.

Teller

LOCAL CONSTRAINTS

CAUSALITY

$c.TransferR(a,n) \xrightarrow{\Diamond} Transfer(AccHandler.Accounts[c],a,n)$

┃ A valid transfer request from the Customer is echoed by a transfer order sent to the AccHandler.

COOPERATION CONSTRAINTS

STATE PERCEPTION

ӁӃ ($AccHandler.Accounts$ / TRUE)

┃ The Teller can always consult the Accounts table maintained by the AccHandler.

ACTION PERCEPTION

ӁӃ ($c.TransferR(a,n)$ / $c \in DOM(AccHandler.Accounts)$)

┃ A transfer request is valid if and only if the customer has an account at the bank.
┃ The Teller knows the identity of the customer responsible for the transfer.

ACTION INFORMATION

ӁӃ ($Transfer(\_,\_,\_).AccHandler$ / TRUE)

┃ In any situation, the Teller sends his transfer orders to the AccHandler.

Figure 2. Constraints on the *AccHandler*, the *Customer* and the *Teller* agents.

Finally, there are two other available headings not used in the example. Under the **Capability** heading, we describe ECA rules. Besides the circumstances under which an action should or should not occur, the ALBERT language also introduces a more non-deterministic characterization where an action is said to be *permitted* under some circumstances (i.e. may or may not happen). This permits us to express easily a statement like "the AccHandler may decide to close the account of a customer when it is in the red". This non-determinism is very important to be captured at the requirements engineering level where we are concerned with modelling real-world aspects. Under the **State Behaviour** heading, it is permitted to express properties related to the historical sequence of information states. For example, a statement like "a customer's account cannot be in the red for more than 1 month" could be straightforwardly mapped in an equivalent formal ALBERT statement.

Cooperation constraints are classified under four headings describing how an agent perceives action performed by other agents (**Action Perception**), how it can see parts of the state of other agents (**State Perception**), how it lets other agents know of the actions that it does (**Action Information**) and how it shows parts of its state to other agents (**State Information**). Perception and information provide the analyst with a way to add a dynamic dimension to the importation and exportation relationships between agents expressed in the declaration part of the specification. The headings are illustrated on Figure 2, e.g., the **Action Perception** constraint of the *AccHandler* specification defines the conditions under which the *AccHandler* agent is influenced by *Transfer* actions of the *Teller* (in this case, if and only if the transfer will not cause an overdraft of more than $2000).

2.2 Understanding Organizational Relationships Using i^*

When redesigning systems to meet new requirements, we usually need to have a broad understanding of the organizational environment and goals, leading to decisions about what changes to make, and which components can remain.

The i^* framework provides understanding of the "why" by modelling organizational relationships that underlie system requirements. Agents are taken to have goals, and use knowhow and resources in their attempts to achieve goals. The framework includes two models. In the Strategic Dependency model, agents are modelled as depending on each other for goals to be achieved, tasks to be performed, and resources to be furnished. In the Strategic Rationale model, the reasoning that each agent has about its relationships with other agents are described. It supports reasoning about alternative ways for meeting goals, and for evaluating them. Agents are strategic in that they are concerned about opportunities and vulnerabilities.

The framework is intended to assist in gaining a deeper understanding about the organizational environment, help explore alternative patterns of relationships (among software, hardware and human components), to discover the implications of these alternatives for each agent, and to help make tradeoff among the alternatives.

The framework has been presented earlier in the context of information systems requirements engineering, business process re-engineering (Yu and Mylopoulos, 1994a), and software process modelling (Yu and Mylopoulos, 1994b).

2.2.1 The Strategic Dependency Model

Figure 3 show a Strategic Dependency model of the banking-by-teller example. The basic relationship is that a customer depends on the bank to have funds transferred from account a1 to a2. The customer also depends on the bank for the transfer operation to be secure, namely, that only he himself (the owner of the account) can initiate a transfer. The unit in the bank that does the transfer — the account handler — depends on the (human) teller to verify the identity of the customer. To accomplish this, the teller depends on the physical presence of the customer in the bank.

The SD model provides four types of dependency links.

- In a *goal dependency*, one agent depends on another to bring about a condition in the world — for example, that funds be transferred (from one account to another). The depender does not care in what way the dependee accomplishes the condition.
- In a *task dependency*, the depender tells the dependee what to do by specifying how. For example, if the account handler specifies the steps that the teller should go through in verifying customer identity, it would be a task dependency.
- In a *resource dependency*, the depender depends on the availability of an entity as a resource, e.g. (the physical presence of) the customer.
- A *softgoal dependency* is similar to a goal dependency except that the condition is not sharply defined *a priori*. What is "secure" is a matter of interpretation. While the bank may provide measures for security, it is the customer who decides whether they are secure enough for his purposes.

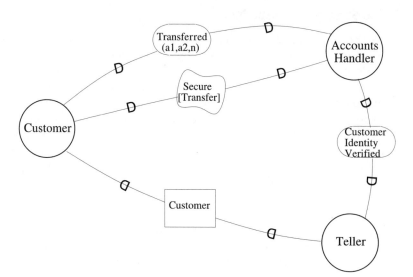

Figure 3.   A Strategic Dependency model of the banking-by-teller.

The SD model provides for different degrees of strength of dependency: *open, committed* and *critical* (Yu, 1995a). The model can also distinguish *agents* from the *roles* that they play and the *positions* that they occupy. In this chapter, we will limit our examples to the basic features.

The SD model can be analysed in terms of opportunities and vulnerabilities. The funds transfer facility offered by the bank enables a customer to, say, cover a cheque using funds from another account. However, in depending on the bank to carry out the transfer, if the bank fails to transfer the funds properly, the customer is vulnerable to the failure, potentially resulting in an overdraft on his account. Agents who are depended on often in turn depend on other agents. The customer's dependency for transfer of funds (and its security) further involves a dependency on the teller to identify the customer, which in turn depends on the physical presence of the customer (see Figure 3).

Modelling organizational processes in terms of intentional dependencies provides a level of description that acknowledges that organizational actors are often able to cope with open-ended situations (such as exceptions) without fully preplanned activity steps (Yu, 1995b). The *i** models are formally represented in the conceptual modelling language Telos (Mylopoulos *et al.*, 1990) and their semantics are characterized by adapting formulations of intentional concepts such as goal, belief, ability and commitment (e.g., Cohen and Levesque, 1990). The underlying conceptual modelling framework allows large amounts of knowledge to be managed along knowledge structuring dimensions such as classification, generalization, aggregation, and time in order to deal with large-scale real-life application domains.

2.2.2 The Strategic Rationale Model

Whereas the Strategic Dependency model gives an external view of how agents depend on each other, the Strategic Rationale model gives a more detailed description of the rationales behind the dependencies. One can answer "why" questions more precisely. There are two main types of relationships: means—ends relationships and task decompositions.

Figure 4 shows that the customer has as a goal that funds be transferred. The means for achieving this end is the task "Request Transfer At Bank". A means—ends relationship suggests that there can be other means for achieving the same end. We show this in the next section. The task of requesting transfer at bank can be further detailed by decomposing it into the subtasks of visiting the bank, and then requesting the transfer in person at the teller.

In transferring funds, the customer also has a number of quality goals (or softgoals) that are desired. He wants the transfer to be secure, quick and convenient, and the service to be friendly. Different ways of transferring funds (i.e., different organizational configurations) may be evaluated as contributing positively or negatively to these goals. In Figure 4, requesting

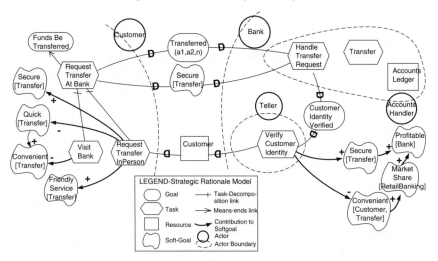

Figure 4. A Strategic Rationale model for banking-by-teller.

a transfer at the bank is considered to be good for security, and is good in terms of friendly service. However, having to visit the bank is bad from a convenience standpoint. It is also negative for quickness, for example, due to long queues at the teller. Softgoals may be correlated with each other. For example, quick service is considered to have a positive contribution to convenience. In general the soft goals form a graph, and their mutual influences can be evaluated by using a qualitative reasoning scheme (e.g., Chung, 1993).

These relationships provide a representation of the rationales because they explain why the dependencies are arranged in a given configuration. When there are alternatives, the softgoals also serve as evaluation criteria. These rationales can also help in coming up with new alternatives for achieving goals (i.e., addressing the strategic interests of the various stakeholders).

Note that the models (SD and SR) are usually incomplete; only items of strategic concern are included in the model (i.e., items that are considered to make a difference in choosing one configuration over another).

3 FROM ORGANIZATIONAL ALTERNATIVES TO SYSTEM REQUIREMENTS

In the above, we have shown how i^* provides an understanding of the organizational relationships in a business domain, while ALBERT is used to specify system requirements. By coupling the two frameworks, one can gain confidence in the ALBERT specifications by linking each fragment of the ALBERT specification to the fulfilment of some organizational goals in the i^* models. Given some organizational goals, the process of obtaining system (functional) requirements is usually far from straightforward. Typically, one would need to go back and forth between organization modelling and system requirements because issues discovered in one level will need to be looked at from the other level. This section shows how the *i** framework and the ALBERT language can be used in conjunction to assist in this process.

Figure 5 shows an initial attempt at considering banking-by-phone as an alternative to conventional teller-based banking. A goal of the bank is to be profitable (see right side of the figure). One way is to increase market share by attracting more business and customers. To do this, banking services should be convenient for the customer. One way to make transfer of funds more convenient is to allow customers to do it over the telephone. From the customer's viewpoint (left side of figure), banking-by-phone is seen to be quicker and more convenient, although it is less user-friendly. A PIN code is proposed (bottom portion of figure) as a means for meeting the goal that the customer be identified in phone banking. The Strategic Dependency model for the proposed banking-by-phone configuration is shown in Figure 6.

At the ALBERT level, Figure 7 shows the new system structure and Figure 8 shows the system requirements specification produced in response to the organizational goals identified above. In particular, at the "Customer" level and "Pbs" (Phone Banking System) agents level, one may notice several changes with respect to the original banking-by-teller system (see Figure 2). These changes pertain to the responsibilities of customers for communicating a PIN code information and of the "Pbs" for discovering the identity of the customer on the basis of the PIN code knowledge.

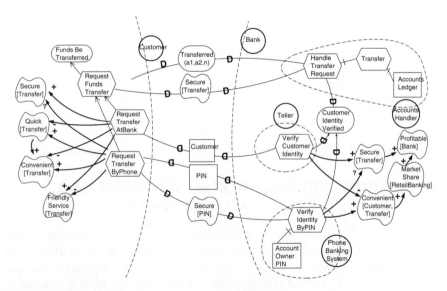

Figure 5. A Strategic Rationale model of banking-by-phone as an alternative to banking-by-teller.

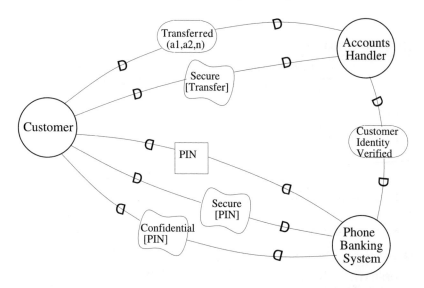

Figure 6.   A Strategic Dependency model of banking-by-phone.

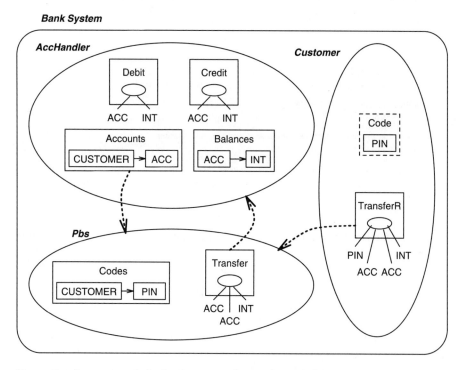

Figure 7.   Structure of the bank system (revised version).

AccHandler

LOCAL CONSTRAINTS
EFFECTS OF ACTIONS
   Credit(a,n): Balances[a] = Balances[a]+n
   ▌ The account a is credited with amount *n*
   Debit(a,n): Balances[a] = Balances[a]−n
   ▌ The account a is debited by amount *n*
CAUSALITY
   $Pbs.Transfer(a1,a2,n) \xrightarrow{\Diamond <1,d} Debit(a1,n); Credit(a2,n)$
   ▌ A transfer order should be followed within at most 1 day, by the corresponding credit and debit operations.

COOPERATION CONSTRAINTS
ACTION PERCEPTION
   XK (*Pbs.Transfer(a,_,n) / Balances[a]>n−$2000*)
   ▌ A transfer order from the Pbs is processed by the BankIS if and only if the resulting balance
   ▌ of the customer's account does not reach more than a $2000 overdraft.
STATE INFORMATION
   XK (*Accounts. Pbs /* TRUE)
   ▌ The Accounts table is always shown to the Pbs.

Customer

COOPERATION CONSTRAINTS
ACTION INFORMATION
   XK (*TransferR(_,_,_,_).Pbs /* TRUE)
   ▌ In any situation, the customer sends his/her transfer requests to the Pbs. He/she validates the transfer with his/her PIN code.

Pbs

LOCAL CONSTRAINTS
CAUSALITY
   $c.TransferR(\_,a1,a2,n) \xrightarrow{\Diamond} Transfer(a1,a2,n)$
   ▌ A valid transfer request from the Customer is echoed by a transfer order sent to the AccHandler.

COOPERATION CONSTRAINTS
STATE PERCEPTION
   XK (*BankIS.Accounts /* TRUE)
   ▌ The Pbs can always consult the Accounts table maintained by the AccHandler.
ACTION PERCEPTION
   XK (_.TransferR(p,a,_,n) / ∃ c, Code[c]=p ∧BankIS.Accounts[c]=a)
   ▌ A transfer request is valid if and only if the PIN code corresponds to the owner of the account to be debited.

ACTION INFORMATION
   XK (*Transfer(_,_,_).AccHandler /* TRUE)
   ▌ In any situation, the Pbs send his transfer orders to the AccHandler.

Figure 8. Constraints on the *AccHandler*, the *Customer* and the *Pbs* agents (revised version).

At this stage in the requirements process, the analyst still has to question himself about the adequacy of the PIN code at the level of security issues (see the question mark on Figure 5). In analysing the ALBERT specification, it turns out that the use of a PIN code by itself does not guarantee the identity of the customer. The action information constraint in the *Customer* specification says that the PIN code accompanying a transfer request is shown to the *Pbs*. The action perception constraint in the *Pbs* agent specification says that a transfer request is valid if and only if the given PIN code corresponds to that of the owner of the account. This set of constraints does not preclude someone other than the account owner from making a valid transfer using the correct PIN code. The security goal is therefore not met.

Returning to the i^* level, because we need to reduce the possibility, for a customer, of using the PIN of another customer, we have to express an additional goal related to the bank's dependency on the customer for the confidentiality of the PIN. This is a softgoal because it does not appear that there are definitive procedures that can guarantee complete confidentiality.

While at the i^* level, one can identify correlations with other goals arising from the need to keep the PIN confidential. For example, having to keep the PIN confidential contributes negatively to convenience since the customer may forget the PIN.

Additional requirements related to the properties of the PIN code may also be identified through this process. For example, if the number of possibilities for a PIN code is large, then it will be more difficult for a customer to use a wrong one. One idea would be to define the procedure in which PIN codes are assigned to customers so that no two customers will have the same PIN code. This would be reflected as a uniqueness constraint in the ALBERT specification.

Other solutions are also possible like those related to complexity (e.g., the number of digits) of the PIN code. Again, these different solutions all have impacts at the i^* level. For example, imposing a 25-digit PIN code has a positive impact on the confidentiality softgoal, but a negative impact on the convenience softgoal for the customer.

Throughout the requirements process, the analyst needs to iterate back and forth between system requirements and organizational requirements in order to deal with their impacts on each other.

4 DISCUSSION AND RELATED WORK

In the above phone-banking example, we have demonstrated that the concept of cooperating agents can offer a good understanding of organizational relationships and goals, and also for stating and analysing requirement specifications. We have illustrated why cooperation needs to be understood in terms of intentional concepts such as knowledge, commitment, obligation and goals (see Yu (1995a) for a discussion of the use of intentional concepts in i^*).

Our two-levelled approach allows us to adopt different concepts of agents at each level that are well-suited to the type of modelling and reasoning for that level. At the level of understanding organizational relationships, we need a notion of agent that recognizes that agents have freedom, and may violate constraints or commitments. One needs to reason about the implications of these violations. The models are used descriptively, to understand the organizational conditions as they are (or might be, in the case of proposed configurations). We need to take a strategic view of agent relationships because new work arrangements alter the configuration of dependencies. The introduction of new systems and/or work processes changes what is possible or not possible, or changes the degree of difficulty in achieving goals. Models at this level tend to be very incomplete, but this is appropriate since only issues that are of strategic significance need to be considered.

At the level of requirements specification, a prescriptive view is more appropriate than a descriptive view. Analysts want to be able to confirm that an organizational configuration has certain desired properties, *assuming* that agents abide by the stated restrictions on their behaviour (the obligations) in a declarative way. The specification level typically requires a much higher degree of completeness, in order to be able to guarantee certain properties. Finer-grained modelling concepts such as states, actions, obligations, information, perception and real-time constraints are appropriate.

Our approach may be compared to other frameworks for requirements engineering which take a multi-agent or organizational perspective. The framework for enterprise modelling of Bubenko (1993) is similar in spirit in several ways. It emphasizes the need to model organizations and their actors, their motivations and rationales (Nellborn and Holm, 1994). It also uses multiple, interlinked models. The informal (but structured) organizational models are linked to more formal specification models. Our approach using ALBERT and *i** is comparable, but adopts a set of intentional concepts explicitly, with more precise semantics. This will allow more computer-based support.

In the KAOS framework (Dardenne *et al.*, 1993), overall goals are explicitly modelled (following the concept of composite systems design (Feather, 1987, 1994; Fickas and Helm, 1992)). Goals are reduced through means—ends reasoning to arrive at responsibilities for agents. The modelling of agents is specificational and prescriptive. Since agents are assumed to conform to prescribed behaviour, one cannot easily analyse strategic relationships and implications.

A number of organization modelling frameworks have been proposed in the organization information systems area (e.g., Blyth *et al.*, 1993). Dependency concepts have also been used for modelling coordination in organizations (e.g., Malone and Crowston, 1994).

The *i** framework differs from these in that it highlights the strategic dimension of agent relationships, and de-emphasizes the operational aspects. Similarly, although multi-agent cooperation has received considerable attention in distributed artificial intelligence (DAI) (e.g., Bond and Gasser, 1988), the emphasis has been on the division of computational work (e.g., the reduction of goals to primitive actions for execution by robots or software programs), and much less on the strategic interests of organizational, social actors (Gasser, 1991). The DAI community has also developed communication and coordination mechanisms and protocols (such as KQML and KIF) which can serve as alternatives to more conventional implementation techniques for meeting the organizational requirements and specifications at the levels described in this chapter.

Finally at the specification level, the ALBERT language is very much in the line of recent formal specification languages designed for the purpose of modelling functional requirements (e.g., MAL (Finkelstein and Potts, 1987), ERAE (Dubois *et al.*, 1991), DAL (Ryan *et al.*, 1991), LCM (Feenstra and Wieringa, 1993) and TROLL (Saake *et al.*, 1993)). The major difference is the application scope of ALBERT related to the modelling of complex real-time cooperative (distributed) systems.

In this chapter, we have concentrated on showing how i^* and ALBERT can work together. Comparisons of i^* and ALBERT to their respective related work and more detailed discussions can be found in Yu (1995a,b, 1997), Yu and Mylopoulos (1994a), Dubois *et al.* (1993b,1994), Du Bois (1995) and Du Bois *et al.* (1997).

5 CONCLUSIONS

As information system development techniques and tools advance, we anticipate that the technical design and implementation stages will occupy a less central place in system development. On the other hand, new systems are becoming more interconnected, and increasingly interwoven into complex organizational processes. The challenge in information system development will shift towards the understanding of organizational environments and needs, and how to make decisions involving technical systems to address those needs and concerns (Jarke and Pohl, 1994).

To this end, we need a clearer understanding of what it means for systems to be "cooperative" (de Michelis *et al.*, this volume). Systems that are merely interconnected, but which may have been designed by different groups, at different times, to serve the purposes and interests of different parties, are not necessarily cooperative. In this chapter, we have argued that a characterization of cooperation requires the use of intentional concepts. Agents and how they relate to each other need to be characterized in terms of concepts such as knowledge, obligation, commitments and goals (Yu, 1995a). Information systems (and other kinds of agents) are cooperative to the extent that they contribute to some larger, overall goals in an organizational context.

To make this kind of understanding and analysis concrete and amenable to support by computer-based tools, we have brought together two agent-oriented modelling frameworks, both based on formal knowledge representation techniques. Each offers a set of capabilities for its respective level of modelling and reasoning. We have demonstrated that a requirements analyst needs to iterate over the two levels of modelling and analysis to arrive at system requirements.

This work is preliminary. We have outlined the approach and illustrated it through a realistic but small example. In ongoing work, we are studying larger real-life cases to test the practicality of the approach. We are elaborating on the steps needed to obtain system requirements from the analysis of strategic organizational relationships, and to identify the types of situations where analysis of the specification would suggest changes to the organization model. There is also ongoing work to link i^* to an agent programming language (Yu et al., 1996).

Another direction for future work is related to the development of knowledge-based tools for supporting the requirements engineering process. In these tools, the two languages — ALBERT and i^* — can be (weakly) coupled by using a common underlying conceptual modelling framework which relates representational objects by knowledge structuring relationships such as classification, generalization, aggregation and time (e.g., as provided by the Telos language (Mylopoulos et al., 1990). This approach may be seen as an extension of the approach adopted in the DAIDA project (Jarke et al., 1992), where three different sets of concepts were used for representing knowledge about the requirements, design, and implementation phases during system development, and which are linked and managed by a common global knowledge base management system.

Languages such as ALBERT and i^* offer new representational constructs appropriate to their respective levels of modelling, adding to the growing body of software engineering and requirements engineering techniques that emphasize the representation of knowledge (Greenspan et al., 1994; Mylopoulos et al., 1997).

ACKNOWLEDGEMENTS

We thank the anonymous referees for suggestions for improving the chapter. This work has been partially supported by the Permanent Joint Commission Canada / French Community of Belgium, the Natural Sciences and Engineering Research Council of Canada, and the Information Technology Research Centre of Ontario.

REFERENCES

Blyth, A.J.C., Chudge, J., Dobson, J.E. and Strens, M.R. (1993) ORDIT: a new methodology to assist in the process of eliciting and modelling organisational requirements. In *Proceedings of the Conference on Organizational Computing Systems — COOCS'93*, S. Kaplan (ed). Milpitas CA. ACM Press, pp. 216–227.

Bond, A.H. and Gasser, L. (1988) *Readings in Distributed Artificial Intelligence*. Morgan Kaufman Publishers.

Borgida, A., Greenspan, S. and Mylopoulos, J (1985) Knowledge representation as the basis for requirements specifications. *IEEE Computer*, pp. 82–91.

Bubenko, J.A. (1980) Information modeling in the context of system development. In *Information Processing 80*, S.H. Lavington, (ed). North-Holland, pp. 395–411.

Bubenko, J.A. (1983) On concepts and strategies for requirements and information analysis. In *Information modeling*, Chartwell-Bratt, pp. 125–169.

Bubenko, J.A. (1993) Extending the scope of information modeling. In *Proceedings of the 4th International Workshop on the Deductive Approach to Information Systems and Databases*, Lloret-Costa Brava (Spain), pp. 73–98.

Chung, L. (1993) Representing and using non-functional requirements: a process-oriented approach. PhD thesis, Computer Science Department, University of Toronto, Toronto, Canada.

Cohen, P.R. and Levesque, H.J. (1990) Intention is choice with commitment. *Artificial Intelligence*, **42**(3), 213–261.

Dardenne, A., van Lamsweerde, A. and Fickas, S. (1993) Goal-directed requirements acquisition. *Science of Computer Programming*, **20**, 3–50.

Dubois, E. (1989) A logic of action for supporting goal-oriented elaborations of requirements. In *Proceedings of the 5th International Workshop on Software Specification and Design — IWSSD'89*, Pittsburgh PA. IEEE, CS Press, pp. 160–168.

Dubois, E., Hagelstein, J. and Rifaut, A. (1988) Formal requirements engineering with ERAE. *Philips Journal of Research*, **43**(3/4), 393–414.

Dubois, E., Hagelstein, J. and Rifaut. A. (1991) A formal language for the requirements engineering of computer systems. In A. Thayse, (ed) *From Natural Language Processing to Logic for Expert Systems*, Chapter 6. Wiley.

Dubois, E., Du Bois, P. and Petit, M. (1993a) O-O requirements analysis: an agent perspective. In *Proceedings of the 7th European Conference on Object-Oriented Programming — ECOOP'93*, O. Nierstrasz, (ed), Kaiserslautern (Germany), LNCS 707, Springer-Verlag, pp. 458–481.

Dubois, E., Du Bois, P. and Zeippen, J.-M. (1993b) Object-oriented formal development of cooperative information systems. In *Proceedings of the ECOOP'93 Workshop on the Application of Object-Oriented Formal Methods*, Kaiserslautern (Germany).

Dubois, E., Du Bois, P. and Dubru, F. (1994) Animating formal requirements specifications of cooperative information systems. In *Proceedings of the Second International Conference on Cooperative Information Systems — CoopIS-94*, Toronto (Canada), University of Toronto Press, pp. 101–112.

Du Bois, P. (1995) The Albert II language: On the design and the use of a formal specification language for requirements analysis. PhD thesis, Computer Science Department, University of Namur, Namur (Belgium). Available at http://www.fun.cediti.be/~pdu/thesispr-uk.html.

Du Bois, P., Dubois, E. and Zeippen, J.-M. (1997) On the use of a formal requirements engineering language — the generalized railroad crossing problem. In *Proceedings of the IEEE International Symposium on Requirements Engineering — RE'97*, Annapolis MD. IEEE Computer Society Press, pp. 128–137.

Feather, M.S. (1987) Language support for the specification and development of composite systems. *ACM Transactions on Programming Languages and Systems*, **9**(2), 198–234.

Feather, M.S. (1994) Composite system design. In *Proceedings of the ICSE-16 Workshop on Research Issues in the Intersection Between Software Engineering and Artificial Intelligence*, Sorrento (Italy).

Feenstra, R.B. and Wieringa, R.J. (1993) LCM 3.0: A language for describing conceptual models — syntax definition. Technical Report IR-344, Faculteit der Wiskunde en Informatica, Vrije Universiteit Amsterdam, Amsterdam, The Netherlands.

Fickas, S. and Helm. R. (1992) Knowledge representation and reasoning in the design of composite systems. *IEEE Transactions on Software Engineering*, **SE-18**(6), 470–482.

Finkelstein, A. and Potts, C. (1987) Building formal specifications using "structured common sense". In *Proceedings of the 4th International Workshop on Software Specification and Design — IWSSD'87*, Monterey CA. IEEE, CS Press, pp. 108–113.

Gasser, L. (1991) Social conceptions of knowledge and action: DAI foundations and open systems semantics. *Artificial Intelligence*, **47**, 107–138.

Greenspan, S.J. (1984) Requirements modeling: a knowledge representation approach to software requirements definition. PhD thesis, Computer Science Department, University of Toronto, Toronto Canada. (Also appears as Technical Report CSRG 155.)

Greenspan, S.J., Borgida, A. and Mylopoulos, J. (1986) A requirements modeling language. *Information Systems*, **11**(1), 9–23.

Greenspan, S., Mylopoulos, J. and Borgida, A. (1994) On formal requirements modelling languages — RML revisited. In *Proceedings of the 16th International Conference on Software Engineering — ICSE'94*, Sorrento, Italy. IEEE & ACM, pp. 135–147.

Jarke, M. and Pohl, K. (1994) Requirements engineering in the year 2001: On (virtually) managing a changing reality. In *Proceedings of the Workshop on System Requirements: Analysis, Management, and Exploitation*, Schloss Dagstuhl, Saarland (Germany).

Jarke, M., Mylopoulos, J., Schmidt, J.W. and Vassiliou, Y. (1992) DAIDA: An environment for evolving information systems. *ACM Transactions on Information Systems*, **10**(1), 1–50.

Malone, T.W. and Crowston, K. (1994) The interdisciplinary study of coordination. *Computing Surveys*, **26** 87–119.

Mylopoulos, J., Borgida, A., Jarke, M. and Koubarakis, M. (1990) Telos: A language for representing knowledge about information systems. *ACM Transansactions on Information Systems*, **8**(4), 325–362.

Mylopoulos, J., Borgida, A. and Yu, E.S.K. (1997). Representing Software Engineering Knowledge. *Automated Software Engineering*, **4** (3), 291–317.

Nellborn, C. and Holm, P. (1994) Capturing information systems requirements through enterprise and speech act modeling. In *Proceedings of the 6th conference on advanced information systems engineering — CAiSE'94*, G. Wijers, S. Brinkkemper and T. Wasserman (eds), Utrecht (The Netherlands), LNCS 811, Springer-Verlag, pp. 172–185.

Ryan, M.D., Fiadeiro, J. and Maibaum, T. (1991) Sharing actions and attributes in modal action logic. In T. Ito and A. Meyer (eds) *Theoretical Aspects of Computer Software*. Springer-Verlag.

Saake, G., Jungclaus, R. and Hartmann, T. (1993) Application modelling in heterogenous environments using an object specification language. In *Proceedings of the International Conference on Intelligent and Cooperative Systems — ICICIS'93*. IEEE CS Press.

Yu, E.S.K. (1995a) Modelling strategic relationships for process reengineering. PhD thesis, Computer Science Department, University of Toronto, Toronto, Canada. (Also appears as Technical Report DKBS-TR-94-6, December 1994.)

Yu, E.S.K. (1995b) Models for supporting the redesign of organizational work. In *Proceedings of the Conference on Organizational Computing Systems*, Milpitas CA. ACM Press, pp. 225–236.

Yu, E.S.K. (1997) Towards modelling and reasoning support for early phase requirements engineering. In *Proceedings of the IEEE International Symposium on Requirements Engineering — RE'97*, Annapolis MD. IEEE Computer Society Press, pp. 226–235.

Yu, E.S.K. and Mylopoulos, J. (1994a) From E-R to A-R — modelling strategic actor relationships for business process reengineering. In *Proceedings of the 13th International Conference on the Entity-Relationship Approach — ER'94*, Manchester, UK. Springer-Verlag, pp. 548–565.

Yu, E.S.K. and Mylopoulos J. (1994b) Understanding "why" in software process modelling, analysis, and design. In *Proceedings of the 16th International Conference on Software Engineering — ICSE'94*, Sorrento (Italy). IEEE & ACM, pp. 159–168.

Yu, E.S.K., Mylopoulos, J. and Lespérance, Y. (1996) A.I. models for business process reengineering. *IEEE Expert*, **11** (4) pp. 16–23.

Part VI

Visionary Approaches

Cooperative Information Systems: a Manifesto

Giorgio De Michelis[a], **Eric Dubois**[b], **Matthias Jarke**[c], **Florian Matthes**[d], **John Mylopoulos**[e], **Michael P. Papazoglou**[f], **Klaus Pohl**[c], **Joachim Schmidt**[d], **Carson Woo**[g], **and Eric Yu**[e]

[a]Università degli Studi di Milano, Italy; [b]University of Namur, Belgium; [c]RWTH Aachen, Germany; [d]TU Hamburg-Hamburg, Germany; [e]University of Toronto, Ontario, Canada; [f]Tilburg University, The Netherlands; [g]University of British Columbia, Vancouver, British Columbia, Canada

Abstract

Information systems technology, computer-supported cooperative work practice, and organizational modelling and planning theories have evolved with only accidental contact to each other. *Cooperative information systems* is a relatively young research area which tries to systematically investigate the synergies between these research fields, driven by the observation that *change management* is the central issue facing all three areas today and that all three fields have indeed developed rather similar strategies to cope with change. In this chapter, we therefore propose a framework that views cooperative information systems as composed from three interrelated facets, viz. the system facet, the group collaboration facet, and the organizational facet. We present an overview of these facets, emphasizing strategies they have developed over the past few years to accommodate change. We also discuss the propagation of change across the facets, and sketch a basic software architecture intended to support the rapid construction and evolution of cooperative information systems on top of existing organizational and technical legacy.

I INTRODUCTION

Cooperative information systems is a relatively young research area whose birth in the early 1990s has been marked by the launching of an international journal, an on-going conference, an international foundation, dedicated special issues in international journals, and numerous meetings and workshops held over the past five years. Given all this activity, we believe that it is time to take a closer look at the area, its premises, primary research challenges and prospects. Also, to better delimit its boundaries, separating topics it covers from ones it does not, thereby offering an identity relative to other more established areas in computer science.

Taking past calls-for-papers for the CoopIS conference (e.g., CoopIS, 1994) as starting point in identifying cooperative information systems, we find them being described primarily as "next generation information systems":

> ... The paradigm for the next generation of information systems will involve large numbers of information systems distributed over large, complex computer/communication networks. This paradigm ranges from the vast and visionary Electronic Superhighway, to the large and complex billing system of a telephone company, and even to the small patient information system in a one-doctor office. Such information systems will manage or have access to large amounts of information and computing services. They will support individual or collaborative human work. Computation will be conducted concurrently over the network by software systems that range from conventional to advanced application systems including expert systems, and multiagent planning systems. Information and services will be available in many forms through legacy and new information repositories that support a host of information services. Communication among component systems will be done in a centralized or distributed fashion, using communication protocols that range from conventional ones to those based on distributed AI. We call such next generation information systems *cooperative information systems* ... (CoopIS, 1994).

Described in such terms, cooperative information systems pose a series of technological challenges which arise primarily because of technological advances (in telecommunications, hardware, software etc.). In contrast, the computer-supported cooperative work (CSCW) area focuses on the opportunities offered by such technological advances to broaden team collaboration across boundaries of place and time, and on the question how this will change human interactions (Roseman and Greenberg, 1996). Yet others argue that research should be driven primarily from a shift in (business) organizational structures away from traditional functional forms towards goal- and customer-oriented processes (Scott Morton, 1991; Keen, 1991; Hammer and Champy, 1993; Hamel and Prahalad, 1994). However, across all these perspectives, it seems that continuous *change* is the one constant theme in all of them. Information technology — used by collaborating groups or formal business organizations — is faced with the task of either learning to cope with change or risk early retirement.

Each of the mentioned areas has addressed only a limited facet of what is needed to understand and realize cooperative information systems. This chapter articulates a vision produced by researchers participating in a collaborative effort between European and Canadian universities, to create an integrated framework for research on cooperative information systems which addresses the mutual impact of continuous change in the system-oriented, group collaboration, and organizational facets of cooperative information systems.

Section 2 of the chapter links the notion of cooperation to that of organizational change. In Section 3, we offer a framework to view and understand cooperation and change in cooperative information systems from three different facets. Sections 4 to 6 describe research challenges arise from each of the facets and survey promising research directions and ongoing projects working towards meeting these challenges. Section 7 ties all three facets together and outlines the impact of change from one facet to the others. The section also discusses research challenges facing the management of change and some possible solutions for them. Given the materials we presented in Sections 3 to 7, we propose a generic architecture for cooperative information systems in Section 8. The final section summarizes our vision of cooperative information systems.

2 COOPERATION AND CHANGE

In distributed systems and cooperative computing, the word "cooperation" has a neutral meaning. *Cooperation* presupposes agents that have goals and can act upon them. Moreover, *cooperation among agents* entails that these agents have some common goals and act towards their fulfillment. More generally, an agent is *cooperative* if she/he/it tends to share goals with other agents in its environment and acts towards the fulfillment of these common goals.

What does "cooperation" have to do with information systems? Information systems can be thought of as collections of human or computerized agents which can carry out actions such as printing a report or requesting information. Moreover, the functional and non-functional requirements of an information system, intended to describe the "purpose" of the system, can be treated as its "goals".

When, then, is an information system cooperative? Consistent with our earlier definition, an information system is cooperative if it shares goals with other agents in its environment, such as other information systems, human agents and the organization itself, and contributes positively towards the fulfillment of these common goals. Cooperation with other information systems presupposes the ability to exchange information and to make a system's own functionality available to other systems. These features are often referred to as *interoperability* in the literature and should be treated as prerequisites to cooperation.

However, cooperation in organizational systems and business processes is more complex than sharing and interoperability. Management and organizational studies, as well as the studies carried on in the CSCW field, focus on cooperation as the basic means through which groups and organizations, while performing for their clients, continuously redesign themselves and their business processes, modify their boundaries, tune their objectives and open themselves to new possibilities (Argyris and Schon, 1978, 1996; Nonaka and Takeuchi, 1995). In this framework, cooperation is not a neutral characteristics of human and automated agents. Rather, it focuses on the basic interactions between the human members of a group and/or an organization. In this sense, cooperation offers a linguistic category for characterizing the process through which they perform together, and together change the organizational structure to which they belong.

The growing complexity of contemporary societies does not allow us to reduce this process to a matter of sharing information, rules and goals. This is because information, rules and goals are created and modified in the same process. Different methods have been proposed in the managerial literature to deal with this complexity (e.g., business process re-engineering, organizational learning, empowerment, knowledge workers and professionals, and network organizations). Despite their relevant differences, all of these methods agree on the necessity of enhancing performance effectiveness, learning capability and communication competence of individuals and groups.

Supporting cooperation, therefore, requires the system to be capable of reflecting both the changes that are decided for its performances and the continuously ongoing changes of the practices of its members. The problem then is not how to build information systems that share goals with their organizational environment, human users and other existing systems at *some time point*. Rather, the problem is how to build information systems that *continue* to share goals with their organizational environment, human users, and other existing systems as they all *evolve*. In short, it is *continuous* organizational and technological *change* that makes cooperative information systems a challenge.

3 A FRAMEWORK FOR RESEARCH IN COOPERATIVE INFORMATION SYSTEMS

This concept of ongoing cooperation and evolution leads to a new vision for information systems. In particular, the paradigm entails that the significance of a cooperative information system lies not in its tangible ingredients such as its hardware or software legacy systems. Rather, it lies in the system's ability to contribute to some goals in a larger social, organizational and technical context. An information system, under the new paradigm, is defined more by its connections and relationships with the outside world than by its internal technological make-up, or even its stand-alone functionalities and capabilities. The identity of an information system can persist over time even as its underlying hardware and software components are continually reconfigured or replaced to adapt to the needs of a changing external environment. A cooperative information system is not a collection of databases, applications and interfaces. Rather, it is an architectural framework which maintains consistency among a variety of computer-based systems, user groups and organizational objectives as they all evolve over time.

We, therefore, envision that research problems and issues in cooperative information systems arise from three areas of concern — systems, group collaboration and organization — and the interactions among them (Figure 1). We call these the three *facets* of cooperative information systems. There has been considerable research focusing on addressing issues in each of these facets. However, in order to provide viable cooperative information system solutions, all three facets must be taken into account and dealt with in a coherent way.

The *systems facet* includes various types of existing information, work-flow and other computer-based systems, developed in terms of conventional technologies such as programming languages, database management systems (DBMS) and workflow systems which are executing on conventional, distributed hardware and software. Typically, these systems were developed in a bottom-up fashion by individuals, groups or even the organization itself and were intended to serve local and often less-than-permanent needs. For cooperation to function within the systems facet, one needs to deal with issues of the heterogeneity of, and thus the incompatibility among systems. Much work has been done under the rubric of system integration, addressing interoperation concerns like data transfer, and semantic and control integration. This is to ensure that all systems within an organization (and sometimes across different organizations) can share data and use each others' functionality, independently of the platform on which they

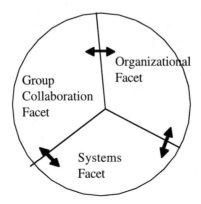

Figure 1.   The three facets of cooperative information systems.

were developed or the one on which they are executing, also independently of their original purpose or origin. The problem that this facet poses to the group collaboration facet is that once built, systems tend to become inflexible, and are not easily adapted to rapidly changing work situations. The systems facet also poses problems to the organizational facet in that traditional system development efforts are costly, involve long lead times, and are hard to manage.

The *group collaboration* facet is concerned with how people working on a common business process or other project — such as co-writing a report — can coordinate their activities, can deal with contingencies, and can change their practices through discussions and learning, as though they were working physically together. The nature and style of work may vary and are often not predictable beforehand. Much progress has been made to address problems in this facet in terms of groupware, organizational computing and other tools. The problem posed to the systems facet is that group collaboration requires a high degree of flexibility and malleability in the systems that support the work. The open-ended, fluid nature of group collaboration is also in constant tension with the more stable, formal and preplanned nature of organizational structuring.

The *organizational* facet is concerned with managing work from a formal organizational perspective, regardless of by whom (the group collaboration facet) or with what technology (the systems facet). It addresses global organizational concerns, including organizational objectives and business goals, policies, regulations and resulting workflow or project plans. This facet has been addressed using models of organizational processes and entities (as in traditional systems analysis), and more recently, models of business rules and policies, and goals and interdependencies among organizational agents. The organizational facet is where system requirements and specifications typically originate. However, subsequent refinements usually take into account group collaboration issues and the constraints and capabilities of the supporting technologies.

This framework is useful for identifying the origins and impacts of change, and thus provides a way to characterize research problems and issues in cooperative information systems. Change can originate in any of the three facets. From the systems facet, a change entails the introduction of new systems that need to be integrated into an existing cooperative information system architecture. Such changes need to be propagated within the systems facet (how can the given system interoperate with other systems within the cooperative information system architecture?); with the group collaboration facet (how can it contribute to human collaborative processes?); and with the organizational facet (how can the new system enhance the achievement of organizational objectives?). Likewise, changes may originate from the group collaboration facet (new business processes, changes in team membership) or from the organizational facet (new objectives, different prioritization of existing objectives). For each of these, the framework suggests a set of questions that need to be answered, such as "How should a change of type X be propagated from one facet to another?" Just as importantly, each facet has its own laws of inertia: for the systems facet, it is legacy systems and the lack of interoperability; for the people facet, it is people wanting to continue doing things the way they were before; for the organizational facet, it is unwillingness to risk change. To deal effectively with change, one has to establish the change vision in a given technical, social and organizational context (Jarke and Pohl, 1993), or, as Ehn (1988) put it, to achieve transcendence while recognizing tradition. We shall return to this question after looking at each individual facet.

4 THE SYSTEMS FACET

While other facets are concerned primarily with the "why", "what" and "who" questions behind cooperative work, the main activities of the systems facet is to specify *how* information is to be processed making best use of existing systems. As will become clear in the sequel, constant organizational change at other facets leads to a strong demand for system solutions where the answers to the "where" and "when" of information processing are delayed as long as possible (leading to *persistence* and *mobility* requirements).

The typical answer to the "how" question provided by traditional information systems and databases research has been to provide *generic systems* (DBMS, fourth-generation languages, repositories etc.) and *expressive data models* (relational, deductive, object-oriented etc.) to improve the productivity of the information system construction process (Atkinson *et al.*, 1990; Stonebraker *et al.*, 1990). Information system construction is often perceived as a software development process centred upon a growing, centralized corporate database to meet the requirements of a specific business task (such as billing, inventory control, or accounting).

The vision of cooperative information systems expands this traditional notion of an information system along two important dimensions. Firstly, it emphasizes the role such an information system takes within a broader context (intra- or cross-organization cooperation) by focusing on its system interfaces to other remote information systems in heterogeneous, distributed networks (*coordination* and *interoperation*). Secondly, it emphasizes the role such an information system plays in the entire life cycle of an organization by focusing on the need for continuous change to accommodate changing organizational demands but also drastic changes in the underlying system technologies (*change management* from a systems perspective).

As a consequence of this broader view, which is driven by recent technological advances such as ubiquitous computing and communication, the system solutions that emerge are based on the decentralized paradigm. Technologies for building repositories of network-linked objects, and mechanisms for partitioning applications and architectures, are emerging to provide network interfaces upon which to construct large-scale distributed applications out of pre-existing, heterogeneous and autonomous components. These consist typically of advanced application building blocks and widely accessible information services, available to applications developers and users. Such architectures exhibit an increased autonomy of change and lead to subsystems with multiple lateral interfaces supporting peer-to-peer cooperation which extend beyond simple (database-centric) client/server configurations.

This shift in system architectures does not imply that the classical database system requirements and modeling requirements can simply be abandoned. Consequently, *system support* for longevity of data, bulk data management and data consistency and integrity continue to be of high relevance for cooperative information systems. However, system cooperation now imposes a series of new requirements concerning the modelling and representation of higher-level functions which include partitioning, placement and migration of applications into distributed components of communications, computation and storage and the allocation of system resources to their execution. Moreover, better mechanisms are needed for the support of long-term business processes that rely on coordination of semi-autonomous legacy systems and applications, system evolution and change management. Some of these issues will be highlighted in the following. In particular, we concentrate on two highly interrelated system dimensions: high-level interoperation and coordination.

4.1 Improved Interoperation

In this section, we identify some of the main technical opportunities, relating to cooperative information systems, which can lead to improved system interoperation and graceful system evolution.

4.1.1 Abstraction from the Underlying System Platforms

This abstraction can be achieved by utilizing problem-oriented, high-level languages and models available uniformly on multiple platforms. Software in standardized, high-level languages (like SQL or ODBC) has the potential to absorb changes in the computing environment (hardware, operating system, system libraries) and to narrow the semantic gap between organizational models and implementation models. Recently, one can also perceive an increased interest in *run-time portability* which goes beyond standard compile-time application portability by enabling active applications (including their bindings to data objects and external resources like windows) to migrate between multiple computers (e.g., connected via the Internet). Interpreted high-level script languages like Tcl, Java, Obliq, Tycoon or Telescript are particularly well-suited to implement such migratory applications (Cardelli, 1994), mobile code (Java, 1995), migrating and persistent threads (Matthes and Schmidt, 1994) or network agents (Wayner, 1994; White, 1994).

4.1.2 Exploitation of Generic Servers

As they are identified, common services — such as persistent data storage, graphical interaction with human users, authentication, network communication, transaction monitoring and workflow management — are usually factored out from individual applications, to be realized using generic off-the-shelf tools such as relational databases, GUI toolkits, RPC services, transaction monitors or workflow engines. Such middleware components (Bernstein, 1993) not only simplify and speed up changes of existing applications but also lift the level of abstraction available for the interoperation between independently developed systems. For example, relational schemata, RPC service descriptions and high-level GUI event specifications often provide a valuable starting point for the interoperation between information systems.

However, when these generic server abstractions are developed over time, the architectural challenge arises: how to make the different abstractions fit together. For example, while VisualBasic nicely integrates programming language and user interface concerns, the interaction with databases via ODBC involves a major paradigm shift which makes information systems implementation in this setting difficult. Integrated database programming languages (Schmidt, 1977) or, more recently, object-oriented databases, solve some of these mismatches, but at the expense of openness and sharing with other kinds of systems. Recent advances in higher-order programming, exemplified in the research arena by Tycoon and in commercial database programming by novel APIs, as well as lightweight interface standards, such as HTML, seem to offer some promise in finally resolving these decade-old issues (Berners-Lee, 1996).

4.1.3 Compartmentalized Applications

Contrary to the architectural rationale of centralized information systems — for example, economies of scale, high level of system consistency, full data integration, division of labour between users and IT department — the rationale of cooperative information systems is to favour small, lightweight, *modular* components and applications that are linked directly to individual organizational needs, goals and structures. As a consequence of this approach, the cost and time required for the initial construction and the long-term maintenance of these applications and of the gateways between these applications can be attributed much more directly to specific business objectives and business processes with positive consequences for project management and business process re-engineering.

It is interesting to note that this *accountability* argument is partially in conflict with the vision of grand unifying system frameworks (*switchboard architectures*). For instance, distributed object systems such as DSOM of IBM (Lau, 1994), DOM of GTE (Manola *et al.*, 1992), CORBA of OMG (1991) and OSF DCE/DME (OSF, 1993) on one hand provide ideal component-ware frameworks, however, they also require a heavy investment to set up and to maintain a common, corporate-wide system infrastructure.

4.2 Liberated Coordination

A severe limitation of traditional information systems is their rigid control model. Essentially, users of an information system are limited to a fixed set of hard-wired transactions or transaction sequences and there is little, if any, support for human intervention or "intelligent" exception handling. To overcome these limitations, the following themes are particularly relevant for cooperative information systems.

4.2.1 Factoring Out Control from Individual Information Systems

Obviously, atomic transactions executed in isolation against a centralized database are not an appropriate mechanism for the coordination of long-term, cooperative human work. As a consequence, there has been significant database research to define and implement richer *synchronization* and *recovery* models (nested transactions, sagas etc.). There is also a growing interest from database researchers in *coordination* models developed in the area of CSCW (Alonso, 1996) and in organizational modelling (business process modeling). Similar to the idea of TP monitors that factor out details of multi-database transaction processing from individual information systems, workflow management systems and active database systems promise to factor out application control logic from individual applications into high-level workflow definitions or declarative rule specifications (Hsu, 1993; Georgakopoulos *et al.*, 1995).

This general theme of eliminating control from applications can also be found in recent developments on the desktop application market. For example, typical stand-alone Microsoft products (Word, Excel, Access) are currently being enriched with *scripting capabilities* with the long-term vision of having a common scripting language (VisualBasic) to coordinate and control integrated application systems that are composed of several of these products (Microsoft, 1994). In light of these developments, it should be mentioned that the shipping of scripts (code mobility) or autonomous agents (thread mobility) may lead to interesting new modes of cooperation and coordination in future distributed information systems (Mathiske *et al.*, 1995).

4.2.2 Integration of Human and System Communication

Advanced e-mail software and novel World-Wide Web (WWW) applications, as well as commercial applications based on groupware platforms like Lotus

Notes and Novell Groupwise demonstrate the *synergy* that can be obtained from the integration of desktop and *communication* tools (like e-mail readers, group calendar managers, telephone and fax systems, bulletin boards, video conferencing, hypertext browsers) with *database* functionality (information retrieval and boolean query functionality, replication, scripting support). More generally, cooperative information systems will have to learn from past research and development in CSCW to make best use of both human and system resources ("agents") to achieve a given business goal. Ideally, such integrated systems support a smooth *transition* between *ad hoc cooperative work* of humans (e.g., for problem solving and exception handling) and standardized, *automated interaction* between autonomous information systems (e.g., via EDI messages or workflow management software).

4.3 Maintenance of Links Between Implementation and Model

Database systems provide explicit information about the database schema itself via *metadata* — schema representations at several levels of abstraction, statistics, access rights, stored procedures, query plans etc. Such information is of particular interest for change management and interoperation tools that have to maintain links to other information system components and to higher-level data models (schema translators, re-engineering tools, gateway generators, IDL stub generators etc.).

Similarly, cooperative information systems have to maintain *explicit links* between individual information system components (applications, agents, transactions, schemata, workflows etc.) and related model components (business objects, business objectives, design decisions etc.) of the organizational facet (Jarke and Rose, 1988) (see Section 6). These links are not only crucial to propagate organizational changes rapidly to the supporting information systems but also to provide a feedback on the organization's performance in terms of the business objectives. For example, it becomes possible to monitor the time and (human) resources consumed by standard business processes that span multiple information systems or to track the probability of exceptions (for instance, because of human interventions) that occur during a certain process step.

Ultimately, cooperative information systems should be able to inspect and modify their own behaviour in the course of their long-term operation in an organization. Such *reflective* systems can be built by using either behavioural reflection or linguistic reflection. With *behavioural reflection*, a system can alter its own behaviour by manipulating its evaluator. One way to achieve this is for an interpreted language to allow access to the internal structures of the interpreter itself at run-time. This form of reflection can be found in variants of Lisp, Prolog or special-purpose research prototypes. In linguistic reflective systems, systems can change themselves directly, rather than the mechanisms of changing a system's run-time behaviour supported by behavioural reflection. A reflective system may, for example, alter the data structure that represents the system itself, alter the compiled code that is being executed or generate new data structures to be interpreted or new code to be executed. These options offer different tradeoffs between flexibility, execution efficiency and assurance of system consistency, which have been studied, for example, in the context of database programming languages (Stemple *et al.*, 1991).

4.4 Information Agents

To achieve cooperative information processing, we must overcome the barriers to building and deploying mission-critical information systems from reusable software components. This can be achieved by assembling information services on demand from a montage of networked legacy applications and information sources. However, it requires locating, reusing, combining, processing and organizing existing chunks of information and application software in such a way that does not impact detrimentally on an organization's operation. We have briefly outlined above some of the requirements, tools and technical opportunities regarding this issue. A promising approach to this problem is to provide access to a large number of information sources by organizing them into a collection of *information agents* (Papazoglou *et al.*, 1992; Knoblock *et al.*, 1994). The goal of each agent is to provide information and expertise on a specific topic by drawing on information from existing information sources and other such information agents. Information agent capabilities typically include interprocess communication mechanisms and services, such as naming, translation, information discovery, syntactic/semantic-reconciliation, partial integration, distributed query processing and transaction management and a variety of other services that can be shared between diverse incompatible information systems.

In the following we will briefly discuss the key components of such information agents.

4.4.1 Agent Organization

Each information agent is another information source; however, it draws on existing information repositories and applications based on organizational and business model components and provides an abstraction of these in the form of a *wrapper*. A wrapper is the appropriate interface code (including translation facilities) that allows an existing information source to be trans-formed into an information agent while allowing it to conform to the conventions of an organization. These wrapper characteristics are largely influenced by the requirements engineering phase of the organizational facet. The wrapper specifies services that can be invoked on data objects (originating from various sources) by completely hiding implementation details. Thus it provides the basis for building new network-based applications by mapping services into a collection of host information systems and applications. The advantage of this approach is that it promotes conceptual simplicity and language transparency. This technological advancement can be achieved, for example, by harnessing the emerging distributed object management technology and by appropriately compartmentalizing existing software and applications.

4.4.2 Brokering Agents

One of the most important functions of an information agent is to find the appropriate information sources and support services (i.e., wrapper-enabled services) in order to fulfil an organizational requirement or a user's needs. To achieve this purpose an agent must have a model of its own domain of expertise, the *agent domain model*, and a model of the other agents that can provide relevant information, the *agent awareness model*. These two models constitute the *knowledge model* of an agent and are used to determine how to process an information request.

Currently there is widespread interest in using *ontologies* as a basis for modelling an agent's domain model (Wiederhold, 1994; Milliner *et al.*, 1995; Kashyap and Sheth, this volume). An ontology can be defined as a linguistic representation of a conceptualization of some domain of knowledge. This ontology consists of abstract descriptions of classes of objects in the domain, relationships between these classes, terminology descriptions and other domain-specific information and establishes a common vocabulary for interacting with an information agent and its underlying information sources. The information sources in the network describe both their contents and their relationship in accordance with an ontology (Milliner *et al.*, 1995). Hence an ontology can be viewed as some form of a knowledge representation scheme.

The domain model does not need to contain a complete description of the other agents' capabilities, but rather only those portions which may directly relevant when handling a request that can not be serviced locally. Each agent is specialized to a single area of expertise and provides access to the available information sources in that domain. The objects and relationships in an ontology do not correspond to the objects described in a particular information source, but rather provide a semantic description of that domain for interaction. Each information source may relate to many information agents. This results in the formations of clusters (or groups) of information sources around domains of expertise handled by their respective information agents. This approach provides conceptual simplicity, enhances scalability and makes interactions in a large collection of information sources become tractable.

Both domain and awareness models may be expressed in some concept representation language such as Loom (McGregor, 1990), or KL-ONE (Brachman and Schmolze, 1985) and be formalized by using concept lattices (Wille, 1992) (a formal method based on a set-theoretical model for concepts and conceptual hierarchies). An example of the use of concept oriented languages for building ontologies can be found in Kashyap and Sheth (this volume).

4.4.3 Agent Communication Languages and Protocols

In order to perform their tasks effectively, information agents depend heavily on expressive communication with other agents, not only to perform requests, but also to propagate their information capabilities. Moreover, since an information agent is an autonomous entity, it must negotiate with other agents to gain access to other sources and capabilities. The process of negotiation can be stateful and may consist of a "conversation sequence", where multiple messages are exchanged according to some prescribed protocol.

To enable the expressive communication and negotiation required, a number of research efforts have concentrated on knowledge sharing techniques (Patil *et al.*, 1992). To organize communications between agents a language that contains brokering performatives can be particularly useful. For example, the Knowledge Query and Manipulation Language (KQML) (Finin *et al.*, 1995) can be used to to allow information agents to assert interests in information services, advertise their own services and explicitly delegate tasks or requests for assistance from other agents. KQML's brokering performatives provide the basic message types that can be combined to implement a variety of agent communication protocols. This type of language can be used for both communication and negotiation purposes and provides the basis for developing a variety of interagent communications protocols that enable information agents to collectively cooperate in sharing information.

4.4.4 Self-Representation Abilities

One of the most challenging problems to be addressed by cooperative information systems is the development of a methodology that opens up the general process of constructing and managing objects based on dispersed and pre-existing networked information sources. Activities such as object integration, message forking to multiple object subcomponents, scheduling, locking and transaction management are until now totally hidden and performed in an *ad hoc* manner depending on the application demands. What is needed is the ability to work with abstractions that express naturally and directly system aspects and then combine these into a final meaningful implementation.

Such ideas can benefit tremendously from techniques found in reflection and meta-object protocols. The concepts behind meta-object protocols may be usefully transferred to cooperating systems. Core cooperative tasks, carried out in an *ad hoc* manner up to now, can be performed using metalevel facilities. These can be used to separate implementation from domain representation concerns and to reveal the former in a modifiable and natural way (Edmond and Papazoglou, this volume). Therefore, information agents may provide a general coordination and policy framework for application construction and management, one that allows particular policies to be developed and applied in a controlled manner. This results in self-describing, dynamic and reconfigurable agents that facilitate the composition (specification and implementation) of large-scale distributed applications, by drawing upon (and possibly specializing) the functionality of already existing information sources.

4.4.5 Application Development

The goal of information agents is to create a collaborative client/server business object environment. The basis for application interoperability can be realized across applications by means of cooperating business and other data objects. Business objects provide a natural way for describing application-independent business concepts such as customers, orders, billing, invoices, payment and so on. Rather than relying on a monolithic application, cooperative information systems applications will consist of suites of cooperating business objects (Brodie, this volume). These should be able to communicate with each other at a semantic level and encapsulate the storage, metadata, concurrency and business rules associated with the specific business entity they describe. Such business rules and objectives are related to the manner that organizational objectives are modelled and are covered in the organizational facet. These objects can then be linked together via scripts written in a variety of scripting languages which are needed to describe and execute arbitrary tasks. This makes it possible to design new kinds of collaborative applications that can be controlled through scripts and semantic events. Semantic events provide a form of messaging that component objects can use to dynamically request services and information from each other.

Scripting is a critical element for allowing developers to automate the interaction of several business object applications to contribute to the accomplishment of a particular common task. This can be perceived as a form of automated workflow, a core aspect of the next generation of business applications. Scripting technology is essential for agents, workflows and cooperative (long-lived) transactions. Scripting languages provide added flexibility as they use late binding mechanisms and can, thus, attach scripts dynamically to component (business) objects. Accordingly, they provide the means for creating *ad hoc* (dynamic) collaborations between components, which is the very essence of cooperative systems.

5 THE GROUP COLLABORATION FACET

In order to effectively support group collaboration, we must take the following two main tasks into consideration. Firstly, analysis of work practice

(De Michelis, 1996a,b) shows that we must ensure that a group of people working together on a common business process or on another project can communicate with each other through the medium they want, coordinate their activities, get the timely information they need wherever it is, and deal with any contingencies that may occur, independent of time and space distances. Secondly, we must be able to locate the same group of people in the (organizational) context of the process to which they participate, so that the information characterizing it is transparent and/or visible to them whenever they need it, and their work space is shaped by it, disregarding any other information about any other process which is not relevant at that moment.

In order to explain the above more clearly, the group collaboration facet describes cooperative information systems within a spatial metaphor. In traditional cooperation, people are either together or not together in space and time. Cooperative information systems, on the other hand, shape much more flexibly the (virtual) space where people cooperate on a work process. Several spatial metaphors, including document replication (Lotus Notes), electronic circulation folders (Karbe and Ramsberger, 1991; Prinz and Kolvenbach 1996), team rooms (Roseman and Greenberg, 1996), or work spaces (Appelt, 1996) have been used in this context.

Since the environment where users do their work and cooperate with each other can be considered as the virtual space inhabited by the users, a cooperative information system can, in fact, be considered as an electronic extension of the physical space inhabited by the users. The physical space of a group is, in general, a distributed space. Inhabitants moving in it can either be in the same place or in different places. If they are in different places, they can communicate either synchronously or asynchronously.

Within the group collaboration context, users can be in the same or different virtual spaces. If they are in the same space, they are sharing the work space. If they are doing things outside the collaboration environment or in a different part of it, then they are in a non-sharing work space situation. However, organizational workers might go through different modes of cooperation when performing an organizational task. Cooperative information systems should, therefore, also support the movements between shared work spaces and distinct (i.e., not shared) work spaces, as well as between synchronous and asynchronous communication.

Research surveyed in this section originates in computer-supported cooperative work (CSCW), an interdisciplinary research area based on the idea that complex work processes are generally cooperative processes, where people distributed in time and space interact through electronic media. CSCW systems (called groupware and workgroup computing systems in existing products) are systems supporting cooperation between human beings.

5.1 The Main Features of the Group Collaboration Facet

The group collaboration facet of a cooperative information system is a means to extend the physical space in which a group of people cooperate, to transform it into a share work space. The most interesting and challenging situation for the use of a cooperative information system is the one where the group is not co-located in a physical place.

There are two types of share work spaces — synchronous and asynchronous. A synchronous work space provides the necessary mechanisms for agents at a distance to interact as if they were face-to-face. Thus, at any point in time, all agents sharing the work space can view and update the same work space concurrently. For example, a video conferencing system creates a synchronous work space for its users where they can see each other and they can point to the same object on the screen. An asynchronous work space, on the other hand, is a work space such that at any point in time, only one agent has access to the work space and only this agent can view and modify what it contains. For example, the channel through which a file folder flows from one person to another is an asynchronous work space.

It is important to consider how the two different share work spaces support their users, in different ways, the awareness of their working context.

5.1.1 Synchronous Sharing

The facilitation of synchronous sharing has raised a number of research challenges, of which we will only discuss two. Firstly, there are interesting cognitive and behavioural considerations when designing a system for a group of distributed users (Mantei *et al.*, 1991). It is impossible to provide an identical face-to-face environment for them because there are too many happenings in a meeting. For example, in the face-to-face meeting everyone may notice that while Joe hands a piece of paper to Chris, Ken's feet are shaking. From this happening everyone may infer that Ken is nervous. Which of these happenings are absolutely necessary for the purpose of the meeting? For example, is it necessary in a distributed environment to let everyone in the meeting know that Joe is sending a note to Chris? If showing body movements (including shaking) is important, then how are we going to support it?

Secondly, there are many technical and behavioural issues related to the development of user interface for real-time sharing (Greenberg and Marwood, 1994; Munson and Dewan, 1994). For example, how can two persons avoid modifying the same sentence of a document they are co-editing at the same time? Or, how are results to be merged, if users concurrently modified different parts of a document.

In both cases, it is evident that synchronous sharing offers a very effective means to support the mutual awareness of the actors of what they are doing, while different strategies for handling information sharing are embedded in the different solutions offered to address the first research challenge mentioned above.

5.1.2 Asynchronous Sharing

Asynchronous sharing means that people are in different locations and their interactions are not in real-time. This type of interaction has been with us for a long time. For example, a government officer writes a letter to a taxpayer, notifying her that she did not pay enough income tax. The taxpayer writes back with additional evidence on why she does not need to pay more taxes. The government officer then sends her an additional form to be filled. The taxpayer fills the form and sends it back. Since these two persons are using regular postal mail (i.e., an asynchronous communication medium), each subsequent letter sent by the taxpayer needs to identify the subject matter and the government officer needs to keep a file of the case in order for him to follow up with it.

It should be clear from the above example that knowing the correct context (e.g., missing income tax payment) in asynchronous interactions is very important. If we use computers to support this type of interaction, contextual information will form a major component of the share work space, and we need a representation for it. Similar to any other knowledge representation problem, such representation needs to be simple but still capture the essence of each context. A common approach in providing semantics for interactions is the language/action perspective (Winograd and Flores, 1986; Flores *et al.*, 1988), which is based on the speech act theory originally developed in linguistics. The fundamental idea behind this theory is that for each possible action, there exists a verb to describe it, and these verbs belong to a small number of speech act categories each of which defines a different pragmatical relation between the conversing persons — using the technical terms in linguistics, each of these speech act categories has a clear and distinct elocutionary point. Most computer-based systems using this approach require users to identify a speech act category for each message they are composing. Many authors demonstrate that it is impossible to be sure that different persons can agree the specification and interpretation of the speech acts they communicate. Suchman (1994), in particular, attributed these difficulties to the unnaturalness of constraining human interactions.

A different approach has been used in the conversation handler of the Milano system (De Michelis and Grasso, 1994). It allows users to bring forth activity templates on which they agree, without forcing them to reduce their utterances to well-defined speech acts. We believe that the language/action approach is promising but needs to accommodate additional contextual information to be usable. In the Milano system (Agostini *et al.*, 1995), for example, each message is linked both to the previous messages of the conversation to which it belongs and to the results of the activities negotiated within it. Moreover, it includes all the relevant documents to identify its context. An alternative solution proposed by Janson and Woo (1996) is to use a double loop learning to aid the specification and interpretation (e.g., if things are unclear, use a sequence of speech acts exchanged previously to specify or to interpret the correct meaning).

5.1.3 Managing the Switches

In an environment where organizational goals change frequently and the environments to which persons can interact are open-ended, it is possible that an originally isolated actor now needs to collaborate with some other persons — to share with them a work space. It is also possible that two persons communicating asynchronously now need to meet face-to-face (i.e., communicating synchronously). In other words, the mode of communication can change. Reder and Schwab (1990) show that these switches between communication media are very frequent.

Electronic work spaces can assist these switches if there is a common standard for creating and using them, or if they share with all the other work spaces the appropriate contextual information. These issues have been studied at a coarse grain of cooperation in information systems for cooperative design (e.g., Jarke *et al.*, 1992a) but the current challenge is to provide lightweight awareness solutions for continuous cooperation (Gutwin *et al.*, 1996; Palfreyman and Rodden, 1996).

The common standard is like a protocol that separates exchanging information from its processing. It can also be viewed as a translator between two incompatible software agents. For example, if agent X needs to share something with agent Y, then the following translation happens:

agent X's representation → work space representation
→ agent Y's representation

This will facilitate previously developed applications (e.g., legacy systems) or agents not conforming to the standard (e.g., e-mail systems) to be able to share. What will be a sufficient standard for the work space is still a research question. In OASIS (Martens and Woo, 1997), for example, the work space consists of a set of forms where a form can either provide information or state an unaccomplished goal.

When the persons involved in a cooperative process continuously switch from one type of share work space to another, it is necessary that, in all of these work spaces, they can access the information characterizing the past history of the cooperative process. This is the contextual information mentioned above. In Milano (Agostini *et al.*, 1996), for example, this information is recorded in a partial order list linking together the e-mail conversation, their associated documents, and the activities performed within a common work process. Similar solutions have also been developed for traceability of cooperative software processes involving multiple hetero-geneous tools (Pohl, 1996).

In the following, we list four different types of switchings and their corresponding problems to be solved or support needed by the computer:

- from distinct work space to share work space (both synchronous and asynchronous): need to determine what information to make available within the work space for sharing and then translate, if necessary, from the individual representations to the work space representation;
- from share work space (both synchronous and asynchronous) to distinct work space: need to determine who gets what information;
- from asynchronous sharing to synchronous sharing: the task-at-hand here is very similar to that of setting up a meeting;
- from synchronous sharing to asynchronous sharing: the task here is akin to the continuation of work after a meeting.

It is important to note that the switching effort between different types of work spaces, from the user's point of view, should be as effective as the continuous modification of the same work space.

5.2 Linkages Between Group Collaboration and Organizational Model

Suchman (1987) points out that people tend to act in a situated manner and employ organizations and plans just as tools which they may or may not use. Thus, there is a continuous interplay between the work practice of the group collaboration facet and the organizational facet. The contin-uously changing work space where a group cooperates, is populated by the objects supporting the various communication media as well as the objects making accessible the context of the ongoing collaboration. Both types of objects are instances of corresponding objects in the organizational model, where they are stored with their specific access rights. Cooperation is performed, therefore, by instantiating some objects from the organiza-tional model. Conversely, to address problems, group collaborators may modify the objects in the organizational model, either at the level of the data stored in them, or at the level of the objects themselves, whenever an activity results in a modification of a role definition, of a procedure definition etc. (Figure 2).

Using the spatial metaphor, cooperative information systems emerge as complex systems where legacy systems are artefacts in the virtual work space of their users, while the cooperation support templates are objects stored in the distributed architecture. While the user work space is charac-terized by the history of cooperation within which users are active at any given moment, the legacy systems are characterized by the information they have accumulated and the communication protocols they support. Cooper-ative information systems have the potential — and the ambition — to build

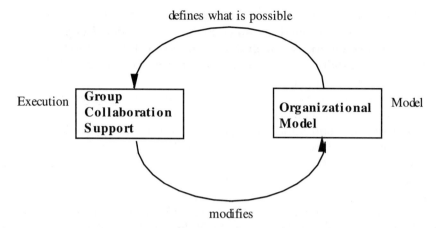

Figure 2. Linkages between group collaboration support and organizational model.

systems which neither reduce human work spaces to information systems nor information systems to human work spaces.

The group collaboration facet is subject to radical changes with the emergence and the diffusion of the Internet as the basis for the creation of computer support for cooperative work. The first experiences of intranet applications as well as the first research projects in this field (such as the European CoopWWW project offering a basic cooperation support infrastructure on the Web) (Appelt, 1996) offer some hints on the type of evolution we may foresee.

6 THE ORGANIZATIONAL FACET

While the group collaboration facet can be best understood from a spatial point of view, the organizational facet can be understood from a linguistic perspective — its objects characterize the lexicon (or ontology) through which the members of an organization conceive and speak of their work (goals, roles, structures, tools, resources, procedures, ...).

The notion of cooperation in the delivery of information services within an organization cannot be fully addressed unless the goals and desires of organizational agents *and those of the organization itself* are taken into account. Agents cooperate when they share goals and work together to fulfil those goals. Computer systems are cooperative to the extent that they contribute to the goals of human and organizational agents.

In traditional systems development, the identification of organizational objectives and the determination of system features and characteristics to meet those goals is usually carried out under the title of "requirements analysis". It is well recognized that defining what software system is to be built before designing and implementing it, is critical to the success of the software system. Another area that has addressed the problem of capturing and accommodating organizational objectives and goals is that of enterprise integration, where research has focused on the integration of production and administrative processes, often in the context of a manufacturing organization.

As we move towards a vision of cooperative information systems, the task of requirements engineering remains crucial, although a number of important adjustments and extensions will be needed. Firstly, both forward and reverse engineering will be required. In traditional software systems development, as well as in enterprise integration, an entire system/enterprise is typically designed from scratch. Under the cooperative information systems paradigm, cooperative information system development does not necessarily proceed uniformly from requirements to design to implementation. There will already be implemented system components that are integrated to some degree (within the systems facet) for some purpose (organizational facet). It is, therefore, important to support both forward and reverse requirements engineering, i.e., from an existing situation to the set of objectives that account for it, and from a new set of objectives to a new cooperative information system.

Secondly, requirements models for a cooperative information system under the new paradigm will potentially cover a much broader scope, since a cooperative information system typically brings together many systems (which may be existing or to be developed). Explicit models that describe what a system is supposed to do and the organizational rationales behind them become even more important since they are important knowledge assets in their own right for the organization, regardless of how they are implemented technologically. As the system evolves (whether to take advantage of technological advances, or to address changing organizational needs), this facet provides, on an ongoing basis, the linkages needed to ensure that the technical systems are meeting organizational goals.

Thirdly, requirements models will have an active role to play throughout the life of a system. Under the traditional paradigm of information system development, requirements definition is usually seen as a phase or step through which one has to go through in order to arrive at the final product — the operational system. Requirements typically appear in a static, printed form, often serving as a contractual document among different stakeholders (users, customers, developers etc.). Once a system is operational, the requirements do not have an active role to play. Under the emerging paradigm, due to ongoing evolution, organizational objectives and systems requirements must be "kept alive" and remain a part of the running system (e.g., in the form of a knowledge base or repository). Otherwise, one cannot ensure that the system(s) are cooperative on an continuing basis. System specifications and requirements are also needed to provide context for interpreting system behaviour.

Within this section we briefly review three areas which can potentially contribute to the organizational facet: enterprise integration, early requirements and systems requirements.

6.1 Enterprise Integration

Enterprise integration is a research area in its own right, focusing on methods, tools and concepts for introducing technology within an organization to improve the dissemination of information, the coordination of decisions and the management of actions; for a recent and thorough account of the field, see Vernadat (1996). Generally speaking, enterprise integration is accomplished through a conceptual model of an enterprise that accounts, at varying levels of detail and from a variety of perspectives, the inner working of the enterprise. In addition, different modelling frameworks come with a variety of tools for creating, editting, and analysing an enterprise model.

Enterprise modelling is generally tackled by offering notations for modelling a variety of organizational information, including organizational structure, business processes and activities, people, resources, tools and expertise, (existing) information system structure and functionality, information sources, their format and their contents. An *enterprise reference model* provides a data dictionary (ontology) of concepts that are common across different organizations, such as products, materials, personnel, orders, departments and the like.

Many reference models have been proposed in the literature and there is ongoing work to create industry-wide standards in Europe, North America and the Far East (Bernus and Nemes, 1996). Some of the reference models mentioned most frequently are:

- **CAM-I** — US-based non-profit group of industrial organizations, striving to establish manufacturing software and modelling standards (Berliner and Brimson, 1988);
- **CIM-OSA** — reference model developed within the AMICE ESPRIT project, used widely in Europe (Vernadat, 1984; ESPRIT, 1989);
- **ARIS** — developed by August-Wilhelm Scheer at the University of Saarland, can be seen as the conceptual counterpart to the highly successful SAP standard software architecture (Scheer, 1994);
- **PERA — The Purdue Reference Model** — developed at the University of Purdue by Theodore Williams, focuses on manufacturing (Williams, 1992).

The CIM-OSA (Computer-Integrated Manufacturing — Open System Architecture) reference model and methodology provides a three-level architecture to describe a manufacturing enterprise in terms of requirements, design and implementation. In addition, CIM-OSA offers a reference architecture, from which particular architectures may be derived for a specific manufacturing process. This architecture was designed so as to support and encourage modularity, abstraction and open-endedness. Currently, these efforts are being followed up by the GERAM attempt to unify the various existing enterprise models, whereas many details are being worked out in numerous domain-specific modelling efforts (e.g., STEP in the production industry, PI-STEP in the process industries, and many others). In some ways, these architectures are similar to the one proposed here, but seem to have a top-down, monolithic flavour which is contrary to the spirit of this manifesto's view of cooperative information systems.

6.2 Modelling Organizational Objectives

In order to relate system functions and behaviours to organizational objectives (and thus to understand the "whys" behind system requirements), a cooperative information system must have suitable representations or models of organizations, and mechanisms for supporting reasoning about them (Bubenko, 1980; Wieringa, 1996).

6.2.1 Representing and Using Knowledge about Organizational Objectives

Traditionally, organizational objectives are treated only during the earliest stages of system development (e.g., during "systems planning"). Although these objectives are used to determine system requirements, there are seldom systematic links from the requirements (or other system models) back to organizational or business objectives. Under the cooperative information systems paradigm, these links (both forward and reverse) will be crucial for ensuring that technical systems continue to meet organizational objectives as they all evolve.

One important obstacle to bringing business objectives into an overall information system architecture is the lack of formal representations for this kind of knowledge. The difficulty in drawing conclusions from such informal bodies of recorded knowledge substantially weakens the cost-benefits of maintaining the knowledge. To understand cooperative systems environments, we need to manage and draw conclusions from large amounts of knowledge covering the business rationales that cut across many systems and business domains.

Recent research in requirements engineering has developed techniques that can potentially contribute to addressing these issues. The explicit representation of goals and their use in deriving requirements (e.g., Feather, 1987; Dardenne *et al.*, 1993; Chung, 1993) is an important technique that can be applied at the level of business objectives. Business reasoning, however, frequently requires more flexible forms of reasoning beyond those supported by traditional techniques (e.g., classical problem-solving techniques in AI). Variations of goal-based reasoning (e.g., Lee,

1992), with additional support such as qualitative reasoning and the concept of satisficing have been developed (e.g., Mylopoulos *et al.*, 1992; Chung, 1993).

6.2.2 Dealing with the Organizational Dimension of Cooperative Information Systems

Adopting a cooperative information systems perspective places special demands on the knowledge representation framework for modelling business objectives and rationales for information systems. Cooperative systems are not merely distributed systems — they are also organizational. They consist of "agents" who relate to each other as a social organization. They share responsibilities, have commitments to each other and may have common or different values and beliefs. While they may cooperate at one level, they can also have competing or conflicting interests at another.

Research on organizational issues of computing (e.g., Kling and Scacchi, 1982; Gasser 1991) has contributed significantly to the understanding of the embedding of computer information systems in organizations. Frameworks that emphasize organization modelling have started to emerge. For example, the Action Workflow model of Medina-Mora *et al.* (1992) highlights relationships among customers and performers. The framework of Bubenko (1993) uses a multi-model approach to link enterprise objectives to system requirements. The i^* framework (Yu, 1995) introduces the concept of intentional dependency for modelling strategic relationships among organizational actors (the Strategic Dependency model). Means–ends reasoning is used to help capture rationales and support reasoning about business objectives and alternative solutions (the Strategic Rationale model).

6.3 Modelling Systems Requirements

Systems requirements describe the observable external behaviour of a system (the "what") rather than internal details about its implementation (the "how"). In the context of cooperative systems where there are multiple heterogeneous agents (software/hardware, humans, devices etc.), it should make clear the responsibilities associated with each individual agent in relation to the "whats" (i.e., what each of them will guarantee).

6.3.1 Representing Systems Requirements for Cooperative Information Systems

At the systems requirements level, we need to determine the system features that will make the achievement of the organizational goals possible. Typically, at that level, these system features will be characterized in terms of the "environment" of the system (i.e., the portion of the real world whose current behaviour is unsatisfactory in some way). Systems requirements will be expressed by describing how the system is connected to the environment in such a way that the behaviour of the environment will be satisfactory. For example, requirements inherent to a library system will be expressed in terms of data and information (e.g., borrowed books, books on shelves, and reservations) manipulated by different actors (e.g., the librarian and the users) belonging to the environment.

Systems requirements should not be confused with the specification of the system itself. The specification of the system belongs to the system facet (i.e., it describes the system by adopting an internal perspective). At this level, a conceptual representation of the system is usually produced in terms of various object classes: active controllers, domain entities (mirroring the problem domain objects) and interface objects. This conceptual representation can be expressed by using semi-formal methods (e.g., OMT, Coad-Yourdon, Fusion, Objectory) or by using more formal methods (e.g., RML (Greenspan *et al.*, 1986), GIST (Feather, 1987), Oblog (Sernadas *et al.*, 1991) and LCM (Wieringa, 1994)).

Requirements languages that can be used at the systems requirements level, on the other hand, should offer the following two facilities:

- The language should offer mechanisms (action/state perception, action/state information) to distinguish the boundary between the system and its environment, as well as the responsibilities associated with each of them. This possibility of making clear the distinction is advocated by several authors. For example, Jackson and Zave (1995) recommend to make a distinction between "indicative requirements" (statements about the environment) and "optative" requirements (statements about the system). An adequate language should, therefore, provide: (i) an ontology including an appropriate concept of *agent*; (ii) mechanisms for expressing different actions and responsibilities associated with their control; (iii) communication mechanisms for describing time-varying information and perception.
- The language should support a *declarative* style of specification which supports a natural mapping (i.e., without having to introduce any over-specification) of stakeholders' informal statements in terms of their formal counterpart. This is due to the possibility offered by the language to model requirements adopting a *God's eye view perspective*, i.e., to express requirements by considering the whole admissible life (the sequence of states of the system) rather than adopting the usual constructive (operational) style where the value of a state at a given moment is computed from the subsequence of past states. For example, we want to express easily a statement like "the borrowing of a book should be followed by its return within the three next weeks". This *naturalness* property is essential

for the purpose of traceability, i.e., to keep a close relationship between the informal requirements and their formal reformulation.

In terms of semi-formal notations, we can say that many existing OORA (object-oriented requirements analysis) methods are trying to incorporate these aspects in their suggested methodology. Describing the role of the system from the external users' perspectives is typically the goal of the *use case* originally introduced in Objectory (Jacobson *et al.*, 1992) and also incorporated in the new Unified Modelling Language (UML). A similar attempt exists in the ROOM (Selic *et al.*, 1994) where *scenarios* are used for capturing the environment behaviour in presence of the system.

In terms of formal notations, recent proposals are the agent-oriented extension of GIST (Feather, 1987) and the ALBERT language (Du Bois *et al.*, 1997). Besides the existence of precise rules of interpretation, it is expected that the mathematical/logical foundations underlying these languages will permit the development of a new generation of tools supporting:

- the verification of requirements produced by the analyst such as the detection of inconsistencies (e.g., leading to deadlocks) and incomplete-nesses (e.g., failure to preclude undesirable system behaviours), as well as the possibility of proving global desired goals at the system requirements level;
- the validation of the requirements against customer expectations by, for example, reformulating the formal requirements for easier interpretation (through natural language generation, or translation to some existing, less formal, notations), or by producing animations (or simulations) to allow customers to explore different possible behaviours of the system, and to check against use cases and scenarios.

6.3.2 An Expanded Systems Requirements Process

The cooperative information systems paradigm implies the need to expand the systems requirements process, since systems requirements must now be linked extensively to organizational objectives on one side (e.g., Yu *et al.*, 1995), and to system designs and implementations on the other (e.g., Chung *et al.*, 1995). Requirements activities may proceed in forward and reverse engineering directions, and may have different scopes at different facets (business unit boundaries need not coincide with system boundaries, and *vice versa*). These activities may include:

- identifying the "why", i.e., business objectives and rationales for the new information system (e.g., the improvement of the management of the borrowings in the library in order to make it more attractive);
- identifying the agents in the environment (e.g., the librarian and the users), together with some assumptions and domain knowledge related

to their behaviour (Jackson and Zave, 1995) (e.g., users are issuing books requests to the librarian and, when available, the librarian removes these books from the shelves);

- mapping business goals to system goals, i.e., goals related to the desired global behaviour of the system (Dubois, 1989; Dardenne *et al.*, 1993) (e.g., to prevent the user from keeping more than three books at once);
- "operationalizing" these system goals by reducing them into constraints that agents can be responsible for through their actions (Feather, 1987; van Lamsweerde *et al.*, 1995) (e.g., the system will raise an alarm when the maximum number of loans allowed is exceeded and the librarian will not give the requested book to the user);
- deciding if the identified agents and their associated responsibilities will correspond to:
  - well-described tasks (or procedures). This will be usually the case for the software part of the system. The description of these tasks is the objective of the system specification activity (which is part of the *systems facet*).
  - loosely defined tasks. The objective here is to provide high-level guidance and leave the decision of execution details at run-time. This is often the case when human agents are involved in the task performance (which is part of the *group collaboration facet*).

7 CHANGE MANAGEMENT

A distinguishing feature of a cooperative information system is that it must ensure *continued* cooperation between the system, the group collaboration and the organization facets. This implies that we must identify where changes come from in each facet, how they propagate and what problems are involved in this.

Based on this analysis, facilities for change management can be discussed which are used to ensure that changes introduced at any facet of a cooperative information system are propagated to all other facets. The importance of change management has been recognized by architectures such as DAIDA (Jarke *et al.* 1992b), CIM-OSA (ESPRIT, 1989) or ARIS (Scheer, 1994) through the interlinking of requirements, design and implementation levels. It is perhaps characteristic of the difficulties of cooperative information systems evolution that commercial environments have not really defined the links in depth, even though some research prototypes, such as the DAIDA and ITHACA (Constantopoulos *et al.*, 1995) environments, have experimented with a richer set of dependency types.

When developing a framework for change management, we follow the famous paper by Ackoff (1967) to distinguish between *active* change management (planned change), *reactive* change management (unplanned change) and *proactive* change management (making a system fit for easy reactive change).

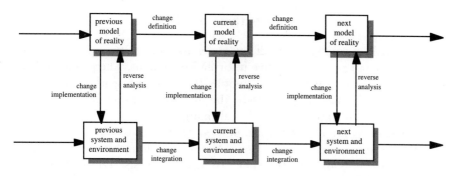

Figure 3.   The change process for cooperative information systems.

A basic framework for continuous change management is shown in Figure 3. The approach shown therein for *active* change management (planned changes) is borrowed from the so-called Carroll cycle, a method which has proven useful in the design of user interfaces (Carroll *et al.*, 1991). In each such cycle, the current reality is reverse-engineered into models to uncover its underlying rationale. Then, a change is defined on the models, and implemented into a new reality, integrating the legacy of the existing context.

Besides these planned changes, there can also be unplanned changes where reality is changed directly, without resorting to any model. Change management then becomes *reactive*, to reverse-analyse such changes into models, thus analysing their consequences and identifying possible follow-up changes. But purely reactive change management will not work. Ackoff (1967) has pointed out that information systems should be designed to cope with such unplanned changes, i.e., measures should be taken to make them *proactive*, not just reactive. This has, in fact, been the goal in each facet discussed in Sections 4–6, but additional measures for proactiveness must be taken at the level of change management across facets.

In Section 7.1, we discuss active, reactive and proactive changes in more detail. The continuous tension between the envisioned change and the perseverance and autonomous activity of existing context has been identified as the main driver for requirements engineering, which was therefore defined as "the process of establishing a change vision in the technical, cognitive, and social context" (Jarke and Pohl, 1993). Reverse engineering as well as re-implementation are significantly facilitated if they can reuse experiences gained in previous cycles. This is why repository technology as a means of not only linking heterogeneous environments, but also as a computerized organizational memory, is playing a central role in change management (Section 7.2). However, a cooperative information system will also need active components to manage the mediation between group collaboration, system change and organizational change. Section 7.3 offers a sketch of such a "coach" for change.

7.1 Perspectives on Change

Let us briefly retrace each facet, in order to identify typical sources and patterns of change in cooperative information systems. The group collaboration facet focuses on *practice* — people, their culture, work practices and interactions. This facet appears to be the most frequent initiator of change. Sources of change may include cultural changes (e.g., a local software development team is augmented by some people in India), different levels of knowledge (e.g., a system like Lotus Notes is no longer used in a closed organization, it is on the Internet), or user interests. Within this facet, change is enabled by the spatial metaphor and the CSCW attempts to make collaboration spaces more flexible.

The organizational facet focuses on *language* — models of organizational structure, goals and policies, processes and workflows, even of information technology. Typically, changes in this facet are initiated by managers (from the group collaboration facet, but with defined organizational roles) or external consultants (with less relationships to the group collaboration facet). They involve policy changes, changes in environmental conditions (e.g., laws), implementation of meta-strategies such as business process re-engineering or total quality management, or the execution of organizational mergers. In this facet, the understanding of change is facilitated by extending the suite of formalisms available to support the full path from organizational goals and dependencies to implementation models.

The systems facet focuses on *technology* — components and coordination tools, mobility, persistence and computational resources. Reasons for change from this facet include technical innovation (e.g., e-mail and WWW) or degradation (our old mainframe finally seems to die!), but they may also include various kinds of maintenance all the way to re-integration and re-architecturing of the whole system. Componentization, liberated coordination, and reflection are identified as main facilitators of change in this facet.

We now turn to change propagation patterns across the facets. It is obvious that changes in one facet might affect all other facets. In this light, it may be surprising that most existing research has focused on only two facets, as indicated in Figure 4.

- Formal organization ↔ system integration ensuring correct implementation of business model changes: this is the classical approach in organizational information systems. A typical example for this kind of change management is the SAP approach which maps organizational reference models to technical reference models, albeit only in the limited sense of parameter variation. The need for supporting this type of change was also recognized by database vendors (Oracle CASE). This kind of change support typically neglects the humans in the organization, i.e., does not (or to an insufficient degree) consider the group collaboration facets.

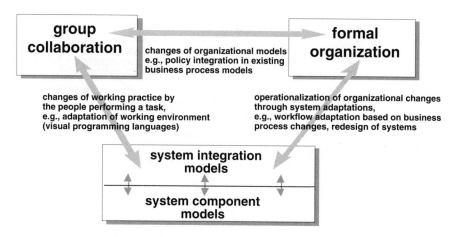

Figure 4.   Three isolated change perspectives.

- Group collaboration ↔ system integration: this is the interface between CSCW and computer science research. Typical examples are OLE, Tcl, visual programming languages; these approaches try to empower the users to adapt their computerized environment according to their individual needs without taking the organization models into account. Thus, changes can be made that are in conflict with, for example, workflow models.

- Group collaboration ↔ organization facet: this has been studied for many years by researchers in organizational behaviour. The fact that all the relevant people in an organization must be considered when changing the organization models is recently more and more recognized, e.g., the involvement of all kinds of stakeholders during the requirements engineering task has gained more attention and is seen as very important. Traceability is seen as an important prerequisite to enable such change support.

To identify more comprehensive change scenarios, we focus on the two extreme cases of active and reactive change management. Both start from the group collaboration facet, but one from people with manager roles, the other from "normal" group members.

7.1.1 Active Change Management

Active changes can have three main goals:

- better system supporting the same "workflow or business process";
- adaptation of system according to particular people performing the process;
- change of current working practice.

Figure 5 depicts a typical active change cycle. Usually, managers supported by consultants initiate the change in the organization models, often by

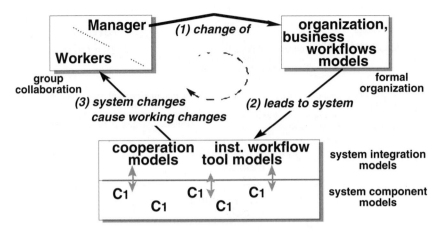

Figure 5.   Active change.

changing some kind of business goal or policy. This change results in the adaptation of existing or the definition of new business process models as sketched in Section 6. Subsequently, the changes in the business process models are propagated to the systems facet, e.g., via workflow models. Such changes can:

- lead to the embedding of new, or the change of existing, system components;
- lead to the change in the system integration models:
  - use of different components for performing the tasks (does not effect the overall working procedure too much);
  - define alternative components that can be chosen by the people performing a task (enables freedoms for the individual to choose a component for a certain task that fits best);
  - application of new collaboration approaches within the workflow (try to achieve the business goal without changing the workflow);
  - new workflow definitions — ordering of tasks, new task steps, additional collaborations, other work distributions etc.

Indirectly, the changes of the cooperative information systems affect the people performing the tasks, i.e., changes of the cooperative information systems leads to new working practice. Of course, there are also active changes which do not change the system at all but are intended to directly influence the work practice.

When looking for formal models or computerized support for such active changes, relevant research can be found in design engineering research, project planning and scheduling, software engineering, and more recently workflow management. For example, Madhavji (1992) categorized software process changes according to the scope they affect, and co-edited a special issue of *IEEE Transactions on Software Engineering* on process change

(Madhavji and Penedo, 1993); very similar studies have also been conducted for dynamic change management in workflow systems by Agostini *et al.* (1994) and Ellis *et al.* (1995). In the area of design as well as software engineering, the use of reason maintenance systems for effective replanning has been extensively studied (Dhar and Jarke, 1988; Petrie, 1993; Chung *et al.*, 1995).

7.1.2 Reactive Change Management

Reactive changes are typically initiated by the people performing the tasks in the organization. They can again result in changes of components or changes of coordination in the systems facet:

- use of other components for performing a predefined task or process step, i.e., such changes do not effect the organizational facet;
- introduction of new components by the user. This change should at least be considered at the systems facet and may also lead to changes in the organizational facet, e.g., a change of the workflow model;
- one-to-many replacements: a component is replaced by a set of components by which the task defined in the business process or workflow model can be better achieved;
- many-to-one replacements: a set of predefined components is replaced by a more powerful component which has the same functionality;
- changes of collaboration models: adapting collaboration models to user specific needs or using a different collaboration technique as the one predefined;
- changes of instantiated workflow models: performing predefined tasks in a different order or performing additional tasks, or other tasks → may lead to unexpected results which may not conform with the goals defined in the organizational facet.

There are also changes of work practice which do not impact the systems facet. A possibly unfortunate consequence of this is that they cannot be recognized as long as they lead to the expected results of the business process or workflow (i.e., no support is needed).

A typical change process initiated by reactive changes is depicted in Figure 6. In contrast to current practice, reactive changes should be considered in the organizational facet, i.e., whenever an reactive change effects an organizational model, this change should be recognized by the people responsible for maintaining the organizational models. The reflection of reactive changes, in the sense of total quality management (Feigenbaum, 1991), have been recognized as an invaluable source for process improvements (e.g., in the experience factory approach studied in software engineering (Oivo and Basili, 1992).

Change support is needed for steps (2) and (3) of Figure 6. In particular, the need for short-term notification and long-term traceability has been recognized especially in design-oriented applications. Notification and

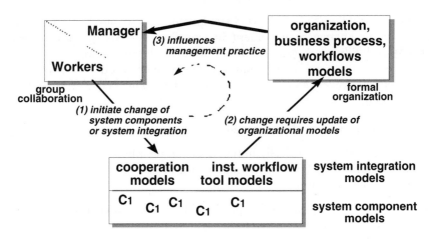

Figure 6.   Reactive change.

more general awareness features are offered by configuration management systems (e.g., Jarke *et al.*, 1992a) and are one of the main foci of CSCW research at the moment (cf. Section 5). The importance of traceability is emphasized by empirical studies (Gotel and Finkelstein, 1994; Ramesh and Edwards, 1993) and mandated by several engineering standards, such as DOD-2167a in software engineering.

7.1.3 Proactive Change Management

To avoid getting overloaded with reactive changes, we must place more emphasis on proactive containment strategies (Ackoff, 1967). Several of these strategies — componentization and control liberation in system integration, generalized work space metaphors in CSCW, and more abstract organizational models avoiding unnecessary over-commitment — introduce user freedoms, without sacrificing the possibility to record aberrations from expected behaviour for process improvement.

Another group of proactive change management strategies is related to the reuse of experiences in earlier change processes. Together with the richer models of early phases in requirements engineering and enterprise modelling, reason maintenance techniques, which have been intensively studied in design and software engineering since the late 1970s (Stallman and Sussman, 1977; Doyle, 1979; Dhar and Jarke, 1988; Petrie, 1993), have emerged as a central technology for dealing with this problem. Repositories, to be discussed in the next subsection, are the main framework for this kind of proactive change management.

A final group of proactive change management strategies which have received less attention so far, are proactive workflow modelling or project planning techniques.

One important aspect is the choice of process models; for example, there is some evidence that artefact-centred process models (e.g., based on the electronic circulation folder metaphor (Prinz and Kolvenbach 1996)) or compositional, situation-oriented process models (e.g., (Rolland *et al.*, 1995)) are more amenable to unforeseen exceptions and process changes than those enforcing an elaborate, strict control structure, such as the initially proposed Petri nets (e.g., Domino (Kreifelts and Woetzel, 1986), FUNSOFT (Gruhn, 1991), SPADE (Bandinelli *et al.*, 1993) or CSCW process grammars (e.g., Glance *et al.*, 1996).

A second aspect is the organization of work within a given process model. For example, (Srikanth and Jarke, 1989) present a decomposition theory for work assignment in project plans that is optimized for containing unplanned changes within as small a subgroup of the project team as possible. Such strategies — about which, in general, relatively little is known so far — enable a rather stable decomposition of responsibilities as well as defined change escalation strategies in case changes with larger impact do occur.

7.2 Cooperative Information Systems Support for Change

Support for change must obviously involve all facets of a cooperative information system: there must be a group collaboration on an intended change, the change must be supported and recorded by organizational change models, and last not least, there must be technological support for change. In this subsection, we focus on the latter.

Technical support for change management has already been partially discussed; in particular, Section 4 presented ways to make system integration more flexible and thus amenable to change. In addition, certain kinds of software agents are being experimented with, that specifically support change in a group setting:

- *Awareness agents* notify managers of relevant *ad hoc* changes and support the adaptation of the organization models; notify workers of organizational changes, explain the changes, guide them in adapting their working practice to the changes.
- *Change integration agents* provide functionalities such as impact analysis, traceability, notification of affected people, and cost analysis.
- *Simulation agents* test changes and their impact before implementing. Since changes are modelled and the system facet is enabled to adapt the cooperative information systems behaviour according to these models, such tests are easier than with conventional approaches (Oberweis *et al.*, 1994; Peters and Jarke, 1996).

The conceptual platform of models and tools, on which such agents provide their service, is typically defined in metamodels and managed in centralized or distributed *repositories*.

Change management demands a global (though specialized) view of all facets and components of a cooperative information system. This change view has to be patched together from several partial models, put together in terms of different notations, at different times and by different people. A standard way of accomplishing this patching together is through meta-modelling. Already mentioned in the 1970s by Abrial (1974), metamodelling has been researched as the prime approach for dealing with the problem of tailoring and linking models since the mid-1980s (Kotteman and Konsynski, 1984). In the early 1990s, a series of workshops and conferences on method engineering has emerged which focus on this problem.

Metamodelling is the activity of creating descriptions of modelling formalisms and possible links between modelling perspectives. The creation of metamodels requires a language in which they are specified, which can in turn be seen as a metametamodel.

Many metamodelling techniques are quite informal and just rely on extensible graphical notations; the aforementioned ARIS system or the RDD-100 traceability environment (Alford, 1990) are good examples. While both of these rely on extended entity–relationship formalisms, object-oriented approaches augment structural descriptions of objects with behavioural ones.

Metamodelling has progressed to the stage where we are beginning to see the first reports on commercial experiences for metamodelling environments where modelling tools are automatically created or linked via logic-based metalevel specifications. For example, the MetaEdit environment of the University of Jyväskylä (Smolander *et al.*, 1991; Kelly *et al.*, 1996) allows the automatic generation of browser/editor interfaces for formal conceptual models from graphical specifications, using a metametamodel called GOPRR which offers Graph, Object, Property, Relationship and Role as basic metalinguistic concepts and a predefined set of constraints.

Based on ideas from semantic networks in knowledge representation, the Telos language (Mylopoulos *et al.*, 1990) allows method engineers to tailor such metametamodels to specific problem domains. Languages like Telos can be used to rapidly create integrated problem-specific analysis and design environments for cooperative information systems. This has been demonstrated in a number of applications of the ConceptBase system developed at RWTH Aachen (Jarke *et al.*, 1995). These metametamodels address, for example, the computer-assisted analysis of the relationships between multiple company departments (Peters *et al.*, 1995), business analysis perspectives (Nissen *et al.*, 1996), software process modelling and traceability approaches (Ramesh and Dhar, 1992; Jarke *et al.*, 1994a; Pohl, 1996). They also facilitate forward and reverse engineering between system specification and implementation (Jeusfeld and Johnen, 1995), and can be linked to metamodels of dynamic simulation models which analyse and predict the behaviour of cooperative information systems (Peters and Jarke, 1996).

Using the principles of metamodelling, *repositories* or *data warehouses* have been proposed as databases that describe other information sources, in order to help either in their usage or in their evolution. A good overview of the questions involved in implementing repositories is given in Bernstein and Dayal (1994). Not surprisingly, technical and ontological extensibility, multiple perspectives and granularities, and a rich set of referential relationships are among the most important features mentioned.

In the NATURE project, a process-oriented repository-centred architecture for change management has been proposed (Jarke *et al.*, 1994b; Pohl, 1996). Its main feature is that it views the trace of an ongoing work process under multiple plans and traceability models, thus enabling the evaluation and control of processes from multiple organizational perspectives as well as the active support by change tools such as planners, decision support systems, and invocation of existing automated components. In the next section, we sketch the vision of a change coach that could operate on such process repositories in order to facilitate the mediation of change between the three facets.

7.3 Coach: an Envisioned Multifacet Cooperation Support Agent

In this section, we provide an example of a multifacet cooperation support agent called "coach". As explained in Section 5.2, the organizational model defines what is possible in group collaboration, while part of the activities in group collaboration can be to modify the organizational model. The coach is, therefore, in charge of facilitating the information exchange between group collaboration support and organizational models as well as managing the propagation of changes between the two, possibly including the systems facet if the changes require, for example, re-integration or re-architecturing of the underlying system. It is an active, autonomous intelligent agent in that it can self-trigger when needed and its behaviour is guided by its own knowledge.

In the following, we present an example scenario to help us explain our vision of the coach. First, we present some background information about the example. Employees of an organization used to follow a particular procedure in order to obtain travel reimbursements. This procedure is specified, with other relevant definitions, in the organizational model. Its main steps are: before leaving — prepare an estimate, submit it for approval both to the project leader and to the head of the department, and if responses are positive, send the signed form to the administration office; after coming back from the trip — calculate the actual expenses (enclosing proof for all of them), submit the documentation for approval both to the project leader and to the department head, and, if responses are positive, send all documents to the administration office for the reimbursement. In other words, the procedure needs a double signature from the person in

charge of the project funds (i.e., the project leader) and the person responsible for the administration of the department (i.e., the department head)
both before and after the trip.

The department head, upon receiving several complaints from her
employees, initiates an investigation of the efficiency of the procedure.
Instead of just getting some historical records or a statistical report, the
coach is able to have a meaningful valuation of the relationships between
the planned and the actual behaviour. This is because the coach is capable
of associating the model (i.e., the procedure definition as specified in the
organizational model) with the enacted workflow (i.e., all instances of the
procedure executed as part of the group collaboration). This example
demonstrates situations where the coach is not representing any particular
facet, but gathering, analysing and integrating multifacet information.

Although not surprising, the outcome of the analysis does show that
the activities to obtain the signatures, both before and after the trip, are
the bottleneck of the procedure in that they consume the most amount of
time. The coach also points out that if the actual trip expenses is lower than
estimated, the project leader's decision of not approving never happens.
Finally, the department head knows that she is not interested in the details,
since she does not have direct responsibility on the project funds, but just
wants to have an overall control. Therefore, she decides to modify the
procedure definition, cancelling the signature of the project leader after
the trip in case of expenses below the estimate, and leaving the approval
of just the department head at the end of the procedure.

Automatically, the new procedure substitutes the old one in the organizational model. Once again, it is the duty of the coach to maintain the
coherence between the model and the enacted workflow. In this case, it
is to propagate the changes from the organizational model to the appropriate facet(s). In doing so, it changes the remaining activities of all *switchable*
instances currently in execution without having to restart them from the
beginning.

The ability to dynamically change all running instances of a procedure
needs further explanation. The change mainly involves three steps:
(1) collect all running instances; (2) assess which of them are switchable;
(3) change those that are switchable to the new workflow definition
without causing errors (e.g., without skipping activities to be performed or
performing an activity twice). Due to the lack of certain domain knowledge,
it is not always possible to automatically determine which running instances
can be switched (e.g., adding new activities to a procedure) (Agostini *et al.*,
1994; Ellis *et al.*, 1995). Under those circumstances, the coach helps the
department head to define switchability policy.

One can argue that the aforementioned three steps can be carried out
by the workflow management system itself and, therefore, having a coach
is unnecessary. However, procedures are part of the organizational model
and, therefore, if we do not want to create a hierarchical link between the

different facets, we need an autonomous agent to perform them. The idea of the coach, and the multifacet cooperation support agents in general, is a way to manage change without complicating the underlying systems in performing their regular activities (i.e., the workflow management system manages the execution of workflows, while the coach manages changes).

Note that most of coach's features are not new. The novelty is rather in recognizing the need, in a distributed and complex environment, for someone to be in charge of tasks that cover several units/applications/sites.

8 TOWARDS A GENERIC ARCHITECTURE FOR COOPERATIVE INFORMATION SYSTEMS

In the preceding sections, we have outlined a framework for identifying and characterizing research problems and issues in cooperative information systems. This clearer picture also enables us to envision possible solutions. In this section, we propose a generic architecture which puts forth a vision of how cooperation and ongoing change can be supported, while addressing all three facets and their interactions.

The purpose of this generic architecture (or architectural model) is to help focus and coordinate our research efforts towards solutions that are implementable within the expected time frame, while allowing for considerable freedom within each subarea of research. The architecture identifies the major architectural layers and component types, what kinds of functions they perform, what information they maintain, and what kinds of interdependencies they manage in order to deal with various classes of changes and modes of cooperation. The generic architecture leaves open many issues to be addressed during specific architectural design (e.g., the interface mechanisms among particular architectural components).

We start with the premise that existing practices with computer-based technologies, such as compilers, DBMSs, and workflow products will continue to exist, get used and evolve on their own for some time to come, partly because of existing investments in legacy systems and human training that cannot be simply written off, partly because of general laws of inertia. The task at hand for us working in this area is not to replace this practice, but rather to augment it. Accordingly, our conception of cooperative information systems is one of providing a value-added layer on top of legacy and other existing systems, thereby ensuring that they continue to fulfill users' information needs and remain consistent with organizational objectives.

The generic architecture thus consists of two layers (Figure 7):

- the base layer — includes information systems that directly provide information services to users;
- the cooperation support layer — a value-added layer that provides facilities for dealing with all three facets, their interactions, and for supporting cooperation and change.

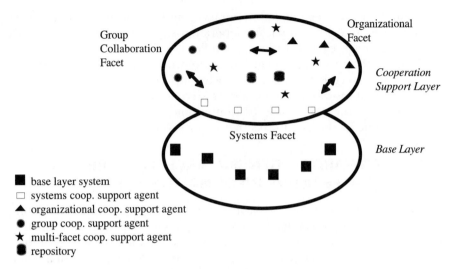

Figure 7.   A generic architecture for cooperative information systems.

As shown in the figure, the cooperation support layer consists of several types of cooperation support agents (or components). The systems, group and organizational agents provide interfaces to their respective facet and interact with each other. The fourth type of agents, the multifacet cooperation support agent, does not represent any single facet. They play a control and/or coordination role among the aforementioned three types of agents (Section 7.3).

Repositories in the cooperation support layer are used to maintain the various types of models and metamodels, their interdependencies, and their relative changes over time (as discussed in Section 7.2).

Finally, the architecture also maintains a set of proximity relations. A proximity relation is defined by the interdependencies among the three facets, involving objectives, people and systems. These may include data and/or control dependencies, visibility relationships (import/export properties), and change interdependencies (what kinds of changes should be propagated in what ways). For example, there is a proximity relation between the "increase profitability" goal (in the organizational facet), the structure of a new team of workers (in the group collaboration facet), and a new system that helps them do their work the "new way" (in the systems facet). This dependence is important to record and keep track of because if anything changes, it will tell us what else is potentially affected. Proximity relations are modelled in the repository and can be used by the four types of cooperation support agents when performing their duties.

This approach of providing a value-added layer for cooperation support is complementary to approaches that attempt to build cooperation and flexibility for change into base layer components (e.g., recent componentized system approaches that use standardized middleware for interoperability and reusability). Our belief is that even with such approaches, there will still be need for value-added components that deal specifically with cooperation and change.

In addition to dealing with cooperation and change, we believe that this architecture is also useful in providing a framework for delivering information services within an organization, in support of business processes, and in aligning them with organizational objectives. Such delivery is based on the execution of legacy information systems and workflows that disseminate, retrieve and distribute information. The systems cooperation support agents compose systems transactions into scripts (or long transactions). Each of these scripts is executing in a distributed fashion and uses the services of several legacy systems. The systems cooperation support agents also deal with issues related to integration and interoperation when executing these scripts. Such scripts are, in turn, executing in support of human collaborative work defined in terms of business processes through the group cooperation support agents. Finally, such work contributes to objectives at the organizational facet.

The generic architecture entails a research agenda that is being pursued by the research teams represented by the authors. We are working towards cooperative information systems solutions that can be deployed in the time frame of five to ten years from now. A number of pieces of the technology already exist as research prototypes and are being further developed in relation to the generic architecture. The architecture assumes that computing environments in the targeted time frame will be highly interconnected, involving heterogeneous systems and networks. High-capacity multimedia network-based computing will be commonplace, making use of local and global networks, which may be wired, mobile or fibre-based. There will be standardization efforts in many areas, but uniformity of standards will unlikely be achieved in most areas. There will be high expectations for performance, reliability and information quality. Socio-economic issues will remain crucial to the success of new technologies, systems and services.

9 CONCLUSIONS

We have argued that the basic issue that needs to be addressed by cooperative information systems as a research area is *organizational and technological change*. We have then reviewed some of the issues which cooperative information systems bring forth and some of the approaches being tried to address these issues. We have also proposed a generic, coarse-grain architecture for systems which is capable of relating legacy systems to human collaborative activity and organizational goals, for purposes of driving information services and guiding change.

The proposed architecture is only a starting point for the research in cooperative information systems and we consider it as a basis for a multi-disciplinary discussion on the subject. It is our opinion that cooperative information systems is a field opening new relevant research challenges to various computer science sub-disciplines and calling for breaking the existing boundaries between them. Some explanations for the above claim are given below.

1. Cooperative information systems, unlike information systems and databases, need to address not only technological issues, such as "How do I build a system that does X?", but also human and social ones ("How does a group of people accomplish task Y?") as well as organizational ones ("How can we meet objective Z?"). Within this framework, it seems to us that the research in information systems cannot conquer the CSCW field as if CSCW systems were mere innovative interfaces for distributed information systems, and that CSCW scholars and practitioners cannot afford to address the typical issues of information systems research as if the latter were mere information sources that users can access during their work. On the contrary, cooperative information systems emerge as newly conceived systems coupling the human process orientation of CSCW systems with the distributed systems orientation of information systems. Cooperative information systems are based on an architecture where the process-oriented domain of human activity and the distributed systems of information processing are two autonomous cooperating modules of one and the same system. Building such systems will require technological as well as social and organizational know-how.

2. The new and growing complexity of the architecture we have proposed for cooperative information systems is based on active and passive components. There is, therefore, the need for a growing number of active components (of intelligent agents) managing the relations between and among the different facets and, in particular, between the group collaboration support module and the organizational model. It is our conviction that the creation of these intelligent agents provides new research issues such as knowledge contextualization for the distributed artificial intelligence field.

3. Cooperative information systems are a new type of systems, oriented to support not only information processing but also change. The design and engineering of cooperative information systems does not appear well supported by the typical techniques and methods emerging from software engineering: it requires on the contrary new methods and tools supporting user participation, continuous changes, and on-line performance evaluation.

ACKNOWLEDGEMENTS

The authors gratefully acknowledge financial support for this collaborative project from the European Commission and Ontario's Information

Technology Research Centre. Particular thanks are due to Alessandra Agostini who contributed to the development of the coach concept. The following people read an earlier version of this chapter and provided numerous constructive suggestions on improving the chapter during a three-day workshop held in Vancouver, Canada on 5−7 August, 1996: Mike Bauer, Alex Borgida, Philippe Du Bois, Tamer Ozsu, Remo Pareschi, Peter Peters, Bala Ramesh, Jacob Slonim and Francois Vernadat.

REFERENCES

Abrial, J.-R. (1974) Data semantics. In *Data Management Systems*, J.W. Klimbie and K.L. Koffeman (eds). North-Holland.

Ackoff, R.L. (1967) Management misinformation systems. *Management Science*, **14**(4), 147−156.

Agostini, A., De Michelis, G. and Petruni, K. (1994) Keeping workflow models as simple as possible. In *Proceedings of the Workshop on Computer-Supported Cooperative Work, Petri-Nets and Related Formalisms*, within the 15th International Conference on Application and Theory of Petri Nets (ATPN '94), pp. 11−23. (Available on request from CTL, University of Milano, email: gdemich@dsi.unimi.it.)

Agostini, A., De Michelis, G. and Grasso, M. (1995) The Milano system. In *A Computational Model of Organizational Context. COMIC Deliverable 1.3*, pp. 163−192. (Available on request from the Computing Department, University of Lancaster, Lancaster LA1 4YR, UK, e-mail: tom@comp.lancs.ac.uk.)

Agostini, A., De Michelis, G., Grasso, M., Prinz, W. and Syri, A. (1996) Contexts, work processes, work spaces. *Computer Supported Cooperative Work: The Journal of Collaborative Computing*, **5**(2−3), 223−250.

Alford, M.W. (1990) Software requirements engineering methodology (SREM) at the age of eleven — requirements-driven design. In *Modern Software Engineering*, P.A. Ng and R.T. Yeh (eds). Van Nostrand Reinold.

Alonso, G. (1996) The role of database technology in workflow management systems. In *Proceedings of CoopIS '96*, Brussels, Belgium. IEEE Computer Society Press, pp. 176−179.

Appelt, W. (1996) CoopWWW — interoperable tools for cooperation support using the World-Wide Web. In *Proceedings 5th ERCIM/W4G Workshop CSCW and the Web*, Arbeitspapiere der GMD 984, GMD, Sankt Augustin, Germany, pp. 95−99.

Argyris, M. and Schon, D. (1978) *Organizational Learning*, Addison Wesley, Reading.

Argyris, M. and Schon, D. (1996) *Organizational Learning II*, Addison Wesley, Reading.

Atkinson, M., Bancilhon, F., De Witt, D., Dittrich, K., Maier, D. and Zdonik. S. (1990) The Object-Oriented Database System Manifesto. In *Deductive and Object-oriented Databases*. Elsevier Science Publishers, Amsterdam, Netherlands.

Bandinelli, S.C., Fuggetta, A. and Ghezzi, C. (1993) Software process model evolution in the SPADE environment. *IEEE Transactions on Software Engineering*, **19**(12), 1128−1144.

Berliner, C. and Brimson, J. (1988) *Cost Management for Today's Advanced Manufacturing: The CAM-I Conceptual Design*, Free Press.

Berners-Lee, T. (1996) WWW: past, present, and future. *IEEE Computer*, **29**(10), 69−77.

Bernstein, P. (1993) Middleware: An Architecture for Distributed System Services. CRL 93/6, Digital Equipment Corporation, Cambridge Research Lab.

Bernstein, P.A. and Dayal, U. (1994) An Overview of Repository Technology. In *Proceedings of the Twentieth International Conference on Very Large Data Bases*, Santiago, Chile, pp. 705–713.

Bernus, P. and Nemes, L. (eds). (1996) *Modelling and Methodologies for Enterprise Integration*, Chapman and Hall.

Brachman, R.J. and Schmolze, J.G. (1985) An Overview of the KL-ONE Knowledge Representation System. *Cognitive Science*, **9**(2), 171–216.

Bubenko, J.A. (1980) Information Modeling in the Context of System Development. In *Proceedings of Information Processing '80*, S.H. Lavington (ed). North-Holland, pp. 395–411.

Bubenko, J. (1993) Extending the Scope of Information Modeling. In *Proceedings of the Fourth International Workshop on the Deductive Approach to Information Systems and Databases*, Lloret-Costa Brava, Catalonia, 73–98.

Cardelli, L. (1994) Obliq: A language with distributed scope. Technical report, Digital Equipment Corporation, Systems Research Center, Palo Alto, California.

Carroll, J.M., Kellogg, W.A., Rosson, M.B. (1991) The Task–Artifact Cycle. In *Designing Interaction. Psychology at the Human–Computer Interface*. J.M. Carroll (ed.): Cambridge.

Chung, K.L. (1993) Representing and using non-functional requirements for information system development: a process-oriented approach. PhD thesis, University of Toronto.

Chung, L., Nixon, B. and Yu, E. (1995) Using Non-Functional Requirements to Systematically Support Change. In *IEEE International Symposium on Requirements Engineering* (RE '95), IEEE Computer Society Press, pp. 132–139.

Constantopoulos, P., Jarke, M., Mylopoulos, J. and Vassiliou, Y. (1995) The Software Information Base: A Server for Reuse. *VLDB-Journal*, **4**(1), 1–43.

CoopIS (1994) *Second International Conference on Cooperative Information Systems (CoopIS-94)*, Toronto, Canada.

Dardenne, A., van Lamsweerde, A. and Fickas, S. (1993) Goal-directed requirements acquisition. *Science of Computer Programming*, **20**(1), 3–50.

De Michelis, G. (1996a) Work Processes, Organizational Structures and Cooperation Supports: Managing Complexity. In *Proceedings of the Fifth IFAC Symposium on Automated Systems Based on Human Skills — Joint Design of Technology and Organization*, Pergamon Elsevier International, New York, pp. 3–12.

De Michelis, G. (1996b) Computer-based systems between people and social complexity. In *Proceedings of the Toshiba Chair Symposium on Human Oriented Information Technology and Complex Systems*, Keio University, Tokio, pp. 1–8.

De Michelis, G. and Grasso, M. (1994) Situating Conversations within the Language/Action Perspective: The Milano Conversation Model. In *Proceedings of the Conference on CSCW '94*, (Chapel Hill, North Carolina) ACM Press, pp. 89–100.

Dhar, V. and Jarke, M. (1988) Dependency-directed reasoning and learning in systems maintenance support. *IEEE Transactions on Software Engineering*, **14**(2), 211–227.

Doyle, J. (1979) A truth maintenance system. *Artificial Intelligence*, **12**(3), 231–272.

Dubois, E. (1989) A Logic of Action for Supporting Goal-Oriented Elaborations of Requirements. In *Proceedings of the Fifth International Workshop on Software Specification and Design* (IWSSD '89), CS Press, pp. 160–168.

Du Bois, P., Dubois, E. and Zeippen, J-M. (1997) On the Use of a Formal RE Language: the Generalized Railroad Crossing Problem. *IEEE International Symposium on Requirements Engineering* (Annapolis, USA).

Ehn, P. (1988) *Work-oriented Design of Computer Artifacts*. 2nd edn Arbetslivscentrum, Stockholm.

Ellis, C.A., Keddara, K. and Rozenberg, G. (1995) Dynamic Change within Work-flow Systems. In *Proceedings of the Conference on Organizational Computing Systems*, Milpitas, CA. ACM Press, pp. 10−21.

ESPRIT Project AMICE (1989) *Open Systems Architecture for CIM*. Springer-Verlag.

Feather, M. (1987) Language Support for the Specification and Development of Composite Systems. *ACM Transactions on Programming Languages and Systems*, **9**(2), 198−234.

Feigenbaum, A. (1991) *Total Quality Control*, McGraw-Hill.

Finin, T., Lambrou, Y. and Mayfeld, J. (1995) KQML as an Agent Communication Language. In *Software Agents*, J. Bradshaw (ed), AAAI/MIT Press, Menlo-Park, Ca.

Flores, F., Graves, M., Hartfield, B. and Winograd, T. (1988) Computer Systems and the Design of Organizational Interaction. *ACM Transactions on Office Information Systems*, **6**(2), 153−172.

Gasser, L. (1991) Social Conceptions of Knowledge and Action: DAI Foundations and Open Systems Semantics. *Artificial Intelligence*, **47**, 107−138.

Georgakopoulos, D., Hornick, M. and Sheth, A. (1995) An Overview of Workflow Management: From Process Modeling to Infrastructure for Automation. *Journal on Distributed and Parallel Database Systems*, **3**(2), 119−153.

Glance, N.S., Pagani, D.S. and Pareschi, R. (1996) Generalized process structure grammars (GPSG) for flexible representations of work. *Proceedings of CSCW '96* (Cambridge, Mass.), ACM Press, pp. 180−189.

Gotel, O. and Finkelstein, A. (1994) An Analysis of the Requirements Traceability Problem. In *Proceedings IEEE International Conference on Requirements Engineering*, Computer Science Press.

Greenberg S. and Marwood, D. (1994) Real Time Groupware as a Distributed System: Concurrency Control and its Effect on the Interface. *Proceedings of the Conference on CSCW '94*, (Chapel Hill, North Carolina), ACM Press, New York, pp. 207−217.

Greenspan, S., Borgida A. and Mylopoulos, J. (1986) A Requirements Modeling Language and its Logic. *Information Systems*, **11**(1), 9−23.

Gruhn, V. (1991) Validation and verification of software process models. PhD thesis, Univ. Dortmund, Germany.

Gutwin, C., Roseman, M. and Greenberg, S. (1996) A usability study of awareness widgets in a shared workspace groupware system. In *Proceedings of CSCW '96* (Cambridge, Mass.).

Hamel, G. and Prahalad, C. (1994) *Competing for the Future*, Harvard Business School Press, Boston, Mass.

Hammer, M. and Champy, J. (1993) *Reengineering the Corporation: A Manifesto for Business Revolution*, HarperBusiness.

Hsu, M. (1993) Special Issue on Workflow and Extended Transaction Systems. *Bulletin of the Technical Committee on Data Engineering*, **16**(2).

Jacobson, I., *et al.* (1992) *Object-Oriented Software Engineering: A Use Case Driven Approach*, Prentice-Hall.

Jackson, M. and Zave, P. (1995) Deriving Specifications from Requirements. *Proceedings of the Seventeenth International Conference on Software Engineering*, ACM Press, pp. 15−24.

Janson, M. and Woo, C.C. (1996) "A Speech Act Lexicon: An Alternative Use of Speech Act Theory In Information Systems". *Information Systems Journal*, **6**(3).

Jarke, M. and Pohl, M. (1993) Establishing Visions in Context: Towards a Model of Requirements Processes. *Proceedings 14th International Conference on Information Systems* (Orlando, Fl), pp. 23−34.

Jarke, M. and Rose, T. (1988) Managing Knowledge About Information System Evolution. In *Proceedings ACM-SIGMOD Conference*, Chicago.

Jarke, M., Maltzahn, C.G.v. and Rose, T. (1992a) Sharing processes: team support in design repositories. *International Journal of Intelligent and Cooperative Information Systems*, **1**(1), 145−167.

Jarke, M., Mylopoulos, J., Schmidt, J.W. and Vassiliou, Y. (1992b) DAIDA: An Environment for Evolving Information Systems. *ACM Transactions on Information Systems*, **10**(1), 1−50.

Jarke, M., Pohl, K., Rolland, C. and Schmitt, J.R. (1994a) Experience-Based Method Evaluation and Improvement: A Process Modeling Approach. In *Proceedings IFIP WG 8.1 Conference on CRIS*, Maastricht, North Holland.

Jarke, M., Pohl, K., Dömges, R., Jacobs, S. and Nissen, H.W. (1994b) Requirements Information Management: The NATURE Approach. *Engineering of Information Systems*, **2**(6).

Jarke, M., Gallersdörfer, R., Jeusfeld, M.A., Staudt, M. and Eherer, S. (1995) ConceptBase — A Deductive Object Base for Meta Data Management. *Journal of Intelligent Informations Systems*, **4**(2), 167−192

Java (1995) *Java: The Inside Story.* http://www.sun.com/sunworldonline/swol-07-1995/swol-07-java.html.

Jeusfeld, M.A. and Johnen, U. (1995) An Executable Meta Model for Re-Engineering of Database Schemas. *International Journal of Cooperative Information Systems*, **4**(2&3), 237−258 (Special Issue on ER '94).

Karbe, B. and Ramsberger, N. (1991) Concepts and implementation of migrating office processes. In Brauer/Hernandez (eds): *Verteilte Kuenstliche Intelligenz und Kooperatives Arbeiten*, Springer-Verlag.

Keen, P. (1991) *Shaping the Future: Business Design Through Information Technology*, Harvard Business School Press, Boston, Mass.

Kelly, S., Lyytinen, K. and Rossi, M. (1996) MetaEdit+: a fully configurable multi-user and multi-tool CASE and CAME environment. *Proceedings of CAiSE '96* (Heraklion, Greece), pp. 1−21.

Kling, R. and Scacchi, M. (1982) The Web of Computing: Computer Technology as Social Organization. *Advances in Computing*, **21**, 1−90.

Knoblock, C.A., Arens, Y. and Hsu, C.N. (1994) Cooperating Agents for Information retrieval. In *Proceedings on the Second International Conference on Cooperative Information Systems* (Toronto, Canada), 122−133.

Kotteman, J. and Konsynski, B. (1984) Dynamic Metasystems for Information Systems Development. In *Proceedings 5th International Conference on Information Systems*, Tucson, Az.

Kreifelts, T. and Woetzel, G. (1986) Distribution and error handling in an office procedure system. *Proceedings of IFIP WG8.4 Working Conference on Methods and Tools for Office Systems* (Pisa, Italy), pp. 197−208.

Lau, C. (1994) *Object-Oriented Programming using SOM and DSOM.* Van Nostrand Reinhold, Thomson Publishing Company, New York.

Lee, J. (1992) A decision rationale management system: capturing, reusing, and managing the reasons for decisions. PhD thesis, MIT.

McGregor, R. (1990) The Evolving Technology of Classification-Based knowledge Representation Systems. In *Principles of Semantic Networks*, J. Sowa (ed), Morgan-Kaufmann.

Madhavji, N. (1992) Environment evolution: the Prism model of change. *IEEE Transactions on Software Engineering*, **18**(5), 380−392.

Madhavji, N. and Penedo, M.H. (eds). (1993) Special Section on the Evolution of Software Processes. *IEEE Transactions on Software Engineering*, **19**(12).

Manola, Heiler, F., Georgakopoulos, D., Hornick, M. and Brodie, M. (1992) Distributed Object Management. *International Journal of Intelligent and Cooperative Information Systems*, **1**(1), 5–42.

Mantei, M., Baecker, R., Sellen, A., Buxton, W., Milligan, T. and Wellman, B. (1991) Experiences in the Use of a Media Space. In *Proceedings of CHI* (New Orleans), ACM Press, New York, pp. 127–138.

Martens, C. and Woo, C.C. (1997) OASIS: An Integrative Toolkit for Developing Autonomous Applications in Decentralized Environments. *Journal of Organizational Computing and Electronic Commerce*, **7**(3).

Mathiske, B., Matthes, F. and Schmidt, J.W. (1995) Scaling Database Languages to Higher-Order Distributed Programming. In *Proceedings of the Fifth International Workshop on Database Programming Languages* (Gubbio, Italy), Springer-Verlag.

Matthes F. and Schmidt, J.W. (1994) Persistent Threads. *Proceedings of the Twentieth International Conference on Very Large Data Bases* (Santiago, Chile), pp. 403–414.

Medina-Mora, R., Winograd, T., Flores, R. and Flores, F. (1992) The Action Workflow Approach to Workflow Management Technology. *Proceedings of CSCW '92* (Toronto, Canada), ACM Press, pp. 281–288.

Microsoft (1994) *Microsoft Office Developer's Kit*. Microsoft Corporation.

Milliner, S., Bouguettaya, A. and Papazoglou, M.P. (1995) A Scalable Architecture for Autonomous Heterogeneous Database Interactions. *21st VLDB Conference* (Zurich).

Munson, J.P. and Dewan, P. (1994) A Flexible Object Merging Framework. *Proceedings of CSCW '94* (Chapel Hill, North Carolina), ACM Press, New York, pp. 231–242.

Mylopoulos, J., Borgida, A., Jarke, M. and Koubarakis, M. (1990) Telos: Representing Knowledge about Information Systems. *ACM Transactions on Information Systems*, **8**(4), 325–362.

Mylopoulos, J., Chung, L. and Nixon, B. (1992) Representing and Using Non-Functional Requirements: A Process-Oriented Approach. *IEEE Transactions on Software Engineering*, **18**(6).

Nissen, H.W., Jeusfeld, M.A., Jarke, M., Zemanek, G.V. and Huber, H. (1996) Managing multiple requirements perspectives with meta models. *IEEE Software, Special Issue on Requirements Engineering*.

Nonaka, I. and Takeuchi, H. (1995) *The Knowledge-Creating Company*. Oxford University Press.

Oberweis, A., Scherrer, G. and Stucky, W. (1994) Income/Star: methodology and tools for the development of distributed information systems. *Information Systems*, **19**(8), 643–660.

Oivo, M. and Basili, V.R. (1992) Representing software engineering models: the TAME goal-oriented approach. *IEEE Transactions on Software Engineering*, **18**(10), 886–898.

OMG (1991) *The Common Object Request Broker: Architecture and Specification*. Document 91.12.1, Rev. 1.1, Object Management Group.

OSF (1993) *OSF DCE Application Development Guide*. Open Software Foundation. Prentice Hall, Englewood Cliffs, New Jersey.

Palfreyman, K. and Rodden, T. (1996) A protocol for user awareness on the World Wide Web. *Proceedings of CSCW '96* (Cambridge, Mass.), ACM Press, pp. 130–139.

Papazoglou, M.P., Laufmann, S. and Sellis, T. (1992) An Organizational Framework for Cooperating Intelligent Information Systems. *International Journal of Intelligent and Cooperative Information Systems*, **1**(1), 169–202.

Patil, R., Fikes, R., Patel-Schneider, P., MacKay, D., Finnin, T., Gruber, T. and Neches, R. (1992) The DARPA knowledge sharing effort. *Proceedings 3rd International Conference on Principles of Knowledge Representation and Reasoning*, Morgan-Kaufman.

Peters, P. and Jarke, M. (1996) Simulating the impact of information flows on networked organizations. In *Proceedings 17th International Conference on Information Systems* (Cleveland, Ohio).

Peters, P., Szczuko, P., Jeusfeld, M. and Jarke, M. (1995) Business Process Oriented Information Management: Conceptual Model at Work. *Proceedings of the Conference on Organizational Computing Systems* (Milpitas, CA.), ACM Press, pp. 216–224.

Petrie, C. (1993) The Redux server. *Proceedings First International Conference on Intelligent and Cooperative Information Systems* (Rotterdam, Netherlands), IEEE Computer Society Press, pp. 134–143.

Pohl, K. (1996) *Process Centered Requirements Engineering*, John Wiley Research Science Press.

Prinz, W. and Kolvenbach, S. (1996) Support for workflows in a ministerial environment. *Proceedings of CSCW '96* (Cambridge, Mass.), ACM Press, pp. 199–208.

Ramesh, B. and Dhar, V. (1992) Supporting systems development by capturing deliberations during requirements engineering. *IEEE Transactions Software Engineering*, **18**(6), 498–510.

Ramesh, B. and Edwards, M. (1993) Issues in the development of a requirements traceability model. In *Proceedings International Symposium on Requirements Engineering* (San Diego, Ca).

Reder, S. and Schwab, R.G. (1990) The Temporal Structure of Cooperative Activity. *Proceedings of CSCW '90* (Los Angeles, CA), ACM Press, pp. 303–316.

Rolland, C., Souveyet, C. and Moreno, M. (1995) An approach for defining ways-of-working. *Information Systems*, **20**(3).

Roseman, M. and Greenberg, S. (1996) TeamRooms: network places for collaboration. In *Proceedings of CSCW '96* (Cambridge, Mass.), ACM Press, pp. 325–333.

Scheer, A-W. (1994) *Enterprise-Wide Data Modeling*, 4th edn Springer-Verlag.

Schmidt, J.W. (1977) Some high-level language constructs for data of type relation. *ACM Transactions on Database Systems*, **2**(3), 247–261.

Scott Morton, M., (ed). (1991) *The Corporation of the 1990s: Information Technology and Organizational Transformation*, Oxford University Press.

Selic B. *et al.* (1994) *Real-Time Object-Oriented Modeling*, Wiley.

Sernadas, A., Sernadas, C., Gouveia, P., Resende, P. and Gouveia, J. (1991) OBLOG — object-oriented logic: an informal introduction. Technical Report, INESC, Lisbon.

Smolander, K., Lyytinen, K., Tahvanainen, V.-P. and Martiin, P. (1991) MetaEdit — a Flexible Graphical Environment for Methodology Modeling. In *Proceedings of CAiSE '91* (Trondheim, Norway).

Srikanth, R. and Jarke, M. (1989) The design of knowledge-based systems for managing ill-structured software projects. *Decision Support Systems*, **5**(4), 425–448.

Stallman, R.M. and Sussman, G.J. (1977) Forward reasoning and dependency-directed backtracking in a system for computer-aided circuit analysis. *Artificial Intelligence*, **9**(2), 135–196.

Stemple, D., Morrison, R. and Atkinson, M. (1991) Type-Safe Linguistic Reflection. *Database Programming Languages: Bulk Types and Persistent Data*, Morgan Kaufmann Publishers, 357–362.

Stonebraker, M., Rowe, L., Lindsay, B., Gray, J., Carey, M., Brodie, M. and Bernstein, P. (1990) Third-Generation Data Base System Manifesto. *ACM SIGMOD Record*, **19**(3), 31–44.

Suchman, L. (1987) *Plans and Situated Actions*, Cambridge University Press.

Suchman, L. (1994) Do Categories Have Politics? The Language/Action Perspective Reconsidered. *Computer Supported Cooperative Work: An International Journal*, **2**(3), 177–190.

van Lamsweerde, A., Darimont R. and Massonet, P. (1995) Goal-Directed Elaboration of Requirements for a Meeting Scheduler. *Proceedings of IEEE International Symposium on Requirements Engineering* (RE '95), IEEE Computer Society Press, pp. 194–203.

Vernadat, F. (1984) Computer-Integrated Manufacturing: On the Database Aspect. In *Proceedings of CAD/CAM and Robotics Conference*, Toronto.

Vernadat, F. (1996) *Enterprise Modeling and Integration*, Chapman and Hall.

Wayner, P. (1994) Agents Away. *BYTE*, 113–118.

White, J.E. (1994) *Telescript Technology: The Foundation for the Electronic Marketplace*. White paper, General Magic Inc., Mountain View, California, USA.

Wiederhold, G. (1994) Interoperation, Mediation and Ontologies. In *Proceedings of International Workshop on Heterogeneous Cooperativer Knowledge-Bases* (Tokyo).

Wieringa, R. (1994) LCM and MCN: Specification of a Control System Using Dynamic Logic and Process Algebra. *In Case Study Production Cell — A Comparative Study of Formal Software Development*, C. Lewerentz and T. Lindner (eds). LNCS, Springer-Verlag.

Wieringa, R. (1996) *Requirements Engineering: Frameworks for Understanding*, Wiley.

Wille, R. (1992) Concept Lattices and Conceptual Knowledge Systems. In *Semantic Networks in Artificial Inteligence*, F. Lehmann (ed), Pergamon Press, pp. 493–515.

Williams, T. (1992) The purdue enterprise reference architecture. Purdue Laboratory for Applied Industrial Control, Purdue University.

Winograd, T. and Flores, F. (1986) *Understanding Computers and Cognition; A New Foundation for Design*, Ablex.

Yu, E. (1995) Modelling strategic relationships for process reengineering. PhD thesis, University of Toronto.

Yu, E., Du Bois, P., Dubois, E. and Mylopoulos, J. (1995) From Organization Models to System Requirements — A Cooperating Agents Approach. In *Proceedings of the Third International Conference on Cooperative Information Systems* (Vienna), University of Toronto Press, pp. 194–204.

Index

Adaptability 51, 52, 55
Agent communication languages and
      protocols 328
Agents 293–312
Aggregation 214–15
ALBERT language 293, 295–303
ALBERT specification 303–7
AlbertCORE 296
Application development 51, 74, 329
Application frameworks 99–100
Application interoperability 15
Approximation 214–15
April language 112, 253–4
      review 115–16
AprilQ 111–36
      broker program 121–6
      cooperation between servers 130–2
      internetting 132–4
      key features 113–14
      macro–layer approach 113
      overview 127–9
architectures xi, 6, 19, 28, 57, 58, 86,
      95–8, 164–6, 353–5
Aspect-oriented programming 65
Asynchronous sharing 332

Base ontology 192–4
Black-box reuse 51–4
Broker agent
      as April process 116–19
      communication scenario 120–1,
      122–3
      forking and using 119–20
Brokerage architectures xi
Business object architecture 95
Business Object Domain Task Force
      (BODTF) 93–4
Business Object Facility 94, 99
Business objects 92–5

C++ 63, 247–50
Carrier Access System (CABS II) 28–9, 32
Change management 342–53
      active 345
      and cooperation 317–18
      CIS support 349–51
      perspectives on 344–9

pro-active 348–9
      reactive 347–8
Class composition 66
Classification 188–90
Classificational object-based data model
      (CODM) 191–2
Client/server architectures 6, 95
Coach 351–3
Commercial off-the-shelf (COTS)
      applications 46–7
Common Business Objects (CBOs) 94
Common ontology 184–7
Communication, human-system integration
      324–5
Compartmentalized applications 323–4
Component developers 51
Component framework 49, 56
Component-oriented software development
      75
Component-oriented software life cycle 74
Component-oriented sofware development
      56
Components 49–78
      and objects 54
      meaning 53
      need for 54–6
      problems addressed by 54–6
Componentware 64–5
Composite concepts 194–5
Composition environment 52, 75
      requirements 66–75
Composition model 51, 58
Composition rules 58
Compositional development 56–8
Compositional methods 74
Computer-supported cooperative work
      (CSCW) xii, 316, 325, 330
Computing environment 19, 22
ConceptBase system 272
Conceptual contexts 140, 146–63
      projection rules for mapping to
            database objects 158–9
Conceptual relationships 195–7
Concurrency 60
Connectors 57
Constraints 297–300
Context 139–78
Context manipulation 153–7

Context representation   148–9, 160–3
    partial   149–53
Contextual descriptions   155–60
Contract   51, 63
Cooperating agents   293–312
Cooperation   xi, 49–50, 233–60
    and change management   317–18
Cooperative federated database system
    (CFDBS)   179–203
    information sharing   185
Cooperative information system (CIS)   xi,
    50, 293–4
    building   90
    change management process
        269–73
    characteristics   7–8
    computing   5
    conceptualization   264
    example   266–8
    facets of   319
    framework for research   318–21
    generic architecture   353–5
    identifying and planning information
        flows   273–82
    in context of modern organizations
        6–7
    maintenance of links between
        implementation and model   325–6
    manifesto   315–63
    model-based evolution process   269
    model-driven planning and design
        263–91
    operational support for information
        flows   282–7
    organizational dimension   339
    quality life cycle   266
    reactiveness to change   265
    research   3–11, 81, 85, 91
    static structure   264
    technologies   3–6
    vision   264, 321
Cooperative modelling, information flows
    273–9
Cooperative processing   247–53
Coordination   324–5
    strategy   270–3
CORBA   20, 37–9, 81, 83–5, 88, 91, 94,
    96, 104, 105, 108, 257–8
Coupling design   281–2
Customized transaction management (CTM)
    technology   103

DAIDA project   310
Data mining   207–31

Data model heterogeneity   181–2
Database   6, 207–31
    interoperation   185
    multiple-layer   209–12
Database management system (DBMS)   24,
    28, 31, 33, 35, 36, 38, 84, 90, 98, 188,
    319
Declarations   297
Declarative style   297
Derived ontology   194–7
Description logic (DL)   150, 175–7
Discovery mediator   199–201
Distributed and cooperative information
    systems (CoopISs)   16, 19
Distributed computing   6, 15
    framework   16, 25
Distributed computing environment plus
    legacy gateway   26
Distributed object architectures   86
Distributed object computational model
    20, 36
Distributed object computing (DOC)
    15–48
    applications   30–3, 46
    benefits   18, 44
    challenge of   16–19
    complexity   17
    deployment status   29–34
    environment   32
    framework   19–24, 23
    GTE's experience   24–9
    industrial-strength, enterprise-wide
        interoperable applications   40–6
    industrial-strength requirements
        34–40
    infrastructure   26, 28, 35
    programming environments   37
    technology   17–19, 26, 27, 34–5
Distributed object management (DOM)   102
Domain model interoperability   45
Domain orientation   20, 23, 42
Domain-specific metadata   139, 142, 145–7
Domain-specific ontologies   140
Domain standardization   21, 43–4
Dynamic classificational ontologies (DCOs)
    179–81, 190–1

Encapsulation   53
Enterprise information system architecture
    82
Enterprise integration   337–8
Enterprise modelling   337
Enterprise reference model   337
Enterprise-scale distributed object systems
    81–110

Export mediator 197–9
Extended transactions 100–4

Framework development 74
Functional behaviour 65–6

Generalization of data 212–15
Generic architecture 353–5
Generic compositions 68–9
Generic servers 323
Generic software architecture 57
Generic synchronization policies 248
Genericity 62–5
Global information infrastructure (GII)
    139, 147, 153, 171, 172
Global information systems (GIS) 139–78
Group collaboration facet 319, 320,
    329–35
    linkages with organizational model
    334–5
    main features 331–4

Heterogeneity of information 181–4
Heterogeneous databases 226–8
Heterogeneous simulation 280
HTTP 105, 106
Hypernym 142, 169–70
Hyponym 142, 169–70

i* framework 295, 296–307
Information agent 4–5, 326–9
Information brokering 327–8
Information flows
    cooperative modelling 273–9
    simulation 279–81
Information frameworks (IFs) 180
Information management techniques 6
Information networks 4
Information overload 139, 147, 153, 171
Information repositories (IRs) 180
Information retrieval 186–7
Information systems, next generation 316
Inheritance 60–1
Inherited anomaly 248
Interface compatibility 57
Interface Definition Language 88
International Foundation on Cooperative
    Information Systems (IFCIS) 10
International Telecommunications Union
    (ITU) 41
Internet 49, 83
    integration of technology 104–6
    resource discovery 187
Internet Inter-ORB Protocol (IIOP) 88

Internet Special Interest Group 105
Interontology interoperation 166–71
    architecture for 164–6
Interontology relationships manager (IRM)
    164–6
Interoperability 15, 317
Interoperable domain frameworks 21
Interoperable life cycle support
    environments 22
Interoperable object models 21
Interoperation, improved 322–4
Intranets 83

Java programs 62, 105

KAOS framework 308
Knowledge-based systems 6, 113
Knowledge Query and Manipulation
    Lamguage (KQML) 111, 114, 115,
    134, 328

Legacy migration 45
Life cycle support environment
    specialization 22

Market share 42
Mediators for information sharing
    197–201
Messaging Service 104, 106
Metadata 84, 139–78
    capturing information content
    144–5
    classification 142–4
    contexts 140, 145–6
    definition 142
    for digital media 143
Meta-information system 5
Meta-modelling 270–3
Meta-object protocols 107, 236–7
Meta-objects 240–6, 255–7
Microsoft Transaction Server 37
Migration architecture 28
Migration challenge 27
Mix-ins 60
Modularity 42
Multicomponent networks 6
Multifacet cooperation support agent
    351–3
Multimedia data 215
Multiple-layer database (MLDB) 209–12
    building 215–19
    construction algorithm 218
    for heterogeneous database systems
    226–8

Multiple-layer database (MLDB) (*continued*)
    maintenance   219–20
    query answering in   220–6
    schema   218–19
Multiple-tier architectures   95–8

Non-functional behaviour   50, 65–6

OASIS   333
Object-based programming languages   59
Object composition   61–2, 66
Object DBMS (ODBMS)   89
Object framework   98, 99
Object Management Architecture (OMA)
    85
Object Management Group (OMG)   20, 83,
    86, 91, 99, 100
Object model family   21, 45
Objectorganizations, need for higher-level
    91–100
Object-oriented features, interference
    59–60
Object-oriented languages   50, 75
Object-oriented software composition
    58–66
Object-oriented systems   75
Object Request Broker (ORB)   86–9
Object Service   85, 86, 88, 89
Objects and components   54
OBSERVER   165–9, 177–8
Ontology   139–78, 184–7
Open systems   49, 50, 75
    software composition for   52
Operational reflection   233, 237
Operational style   297
Organizational alternatives   303–7
Organizational facet   319, 320, 335–42
Organizational models   293–312
    linkages with group collaboration
    334–5
Organizational objectives, modelling
    338–9
Organizational relationships   300

Persistence   60
PIN (personal identification number)   296,
    306–7
Proxy objects   250–1

Query answering in multiple-layer database
    (MLDB)   220–6
Query processor   164, 166

Real-world semantics (RWS)   148
Reflection   107–8, 233–60

Reflective capabilities   107–8
Relevance factor (RF)   199–201
Request for Proposal (RFP)   89, 94, 104
Request-commit-perform-evaluate cycles
    286
RICHE   43
    ROK framework   237–46, 248
    characteristics   238–40
    implementation   253–7
    meta-layer components   240–6
    meta-object support infrastructure
    250–3
    systems development and
    administration   247–8
Run-time behaviour   72–3

Scalability   166
Schema correspondences   141
Semantic heterogeneity   139–78, 183–4,
    207–31
Semantic interoperability   23, 42, 81,
    163–71
Semantics   xi
Server objects   251
Simulation   279–82
Simulation repository   281–2
Software architecture   57
Software composition for open systems   52
Software development subsystems   280
Software reuse   50
SOM   257–8
STL (Standard Template Library)   62–3
Strategic dependency (SD) model   295,
    301–3
Strategic rationale (SR) model   295, 302–3
Surrogate objects   251
Switching   333–4
Synchronous sharing   331
Synonyms   166–9
System support   322
Systems facet   319, 321–9
Systems requirements   293–312
    expanded process   341–2
    modelling   339–42

Technology adoption life cycle   17
Telecommunication workflows   101
Terminological relationships   140, 163–71
Three-tier architectures   96–8
Total quality management (TQM)   96–8,
    266
Transaction Specification and Management
    Environment (TSME)   103
Transactional workflows   102

Variability   51, 52, 55
Visual composition environment   67–8,
    70–3
    current research   73
Visual composition support   71–2
    adaptability to composition model
    73

White-box reuse   51, 52–3
WibQuS meta-model   281

WibQuS project   266–8, 282, 284, 286
Workflow management systems (WFMS)
    31
Workflows   100–4
World Trade Organization   41
World Wide Web (WWW)   105, 106, 182,
    189, 324